Big Ten Football

Other books by
Mervin D. Hyman and Gordon S. White, Jr.

COACH TOM CAHILL: A MAN FOR THE CORPS

JOE PATERNO: ''FOOTBALL MY WAY''

Big Ten Football

ITS LIFE AND TIMES, GREAT COACHES, PLAYERS AND GAMES

**Mervin D. Hyman
and Gordon S. White, Jr.**

Macmillan Publishing Co., Inc.
NEW YORK

For

Rachel, Lisa and Lauren

and

John W. and Gordon S. III

Macmillan Publishing Co., Inc.
866 Third Avenue, New York, N.Y. 10022
Collier Macmillan Canada, Ltd.

Library of Congress Cataloging in Publication Data
Hyman, Mervin D
Big ten football, its life and times, great coaches,
players, and games.
Includes index.
1. Intercollegiate Conference of Faculty Representatives. 2. Football—History. I. White, Gordon S.,
joint author. II. Title.
GV958.5.I55H95 796.33'263'0973 77-9306
ISBN 0-02-558070-1

First Printing 1977

Printed in the United States of America

Contents

Acknowledgments

In writing this book, it was obvious early on that we had undertaken a monumental task in sorting out the history, anecdotes, and memorabilia and in exploring the fascinating combination of myths and facts which are a part of Big Ten Football. It also was obvious that we would have to seek assistance from many sources, and dozens of people were liberal and extremely helpful with their cooperation. It is impossible to list them all, but our appreciation for their aid is no less sincere. However, there are some whose help must be acknowledged.

First, of course, there were the sports information directors of the great universities who have been and are a part of the Big Ten—Fred Stabley of Michigan State, the dean of the nation's S.I.D.'s; Will Perry of Michigan; Tom Miller of Indiana; Jim Mott of Wisconsin; George Wine of Iowa; Dick Kubick of Chicago; and former sports information directors Ted Haracz of Purdue; George Beres of Northwestern; Otis Dypwick of Minnesota; Norm Sheya of Illinois and his assistant, Jim Flynn. Also, Mike Krauss, director of the Office of Public Information at Chicago, and Sam Akers, public relations director of the Tournament of Roses. Without their contributions of pictures, clippings, records, facts, figures, and, in some cases, memories, it would have been impossible for us to write this book.

Most of the pictures in this book, except those where on-page credits are noted, appear with the permission and through the courtesy of the Big Ten office and the athletic departments and sports information directors of the former and present universities of the Conference—Chicago, Illinois, Indiana, Iowa, Michigan, Michigan State, Minnesota, Northwestern, Ohio State, Purdue, and Wisconsin. We acknowledge their cooperation with gratitude.

We are indebted, too, to Athletic Director Don Canham of Michigan and Athletic Director Dave Nelson of the University of Delaware, whose reminiscences of his days as a Michigan teammate of

Acknowledgments

Tom Harmon and Forest Evashevski provided a rare insight into college football of that era. And to Kaye Kessler of the Columbus *Citizen-Journal* and Jim Benagh of the Detroit *Free Press*, writing colleagues who were helpful in many ways.

We also are deeply appreciative for the assistance and encouragement we received from the Big Ten Conference office, particularly from our old and good friend, Commissioner Wayne Duke, Assistant Commissioner John D. Dewey, and Jeff Elliott, director of the Big Ten Service Bureau.

Perhaps we owe most of all, however, to our long-suffering wives, Ruth and Jane, who endured so many lonely months listening to the incessant banging of typewriter keys as we researched, wrote, and re-wrote through the seemingly long days and endless nights. We are grateful for their patience and understanding.

To all of them—and to those we neglected to mention—we express our sincere thanks.

Mervin D. Hyman
Gordon S. White, Jr.

Big Ten Football

ONE

From Roses to Rags

It was January 1, 1977. After two days of rain, a bright California winter sun shone down on beautiful downtown Pasadena, warming the hundreds of thousands who swarmed the streets of the quaint city watching one of the nation's most famous spectacles, the annual Rose Parade.

Riding proudly at the head of the extravagant parade were cowboy film star Roy Rogers and his wife, Dale Evans, the first husband-wife team ever to be named Grand Marshals of this prestigious event. Among the others who had been given this honor were three presidents of the United States, Herbert Hoover, Dwight D. Eisenhower, and Richard M. Nixon.

Even while their attention was focused on Rogers and Evans and the scores of beautiful flower-bedecked floats which passed in review, most of the spectators had their minds on the grand climax of the Tournament of Roses which would take place several hours later, the Rose Bowl football game between the University of Southern California and Michigan.

Long before the 2 P.M. kickoff, more than 106,000 fans would suffer their way through the endless traffic jams to the picturesque stadium, which nestles comfortably in the Arroyo Seco, bounded by the residential streets of Pasadena on one side and the San Gabriel mountains on the other. Thousands of cars would fill the spacious parking lots around the stadium and surrounding streets. Huge banners and signs proclaiming the partisanship of the fans—"Trap the Wolves," "Trample 'Em, Trojans," "Go, Wolves, Go," "Ring Ricky's Bell," an obvious reference to USC's All-America tailback, were just a few—would be displayed on campers, small trucks, station wagons, and chartered buses. The traditional tailgate parties, some as elaborate as a formal Saturday-night dinner party with candles decorating the bridge tables, would begin with a never-ending flow of Bloody Marys and very, very dry martinis priming the juices of the fans for the gala event ahead.

It was all window dressing for what has become a traditional struggle between the champions of the Big Ten and the Pacific Eight conferences. It was even more so this year because there was just a chance that the winner would come out of the action with the national championship. Only undefeated and No. 1-ranked Pittsburgh, which was scheduled to meet Georgia in the Sugar Bowl earlier in the day, stood in the way of that possibility. Michigan was ranked No. 2 and USC No. 3, and a Georgia victory would give the Rose Bowl victor a shot at the title. As it turned out, that chance disappeared even before the opening kickoff when it became known that Pitt had clobbered the Southeastern Conference champions, 27–3.

However, that hardly diminished the importance of the Rose Bowl game. USC, coming in with a 10–1 record, had recovered from an opening game 46–25 upset by Missouri to roll over ten straight opponents, including a 24–14 win over UCLA to win the Pac Eight title and a season-ending 17–13 win over Notre Dame. And the Trojans had done it with a forty-one-year-old rookie coach, John Robinson, who had succeeded John McKay when the longtime USC leader deserted the college ranks after the 1975 season to coach the expansion Tampa Bay Buccaneers of the National Football League. However, Robinson had prepped well for his first head coaching assignment, serving for thirteen years as an assistant at Oregon, three more as McKay's offensive coordinator at USC, and one season with the Oakland Raiders under old friend Coach John Madden.

Robinson demonstrated that he could be both serious and indulge in some dry humor. He told everyone who would listen that he was going to make the USC quarterback position more important, his team would move the ball, and he intended to have a good defense. He also told them that one reason he had returned to USC was "I really missed the Trojan horse. The horse, the band, and all those song girls. . . ."

Michigan, ranked No. 1 in several preseason polls, had reached the Rose Bowl with a similar 10–1 record. Along the way, the Wolverines had smashed Stanford, 51–0; Navy, 70–14; Michigan State, 42–10; Northwestern, 38–7; Indiana, 35–0; Minnesota, 45–0;

Illinois, 38–7; and then overwhelmed old nemesis Ohio State, 22–0, in the "big one." However, a 16–14 upset by Purdue had cost Michigan its No. 1 ranking and put the Wolves into a tie with Ohio State for the Big Ten title.

Michigan also brought an impressive set of statistics to Pasadena. The Wolverines led the nation in total offense with 4,929 yards, in rushing with 3,989 for a 362.6-yard-per-game average, in scoring with 38.7 points a game, and they were tied with Rutgers for giving up the fewest points—7.4 per game. True, Michigan's opposition, with the exception of Ohio State, was mostly of the marshmallow variety, soft and mushy.

Coach Glenn (Bo) Schembechler was making his third trip to the Rose Bowl since he began coaching at Michigan and he had something less than fond memories of his two previous visits. In 1970 he suffered a heart attack on the eve of the game and his team lost to USC, 10–3. In 1972 Stanford edged his Wolverines, 13–12. So, despite his team's apparent strength and the fact that it was a six-point favorite, Bo had to be somewhat apprehensive about the outcome.

Then there was all that pregame talk about Michigan's landlocked offense. In defense of his style of play, Schembechler told interviewers, "You all talk about passing and I agree that every team should be able to pass. But in our league, Ohio State and Michigan believe in the run first and the pass second. I don't see many pure passing teams coming in first."

Little did Schembechler know then that it was the pass—USC's success with it and Michigan's failure with it—that would do in the Wolverines on New Year's Day.

Bo also appeared to be more relaxed and patient than he had been in the past. For example, in his final press conference before the Michigan–Ohio State game, he opened the proceedings by announcing, "We'll run a triple reverse on the opening kickoff. Then we'll throw a bomb." That was like Ronald Reagan's saying he was going to run for office as a liberal.

Schembechler wasn't quite that flip in Pasadena, but he was available for interviews, was pleasant and affable, and answered questions willingly. Three days before the game, however, Bo began tightening up his procedures. He switched practice sessions to the afternoons, cut down on his players' free time, and eliminated all player interviews. One Michigan player was disciplined for watching television after the 11 P.M. curfew.

"Everybody else out here is on vacation," grumbled Bo. "That's no way to get ready for a football game."

Each team had its collection of All-America and All-Conference stars. USC's best were tailback Ricky Bell, offensive linemen Marvin Powell and Donnie Hickman, defensive tackle Gary Jeter, linebacker Clay Matthews, and defensive back Dennis Thurman. There also were quarterback Vince Evans and his two favorite receivers, Shelton Diggs and Randy Simmrin.

Michigan's outstanding players were Rob Lytle, who alternated between fullback and tailback; wingback Jim Smith, also one of the nation's leading punt returners; quarterback Ricky Leach; guard Mark Donahue; linebacker Calvin O'Neal; and Greg Morton, a 230-pound tackle who talked to plants (his favorites were Phyllis, a philodendron, and Claudia, a purple passion plant).

What everyone was looking forward to, however, was the expected running duel between Bell and Lytle, a pair of runners who made almost everyone's All-America team. Early in the season, Bell had been the leading challenger to Pittsburgh's Tony Dorsett for the Heisman Trophy. Quick, hard-hitting, and slinky in the open, he had piled up 1,008 yards running, including 347 in fifty-one carries against Washington State, in USC's first five games. Then Bell hurt his hip against Oregon State, twisted his ankle against California, and was used only sparingly against Washington. He returned for full-time service against UCLA and Notre Dame and finished the season with 1,417 yards rushing, fourteen touchdowns, and a distant second to Dorsett in the balloting for the Heisman Trophy.

Lytle, maybe even a mite faster and just a little bit tougher as an inside runner, had survived all kinds of punishment without serious injury. A modest young man with thick, reddish-blond hair, light freckles, sleepy-looking eyes, and a quick, toothy grin, he came into the game with 1,402 yards and thirteen touchdowns, and a career total of 3,250 yards, more than any other back in Michigan history, including the legendary Tom Harmon.

However the confrontation between Bell and Lytle never took place. On USC's fifth offensive play, a little more than four minutes into the game, Ricky had his bell rung. He boomed off his left tackle for 6 yards and a first down, and then wobbled off the field. He didn't play again and it was announced that he had suffered a concussion.

Fullback Dave Farmer, on the bench at the time, later described what happened on the play that leveled Bell. "The strong safety came up and hit him head-on," said Farmer. "Then the weakside linebacker whacked him from the rear. Ricky's head snapped like a rubber band. It was a classic case of whiplash. He was really hit!"

After the game, Bell, still groggy, said he didn't remember getting hit. "It was like a dream," he said, "a real bad dream."

Bell's loss was sub tailback Charlie White's—and USC's—gain. White, a six-foot, 180-pound freshman and one of those always-plentiful Trojan speedsters, took over for Ricky in grand style. A wispy type with good balance, he ran for 114 yards, scored on a 7-yard run, and generally comported himself in a manner which indicated that he was up to continuing the tradition of great USC tailbacks.

But it was Evans, the much-maligned quarterback of a year earlier, who turned out to be the hero of the afternoon. He did what Michigan's Leach couldn't do. He ran *and* he passed, and very well indeed. So well that he completed fourteen of his twenty passes, eight to Diggs, the sticky-handed flanker who couldn't miss. Two of Evans' tosses led to scores, one on his own 1-yard bootleg sweep of left end and the other on White's 7-yard dash. All the left-handed Leach could do, once he began throwing in desperation, was complete four of twelve tries.

Although Michigan scored first on Lytle's 1-yard dive in the second quarter for a 6–0 lead, the Wolverines were soon forced to play catch-up without the weapons necessary for that kind of game. Evans' touchdown and Bob Woods' placement just before the half put Southern Cal ahead 7–6, and after that Michigan just couldn't mount a meaningful drive. Leach's passing wasn't up to the occasion and White's touchdown with 3:03 to go in the game, following another long Evans pass completion, gave the Trojans a 14–6 victory.

It was the Big Ten's seventh loss in the last eight Rose Bowl games and, hopefully, gave the conference some food for thought. Perhaps Schembechler and Woody Hayes, the two leading conservatives in the Big Ten and the only ones to bring their teams to Pasadena in the last nine years, will have to do some retooling of their offensive ways if the Big Ten is ever to win again in the Rose Bowl. Meanwhile, later that night, Hayes' Ohio State team found someone it could outbang on the ground in the Orange Bowl and defeated Colorado, 27–10.

"A one-dimension offense" was the way USC alumnus O. J.

Simpson, an expert in those matters, described the Michigan attack, and not even the most rabid Wolverine was ready to argue with him.

Schembechler, despite his disappointment, was gracious after the game. "They deserved to win," said Bo. "I think they're the best football team I've seen this year. I have no vote for the national championship, but if I did I certainly would vote for USC."

Asked if he agreed with Schembechler, USC's Robinson answered, "Damn right I do." And then, with a grin, John said, "We all took a vote on the way to the locker room and the USC poll voted us Number One."

The Associated Press and United Press International voters didn't agree, however. Both polls gave the national championship to Pittsburgh, the first Eastern team to win the title since Syracuse in 1959.

Two years earlier, on January 1, 1975, the scene was the same but the cast was different. It was the third straight time, and the fourth since 1969, that Ohio State's Woody Hayes and USC's John McKay would be the protagonists in college football's oldest and most prestigious postseason bowl game. The two previous encounters had both resulted in one-sided decisions, USC winning 42–17 in 1973 and Ohio State romping 42–21 in 1974. In 1969 the Buckeyes had triumphed 27–16, giving Hayes a 2–1 edge over McKay in the Rose Bowl and 4–2 overall, including three regular-season games.

USC, coming into the game with a 9–1–1 record, had rebounded from a desultory start, that included an opening game 22–7 upset by Arkansas and a 15–15 tie with California, to romp over its last four opponents—Stanford, Washington, UCLA, and Notre Dame. The Trojans had captured the fancy of the nation with their comeback in the season's final game when they overcame a 24–0 deficit to rout the Irish 55–24.

Ohio State had reached the Rose Bowl through a more intriguing set of circumstances. The Buckeyes had marched relentlessly over their first eight opponents and then were upset by a fine Michigan State club, 16–13, in a controversial ending that saw the Bucks denied the winning touchdown when the officials—and Commissioner Wayne Duke—ruled that time had expired before the final play went off. However, Ohio State came back to win its last two games, beating Iowa by 35–10 and Michigan by 12–10. The victory over Michigan gave Ohio State a tie with the Wolverines for the Big Ten title and set off a furor over which team would be selected to represent the conference in the Rose Bowl.

A year earlier the same two old bitter rivals, both unbeaten, had battled to a 10–10 tie to finish in a deadlock for the championship. Everyone expected that Michigan would get the nod to go to Pasadena from the conference athletic directors, but the vote went in favor of Ohio State by a narrow margin, inspiring unofficial charges by Michigan's Bo Schembechler that Commissioner Duke had "rigged" the voting. While not everyone went quite that far in their anger over the vote, Michigan supporters—and some others in the Big Ten—were quite outspoken in claiming that the Wolverines had indeed been "robbed." The rumblings in the Midwest had not yet subsided from that decision when the athletic directors again voted for Ohio State to represent the conference in the 1975 game. However this time there seemed to be more justification for their conclusion than there had been a year earlier. After all, the Buckeyes *had* beaten Michigan, however narrowly, in their head-to-head confrontation.

So the stage was set. California braced itself for Ohio State's Woody Hayes, who had not exactly endeared himself to West Coast football fans and the press in his previous six trips to the Rose Bowl. Woody hadn't always been a gracious loser—or a gracious winner either, for that matter. On at least a couple of occasions he had brusquely demeaned his Pac Eight foes by claiming that several Big Ten also-rans were tougher. He had been surly with some writers, including one or two of his own from Columbus, and had been accused of striking a photographer after the 1973 game. Woody had been just as tough with his players. He had cloistered them from the press, once even putting them in a monastery the night before a game. His players had not been permitted to visit Disneyland, that California wonderland, and they had about as much freedom as a lifer at San Quentin. In fact one year Hayes had a minor rebellion on his hands because of his strict disciplinary methods.

But all was sweetness and conviviality when Hayes came west for the 1975 game. From the moment he stepped off the plane in Los Angeles and received a rose from the Rose Bowl queen, Woody was amiable and approachable. Even his disciplinary values seemed to have changed. Jeff Prugh of the *Los Angeles Times* wrote, "When Woody Hayes was asked the other day about a curfew for his Ohio State football team, he hardly sounded like the ogre critics portray him to be. 'Oh, we will have a curfew,' the coach said nonchalantly. 'I'm not sure yet when it will be. Maybe midnight or maybe one o'clock. I don't know. We'll talk that over with the players and see what they want to do before we decide.'

"Was that Woody Hayes talking? What has happened to iron-fisted authoritarianism? Or strength through adversity? Has Hayes gone soft?"

There were other changes, too. The Buckeyes spent Christmas Day at the beach, once a Woody Hayes no-no. They were allowed to use breakfast money to buy pizza and they practiced only once a day instead of twice.

No, Woody Hayes hadn't gone soft. But he was presenting a new image to West Coast sportswriters. He simply oozed with charm and went out of his way to be downright pleasant to some of the same men who had pilloried him in print in other years. What's more, he didn't push a single photographer, and even smiled for them. He answered questions willingly and brought some of his players to press conferences. He appeared at luncheons and banquets when he was supposed to and said things like, "I'm very glad to be here again."

The only time Woody bristled, and even then it was good-naturedly, was when a writer asked him if he had mellowed since his heart attack the previous winter. Woody's response, with a mischievous smile, was a hearty "Hell, no!"

Maybe Woody Hayes was never going to make it as Mr. Nice Guy, but he sure was giving it one hell of a try.

Meanwhile John McKay was his old witty and quotable self. The crafty, white-haired McKay, who had revolutionized college football in 1962 when his Trojans won the national championship with an innovative power-I offense, enchanted even the Columbus writers with his one-liners.

The inevitable question about coaching his own son John, a marvelous pass receiver, brought this reply from McKay: "The crowd used to yell 'there's that idiot McKay.' Now they yell 'There's that idiot McKay playing his idiot son.'"

It was all good, clean fun, of course, and Johnny McKay was simply being himself.

What everybody *really* was waiting for, however, was the head-to-head, yard-gobbling duel between Archie Griffin, Ohio State's Heisman Trophy winner, and Anthony Davis, the equally heralded

USC halfback who had wound up his senior season by personally running roughshod over Notre Dame in that frenetic comeback, including a 102-yard kickoff return for a touchdown, among his contributions to the tremendous victory. Griffin, of course, had just finished his third straight spectacular season, gaining 100 yards or more in his last twenty-two games and winning acknowledgment as the best college football player in the land. Trojan adherents, naturally, disputed the decision by the Heisman Trophy voters, claiming that their "A.D." was every bit as good as Griffin, if not better. Unhappily the duel never did materialize. Davis was knocked out of the game in the second quarter with an injured sternum and badly bruised ribs after he had run for 67 yards, and Griffin's contribution was a "mere" 75 yards rushing and no touchdowns.

Many of the players on both sides were in their third straight Rose Bowl game against each other so there was little chance that the pressure would get to them. In fact it was more like a gathering of old friends, except for one thing: these "old friends" were bent on committing mayhem on each other in full view of 106,721 spectators, the second-largest crowd in Rose Bowl history.

There was another element that contrived to make the game doubly important. With unbeaten Oklahoma (ranked No. 1 in the Associated Press poll but unranked in the United Press International poll because it was on probation) unable to play in a postseason bowl, while Alabama (the only other undefeated major college team and ranked No. 1 by UPI) was scheduled to play Notre Dame in the Orange Bowl, there was an outside chance that the Rose Bowl winner might *just* have a shot at the UPI national championship—*if* Notre Dame upset Coach Bear Bryant's Crimson Tide on New Year's night in Miami. Neither Hayes nor McKay wanted to talk about the possibility, but you can bet they were thinking about it.

For almost two quarters the game hardly appeared to be a matchup of two of the country's five best teams. Fumbles, pass interceptions, and just plain mistakes hounded both teams as they strove fruitlessly to take command. USC was the first to score, on a 30-yard field goal by Indonesian-born Chris Limahelu in the opening quarter.

Then came one of the weirdest plays of the year. With the ball on the USC 17-yard line, Jim Lucas, the Trojan punter, muffed the snap, calmly picked up the ball, and ran 16 yards for a first down, prompting Coach McKay to say to the press jokingly after the game, "Gentlemen, we've got the worst punting game in the history of college football. I've decided to change Jim [Lucas] to a running back. The way he moved with the one he missed was our best run of the day."

Lucas, however, didn't move quickly enough a few moments later. This time Ohio State's Tim Fox stormed through to block Lucas' punt and, suddenly, the Buckeyes had the ball on the Trojans' 17-yard line! So what happened? On the third play Archie Griffin fumbled the ball away on the 2-yard line, the first of two bobbles he made in the game. It was enough to make Woody Hayes see red— USC red—on the sidelines.

Ah, but there was more to come. Anthony Davis, who had gone out of the game with an injury minutes earlier, was back in and, on the first play, *he* fumbled and tackle Nick Buonamici recovered for Ohio State on the 6-yard line. That was enough to make John McKay see red—Ohio State scarlet red.

Meanwhile there was a minor uprising on the Ohio State sideline. Champ Henson, smoldering over the decision of Coach Hayes and his assistant George Chaump to start Pete Johnson at fullback, leaped off the bench, charged the coach, and yelled, "Woody, if you want that son-of-a-bitch in the end zone, then put me in!"

Hayes obliged and Henson angrily bulled his way for 4 yards to the 2. On the next play he slammed up the middle for a touchdown. Tom Klaban's successful kick made it 7–3, Ohio State, but Henson was still fuming. As he came off the field he bitterly gave an obscene gesture to an assistant coach and screamed, "You tell them to shove it. They said I couldn't take it in. Well, I showed them something, didn't I."

There was even more, too, before the first half was over. USC came storming back on Haden's passes to McKay and tight end Jim Obradovich, and soon it was fourth down and five to go on the Ohio State 22-yard line with nineteen seconds remaining in the first half. Limahelu was called in to do his specialty and his 39-yard placement kick sailed through the goal posts. Three points for USC, cutting the Ohio State lead to 7–6.

But wait a minute. A Buckeye was offside on the play. Coach John McKay had an important decision to make. Take the three points or give it up in favor of the penalty and a first down on the Ohio State 17 and a possible shot at a touchdown that would give

USC the lead going into the locker room at halftime—or at the very least, another field goal by the usually accurate Limahelu. McKay, typically, decided to gamble and it was a decision that, for a long while, looked like it would cost him the game.

After three pass plays USC was on the 6-yard line with only four seconds to play. So in came Limahelu again to try to retrieve the three points that his coach had given away seconds earlier. This time it was a mere chip shot from the 14-yard line, the kind Chris had made time and again all season long. However, he missed, the ball going wide to the left as the half ended with Ohio State leading, 7–3.

Later McKay admitted there were several times he had second thoughts about the decision to give up the sure three points but, in his inimitable way, he shrugged it off. "Just call me Mr. Lucky," said John.

When the teams returned to action for the second half Davis was out of the lineup, never to return for the rest of the game. A jarring tackle by Ohio State's Pete Cusick late in the second quarter had injured his sternum and bruised his ribs and A.D. spent the rest of the frantic afternoon on the sidelines being consoled by a couple of onetime USC Heisman Trophy winners, O. J. Simpson and Mike Garrett.

Despite Davis' absence the game suddenly changed from a duel of fumbles and bumbles to the exciting matchup it was supposed to be. First, USC scored on quarterback Pat Haden's 9-yard pass to Obradovich and Limahelu's placement kick, to take a 10–7 lead. Then the Buckeyes came back on quarterback Corny Greene's 3-yard end sweep and, a few minutes later, on Klaban's 15-yard field goal to go ahead 17–10 with only 6:38 to play. It appeared that the momentum had gone over to Ohio State, but that, as it turned out, was only wishful thinking on the part of the joyous Buckeye fans. USC wasn't quite finished with the visitors from the Midwest.

It was obvious to everyone, including the Ohio State coaches and players, what USC's final-gasp battle plan would be—a barrage of passes from the talented Haden. But wily Coach John McKay didn't play it that way. While the Buckeye defense braced itself for the expected aerial attack, the Trojans, after returning the kickoff to the 17-yard line, stayed on the ground. Haden sent Allen Carter, maybe the best backup tailback in the country, and fullback Dave Farmer ripping through the line for short but valuable yardage as the minutes and seconds ticked off on the clock. They picked up three first downs, the last one on the OSU 38. Then, with only 2:03 left, Haden went for the bomb. He threw a perfect strike to McKay, who outmaneuvered Steve Luke, the Ohio State defender, and made a leaping catch in the right-hand corner of the end zone for the touchdown that pulled the Trojans within one point of Ohio State, 17–16, while the mostly home-team crowd went delirious with joy.

Now John McKay had one of the biggest decisions of his college coaching life to make. Go for the extra-point placement kick and an almost certain tie, or go for two points and a possible victory. Everyone in the stadium, *including* Woody Hayes, knew what McKay's decision would be. The cocky little guy who had both won and lost on similar gambles in his lifetime—including one that failed and cost him a 14–13 loss to Purdue in this same stadium eight years earlier—didn't hesitate even a single second. And Woody Hayes, standing helplessly on the opposing sideline, knew exactly what John McKay would have his team do. Pat Haden would almost surely throw the ball.

USC lined up in its regular power-I formation, except that side receiver John McKay and flanker Sheldon Diggs were both split to the right side. Haden, after the snap, took off to his right while McKay went for the corner and Diggs ran a little curl pattern inside. When Diggs' defender made a move to come up on Haden, Pat simply dumped the ball off into the end zone, where Diggs went to his knees and gathered it in for the two-pointer that put USC ahead 18–17. John McKay's gamble had paid off in one of the most thrilling finishes the staid old bowl has ever seen.

And before that New Year's Day was over, the Trojans were to add still another feather to their already-overflowing caps. That night Notre Dame upset unbeaten Alabama in the Orange Bowl, 18–11, boosting USC to No. 1 in the UPI poll and giving it the coaches' version of the national championship. Unbeaten Oklahoma remained No. 1 in the final AP poll.

Despite his obvious disappointment, Woody Hayes' new West Coast image prevailed after the game although his antics on the sidelines during the action were reminiscent of the Woody Hayes that Californians had learned to love to hate. At various times he had thrown down his glasses and stomped around them in disgust, torn off his baseball cap and windbreaker and thrown them to the ground, and, in the fourth quarter, Woody punched linebacker Arnie Jones in the chest on the sidelines and shook him by his face mask. Hayes said later, "I did it to get him fired up."

Woody answered questions patiently and graciously for almost fifteen minutes, surprising the writers who expected him to be his old irascible self after the defeat.

"We lost to a team that was just about one point better," said Hayes. And then he wished *all* the writers a Happy New Year before striding off into the Pasadena dusk.

Just a year later, on January 1, 1976, Woody Hayes and his Buckeyes were back in Pasadena. This time, however, things were a little different. Ohio State, unbeaten in all eleven of its regular season games, was No. 1 in both the AP and UPI polls, and Hayes had been voted the Football Writers Association's Coach of the Year. And, for the first time in four years, the Buckeyes' opponent would not be USC. The Trojans had dropped their last four games after Coach John McKay announced that he was leaving sunny California and college coaching to join the pros in 1976, and USC had to be satisfied with a bid to play in the Liberty Bowl. There was one other thing that was different. The Big Ten also had changed its postseason policy to permit runners-up to accept bids to other bowls, and Michigan, beaten only by Ohio State but tied by Stanford and Baylor, was in the Orange Bowl against once-defeated and No. 2–ranked Oklahoma.

For UCLA it was the Bruins' first appearance in the Rose Bowl since 1966, the year they upset Michigan State 14–12 after losing to the same Spartans in the season's opener. Hardly anyone gave UCLA a chance. After all, hadn't Ohio State thrashed the Bruins 41–20 during the regular season, and didn't the Bucks still have Archie Griffin, who came west with a second Heisman Trophy tucked under his arm, the first player in history to win that coveted award twice? And then there was Coach Hayes, who had it all over second-year UCLA Coach Dick Vermeil in experience.

Once again Woody put his best face forward during the pregame exercises. He smiled a lot, had his picture taken patting one of Snow White's dwarfs at Disneyland, and good-naturedly lectured the press on American history, Lana Turner, the cleanliness of Disneyland, General George Patton, and other pertinent subjects. It was obvious that Hayes felt pretty good about his team and he indicated privately that this might just be his best club ever at Ohio State, even superior to the 1954 bunch that featured Hopalong Cassady or the 1968 – 69 – 70 teams led by quarterback Rex Kern.

"It's a closer team," Hayes said, "much closer than last year's team."

It certainly looked that way in the first half when Ohio State, a two-touchdown favorite, did everything but put UCLA through a wringer. The Buckeyes, even though Griffin broke a bone in his left hand on the third play of the game (he still played the entire game), controlled the ball for almost twenty-one of the thirty minutes, out-rushed the Bruins 115 to 9 yards, and led in first downs eleven to two. Ohio State should have been leading by a ton but, somehow, the only score the Bucks had been able to muster was a 42-yard field goal by Tom Klaban. However, it seemed to be just a question of time before OSU would convert its field superiority into touch-downs and roll to the national championship everyone expected it to win.

But a funny thing happened to the Bucks on the way to the na-tional title. They blew it. In just thirty minutes, they let the inspired Bruins take the ball game—and the whole season—away from them. All of a sudden John Sciarra, the UCLA quarterback who wasn't supposed to be much of a passer, was throwing the ball left and right, long and short, and with the accuracy of a Fran Tarken-ton. And the UCLA running attack was rolling along relentlessly like a runaway tractor.

UCLA took the second-half kickoff and promptly moved 62 yards to set up Brett White's game-tying 33-yard field goal. Then, in quick succession, nonpasser Sciarra threw for 16 yards and 67 yards to flanker Wally Frank, who showboated his way into the end zone on both occasions and, zap, the Bruins had a 16–3 lead!

Despite the surprising turn of events, Ohio State wasn't through, at least not yet. The Buckeyes, doing what they do best, sent Griffin and Johnson banging through the UCLA line on a 65-yard march, with Johnson bulling his way the final 3 yards. Then Craig Cassady, son of Hopalong, the Heisman Trophy All-America of the 1950s, intercepted a Sciarra pass and a subsequent penalty against UCLA for a late hit put the ball on the Bruin 35-yard line.

Shucks, everybody in the crowd of more than 105,000 knew what Woody Hayes would do now. A pitchout to Archie, Johnson bulldozing up the middle out of the Robust T, and maybe a reverse with wingback Brian Baschnagel carrying, something he had done so well so often the last three years. Instead, there was quarter-back Corny Greene, who had been passing horribly all afternoon, back to throw on first down, almost a heresy in Woody Hayes' game plan. Greene, under a strong rush, floated the ball into the air like a wounded duck and it was picked off by an alert Bruin. Minutes later Wendell Tyler, a 9.6 sprinter, broke loose for a 54-yard run that put joyful UCLA ahead for good, 23–10.

What happened to turn the Bruins from first-half tabbycats into a bunch of superstars?

"We just came in at halftime, ate a little raw meat, and spread some gunpowder on everybody's dish," explained UCLA nose guard Cliff Frazier.

With eight seconds to go and UCLA running out the clock near the south end zone, Woody Hayes trudged forlornly across the field to congratulate UCLA's Dick Vermeil. "Congratulations. We just screwed up," said Hayes to his jubilant thirty-nine-year-old coaching rival.

Hayes was back to his old inimitable self after the game. He refused to talk to reporters or permit his players to be interviewed. Instead, Woody sat morosely in the locker room for almost an hour, talking to no one as he reflected on what might have been one of his finest hours, until finally he sneaked out and into the team bus.

The only comment came from Assistant Coach George Hill, the defensive coordinator, who simply said, "They just kicked the hell out of us."

That night the Big Ten suffered a second blow when Oklahoma beat Michigan 14–6 in the Orange Bowl, and a couple of days later the Sooners were voted No. 1 in both the AP and UPI polls. It just might have been the blackest day in Big Ten football history.

Ohio State and Michigan would be back again and again in the Rose Bowl and other postseason extravaganzas, but how many more opportunities would the then sixty-two-year-old Woody Hayes get to win a national championship?

Officially it all started back in 1947, after the Big Ten and the then Pacific Coast Conference entered into a formal contract for its champions—or, more properly, its representatives—to meet annually in the Rose Bowl. Unofficially it *really* started way back in 1902 when Michigan's unbeaten 1901 Point-A-Minute team was invited west to play Stanford on New Year's Day, 1902, in a game that was to be part of a Tournament of Roses celebration.

Unhappily for Californians, Michigan polished off Stanford,

49–0, spoiling the whole fiesta and giving the folks of Pasadena some second thoughts about what sport to include in their celebration. Publisher Ron Chapin noted in his *Pasadena News*: "Several thousand Dutchmen and Britishers engage in several years of bloody fighting for the possession of a government and don't get an encore. Twenty-two striplings argue for an hour over the progress along the ground of an inflated hog's hide, and law-abiding citizens bound up and down on the seats of their trousers, while demure maidens hammer plug hats down over the ears of their escorts with their parasols."

The next year, the Tournament of Roses committee switched to polo and that proved to be an even greater flop than football. It was far too refined and effete for Californians. What they wanted was something simple yet exciting. What they got the next New Year's Day in the Rose Bowl was chariot racing. Yes, chariot racing.

For the next thirteen years the Ben Hurs of that time raced their chariots up and down the turf of the stadium. But interest in the biblical sport eventually waned and in 1915 the Tournament of Roses committee, by this time over the shock of Michigan's trouncing of Stanford in 1902, decided to have another go at football. Unbeaten Washington State was picked to represent the West on January 1, 1916, and the Cougars invited Brown, an Eastern team with an unimposing 5–3–1 record and a star halfback named Fritz Pollard, who had received good notices back home. Brown also had a little-known guard named Wallace Wade, who was later to coach five teams from Alabama and Duke in the Rose Bowl.

To add a bizarre touch, the Washington State players who practiced in the Los Angeles area took time out to make $100 a day each as extras in, of all things, a movie called *Tom Brown of Harvard*. Despite their pregame highjinks, and amid reports that the Cougars had pooled their money to bet on themselves, the Westerners won, 14–9. That was the beginning of the oldest postseason college football bowl game in the country.

The game continued as an annual affair between a representative Western team and an opponent from another section of the country, but it wasn't until 1921 that a Big Ten team made its appearance again in the Rose Bowl. Unbeaten Ohio State, the conference champion, was invited to play California and the Bears promptly overwhelmed the Buckeyes, 28–0. That was the game that caused the Big Ten officially to ban postseason competition for its football teams. Perhaps the timing was only coincidental, but it seemed that the conference was trying to avoid being embarrassed again.

Through the years many attempts were made by various Big Ten schools to have the ban rescinded. Finally, in September 1946, under the leadership of Commissioner Kenneth L. (Tug) Wilson, the conference voted for a five-year agreement with the Pacific Coast Conference for its champions to meet annually in the Rose Bowl. The Big Ten, however, insisted on several restrictions, including an important one that prohibited its schools from playing in the Rose Bowl two years in a row. Because of that rule there were several times in the ensuing years when the Big Ten was represented by a runner-up while its champion stayed at home. Then, for the 1973 game, the Big Ten shook off its fuddy-duddy attitude toward postseason competition and that policy was changed.

The agreement survived until 1958, when the Pacific Coast Conference expired in a cloud of scandal. When the West Coast schools regrouped a year later under the banner of the Athletic Association of Western Universities, better known as the Pacific Eight, the Big Ten agreed not to sign a new pact but to allow individual schools decide whether or not to accept bids to the Rose Bowl.

That rather obtuse policy was responsible for one of the greatest rhubarbs of all time in a conference noted for its rhubarbs. The 1961 Ohio State team, unbeaten but tied by Texas Christian University, all but had its bags packed when the OSU faculty, which in those days did the voting, turned down the invitation. Needless to say, the decision set off a hue and cry that was led by Coach Woody Hayes. It also, ultimately, resulted in a new agreement between the Big Ten and the Pac Eight, one which eliminated the right of refusal by the individual schools.

While there have been many memorable Rose Bowl games over the years, that first one, in 1947, has a special place in Big Ten history. Illinois, the Big Ten champion, led by pint-sized Buddy Young and Julie Rykovich, trampled UCLA, 45–14, before 93,000 fans, one of the largest crowds ever to see a college football game. About the only thing the humiliated Bruins had to cheer was a 103-yard kickoff return for a touchdown by Al Hoisch.

For the next dozen years or so it seemed that the postseason rivalry between the two conferences was one of the greatest mismatches of all time. Michigan's national champions romped over

USC 49–0 in 1948; Northwestern, the Big Ten runner-up (Michigan won again but couldn't return to Pasadena because of the "no-repeat" rule), squeezed past California, 20–14, on Ed Tunnicliff's 45-yard touchdown run in the final seconds in 1949; Ohio State eked out a 17–14 win on Jimmy Hague's field goal in 1950; Michigan handed Cal its third straight Rose Bowl loss, 14–6, in 1951; and Illinois whomped Stanford 40–7 in 1952.

USC finally broke the Big Ten's six-game winning streak when it squeaked by Wisconsin, 7–0, in 1953, but the visitors from the Midwest promptly began another five-game string in 1954 when Michigan State, led by halfback Billy Wells, stormed from behind to overtake UCLA, 28–20. Two years later the Spartans were back again, winning this time, 17–14, on Dave Kaiser's 41-yard field goal with only seven seconds to play.

After winning only once in the first thirteen games, West Coast teams suddenly began to be more of a match for their rivals from the Big Ten. Washington got them rolling with a 44–8 win in 1960, and since then the Pac Eight has had the upper hand in victories. But winning has rarely come easy for either conference's representatives and some of the games have been wild and woolly.

Perhaps the wildest of all was the 1963 game in which Wisconsin quarterback Ron VanderKelen, who wasn't exactly an unknown going into the game with USC's national champions, put on a fantastic performance. He had broken the Big Ten record for total offense with 1,237 yards, 1,009 passing and 228 rushing.

USC, however, was the best team in the nation. Coach John McKay's club had swept past all opposition with relative ease and now, going into the fourth quarter of the Rose Bowl game, the Trojans had a seemingly safe 35–14 lead. Then Ron VanderKelen and his Badger teammates staged one of the most remarkable rallies ever seen anywhere. Ron's passes began to hit with unerring accuracy and suddenly Wisconsin was back in the ball game as 98,698 fans in the lovely Pasadena oval looked on in astonishment. When that last quarter was over Wisconsin had scored twenty-three points on three touchdowns and a safety. VanderKelen had completed thirty-three of forty-eight passes for 419 yards, still a Rose Bowl record, thrown for two touchdowns, and run 17 yards for another score. It was, by far, the greatest individual performance ever seen in the hallowed old bowl but, unhappily, Ron and his fighting Badgers came up short. They couldn't quite catch USC and lost, 42–37.

There have been other thrillers, too, like Purdue's 14–13 win over these same Trojans in 1967 when Coach McKay gambled for two points and victory and blew it on an end-zone pass interception by the Boilermakers' George Catavolos. Then there were Stanford's back-to-back upsets, over Ohio State, 27–17, in 1971, and Michigan, 13–12, in 1972, on Ron Garcia's 31-yard field goal with twelve seconds to go.

All in all, through the years it has been a satisfying relationship for both conferences and one which will probably endure for many more years. Big Ten Commissioner Wayne Duke and Pac Eight Executive Director Wiles Hallock are both firmly committed to keeping the annual rivalry going. Everyone has made a pile of money from the gate receipts and the television money, both of which keep going up each year. For the 1977 game the gross came to some $5 million, and the total loot divided up by Southern California and Michigan and their respective conferences, after expenses and Pasadena's 15-percent cut, was around $4 million, tops among all the bowls.

No wonder Duke and Hallock grin and bear it, whether their teams win or lose.

What has made it even more interesting is that some of college football's greatest teams and players have displayed their wares in the Rose Bowl. In 1971 Joe Hendrickson, sports editor of the Pasadena *Star-News*, conducted a poll of twenty-two sportswriters from all over the country to select an All-Time Fifty-Year Rose Bowl team. Nine Big Ten athletes were named to the first team—halfback Buddy Young of Illinois (1947), end Pat Richter of Wisconsin (1963), tackle Al Wistert of Michigan (1948), and guard Alex Agase of Illinois (1947) on offense; and tackles Alex Karras of Iowa (1957) and Carl Eller of Minnesota (1962), middle guard Jim Stillwagon of Ohio State (1969–1971), and cornerbacks Leroy Keyes of Purdue (1976) and Jack Tatum of Ohio State (1969–1971) on defense. The second team listed center Dan Dworsky of Michigan (1948) on offense and ends Charles (Bubba) Smith of Michigan State (1966) and Ellis Duckett of Michigan State (1954), tackle Bobby Bell of Minnesota (1962), linebacker Dick Butkus of Illinois (1964), and safety John Charles of Purdue (1967) on defense.

Along with the West Coast greats, players who have starred in the Rose Bowl would make anyone's "Who's Who" of college football.

TWO

How It All Began

A quarter-century after Rutgers and Princeton met in the first college football game in 1869, the game, the players, and demands for victory were getting out of hand. Football spread rapidly from its Eastern beginnings to reach the Middle West, South, and even Far West. Fans wanted then what they want today. They wanted nothing but a big winner. The results were just as they are today—abuses.

As is also the case so often these days, the colleges got publicity for victory, criticism for defeat, and a lot of noise surrounded the football games and football preparations. And like today the noise of all this football activity seemed to reach the ivory towers of the college presidents long after the harm was done.

There are tales of players who were not students. They were hired and paid for their participation on the gridirons of the country. These were the men who helped create the legends of the monsters dug up from the coal mines to be outfitted in football uniforms and run rampant over the fields of play. There obviously was validity in these tales. All of the big tackles may not have come from coal mines, but many of them did, and many were outsized human beings who had no intentions of getting inside a classroom, and stuck to those intentions.

The result was reform. If colleges were to represent their football teams as being a part of the college program and represent the sport as one played by the young men of the student body, the coal miner–nonstudent would have to go back to his digging and leave the game to the boys. Well, it was something like that. Reform was needed.

Of course reform often indicates original control that gets out of hand and needs a strong leadership to harness violations of some sort. In many cases, however, there was no control to begin with in college football. Students began the game of football. Students were coaching many of the teams. It was a situation of no faculty control over something that was fast becoming more important in college life than those humanities courses.

Some colleges hired men to coach football teams, men who were in most instances totally unrelated to the faculty or to the administration of the colleges. These coaches were for the most part just muscle men who were told to go out and lead the boys in their games. Many of the abuses came from no control over the students but even more so from the uncontrolled hired coaches, who did anything they wanted to win. After all, in those days, too, a coach could lose a job by losing too many football games.

Word of these football irregularities, nonstudent players, suspect coaching activities, and win-at-any-price attitudes finally got through the big oak doors of the university presidential offices. At first it was just an inkling of something that might be amiss. Then football persisted in making itself heard about throughout the land so that the noises began giving university presidents some headaches. When that happened and the presidents began worrying about such things, they sometimes acted.

After all, these presidents could read their own campus newspapers, which often spoke of the professional players used by the opponent. These campus papers reported the fights, the cases of players who were not enrolled at the college they represented. There were the stories of the athletes who played football for one college and baseball for another.

By the year 1894 baseball was the primary sport, with football fast catching up in interest. The first intercollegiate sports event had been a rowing race between Harvard and Yale, and rowing was a big thing for college rivalries, particularly in the East. And all sports had their problems of using "ringers" in the lineup.

When there was enough of this sort of thing reported and enough noise made of it, James H. Smart, president of Purdue University, became troubled. At least he became more troubled than many other presidents. Purdue was and is a state institution in Indiana. Rivalries between state colleges and neighboring state colleges in football became more than just games. They became battles. This sort of thing still persists. But at that time President Smart felt it might be wise to see what controls could be placed upon the operations of intercollegiate athletics. Where better to start than with a group of his neighboring institutions that were Purdue's rivals in football and other sports?

The problems involved were numerous. It was a new thing to deal with in campus life. It was something not governed by traditional attitudes toward education. It involved outside pressures from alumni and just plain fans who were citizens of one state wanting to see the state next door brought to its knees.

But President Smart felt strongly that something could be done, so he invited a half-dozen university presidents to meet with him. This first intercollegiate athletic summit meeting took place in the Palmer House in Chicago, January 11, 1895. The results were momentous. From this gathering the nation's colleges learned that they could do something to harness the thousands of student athletes into teams that were more a part of the institutional life than a part of a professional league of tramp athletes dressed up to look like college teams. Colleges have since found they have a difficult time keeping things in line, but from that Palmer House meeting came basic ideas for university control of athletics.

The seven universities represented were Purdue, Michigan, Northwestern, Minnesota, Illinois, Wisconsin, and Chicago. Northwestern and Chicago were private institutions that competed against the other five in sports. It was the beginning of the Big Ten although the organization that came out of that meeting was called the Intercollegiate Conference of Faculty Representatives, and three more colleges had to join up later to make seven small ones into the Big Ten.

The biggest achievement of this meeting was to place the faculty in control of athletics at an institution. This was a new concept. It was adopted later by other colleges and even by a national group after the turn of the century. Faculty control of athletics in 1895 was a radical step but became the strong point of this first formal meeting of a group of colleges for the purpose of direction of athletics.

These presidents set down a list of twelve rules to be the guidelines for this new intercollegiate sports organization. These rules, in the years to come, were followed, violated, criticized, and changed. But whatever is said of the Big Ten, it was from its seven charter members that the methods of dealing with intercollegiate athletics throughout the nation evolved. It wasn't until more than half a century later that the Ivy League group formalized itself under what is known as the Presidents' Agreement of 1954. After

1895 many another college athletic organization developed and set up rules for conduct between member colleges, and even for conduct against colleges not members of a given group.

The twelve rules that came out of the Palmer House meeting in January of 1895 were:

1. Each college and university which has not already done so shall appoint a committee on college athletics which shall take over general supervision of all athletic matters in the respective college or university, and which shall have all responsibility of enforcing the college or university rules regarding athletics and all intercollegiate sports. [This is the important faculty representative rule.]

2. No one shall participate in any game or athletic sport unless he [no Women's Lib at this time] be a bona fide student doing full work in a regular or special course as defined in the curriculum of his college; and no person who has participated in any match game as a member of any college team shall be permitted to participate in any game as a member of another college team, until he has matriculated in said college under the above conditions for a period of six months. This rule shall not apply to students who, having graduated at one college, shall enter another college for professional or graduate work.

3. No person shall be admitted to any intercollegiate contest who receives any gift, remuneration or pay for his services on the college team.

4. Any student of any institution who shall be pursuing a regularly prescribed resident graduate course within such institution, whether for an advanced degree or in one of its professional schools, may be permitted to play for the period of the minimum number of years required for securing the graduate or professional degree for which he is a candidate.

5. No person who has been employed in training a college team for intercollegiate contests shall be allowed to participate in any intercollegiate contest as a member of any team which he has trained, and no professional athlete or person who has ever been a member of a professional team shall play at any intercollegiate contest.

6. No student shall play in any game under an assumed name.

7. No student shall be permitted to participate in any intercolle-

giate contest who is found by the faculty to be delinquent in his studies.

8. All games shall be played on grounds either owned by or under the immediate control of one or both of the colleges participating in the contest, and all games shall be played under student management and not under the patronage or control of any other corporation, association, or private individual.

9. The election of managers and captains of teams in each college shall be subject to the approval of its committee on athletics.

10. College teams shall not engage in games with professional teams nor with those representing so-called athletic clubs.

11. Before every intercollegiate contest a list of men proposing to play shall be presented by each team or teams to the other or others, certifying that all the members are entitled to play under conditions of the rules adopted, such certificate to be signed by the registrar or the secretary of the college or university. It shall be the duty of the captain to enforce this rule.

12. We call upon the expert managers of football teams to so revise the rules as to reduce the liability to injury to a minimum.

Not only was this a landmark meeting and set of rules for intercollegiate athletic conduct, but the presidents spelled out just what was troubling them about sports in colleges in this catechism for sports. Note, for instance, Rule 3, which prohibits professionalism in college sports involving these seven institutions. Obviously, word had gotten to these presidents that some of the athletes representing their universities were getting paid for their services. And in those days it wasn't even under the table. It was for all to see and hear about.

Rule 6 is interesting in that one of the practices was to have a man play for a number of colleges under the name of Tom Smith at college *A*, the name of Bill Jones at college *B*, and Raphael Arnswager at college *C*. It was such a joke that knowing fans recognized the man wherever he played.

Rule 7 puts into force the idea of "satisfactory progress toward a degree," which was later adopted by other such groups and uniformly established the idea that failing grades were sufficient cause to put a young man off a team.

The twelfth and final rule in this new organization was a hint of bigger things to come. Obviously, the injury lists were bothering the college presidents. Eventually the intercollegiate football injury lists bothered the president of the United States. It was about a decade after the Palmer House meeting that President Theodore Roosevelt practically ordered the colleges of the nation to put a stop to the great number of football injuries or he would put a stop to the game of football.

The colleges responded in 1906 by forming the National Collegiate Athletic Association, which was originally formed to establish strict rules for the game of football and then for other sports. Through the years the N.C.A.A. has become much more than just an organization to set up game rules. It has become the master conference, the master group for servicing intercollegiate athletics, and a driving political force for college athletics. The N.C.A.A. has also become a lot of things some people don't like. It has been called a lot of things it is not. But the N.C.A.A. followed some of those basic concepts of President Smart and his colleagues in forming a constitution for a national intercollegiate athletic organization.

The N.C.A.A., for instance, is based upon a concept of amateur athletics as spelled out by that Rule 3 of the Palmer House meeting. Some question modern "amateur" rules of the N.C.A.A., which allow a person to receive a scholarship worth thousands of dollars if the "student-athlete," as the N.C.A.A. calls the person, is recruited by a college for the purpose of playing a sport for that college.

The N.C.A.A. stipulates in its constitution that a student-athlete must be making "satisfactory progress toward a degree" in order to be eligible for whatever team he is playing on. That comes from Rules 4 and 7 of the original Big Ten rules.

Neither the N.C.A.A. nor the Big Ten work just the way it was originally intended. But, for some reason or other, each of these groups and the other intercollegiate conferences, associations, and leagues work. Maybe they don't perform too well at times and maybe the college presidents don't seem to care at times. Also, coaches and players work full time to find ways of getting around the rules in some cases. But the meeting in the Palmer House in 1895 was the start of something big—organized intercollegiate athletics as we know it today, with the faculties having something to say about the conduct of sports on and off their campuses.

THREE

And Then They Grew

Now that the presidents of these seven universities had taken steps to get control of an unruly situation, they had to sell the idea back home at the campus level. It wasn't an easy task. Nothing new may be too easy, particularly when it means someone has to do a little more work. But these presidents went back home with the idea of giving their institutions time to read and digest and then send the faculty representatives for athletics back to meet with each other within a year.

The University of Chicago, always up to something new, had a built-in faculty representative for athletics. This university, relatively new in the academic world, had hired a man to be its supervisor of sports some time before President Smart of Purdue launched the Palmer House meeting. The man at the University of Chicago was a professor on the faculty since the institution dignified sports by giving him that status. He was Amos Alonzo Stagg.

For years Stagg and his fellow faculty representatives from the other institutions of this new Midwest conference formed and molded the rules of intercollegiate competition and eligibility that they wished to go by. Progress was rapid, and the day was coming when others would be eager to join the league.

Indiana University and the University of Iowa were admitted to the little group in 1899, which led to the first shortening of the title of the group to the obvious—the Big Nine. It was not until 1912 that the tenth member joined the fold—Ohio State University.

However, when Ohio State joined up it kept the group at nine members for a while because Michigan, upset with scheduling rules that limited a team to five football games a season, left the group in 1907, not to return until 1917 when, for the first time, the league was what it is now known as—the Big Ten. There were ups and downs, ins and outs, and another long period when the Big Ten got smaller in size by one. The University of Chicago dropped intercollegiate football after the 1939 season and eventually dropped out of the Big Ten. Without football you aren't much in the Big Ten or Nine or whatever. Chicago formally withdrew from the Big Ten on March 8, 1946.

Michigan State University, always eager to to join up with the conference no matter what the number of college members, finally got its wish in 1949 and, with plenty of help from Michigan politicos, was admitted to the league and it once again became the Big Ten. The Michigan State entrance into the league is a story of beating back the objections of the University of Michigan. This political struggle to admit Michigan State has left jealousies of long standing that were quite evident in the vote to send Ohio State instead of Michigan to the Rose Bowl after the Buckeyes and Wolverines played a tie at the end of the 1973 season. This tie game kept the teams in a deadlock for the league title and Michigan was expected to go to the Rose Bowl. But the vote of 6–4 was in favor of Ohio State, and Michigan State voted for Ohio State to go to the Rose Bowl.

From the original group of seven through the days of nine members, ten members, nine again, and eventually ten again, the league was always doing something to regulate its problems through its faculty athletic representatives. There were the rules barring training tables, rules permitting training tables, rules establishing grants-in-aid for athletes, rules governing academics, and rules that were violated or ignored.

One of the original seven presidents to attend the founders' meeting of the Midwest league was J. B. Angell of the University of Michigan. Ten years after the 1895 meeting, President Angell still held forth in Ann Arbor, Michigan, and from there he cried for more reform. Things were obviously getting out of hand again despite the efforts of the beginners to form the "Big Seven." Injuries were on everyone's minds, including President Roosevelt's and President Angell's.

The University of Michigan chief executive spoke out like a man for all times in intercollegiate sports. His words could have been uttered today or yesterday instead of the day before yesterday when he said them.

Speaking in 1905, J. B. Angell said, "The present conditions [in college athletics] constantly hold before the students and before the world false ideals of college life. The university is necessarily viewed in a wrong perspective. It is looked on as training men for a public spectacle instead of quietly training men for useful intellectual and moral service while securing ample opportunity for reasonable athletic sports. ''

President Angell thus did not call for an end to college athletics, but for more reform. The result was a busy year of work by the faculty representatives of the conference who met in January and again in March. This group established regulations that said one year of residence was necessary for athletic eligibility, thus the idea that a freshman could not play on a varsity team. An athlete was not to play more than three varsity years. No graduate student would be eligible. Training tables were prohibited and ticket prices were set at fifty cents for students and faculty members. Also, the football schedule was set for five games a season.

Ironically, this five-game football schedule is what upset the University of Michigan powers. Although it was President Angell of Michigan who started the second reform movement within the Midwestern group, it was his own institution that could not live with the resulting rules and regulations. So the Wolverines dropped out of the Big Nine. This put the number at eight, until Ohio State entered. By the time Michigan reentered the group, the football teams were playing seven games a season.

Michigan's primary complaint was that it had found another market for games—rivalries with some Eastern opponents. Cutting back from thirteen games in 1904 to five games the next year crimped the Wolverines too much, so they withdrew in 1907.

The three-year rule of eligibility also played a part in Michigan's decision to withdraw from the league. But one thing became even clearer than ever before about the makeup of the Big Seven, Big Nine, or Big Ten—it was a group of colleges that were natural field rivals but naturally needed each other to regulate intercollegiate athletics in their own backyards. Michigan had to come back just as naturally as Ohio State had to join up eventually. The N.C.A.A. was not really strong at the time, and the local league such as this Big Something concept was what worked best for all.

But problems continued, and they continue today as surely as there are difficulties in operating any large group of people or institutions that band together for what they believe to be their own good. As always happens in big-time college athletics, the coaches and the athletic directors, jealous of the power they gained and of the attention they drew to their universities, came into natural conflict with the faculty representatives or other faculty members at these big colleges. At times the faculty reps lost all control over their own coaches and athletic departments. Woody Hayes, for instance, became so powerful that he tended to act as if he were untouchable. Even Woody, however, learned that the Big Ten, as a group, would sit on him if need be.

Scandals occur from time to time in any such group and the Big Ten was no exception. In intercollegiate athletics it is, like everywhere else, simply cases of men trying to get around the rules and laws set up to govern them in their conduct.

In 1912 the conference took steps to prevent its faculty representatives on athletics, those men who govern the coaches and athletic departments, from being touched by any bit of corruption. The Big Ten voted to prohibit the faculty representatives from receiving any pay for this job that was actually above and beyond the call of academic duties. After all, faculty representatives in the Big Ten have come from all types of teachers and professors—law, science, arts, etc.

The ugly head of the alumni began to be impressed upon the Big Ten as something that was up to no good. Feeling that the most difficult aspect of many of the problems was control of eager alumni, the conference formed an alumni committee in 1923. That was the year that Red Grange charged into the attention of sports fans across the nation—big No. 77, the Galloping Ghost of Illinois. So it is little wonder that few people paid attention to the formation of an alumni committee set up by the Big Ten to control those overzealous graduates who wanted to get their hands into the athletic situation, recruit players for their schools, and generally cause havoc as they have done elsewhere in college athletics.

While Red Grange has been long remembered for his exploits on the gridiron, the new alumni committee established by the Big Ten didn't last very long. It didn't work and was quickly forgotten and eventually dropped.

Six years later, in 1929, the Big Ten took the most serious action against a member institution in its history by suspending the University of Iowa. This grew out of one of those struggles between the Hawkeye athletic people and the university administrators. It became quite heated and was one of the most messy Big Ten situations in its history, certainly the worst problem the conference had faced from its inception in 1895 until that day in May 1929, when the Hawkeyes were put out of the league.

The crimes for which Iowa coaches and athletic personnel drew punishment upon the university consisted of "infractions of an athletic nature." That is polite language for giving athletes a share of the commissions on the sale of yearbooks, utilization of a businessmen's slush fund to subsidize athletics, refund of tuition fees to athletes, and the failure to certify athletes as bona fide students.

Iowa was reinstated to the Big Ten nine months after its suspension. One of the primary reasons for this was that some Hawkeyes had done some hawking of their own and come up with charges against all nine other Big Ten schools that sounded uncomfortably like the charges used to suspend Iowa from the league. Possibly Iowa had cleaned house, too.

Iowa was not to go on from there as clean as a hound's tooth after that reinstatement, however. The Hawkeyes were called up on the carpet by the Big Ten again in one of the post–World War II scandals that cropped up all over the conference in the big days of the fifties and sixties.

One of the prime reasons for the 1923 decision to control alumni and the 1929 case against Iowa was that in 1922 the Big Ten took another of those steps that was a first in intercollegiate conference athletics. On June 2, 1922, the Big Ten announced the appointment of Major John L. Griffith as the league's first commissioner. This was a unique move in American college athletics, and one to be followed by almost every formal intercollegiate conference. Only the Ivy League among the major playing conferences does not have a chief executive hired specifically to oversee the operation of league activities and coordinate the many facets of scheduling, competitions, and penalties. The Ivy League is run by the presidents of the eight Ivy schools, and each year a different president heads the conference. Griffith served until his death on December 7, 1944.

The former army officer was hired by the Big Ten in 1922 to "serve as a general secretary, promote educational campaigns on amateurism, and carry on investigations regarding intercollegiate athletic problems." Faculty representatives still ran the Big Ten as sort of a board, but the day-by-day nitty-gritty was handled by Griffith and his successors—Kenneth L. (Tug) Wilson (1945–1961), William R. Reed (1961–1971) , and Wayne Duke (1971–   ).

Griffith brought a bit of the overseer touch to the league and such hanky-panky as the Iowa incident began to be looked upon with disfavor. Again in 1936 the Big Ten threatened to expel one of its members. This time the culprit was Wisconsin.

The Badgers ran afoul of Commissioner Griffith and the Big Ten officials and faculty reps because the Wisconsin Board of Regents took it upon itself to fire the football coach and athletic director. Under the Big Ten system, well established by this time, the faculty was the body that should take such action. When the Wisconsin faculty satisfied the other members of the Big Ten that it had the Wisconsin situation back under control, the other nine league members withdrew their threat to suspend the Badgers. Actually, one of the league's most famous coaches, Harry Stuhldreher, was hired by the Wisconsin Board of Regents as football coach and athletic director in 1936 to succeed both Dr. Clarence Spears, the coach, and Dr. Walter Meanwell, the director of athletics. Stuhldreher was, of course, one of the Four Horsemen of Notre Dame, the most famous backfield in the history of college football.

Stuhldreher remained Wisconsin football coach through the 1948 season so that perhaps the Board of Regents got its cake and enjoyed eating it, too.

All was not trouble, scandal, and problems of rule violations, however, in the Big Ten as the body tried its best to grow up with the times—times that put ever-increasing demands for success upon the college coaching personnel and departments of intercollegiate athletics. New things were happening in sports and in football in particular in college competition, and the Big Ten met some of the problems quite well and established landmark regulations that were to be followed by other such leagues after the Big Ten thought of them.

At the spring meeting of the Big Ten in 1927 the members voted to stop raiding other institutions for successful coaches. Or at least voted to make such a raid well known so the defenses could be put up against personnel shifts. The Big Ten required from that day on that members should not employ coaches from other Big Ten institutions without first obtaining permission to negotiate from the employers of such coaches. This idea has spread and is generally accepted as good practice, and the N.C.A.A. now has rules governing raiding of coaching personnel.

In 1935 the Big Ten took a very important step that would have much more far-reaching implications than thought of at the time.

Members set down regulations governing broadcasting rights to home conference football games. Television was a long way off, but these radio rights set the pattern for TV rights that have become, nationally, the single biggest source of revenue for those football and basketball colleges strong enough to entice the networks to televise them.

In 1938 the Big Ten got back to the eating question and voted to reestablish training tables for football players.

The Big Ten was moving to keep control of what it had established—a league of colleges with similar problems and a need for group answers to those problems. As the threats of war rumbled over the world in the late thirties, the Big Ten felt happy and sure of itself entering a modern era about 1939. A system of athletic scholarships was accepted by the conference. Most athletes had been supported with jobs up to this point, jobs that that sometimes did not seem too difficult, although some players, such as Dave Nelson, the Michigan quarterback in the backfield with Tom Harmon, insists to this day that he worked very hard in the university cafeteria. Nelson went on to become an award-winning football coach and athletic director at the University of Delaware.

FOUR

The Big Ten's Dirty Linen

The biggest troubles in the Big Ten were to follow the Second World War when intercollegiate sports became bigger and, some say, better. The league changed some of its attitudes and still moved forward despite having to spank members now and then for transgressions. By this time the N.C.A.A. was growing in strength also, and the national organization looked down on some of the mischievous activities of various coaches and directors of athletics.

The first of the the big postwar scandals in the Big Ten involved the league's newest member—Michigan State. The Spartans got in trouble over one of the oldest of intercollegiate difficulties—the slush fund used to pay athletes under the table. This little slush fund was called the Spartan Foundation of Lansing, Michigan. There was evidence that $3,800 had been given to Michigan State athletes. The slush fund was credited with having assets of over $38,000.

Taking what was for them rather stern steps, the Big Ten members slapped Michigan State on probation on February 22, 1953. The conference listed the disciplinary action against Michigan State "for its delinquencies in permitting to exist an organization, the Spartan Foundation of Lansing, known to have solicited funds for the assistance of Michigan State athletes . . . ."

Michigan State immediately ordered the end of the Spartan Foundation, so the Big Ten members lifted the probation against the Spartans less than a year after the punishment was imposed. On December 10, 1953 Michigan State was back in the good graces of its fellow members.

Slush fund groups were all over the nation in college athletics.

Alumni and local fan groups ran them, and the colleges were having troubles controlling these eager ones who thought nothing of paying an athlete for a day's good work on the gridiron. A touchdown had a set price. Tackles were worth so much each. And so it went as slush funds grew. But the Spartan Foundation stopped.

A similar situation occurred just three years later involving Ohio State. Coach Woody Hayes, after a story in *Sports Illustrated* revealed some irregularities in the Buckeye football program, drew the ire of the Big Ten. The result was that Ohio State was put on a year's probation. The Buckeyes were declared ineligible for the Rose Bowl for a year "for irregular financial assistance to football players by the coach." It was all just another way of doing the same thing that Michigan State had been doing—paying football players who are supposed to be amateurs.

It was April 26, 1956 when Commissioner Tug Wilson placed Ohio State on probation, saying that "an investigation disclosed serious irregularity in the off-campus work program for football players as well as admitted loans of money to players by the football coach, Woody Hayes." This action was taken by the commissioner following his staff's detective work—the members did not vote this probation for Ohio State. The commissioner had the right to do this, and was obviously using more power to enforce the honest aims of the conference.

Hayes, however, refused to provide an accounting of the assistance he had furnished to players from personal funds, Tug Wilson explained. But, the commissioner said, "He acknowledged assistance to unnamed members of his squad in amounts of approximately four hundred dollars annually over a period of five years." This meant that Woody Hayes had been doing this nefarious bit of payment from the time he took over at Ohio State as head coach in 1951. Hayes' five-year payments covered the seasons of 1951, 1952, 1953, 1954, and 1955 before the heavy hand of Tug Wilson came down on him in the spring of 1956.

When Ohio State was placed on probation, Tug Wilson told how Buckeye football players were given jobs through the football coaching staff's help and that they were paid for work not performed during the season. The idea was as old as college football rules against such illicit payment to amateur athletes.

But Hayes yelled that Ohio State was being made a scapegoat in the investigation. Although Woody complained loudly, Ohio State sat out the probation after winning the Big Ten football championship in 1954 and 1955. In fact, the day that the probation was handed down by Commissioner Wilson, Woody took his team through a spirited spring football practice session and promised each of his players a reward in payment at the end of the day—a milkshake.

In 1975 it was reported that Hayes blew the whistle on Michigan State for recruiting violations—although some Spartans preferred to put the blame on Michigan—and Woody even said, "One of the reasons we will enjoy playing Penn State again [a new series started in 1975] is that we know they, unlike some others, recruit honestly." In 1976 the N.C.A.A. subsequently found Michigan State guilty of thirty-four recruiting violations and socked the Spartans with a three-year probation, an action which also caused Coach Denny Stolz to lose his job.

Hayes, speaking at the Big Ten's annual football kickoff luncheon in Chicago in July 1976, warned his coaching colleagues, "If I catch any of you cheating, I'll turn you in!"

Then Hayes freely admitted what many had suspected. Obviously referring to Michigan State, Woody said, "Did I turn in the team that cheated in our league? Damned right I did! And I'll do it again if necessary."

Darryl Rogers, Michigan State's new coach, responded with a quip. "I'd really like to thank Woody for turning us in—otherwise I wouldn't be here."

Later, Rogers said, "This is the first time I've met Woody Hayes, and I've never been in Columbus, but I don't like either of them."

For some time, however, Woody Hayes had difficult struggles with members of the Ohio State University faculty. There was a running battle to keep the Buckeyes away from the Rose Bowl no matter what the Big Ten, as a conference, decided to do with that postseason game. For a few years this became a real battle in Ohio, and eventually it threatened the foundations of the Big Ten itself.

Speaking in 1959 when the Big Ten Rose Bowl contract was being discussed for the umpteenth time, Dr. Frederic Heinberger, an Ohio State vice-president, said, "The faculty position of being against renewal of the Rose Bowl contract is likely to remain as is for some time to come." Heinberger, a vice-president in charge of academics at Ohio State, was saying that Ohio State's faculty, fed up with having the tail wag the dog, so to speak, and bothered with the tag of Columbus' being "The Football Capital of the World," was not going to take kindly to the Rose Bowl or big-time football anymore. Similar rumblings were being heard from Northwestern at this time, although not because of any particular scandal involving the payment of money to athletes such as was the case at Ohio State. Faculties here and there were just getting tired of the power being used by football coaches and the whole football scene on campus. Actually, the faculties were speaking out for the control over athletics they were supposed to have in this conference.

The mistakes of the football coaches, and serious problems in the breakup of the old Pacific Coast Conference at about the same time, brought all of these issues to a head and the Big Ten waged a knockdown internal fight over whether to continue playing in the Rose Bowl game or not.

The Big Ten received formal notice on Demcember 12, 1958 that the Pacific Coast Conference was being dissolved. This was even more reason to stop the Rose Bowl connection and so the struggle was joined. But, eventually, the Rose Bowl game remained a part of the Big Ten scene in conjunction with the Pac Eight Conference, which grew out of the breakup of the old Pacific Coast Conference. The forces for big-time football in the league had a narrow escape, however, while the issue was being resolved.

At the time that Tug Wilson slapped Ohio State with a one-year probation, the Big Ten was going through a self-appraisal operation, one of those studies by a committee from within the organization. This committee was appointed in December of 1955 and made its report to the Big Ten faculty representatives in August 1956, shortly after the penalty was handed out to the Buckeyes. A new Big Ten concept came out of this report, a concept destined to cause more internal fighting within the conference than just about any other single move ever made by the famous old league. It was the idea of granting athletic scholarships to young men on the basis of need. That is, an athlete was to pay as much as his family could afford to pay, according to a system of tables devised by some experts on education and income. No longer was the athlete to get a free ride on an athletic scholarship. If his family was wealthy he might even have to pay his entire cost of education, room, and board.

Thus, on December 8, 1956, the Big Ten approved the policy of granting financial assistance to an athlete on a basis of demonstrated need. Two months later the Big Ten created a Financial Aids Service to determine what a family would pay and what the college would pay to an enrolled athlete. And all hell broke loose in the Big Ten for a number of years over this one thing—the need factor.

Within days, apparently, the need factor was undermined by at least one coach attempting to get around the problem. It is strongly suspected that many more coaches started immediately to cut corners on the need factor, but one was caught almost before the ink was dry on the Big Ten agreement to award scholarships to athletes on the basis of family need. This time the school was Indiana University, and the coach was Phil Dickens. The Big Ten ordered Indiana to suspend Dickens for one year or else the Hoosiers would not be considered a school in good standing within the conference. President Herman B. Wells of Indiana University said his institution would comply, and so Dickens was suspended for illegal aid to athletes.

Specifically the conference claimed that several athletes were offered free room, board, and tuition, plus a sum of money per month for incidental expenses, without regard to need. Dickens was the person, the conference contended, who made the offers to the prospective football players. Thus Dickens, who had just gotten the job at Indiana as football coach, succeeding Bernie Crimmins, was ordered by the Big Ten "not to perform any of the professional duties or functions of a member of the football staff" and specifically "not [to] have contact with any prospective student."

President Wells backed up his coach, to a degree, saying, "The university administration and athletics committee have great confidence in the character and professional ability of Dickens and believe that he and his staff will build, in time, a highly successful football program at Indiana." Wells was wrong.

Maybe the Big Ten had created a monster it could not control in the need factor. Eventually a decline in the power of Big Ten football was considered by some to be the direct result of the need-factor scholarship. Coaches contended that other leagues, particularly the Big Eight, were able to attract large numbers of top high school athletes because they were giving full athletic scholarships while the Big Ten schools were limited to partial scholarships for their athletes.

But the Big Ten saw immediate problems of cutting corners within its own group as illustrated by the Dickens case. So, in September 1957, the faculty representatives employed a man to be the "examiner." This man was John D. Dewey, and his duties were to make regular inspections of intercollegiate athletic practices at member institutions, and particularly of the administration of financial aid. Dewey was to report his findings regularly to the commissioner and to the Big Ten faculty representatives.

Following the 1957 football season, the Big Ten lifted the suspension of Dickens. He had served just two weeks short of five months of a suspension which was supposed to be a one-year penalty. But the Dickens-Indiana situation was far from finished. The Hoosiers never really did straighten things out, and within three years Indiana was in a peck of trouble with the N.C.A.A. and the Big Ten, and Dickens was at the center of the problem again, accused of doing more of what he had been penalized for in the first place.

Indiana was handed a four-year probation by the N.C.A.A. in March 1960. This was one of the stiffest penalties ever handed down by the N.C.A.A. up to that time. And it stemmed from illegal payments to athletes in 1957 and 1959 under Dickens' coaching at Indiana. Four months later the Big Ten also jumped on the Hoosiers, and Tug Wilson handed Indiana a conference probation that was not lifted until May 1961. This, again, was slightly less than a year of Big Ten penalty. But this time Dickens lost his job and the university remained on the long probation by the N.C.A.A. It was not a pleasant situation for Indiana or the Big Ten.

Just before the Big Ten's commissioner slapped Indiana with its second conference penalty in less than three years, the Big Ten began moving toward elimination of the need factor in scholarships. Obviously, the men of the Big Ten were unable at this time to operate well under this program. Dick Larkins, then the athletic director at Ohio State, said, "I was opposed to the need factor at first. We had a good work program at Ohio State. The community paid the cost of it in jobs [for athletes]. Now we have to pay the whole thing. I'm still not opposed to the grant-in-aid [athletic scholarship], only to the need factor. I think we should be able to get a boy if his dad's a millionaire or if he's dead broke."

Duffy Daugherty, the Michigan State coach who was enjoying great successes in those days of Spartan football, said, "I think they are finally beginning to realize that this isn't the Ivy League and that you can't run things that way. The Ivy system is all right, but remember—most of them are private schools. State legislatures aren't going to give these schools in the Big Ten the money to run their athletic programs."

Daugherty was hoping for a return to the job work programs. The big problem with those systems of aid to athletes was that some of the work was never done although the athletes were paid for the work. And there were those strange jobs such as "winding an eight-day clock" and "watching football stadiums to see they aren't stolen."

Need was on the way out in the Big Ten. It just had not worked. But it was not to be replaced by the old work program of assistance. On December 7 and 8, 1961 the Big Ten approved a set of rules eliminating the need factor from scholarship assistance to athletes and replaced it with what became the full grant-in-aid for athletes.

Some years later in still another N.C.A.A. debate on the need factor, Michigan State's Daugherty said, "Don't bring in the need factor. We [Big Ten] had need once, as you know, and we don't want to have to cheat again." Ergo, coaches cheated under the need factor.

At the time that Indiana was severely penalized by the N.C.A.A., a Chicago sports reporter close to the Big Ten scene said, "Whenever a new coach comes into the Big Ten, all other schools brace themselves for the jolt of his recruiting techniques. The reason is he has four years in which to produce a good team. His success depends largely on how well he recruits in his first year or so; those recruits will be the boys who will make or break his team four years later. Early in the 1950s Indiana hired Bernie Crimmins away from Notre Dame because he had been in charge of Notre Dame recruiting. But Crimmins recruited strictly according to the rules. His teams were unsuccessful and Dickens was brought in.

"Within a very short time there was talk among recruiters in Chicago of the jolting aggressiveness of Indiana's recruiting. This happened at a bad time. The Big Ten had just imposed its grant-in-aid rules, which demand that a parent pay as much of a boy's education as he could afford. The conference was under pressure to prove that the new system would work. That meant it had to crack down on violations to show it meant business. So it cracked down on Dickens in the summer of 1957 and ordered him suspended."

A recruiter from another Big Ten school said, "Let's face it, we all do a little bit for the kids on the side. You almost have to these days if the kid is any good at all."

Meanwhile Tug Wilson retired and Bill Reed, the assistant commissioner and a former navy officer, was named to succeed Wilson as Big Ten commissioner. Reed was to have his days in court with those who violated the letter of the law and with those who skirted around the law but tried so hard to look clean and pure.

Reed had his biggest rules violations problems with the University of Illinois, the next Big Ten member to really stumble over the regulations of recruiting—and about every other regulation one could mention. The Illini made a mess of things, to put it simply.

The whole Illinois situation might have been kept quiet if it weren't for an unhappy assistant athletic director who thought he should have been named athletic director when the position became vacant. When Doug Mills, the Illinois athletic director, retired in 1966, the university was considering the appointment of the very popular football coach, Pete Elliott, to be both athletic director and football coach. This did not sit well with Mel Brewer, who had been Mills' assistant. As a result Brewer took to the University of Illinois president, Dr. David D. Henry, a complete record of expenditures made from a slush fund for athletes over the years since 1961 when the Illini lost every football game they played that season. The slush fund, again—here was that old form of help for athletes to pay them for work done on the gridiron. This slush fund, allegedly operated by the football and the basketball staffs for their players, was also unique in that it was one of the best-documented slush funds in collegiate history. It was sort of like the Nixon tapes—a record that indicted the record keepers.

Elliott was a man so highly thought of that he had been offered the job as athletic director at Northwestern during his career at Illinois. He had taken the losing Illini to a winning position in Big Ten life and to the Rose Bowl game in 1964. But suddenly the bubble burst and, like the Watergate scandal of many years later, Illinois had its own athletic Watergate in 1967.

The eventual ruling was that Illinois had to fire Elliott and its head basketball coach, Harry Combes, and an assistant basketball coach, Howard Braun. The university also was placed on probation and a number of Illinois players were permanently suspended. This action took place over a period of months in early 1967 and the N.C.A.A. also got into the act by placing Illinois on probation.

New to the serious penalties inflicted were the actions taken against the athletes, who were found guilty of violations, too. This was the most important infractions case on the eventual road to the N.C.A.A.'s enacting legislation that made it possible to punish a student-athlete as well as a coach or other member of a university staff. For a long time the athlete was not penalized. The institution and/or the coaches and athletic officials were the only persons so penalized.

So on March 4, 1967 the Illinois case was given its final Big Ten treatment when the conference ruled seven athletes ineligible, five of them permanently, for receiving illegal financial aid from slush funds. This was the wrap up by the conference faculty representatives, who took the final action themselves. Commissioner Reed did the investigating but it was obviously so serious a matter that the league faculty reps took the penalty action into their own hands. The coaches, Elliott and the others, had already been ordered out by these faculty representatives.

The strange set of records that served eventually as the nails in the Illinois coffin were allegedly kept by the coaches. There weren't huge payments to each athlete in question. It was a drib here and a drab there that, however, mounted up to about $21,000 given out in sums as little as $5 at a time. These were the records that Mel Brewer carried into President Henry's office on the fatal day.

President Henry and Illini from coast to coast yelled for mercy, saying the penalties were too harsh. Everyone said the old thing—"Everybody is doing it." That was the defense in Watergate years later. Well, everybody may have been doing it, but everybody didn't keep records. Illinois had still not fully recovered from this blow to its athletic programs by the time of publication of this book, a decade after the Elliott case.

Through all these pains of sin and power football, Big Ten faculty members continued to voice their objections to the things football meant to these major institutions of learning.

In 1959 a magazine survey of some professors throughout the Big Ten picked up some choice remarks by men well known in academic fields and elsewhere for their achievements.

Dr. James Van Allen, who had a belt named after him way out in space, was on the Iowa faculty. He said, "Football is a box connected by a thread to the university. The box is opened on Saturday, the players come out, perform, then go back in the box. They aren't really students. But I like football and it occurred to me one afternoon in the stadium, 'Why isn't this professional? It's a big show.'"

Harold McCarty, a professor of geography at Iowa in 1959, said,

"Football is a nice show, a circus. They're not our boys out there anymore. Faculty people go through three football phases— enthusiasm, cynicism, and indifference. It's like the seven ages of man."

Dean Athelstan Spilhaus of Minnesota said, "Football has run each and every one of the Big Ten schools at one time or another. Now we have a more sensible attitude toward it. But we haven't gone far enough. I will not dilute my time for football. It gains support, but with the wrong kind of people. You place yourself in the hands of pressure groups."

But this same magazine survey also found, to its surprise, that of forty professors interviewed not one among them reported a single case in all their teaching experience of athletic department pressure to give an athlete a good grade. This sort of demolished one of the oldest clichés about Big Ten and other college football. Yet this survey did come up with many a professor complaining about good students being shunted off into easy courses and away from the more difficult science and engineering studies the student-athlete might have wished to take.

Still, the faculty representatives tried to run the Big Ten the way it was originally intended. But other faculty members accused these faculty reps of being too close to the athletic departments to see the wrongdoings of their coaches and athletic administrators.

Following the Illinois scandal, Professor Samuel K. Gove of the Illinois Faculty Senate Committee on Athletics said, "With these revelations it seems that our committee must take a much more positive role to assure that we do have complete faculty control of athletics—a requirement for membership in the Big Ten. Although the Big Ten Conference has determined that each institution shall determine what constitutes full and complete faculty control, it is incumbent on each institution to examine its own conscience in this regard."

FIVE

Michigan's Point-A-Minuters

Fielding H. (Hurry Up) Yost became the football coach at the University of Michigan in 1901 and the Wolverines began to hurry up right by opponents so much so that this Michigan team earned the first well-known nickname for a college football team—the "Point-A-Minute Team." Actually that was overrating the accomplishments of this Michigan team that went on to play in the first Rose Bowl game, January 1, 1902. But the name stuck through the 1905 season so that the "point a minute" was more an era or span of time in Michigan football history than one team. Some of the men who played in 1901 were not on the team that played in following seasons, although the Wolverines kept rolling up high scores week after week against whatever opposition they met.

To be truly a point-a-minute unit, a team would have to score seventy points per game from 1901 to 1905. The game of college football lasted seventy minutes in those days, a drop of twenty minutes per game from the former ninety minutes needed to play football. The seventy-minute rule was established in 1894, and it was not until 1906 that a football game was again trimmed down a bit to the modern sixty minutes allotted for the action. Michigan scored 550 points—including 49 in the postseason Rose Bowl game—in that first season of Point-A-Minute action to a total of zero for the opposition in eleven games. This gave Yost's first Michigan team a per-game average of fifty points a game, something short of a point a minute but nevertheless very impressive.

Of course, during a given game now and then these Wolverines managed to score considerably more than a point a minute, and in one contest they ran up nearly two points a minute by edging Buffalo University, 128–0. In that first season of high-scoring production Michigan beat the opposition by the following scores: Albion, 50–0; Case, 57–0; Indiana, 33–0; Northwestern, 29–0; Buffalo, 128–0; Carlisle, 22–0; Ohio State, 21–0; Chicago, 22–0; Beloit, 89–0; Iowa, 50–0; and Stanford in the Rose Bowl, 49–0.

The heroes of this first Point-A-Minute team for Michigan were Neil Snow, the fullback who scored five touchdowns against Stanford in that initial Rose Bowl; Willie Heston, a halfback who was the best of the runners; and Boss Weeks, Dan McGugin, Dad Gregory, and John Hernstein. A couple of years later there came to Michigan a big center known as "Germany." This middle-of-the-line monster was Adolph Schulz, who was the best center in football history to that time.

These Michigan teams still hold the intercollegiate record for a major college nonlosing streak. In other words, these Point-A-Minute Wolverines went for fifty-six games without a loss. No team has done that since, and it is rather certain that no team did anything like it before the turn of the century when records were not that well kept. The streak ended on the final day of the 1905 season in much the same way that Michigan had treated most of its opponents during the streak. The Wolverines were shut out and it was Amos Alonzo Stagg's Chicago team, possibly the best he built, that blanked Michigan, 2–0.

Statistically, the Michigan team created new numbers for football fans that they had never dreamed of before. For instance, in the first year of this Point-A-Minute barrage, Michigan ran for 8,000 yards (no forward passing yet, remember). That is between four and five miles that season. In the five seasons of Yost's high-scoring machine, Michigan scored 2,821 points to just 42 for the opponents. Michigan did actually get over a two-point-a-minute ratio in the fourth season of this express-train team when the Wolverines got by West Virginia, 130–0.

Besides being known for such a high-scoring threat and living up to the reputation for a long time by college football standards, Michigan caused or took part in three significant strategic changes of the game. Two of them were Yost's offensive ideas to utilize Willie Heston, who tore apart defenses by running around them more than bowling them over. The third was a defensive strategy to stop Michigan—and it worked.

During that initial Rose Bowl game, Heston carried the ball on the first known bootleg play in football. With most of the team lined up and headed one way, Heston was given the ball and ran the other way. On his first try of this play against Stanford, he went left for 40 yards and a touchdown in the 49–0 triumph.

Heston was so capable at running either way that Yost, in his first season as Michigan coach in 1901, devised the initial tailback play in football. This put Heston behind center, or near the center of the backfield, and he was given the ball so he could run either way. To this day that is the proper use of a tailback—to go right or left. It is one of the strengths of modern I-formation football.

But, as has happened so often in the history of football, someone stayed up nights trying to devise the defensive answers to stop the strong team. Michigan drove coaches to the midnight-oil routine and it was Dr. Henry Williams, the Minnesota coach, who burned it with success. It is said that he collaborated with Pudge Hefflefinger, Yale's most famous football player before the turn of the century, to come up with a defense to stop Michigan's Point-A-Minute men.

In those ancient days of football strange things were done. That is, by modern standards they were strange. Since the forward pass had not been developed, teams only defended against the running back. This meant that defensive teams put most of their players at or right near the line. In fact, most teams played nine-man lines, with only two defenders in the backfield. What made Heston so potent was that he got by the line of scrimmage very often, with good blocking in front, and then simply outmaneuvered the two defensive backs by himself. So Dr. Williams wanted something to answer this threat of Heston's.

Conceding Heston would get by the line many times, Williams felt it was a waste to put nine men in the defensive line and leave the backfield unprotected. So he put four men in the defensive backfield, cut the defensive line to seven, and planned to bottle up Heston when the Michigan speedster reached the defensive secondary. Thus was born the diamond, four-man defense, and it stopped Heston just enough so that in the eighth game of the 1903 season Michigan and Minnesota struggled to a 6–6 tie, a major moral victory if ever there was one. This, for Minnesota, was not at all like kissing your sister. It was an achievement of great note even though Michigan went on to win twenty-six more games in a row before the Chicago triumph of 2–0. Of course Minnesota was also a powerful team and the Big Ten was being dominated by the Wolverines and the Golden Gophers at the time they met and tied. But Michigan's streak ended and that's what counted. The Gophers and Wolverines met only one other time during the Point-A-Minute era and Michigan beat Minnesota, 23–6, in the finale of the 1902 season.

The tie game in 1903 was also cause for the beginning of a tradition—a tradition based upon a Little Brown Jug. The 6–6 tie was played at Minnesota and it seems that the trainer for the Michigan team left behind one of the jugs he used to keep water for the Wolverines to drink during the game. The Minnesota trainer picked it up and, when asked to return it, told Michigan people to "come and take it back."

The Little Brown Jug is just that—a little brown jug, such as one sees in pictures of hillbillies sucking on their corn whiskey. Ever since that 6–6 tie, when Michigan and Minnesota meet in football it is for the right to possess the Little Brown Jug for another year. Michigan trainers have, after all, found new containers for their water since that time. This is the oldest college trophy of its type in football, and has been copied in idea and style since. Most notable among other such trophies is the Old Oaken Bucket, which goes to the winner of the Indiana-Purdue football game each year. This was first presented by Purdue and Indiana alumni in 1925. There is also the turtle (a model of the original live one) known as Illibuck, which goes to the Illinois–Ohio State football winner, and the Paul Bunyan Axe for the victor in the Wisconsin-Minnesota game. The Sweet Sioux Tomahawk is a trophy for the Illinois-Northwestern football winner and, of all things, the Old Brass Spittoon for the Michigan State–Indiana game winner. The Purdue-Illinois Cannon goes to that game's winner. A bronze statue of a prize pig is awarded to the Iowa-Minnesota winner.

Thus Michigan, with a high rate of scoring production, became the first team with a name for its accomplishments, the first great power from the organized Big Ten, and helped establish the first trophy hunt in college football. Not bad for a young coach named Yost in his first few seasons.

Also, Michigan was involved in what might be the first "game of the century" on that Thanksgiving Day in 1905 when more than 25,000 persons were attracted to Marshall Field in Chicago to watch Amos Alonzo Stagg's Chicagoans beat Fielding Yost's Michiganers, 2–0. It was the first of the famous streak-enders that have all been known as "the game of the century" by someone or other. The game was settled when Michigan's Denny Clark, trying to run a punt back from his end zone, was tackled and driven back into the end zone for a safety. Stagg once said, "We had won on an error of judgment and we had been lucky to do it." An indication of the defensive struggle in that game is that Chicago punted twenty-two times and Michigan twenty-nine times. Of course, football was still being played under rules calling for 5 yards in three downs, and the field was 110 yards long. The forward pass was a year off.

That game ended what was the first major set of achievements by a team from the organized Big Ten Conference. Michigan was the likely one to be the first real power of the league since the Wolverines had long been enchanted by the game of football and, well before the formation of the Big Ten, had traveled east to find good competition. On one late nineteenth-century venture, Michigan met the three powers of the time—Harvard, Yale, and Princeton—in a six-day period and lost all three games, but not without giving a good account of itself. That was in 1881, fourteen years before the Palmer House meeting that created the Big Ten.

Shortly after the formation of the new league in the Midwest, two games made such big impressions on the Eastern football experts that no one was going to continue to scorn the achievements of those teams from the fledgling conference, the league that was a new concept in college athletics. The first of these impressive efforts by a team from the Big Nine took place in 1898 in Franklin Field in Philadelphia between Stagg's Chicago team and a powerful University of Pennsylvania team. Chicago led, 6–5, at halftime, after taking a 6–0 lead in the first few minutes of play. Penn eventually won, 23–11, but Chicago had done its job as messenger of things to come later out of this new league. Clarence Herschberger was the star of the Maroons, who were coached by a former Yale player, Stagg.

The next game that carried the message East for the Midwest conference was in the Yale Bowl one year after the Franklin Field contest. This time it was Wisconsin that lost to Yale, 6–0, but not before Pat O'Dea, an Australian, kicked the ball so well that Yale fans were totally awed by this Badger booter. The rest of the Wisconsin team did plenty of work to hold mighty Yale through most of the game.

These were individual game achievements, and important ones for the new league's prestige. But it was for Michigan to make the deepest impressions by sustaining over the Point-A-Minute era a strength that made every one of the nation's football fans take notice of Midwestern football.

Michigan's Point-A-Minute period ended the year that President Theodore Roosevelt objected strongly to the college football scene, virtually ordering changes in the rules to safeguard the players, who punched and kicked and gouged as much as any other thing they did on the field of action. In the 1906 rules changes for safety there also evolved a new little item in football—the forward overhand pass. And the Midwestern teams took to it right away. Long before Gus Dorais of Notre Dame made the pass famous in the 1913 game against Army, the Big Nine teams were using the pass effectively. St. Louis University may actually have been the first to throw the pass a lot, or maybe it was Marietta under Coach Henderson E. Van Surdam. No matter, Stagg had a number of pass plays for his team in the 1906 season. He withheld these plays to save them for Minnesota in the big game that would help decide the Big Ten championship that season. Stagg's great quarterback, Walter Eckersall, was to throw the ball and beat the mighty Gophers in another of those "games of the century."

Unfortunately for Chicago the weather did not cooperate and it rained and rained on Friday and Saturday of the November weekend of this game. Stagg never let his team pass in the rain and mud of that football afternoon and Minnesota won, 4–2. A week later, however, Chicago had no reason to keep its pass under wraps and Eckersall had a big fling throwing the ball around to trounce Illinois, 63–0. But it was too late and Minnesota finished undefeated in the league, along with Wisconsin and Michigan. Chicago had only one league loss in four games.

That was Michigan's last Big Nine football season for eleven years, and Wisconsin, the team at the top of the league standings in 1906 with three victories and no defeats, almost withdrew as the faculty struggled with the issues of power football. The Badgers remained although, from that point until the return of Michigan in the 1917 football season, they gained only one conference title—the 1912 championship. Northwestern had dropped out of football for the 1906 and 1907 seasons, but returned to the gridiron in 1908 following strong protests by students and alumni to put the Purple players back in action.

Chicago won the conference title in 1907 and 1908 and no league team managed back-to-back championships until Ohio State joined the conference for the 1912 season and took the titles in 1916 and 1917. But Chicago and Minnesota were the teams that were consistently up near or at the top in those years just before the First World War. One of Minnesota's reasons for success was the development of the shift by the offensive team. Some persons say Stagg invented the shift. Others say it was Dr. Henry Williams, the Minnesota coach, and some still mistakenly claim Notre Dame was the original shift team. Notre Dame may have made it more famous than anyone else, but Williams was undoubtedly the first very successful coach to use the shift, as Minnesota won six of seven games in 1910 and won both of its league games that campaign.

Illinois was the league champion in 1910 despite the Minnesota shift as the Illini had their first undefeated season at seven victories, and went 4–0 in league action. Illinois was also the conference champion because Minnesota got involved in one of the first games involving a major dispute that had people buzzing for years. It was centered around the Minnesota-Michigan game, actually not a league game since the Wolverines were out of the league at the time. But the 6–0 loss tarnished the Gophers' slate enough so that Illinois was declared league champion.

Gopher fans insist the Minnesota-Michigan game should have ended in either a 6–0 Minnesota victory, or, at worst, in a 6–6 tie. But Michigan got the 6–0 decision for the Little Brown Jug. It happened this way: Rules in those days limited a forward pass to a toss of no more than 20 yards in the air. Michigan scored in a drive that involved two long passes, each of which was more than 20 yards in the air according to Minnesota players, coaches, and fans. They claimed one was as long as 30 yards. Then Minnesota apparently scored a touchdown when a blocked Michigan punt was picked up by Leonard Frank of Minnesota, who ran the ball across the Wolverines' goal line. An official, however, called the touchdown back saying the ball was dead. It was just another bit of contention in the long history of the Little Brown Jug.

Minnesota was, of course, using the shift against Michigan that unfortunate day for the Gophers. This was an offensive maneuver that changed football thinking and simply involved lining up one way and quickly jumping into something else before the defense could even get adjusted to what it first saw. Tackles in the Minnesota shift lined up behind the line of scrimmage, and the signal to shift sent them into the line that was unbalanced. The backs also shifted with the signal, and the powerful Minnesota Gophers, stronger than most teams they played, had the added advantage of one of the first major twists in offensive thinking in many years. It was another Yale man, Dr. Williams, who came up with it and won with it so much that shifting became standard operating procedure with many teams. But, like anything else, if the players were good the gimmicks would work. If the players were not good, little would help them win. Minnesota players such as John McGovern were awfully good.

Minnesota was also involved in the biggest upset in the conference during its first twenty years of existence. And, once again, the Gophers were the losers. This was the 1916 surprise victory by Illinois over the mighty Gophers of Minnesota, 14–9. Although Bob Zuppke had been at Illinois for four years when this happened, the unexpected triumph by the Illini made the little Dutchman a nationally known figure, with his witty style of talk and his widespread formations that confounded the opponents' defenses as much as the Minnesota shift had troubled Gopher foes.

Zuppke had taken the Illinois coaching job in 1913, and the following season he gave Illinois its second undefeated season with a team he often insisted was better than the great teams of Red Grange at Illinois a decade later. Zuppke called on a spread offense—not completely new since flankers were being employed on pass receptions by this time. But Illinois' spread was a total wide formation involving all linemen and backs. And this Illinois team of 1914 was exceptionally capable of doing what its coach wanted since it included talented athletes like George (Potsy) Clark, Harold Pogue, Bart Macomber, and Gene Schobinger, the men who made up the backfield.

Illinois remained strong in the 1915 season and fought Minnesota to a 6–6 tie that resulted in the Gophers and Illini tying for the league championship. Bernie Bierman was ailing with a sprained ankle hurt prior to the 1915 Illinois game, so this limited Minnesota's running attack. But a year later Minnesota was rated much stronger than Illinois and the Illini were to be just another of the Gophers' victims on their way to the Big Nine championship. But Zuppke fired his team up. Pep talks and halftime lectures worked in those days. He also called for an even wider than normal spread formation that included eleven men on the line from side to side of the gridiron before a shift sent them into a less widely spread set before the snap. Minnesota was confounded and lost, 14–6, in what cost the Gophers the title.

This enabled Ohio State, the newest member of the league, to win its first Big Nine championship. The Buckeyes repeated in 1917 for what became the first Big Ten football title, because in that year the league was finally a group of ten teams—Ohio State, Minnesota, Northwestern, Wisconsin, Chicago, Illinois, Indiana, Iowa, Purdue, and Michigan. Strangely enough, in Michigan's return to the conference the Wolverines were very strong and had an 8–2 season. But they played only one conference foe and lost, so that Michigan finished at the bottom of the Big Ten its first year back in the fold.

Charles (Chic) Harley, a superb halfback, was the main reason Ohio State won conference titles in 1916 and 1917. He also was responsible for giving the Buckeyes their first victory ever over Michigan in 1919. That series between Ohio State and Michigan was to become one of college football's most famous and bitterly contested each year.

This was a fitting start for the postwar era in college football. Something new—the years of glorification of the American sports hero were dawning. College football players were to be among these highly publicized superhumans, whose best-known figure was a potbellied, skinny-legged, heavy-drinking baseball player—Babe Ruth.

The Roaring Twenties

The days of the flapper and of prohibition were about to start, and with them came that decade of some of the most outstanding athletic accomplishments ever witnessed—the big college games of the twenties. So many of them took place in Big Ten Conference play, or involved a team from the Big Ten, that this Midwestern league has much more than its share of the glory of the twenties. It was a big decade for the famous coaches, who also had their representative group from the Big Ten. But games are the things that establish player and coach alike as worthy or not worthy of recognition.

Two games stand out as the high points for an individual—Red Grange, the Galloping Ghost of Illinois. One was Grange's sensational and still-unmatched performance against Michigan in 1924, when he scored the first four times he carried the ball and then came back to run for a fifth touchdown and pass for a sixth in a 39–14 victory over the Wolverines. The other was against the University of Pennsylvania in 1925. Red, miffed at the lack of attention his exploits had received in the East, was really out to show the skeptics that Red Grange did what Midwesterners said Red Grange could do. Well, he showed them, all right, scoring three touchdowns and rolling up 363 yards as the Illini won easily, 24–2.

Back in 1922, a year before Red Grange became the talk of the Big Ten and the nation, a mighty Chicago team of the Big Ten lost in one of the most memorable nonconference games of the twenties. Strangely enough, most of the well-remembered nonconference games involving Big Ten teams were marked by a losing effort by the Big Ten unit involved. The first of these long-to-be-remembered clashes took place on October 28, 1922 at Stagg Field, the arena named for the coach of the Maroon.

Chicago was to finish the season in a tie with Iowa and Michigan for the Big Ten title. Iowa was the acknowledged power of the conference following a championship season in 1921, and Chicago was just about as strong. It would be nothing for the Maroon to handle a slight invasion from the East, or would it?

The *New York Times* report of the game said, "Princeton avenged its setback at the hands of Chicago last season by defeating the Maroon eleven at Stagg Field this afternoon in the most sensational intersectional battle of football history. Apparently beaten beyond all hope of even their most enthusiastic admirers at the end of the third period, when they were trailing by 18–7, the fighting Tigers staged a desperate rally and rose to a glorious triumph by a score of 21–18."

Years later a Navy team was called "A Team Named Desire." This Princeton team was given the title of "Team of Destiny" after this biggest of all intersectional upsets to that point. Just to show how much Princeton made up in that wild fourth period, the Tigers were behind by eleven points early in the final stanza when, following a punt by Chicago, Princeton began working its way back from its own 2-yard line.

Members of that come-from-behind team of Old Nassau included Charlie Caldwell, who was later to coach the Tigers to some of their finest hours in the early fifties. Caldwell and a whole bunch of Princeton tacklers stopped Chicago on the final play of the game when the Maroon attempted to get over center from the Princeton 1-yard line. Stagg wrote, "Never before or since has Chicago lost a game which it tucked away so safely."

Michigan got over the drubbing it took from Red Grange in the new Illinois Stadium in 1924 and developed under Coach Fielding Yost into one of the strongest teams ever organized in the Big Ten. In fact, Hurry Up Yost insisted that his 1925 pack of Wolverines was better than his Point-A-Minute groups of more than two decades before the midtwenties. And it was a conference game that proved his point and amounted to one of the epic struggles in Big Ten league play.

Michigan had gotten by five opponents undefeated before facing a strong Northwestern team. Crowds were getting bigger and bigger each year and Soldiers Field in Chicago was expected to have

75,000 persons for the Michigan-Northwestern affair. It rained before the start of the game and by kickoff it was cold enough to turn that rain into a sleet. A strong wind whipped off Lake Michigan and 40,000 of the 75,000 who bought tickets showed up to take their chances in the bad weather.

Michigan's heroes of the time were Benny Friedman and Bennie Oosterbaan, who made up one of the first famous passing combinations in college football. Friedman throwing and Oosterbaan catching were a terror to all foes. But this time the real foe was the weather. Yost's powerhouse was stymied when its finest weapon was unable to work. Tiny Lewis booted a field goal for Northwestern in the first quarter after the Wildcats recovered a fumble by Friedman. That was the winning score, as Northwestern beat Michigan, 3–2, in a highly touted game that never really had a chance to become more than a struggle against the elements.

Michigan went on to win the Big Ten title because the Wolverines had five victories against one league loss while Northwestern had three victories against one Big Ten loss. This 1925 season concluded with another highly publicized meeting that took place in Columbus, Ohio. It was Red Grange's varsity finale for Illinois and the Illini beat Ohio State, 13–7. But Grange did not score, one of only five games in which he failed to score a touchdown for Illinois in his undergraduate days.

Tiny Lewis, the hero of the cold and rainy upset over Michigan in 1925, led Northwestern to its first real recognition as a power in the land of football during the 1926 season. These Wildcats under Coach Glen Thistlewaite had Northwestern's first undefeated season within Big Ten Conference play. But they suffered one loss—a 6–0 decision to mighty Notre Dame. Nevertheless, Northwestern shared the Big Ten title with Michigan in 1926 because both teams won all five of their games and they did not meet.

But 1926 was also a season of one of the most unusual scheduling situations in Big Ten history—a throwback to days before the league was organized and a situation never to be repeated. Michigan and Minnesota played each other twice in 1926.

Michigan won both games, just getting by in the second one, 7–6, when Oosterbaan picked up a Minnesota fumble and ran it 55 yards for a touchdown and Friedman kicked the winning extra point. One of the reasons for two meetings between Minnesota and Michigan was that the Gophers were getting a reputation as playing rather rough. This reputation lasted a long time, but in 1926, in order to complete a full eight-game schedule, Fielding Yost of Michigan agreed to play Minnesota twice. The first game was held in Ann Arbor, Michigan, and the second at Minneapolis. In a new use of telegraph, fans in Minneapolis watched as two scrub teams acted out the plays that took place in Ann Arbor following Western Union reports of the action.

This interesting 1926 season also included one of the very early major battles between Michigan and Ohio State. It was a classic Buckeye-Wolverines set-to at Columbus, Ohio, where the stadium in those days held seats for 65,000 persons. But reports have it that about 90,000 squeezed in for this Michigan–Ohio State match. Yost's powerhouse was favored, of course. But it wasn't until it was over that Michigan was able to escape with its life and a slim 17–16 triumph. Unfortunately for the Buckeyes, Meyers Clark missed the tying extra point with just a few minutes remaining in the game after Ohio had scored a touchdown to get within a point of the Wolverines.

The twenties ended happily for the Boilermakers of Purdue, who had their first undefeated season in 1929 and their first Big Ten title. Jimmy Phelan was the coach of this Purdue championship team that held all but one Big Ten rival scoreless. Michigan was the team that managed sixteen points against the Boilermakers. But Purdue was up to that and more in a big game, and won, 30–16. This win was also a long time in coming for Purdue since it marked the first football victory by the Boilermakers over the Wolverines since 1892, three years before the formation of the league.

SEVEN

The Big Games of the Thirties

The depression years of the thirties and those years just prior to Pearl Harbor meant just more greatness for the Big Ten in the way of games and national recognition. It was also a twelve-year period (1930–1941) that saw one team dominate the league for a while like no other team had since the days of the Michigan Point-A-Minute men. This new power was Minnesota, a team to be guided by Coach Bernie Bierman to the heights. Taking over in 1932 at Minneapolis, Bierman built such strong machines that the Gophers won or shared the Big Ten title six of the eight years from 1934 through 1941.

This was quite an accomplishment considering that Minnesota had to win championships by beating out powerful teams like Michigan with Tom Harmon and Forest Evashevski, and the always-threatening Ohio State.

Although Minnesota was involved in some classic tests to prove its right to be king of the Big Ten hill, the Gophers were not involved in the two most famous football games involving the Big Ten in the thirties. Ohio State was involved in each of them, and in each case the Buckeyes lost to a nonconference foe.

It may be that the 1935 Ohio State–Notre Dame football game was the most outstanding college football game ever played. Certainly some of the people present in Ohio Stadium on November 2, 1935 will claim so to their dying day. Allison Danzig, reporter par excellence and historian of collegiate football, tennis, and rowing for five decades with the *New York Times*, considered this game to be one of the five greatest ever played. Upon his retirement from the Old Gray Lady, Danzig was presented with a bronzed replica of the front page of the Sunday *New York Times* sports section from November 3, 1935 which led with his magnificent account of the Ohio State–Notre Dame game.

Francis Schmidt had taken over at Ohio State as the head coach in 1934, and Elmer Layden, one of the famed Four Horsemen in Notre Dame's great backfield, was coaching the Irish. Schmidt had established a wild and furious attack for the Buckeyes that had them scoring in big numbers. Notre Dame was strong but not thought to be as strong as the power-packed Buckeyes, who went on to tie Minnesota for the Big Ten title in 1935. Each of these teams went into the big game at Columbus undefeated, with Ohio State posting four victories and Notre Dame five. The buildup was about the biggest for a single game in college history and, despite deep depression conditions, scalpers were getting an unheard-of $50 per ticket.

It was also the first time that Notre Dame and Ohio State had ever met in a football game, adding to the enthusiasm for the big event at Ohio Stadium. Here is the way Danzig saw it for the *New York Times*' readers:

One of the greatest last-ditch rallies in football history toppled the dreaded Scarlet Scourge of Ohio State from its lofty pinnacle today as 81,000 dumbfounded spectators saw Notre Dame score three touchdowns in less than fifteen minutes to gain an almost miraculous 18–13 victory in the jammed Ohio Stadium.

Not since the Thundering Herd of Southern California spotted the Ramblers 14 points going into the final period at South Bend in 1931 and won by 16–14 has football provided so magnificent a comeback as this game team of Elmer Layden's staged here in the presence of a crowd that paid a quarter of a million dollars at the gate.

Trailing 13 to 0 at the end of the third quarter after being manhandled in fearful fashion for the first half by 220-pound Gomer Jones and his giant mates in the Scarlet line, Notre Dame looked to be so hopelessly beaten that no one in the huge throng conceded it the barest ghost of a chance. The fact that the Ramblers had five times threatened to score and been found wanting on each occasion left their adherents with a feeling of futility of their cause.

And then the incredible happened and happened so fast and furiously, as the lionhearted, blue-shirted players from South Bend became so many swirling, insensate fire-eaters, as to leave the vast assemblage stunned.

In the space of a few minutes, with the stadium clock ticking off the precious remaining moments in the gathering dusk and threatening to save the stampeded home forces from the rout, a team that looked to be irretrievably doomed struck thrice through the air and worked a miracle that brought pandemonium in the Notre Dame stands.

Andy Pilney, the artisan of Notre Dame's victory over Navy with his deadly throwing arm, was the hero of this football battle of the year between two of the mightiest forces in the land. It was Pilney, with his superb passing and his swirling, fearless running from scrimmage and in returning punts, who almost providentially saved the day for the Blue and Gold in a game that was expected to be dominated by Ohio State's sensational sophomore, Joe Williams.

With hardly a minute to go and the score 13 to 12 in the Buckeyes' favor, Pilney broke loose on a dazzling broken-field run of 32 yards after trying vainly to get off another pass, downing the ball on Ohio State's 19-yard line. The cheers that greeted this last brilliant effort by the Notre Dame back died abruptly as he was seen to lie stretched out just over the sideline.

A stretcher was brought out and Notre Dame's hopes looked to be sunk as he was carried out of the enclosure and placed in an ambulance. But thirty seconds later Wayner Milner was receiving the winning touchdown pass from Bill Shakespeare in the end zone, and the joy of the bedlam-struck Notre Dame cheering section became totally unallayed when it was learned that Pilney had suffered no more than a torn ligament in his leg.

And so on went the report of just about the most amazing comeback struggle in the annals of college football.

Four years later Ohio State was to win the Big Ten title outright for one of the two breaks in Minnesota dominance of the Big Ten from 1934 through 1941. And during the 1939 season Ohio State worked to a point of being ranked No. 1 in the nation in the Associated Press weekly poll which was becoming an accepted guide for the relative strengths of teams from coast to coast. While the Buckeyes were sitting high atop the football world, they had a slight pause in their Big Ten battles to dispose of an Eastern rival that got on the schedule somehow. It was Cornell that was providing Ohio State's opposition in the fourth Buckeye game of the 1939 campaign at Ohio Stadium. The Big Red would provide no difficulties. After all, Ohio State had just beaten mighty Minnesota in a real struggle of Big Ten powers the week before, 23–20. In that big game the Buckeyes came from behind to beat the defending league champion Gophers and thus assured themselves of the eventual 1939 Big Ten crown.

Cornell was the best of the Ivy League teams and also the best in the East. But by this time in college football history the East was no longer the big place for the big teams with the big records and the impressive national rankings as much as was the Midwest. So Ohio State was an easy pick to win. The trouble was, however, that Cornell won.

Ohio State, led as usual by quarterback Don Scott, halfbacks Jim Strausbaugh and Frank Zadworney, and fullback Jimmy Langhurst, got off to an early 14–0 lead in the first quarter. That's how it was supposed to happen. But within a few minutes things changed as Walt Scholl, a little halfback, scampered 79 yards for a Cornell touchdown. Then Scholl threw a long touchdown pass to Swifty Bohrman and the game was tied, 14–14. Shocked by the men from upstate New York, Ohio State didn't recover and Cornell got a touchdown and field goal in the second half to beat the mighty Buckeyes, 23–14. As time went by it was apparent that this was no upstart Cornell unit that beat the mighty Buckeyes because the Big Red went on to win all of their eight games in 1939 and established a winning streak of eighteen games in a row. Cornell even got to be ranked No. 1 in the nation before the famous fifth-down, 3–0 loss to Dartmouth in the next-to-last game of 1940. This eighteen-game winning streak also included another big victory over Ohio State. The 21–7 decision over Ohio State by Cornell in 1940 put the Big Red at No. 1 in the nation. These two Cornell–Ohio State football games were the only ones between these institutions. It seems unlikely they will ever meet again, certainly not in the twentieth century.

Thus Ohio State kept up the unfortunate pattern of losing efforts in the most outstanding nonconference games involving Big Ten teams. Yet even the losing team was great in its play in that loss to Notre Dame in 1935 and that loss to Cornell in 1939. The fact that each team was so good made the game what it was in each instance.

When the thirties started it was a time for a couple of familiar names at the top of the Big Ten to continue their positions up there, and Northwestern and Michigan tied for the Big Ten title in 1930. But going into the final game of the season, Northwestern was reaching even higher than just the Big Ten championship. The Wildcats were unbeaten, as was Michigan, and were going against a good Notre Dame team that was also undefeated. "Hard Luck" Hank Bruder, who had been plagued by injuries throughout his career at Northwestern, was returning after being sidelined with smallpox. Late in the game against Notre Dame, Bruder had more hard luck as he fumbled on the Irish 1-yard line. There were seven minutes remaining in a scoreless contest. Notre Dame recovered that fumble by the unfortunate running back, and shortly afterwards Marchy Schwartz ran 27 yards for Notre Dame's winning touchdown in a 14–0 victory, just another big loss for a Big Ten team in a big and important nonconference game.

The 1933 season was Michigan's last one atop the Big Ten for many years to come. But it was blemished just a mite by a scoreless tie with the Minnesota Gophers, who were being shaped into the strong power that Bierman was building. The Wolverines finished the campaign with five Big Ten victories against just that tie with Minnesota. Minnesota also went undefeated in the league in Bierman's second season as head coach at Minneapolis. But that 0–0 tie with Michigan in the game for the Little Brown Jug was just one of four ties that Minnesota played in 1933.

This Minnesota-Michigan game was a hard-hitting affair that was something like the three famous Fordham-Pittsburgh scoreless ties to be played during this same period. Minnesota may have felt some big changes were really taking place under Bierman despite this 0–0 tie, however. The Gophers had lost nineteen straight Little Brown Jug games to Michigan.

Then came 1934, the year when Minnesota reached the strength that marked the Gophers for seasons to come. It was this 1934 squad that was the strongest ever seen in Minneapolis and was even rated by some as the most powerful college football team ever put together since Rutgers and Princeton met in 1869. The Gophers were called a machine, Bierman's Monsters, and lots of other things. The personnel was much the same as the 1933 team that "suffered" four ties. But one year older and wiser and more capable, the 1934 Minnesotans were devastating. The proof positive of this came in the 34–0 victory over Wisconsin in the season finale that concluded one of the finest years a college team ever had.

Glenn Seidel was the quarterback of this Minnesota team that went unbeaten in 1934. He was an exceptional student in the school of engineering. Bud Wilkinson, who would later earn national fame as coach of the powerful Oklahoma Sooners in the post-World War II era, was one of the guards. This corps of strong Minnesota blockers in the line also included a guard, who was the last of a vanishing type in football. He was Bill Bevan, the last known player in the Big Ten to play without a helmet.

One of the strengths of this Minnesota team was that it had

unusual depth with talent. Players were no longer being asked to play all sixty minutes, although they still played what is now known as one-platoon football so that a player was on offense and defense. The first two-platoon, or offensive and defensive units, style didn't come into the picture until the midforties. With depth, however, Bierman could relieve his starters and at center Minnesota had a pair of strong men—Dale Rennebohm and Earl Svendsen. No one ever really decided which one was the better of the two. There was depth in the offensive backfield also, with runners such as Pug Lund, the team captain; Babe LeVoir, who was a halfback and also took over at quarterback for Seidel now and then; and Julie Alfonse and Art Clarkson. And this strong team had two hammer-like fullbacks—Sheldon Beise and Stan Kostka.

Wilkinson, incidentally, played in Minnesota's line in the mid-thirties when a chubby but powerful center, Gomer Jones, played for Ohio State. Jones became an assistant to Wilkinson at Oklahoma and eventually succeeded him as head coach but, unfortunately, never had the success Wilkinson enjoyed with the Sooners and lasted only a couple of seasons.

Minnesota's mighty team just kept rolling on over Midwestern and other foes through the 1935 season and was beginning to resemble a rampant tank. The Golden Gophers weren't particular who they stomped on. Bierman went into the 1936 season with the public endorsement of championship predictions for his Minnesota team again. Would it ever stop? Well, Bierman never wanted it to end and he made a big move in personnel to prevent any end to this magnificent victory string. He moved Wilkinson, a man with an obvious brain and sense for football, from guard to quarterback where he was an additional punch as a fine blocking quarterback in the powerful single wing. So Minnesota just kept winning and, despite some troubles, opened the season by edging Washington, 14–7, on the West Coast. Then came victories over Nebraska, Michigan, and Purdue. The machine was well oiled and working to perfection—but there was a catch. Lynn (Pappy) Waldorf was the catch. Waldorf had just taken over the coaching job at Northwestern, and Minnesota had the Wildcats coming up for game number five of the 1936 season.

Northwestern hadn't really been heard from since the confusing days of the 1931 season. Those charity games were long forgotten and Minnesota was not about to display any charity toward Northwestern on October 31, 1936 at Dyche Stadium in Evanston, Illinois. Northwestern, on the other hand, wasn't looking for any charity although the Wildcats obviously got a big break in this game that was played in the mud of a rainy day. The Big Ten title was obviously on the line although it was only midseason. Everyone knew this game would tell the tale since Waldorf had done wonders with the Purple Wildcats and taken them into the Minnesota game without a loss.

Through the slime and mud of a very wet football afternoon, Minnesota and Northwestern played a slugging, defensive battle for the first half, and entered the third period with a scoreless tie. Then Northwestern got the ball deep into Minnesota territory when the break came. An official threw a flag against Minnesota for roughness and the 15-yard penalty put the football at the Gophers' 1-yard line. Steve Toth, the Northwestern fullback, managed to power and slide through the wet, locked lines tangled in the usual goal-line-plunge situation. He scored a touchdown—the only six points of the game. This 6–0 Northwestern triumph ended Minnesota's string of twenty-eight games without defeat that went all the way back to the 1932 season. Northwestern thereby won the Big Ten title, and with Ohio State's 1939 Big Ten championship, these were the only two breaks in Minnesota's hold on the conference crown for eight seasons.

Minnesota rebounded the next year, as expected, and won the Big Ten title in 1937, 1938, 1940, and 1941. The Gophers did this even though Michigan hired Fritz Crisler to take control and coach the Wolverines, and despite the fact that Michigan had Harmon. Tom Harmon never played on a Big Ten championship team and never played on a team to beat Minnesota. In fact, he never scored against the Gophers in his three varsity seasons.

But Harmon and his mates played some thrilling games that included major triumphs over Penn and Yale to make believers of the Eastern skeptics the way Red Grange had done. One of the Ohio State games, though, was a classic of Harmon action with the help of his favorite blocking back, Forest Evashevski. This was the 1939 Ohio State–Michigan game in Harmon's junior season. Trailing 14–0. Michigan came back to tie the game as Harmon scored one touchdown and passed to Evashevski for the tying score. With three minutes to go, Fred Trosko ran for the winning touchdown on a fake-field-goal play.

Little Davey Nelson was the quarterback with Harmon and Evashevski. Years after his playing days, Nelson said he never got hurt "because I always just threw the ball back to Evy or Harmon and then fell down."

EIGHT

Games of the Century

Big Ten football, like everything else in this country, didn't suddenly return to normalcy immediately after World War II. Proof of this was that Indiana University went undefeated for the first time in its history and won the Big Ten title in the 1945 season just a few months after Japan surrendered. The Hoosiers had good football players. But the long-standing powers of the league didn't have their usual complement of strong boys to keep up with the likes of Ted Kluszewski, Ben Raimondi, and others, who were well directed by Coach Alvin (Bo) McMillin. Indiana hasn't won a Big Ten title outright since that time, and only once, in 1967, did the Hoosiers manage to share a crown as they finished that campaign in a three-way tie with Minnesota and Purdue but got the Rose Bowl trip—and lost.

Things began to return to the way fans expected during the late forties, however, even though Illinois was a bit of a surprise as the 1946 Big Ten football champion and the first representative of the league in the Rose Bowl under the new agreement with the Pacific Coast Conference that began a long postseason pact that still stands. By 1947 Big Ten and other football was back in full swing, moving into a new era of T-formation passing attacks as never seen before, with players and coaches who had ideas of doing things in new ways and maybe even better ways than before.

For the next twenty-five years the crowds would become ever larger, the games would loom as ever more important, and the excitement would increase with every season. And the Big Ten would have its serious problems that would have telling results on the field of play while coaches continued to grumble about being hampered in their quests for victory after victory after victory and victory at any cost.

Michigan State replaced Chicago in the Big Ten at the end of the forties and was first counted in the Big Ten football race in the 1953 season. And it was Michigan State that took part in the most highly publicized game following World War II. It was that game with Notre Dame in 1966, the game that became practically a joke in the newspaper business as the "ultimate game of the century." Oh, there would be Ohio State–Michigan games after that considered, by some, to be even more important each year. But the Michigan–Ohio State thing became so much of an annual "big game," and was usually played in such a fashion of "hit and slug it out" by Woody Hayes and Bo Schembechler, that no one could really expect the Wolverines and Buckeyes to be teams for the "game of the century" every year. Unfortunately for Duffy Daugherty's Spartans of Michigan State, they ended in the famed 10–10 tie with Notre Dame in that game of 1966. This was another nonconference game in which the Big Ten team did not win but, in this case, the Big Ten team came out looking better than the opponent, Notre Dame, which was criticized for not trying hard enough toward the end to win this game that was for No. 1 in the nation. Notre Dame kept the top spot by the tie.

But long before Michigan State met Notre Dame in the big one, in fact seventeen years before that contest, Michigan and Ohio State were at it in the major game of the season within the conference. As so often happened before and after, these two archrivals struggled as if in a battle to the death, and when the 1949 game was over Ohio State got a trip to the Rose Bowl. But Ohio State didn't get a victory that day against Michigan. This Ohio State–Michigan season finale was at Ann Arbor and the home forces had a 7–0 lead late in the fourth quarter. The Buckeyes scored, however, and a tie would send them to the Rose Bowl. All they needed was the extra point. But Jimmy Hague's placement was wide and Ohio State fans were without hope. But then, there on the ground was one of those tell-tale flags that officials throw now and then. It was one flag toss too many for Michigan, which was detected with a man offside. Hague got another chance at the conversion and this time he didn't miss. Ohio State won the trip to the Rose Bowl because Michigan had gone after the 1948 season as the Big Ten champion. But Ohio State didn't beat Michigan's football team that day. Some years later, in 1973, a tie between these two mighty rivals would lead to the loudest screaming and hollering the league had ever seen.

Again, in 1950, it was the Ohio State–Michigan game at the end of the season that was the thriller, the big game for the title and the Rose Bowl scene. But this time, as never before, conditions played a part in the outcome as much as the players. Ohio State was a power in this, Coach Wes Fesler's final season at the Buckeye helm. Vic Janowicz was the star and was helped by a bunch of players who were better than most in the country. The Buckeyes lost in an upset to Kyle Rote and his Southern Methodist University team in the nonleague opener of 1950. But soon Ohio State was rolling and the Buckeyes scored an 83–0 victory over Iowa while scoring 230 points in a five-week span. Then, another upset, as Illinois surprised the Buckeyes a week before the Michigan game. But Ohio had a chance to go to the Rose Bowl with the expected triumph over a fair but not great Michigan team.

That was the game they called the Snow Bowl because it was played in a blizzard which socked in the city of Columbus and produced the most horrible playing conditions ever experienced in any college football game. Unhappily for Ohio State, whose athletic director, Dick Larkins, made the decision to play the game, even under such adverse conditions, the Buckeyes lost, 9–3, when Michigan blocked two of Janowicz's kicks. It was a tough way to lose a chance to go to the Rose Bowl.

Michigan State did not become part of the Big Ten football race until 1953, but in 1951 was a member of the league awaiting the usual four-year entry period. Athletes enrolled before league entrance would be out of the institution and all athletes playing would be under Big Ten Conference regulations by 1953. Yet in 1951 the Spartans, under Coach Biggie Munn, sent chills through the regular lodge of old members as these Spartans trounced everyone in sight and won all nine games with such outstanding performances as a 35–0 triumph over Notre Dame. But it was the 24–20 victory over Ohio State that made opponents shudder at what Michigan State could do when forced. Al Dorow was the quarterback of Munn's multiple offense that used double-wing and single-wing, et al. Trailing 20–17, with just a few minutes remaining in the game. Dorow called on razzle-dazzle at its best and it worked. Taking the snap from center, Dorow pitched wide right back to Tom Yewcic as the entire Spartan team moved right to give Yewcic the big strength for a sweep. The entire team minus one went right with the tailback. The one exception was Dorow, who took off alone to the left and got behind the Ohio secondary before anyone on defense could correct the move to take Yewcic. Yewcic then stopped and passed long to Dorow who scored the winning touchdown easily. These Spartans were on their way to a long time of power in the Big Ten, and everyone who saw that victory over Ohio State knew the league was going to undergo some changes in the football standings starting with the 1953 season. That's what happened as the Spartans tied for the league title their first official season of 1953 and went to the Rose Bowl.

Michigan State went on through the 1952 season undefeated and was ready to enter official Big Ten play in 1953 riding the heights of a two-season-plus winning streak. Now that the terrible Spartans were part of the official family they were all geared up to treat the other nine members with very little brotherly love. It was expected to be onward and upward for Biggie Munn and company in 1953, even though this would turn out to be Munn's final season as coach of the green and white Spartans of Lansing. This 1953 season also marked the return to one-platoon football from the short experiment with unlimited substitutions. Players who had rested while the other half of the team worked suddenly found themselves going on offense and defense. But Michigan State's players were good enough to do the job. And so were Illinois' players that good. The Illini were able to call on J. C. Caroline, the Big Ten's best runner that season. These two teams finished in a deadlock for the Big Ten crown and Michigan State got the Rose Bowl bid because, of course, the Spartans had never gone as a Big Ten representative before.

Michigan State, however, did not get through the season without finally suffering a loss. And the defeat came from a most unexpected source—Purdue. This was a 6–0 victory by the Boilermakers in the biggest Big Ten upset of many seasons. It ended Michigan State's twenty-nine-game winning streak and proved that even the Spartans were human, ordinary Big Ten football players. But Purdue has been upsetting people for so many seasons those Big Ten folks should get used to it. Michigan State learned the hard way, and finished with a 9–1 season mark and 5–1 league record, the same as Illinois.

Now came Woody Hayes front and center with the Ohio State Buckeyes, who were to have the stamp of this stern coach for three decades. It was 1954, Hayes' fourth season as head coach at Columbus, Ohio, where nothing had really been distinguished about the Buckeyes to the casual eye. But Woody had been building and was now going to strike with a powerful line and a bunch of good backs. This Ohio State team had Jim Parker in the line, one of the youngest men to be named to the Football Hall of Fame, and Howard (Hopalong) Cassady, a runner par excellence. And where should a good Ohio State season be concluded but with Michigan? So there in Ohio Stadium in Columbus, Hayes and company enjoyed one of his many big days against a good Michigan team by beating the Wolverines, 21–7. It gave the Buckeyes a perfect record, the first of many for Hayes at Columbus, and sent them off to the Rose Bowl again.

Ohio won the title again the following year but, under the Big Ten's funny rules, was not able to succeed itself in the Rose Bowl, so Michigan State, runner-up in the league, went west.

Forest Evashevski was the next coach to make his mark at the top of the Big Ten heap and the former Michigan star did it with the Iowa Hawkeyes, who had not won a title for thirty-four years. Going into the last two Big Ten Conference games of 1956, Iowa was known as a strong team but first Minnesota and then Ohio State were favored to beat these Iowa players. It took only two touchdowns—one in each game—for Evashevski's wing-T Hawkeyes to do their work in a couple of surprises and get the Rose Bowl trip.

Early in the contest with Minnesota the Gophers fumbled and Iowa recovered. Fred Harris scored to end a 38-yard move after the change of ball, and then Iowa held for fifty-five minutes to win, 7–0. A week later Iowa went against Woody Hayes' boys, who had won their last seventeen Big Ten Conference games. In the third period of that game Iowa marched 63 yards for a touchdown and again held for the remainder to get a 6–0 triumph. This put the Hawkeyes in the Rose Bowl. Evashevski didn't last at Iowa as long as he wanted to because of many problems, but he had another Big Ten championship in 1958 and tied for the title in 1960, his final year coaching the Hawkeyes.

The big games in the Big Ten always seemed to have an element of surprise or something totally unexpected. It wasn't always that the big game was an upset, but it was a bit of a surprise now and then how the final score was achieved. Yet there was to be another of those surprises in nonconference play, one of those many upsets from the team intruding upon the strength of the Big Ten. It was again Ohio State that was shocked by Penn State, 7–6, in a 1956 game. And this only set the stage for a game seven years later.

Woody Hayes had gotten the mighty Bucks back up on top in 1957 and 1961. His was another of the strong Ohio State teams in

1963 when the Nittany Lions of Penn State shocked the Buckeyes again with a 10–7 triumph. And this, in turn, made things even more interesting for a nonconference meeting with Penn State again in 1964. This time Woody Hayes was ready and had a team undefeated through its first six games and ranked No. 1 in the nation. Penn State this time would be no problem. Rip Engle would take his Penn Staters to Columbus, Ohio, and these Buckeyes would show them a thing or two—or would they?

The night before the game, Joe Paterno, then an assistant coach to Rip Engle at Penn State in those days, joined Jim Tarman, the sports information director, and Jim O'Hora, another assistant coach, for a beer in the cocktail lounge of the motel where they were staying in Columbus. "I know we can't possibly win," said Tarman, "but we're not going to be humiliated, are we?"

Paterno answered matter-of-factly, "We're going to shut out Woody."

Paterno was right. Penn State won, 27–0, in one of the biggest upsets ever turned in against a Big Ten team from the outside world. Later Paterno explained why he had been so certain of a victory: "Actually, Woody had gotten into a pattern with his offense. After studying the films and our scouting reports, we felt we could tell which side they were going to run to without any chance for error."

NINE

The Seventies—A Time for Buckeyes and Wolverines

Indiana, Minnesota, and Purdue tied for the Big Ten football championship in 1967, and the Hoosiers, under Coach John Pont, went on to lose to Southern California, 14–3, in the Rose Bowl. Pont enjoyed such honors as Coach of the Year and Indiana and Purdue were ranked among the top ten teams in the nation.

And so ended the story of success for eight of the Big Ten football teams for many years to follow. From that time on Ohio State and Michigan dominated the Big Ten as no two teams have controlled a single college football league. It became laughable to those watching from the outside as year after year the Buckeyes and Wolverines seemed just to go through the motions of playing everyone else in the Big Ten only as prelims to the main event—the Ohio State–Michigan game before about 86,000 in Columbus or over 100,000 in Ann Arbor. Of course there was the ever-present ABC Sports telecast of the game each year that was viewed by millions across the nation.

From 1968 through 1976 either Michigan or Ohio State or both won the Big Ten title. Only once in that time did one of these powers finish lower than second, and that was 1971 when Michigan won the crown and the Buckeyes were tied for third behind Northwestern, which was runner-up.

Many factors contribute to such long success in college athletic teams where the personnel is constantly changing because of graduations or academic attrition. But, obviously, the rich got richer in this case. Teams win with athletes, and the best athletes going to the Big Ten football teams seemed to keep going to either Ohio State or Michigan.

Bob Blackman, who tried for six years in the futile Big Ten

struggle by the also-rans in this period, summed it up well when he was fired at Illinois after the 1976 season and returned to the Ivy League to take the head coaching job at Cornell. The former Dartmouth coach said, "You're a coach at Illinois or another school in the Big Ten other than Ohio State and Michigan and you have recruits onto the campus sometime in January or February to try to sell your school and football program. These young high school athletes talk to your team players, who are thinking other than football now. They may even want to forget it because they had a losing season that recently ended. Your football players are concerned with classes and other things, and the weather is cold and the campus bleak in the winter. Just what impresssion do you think the high school boy has from that visit?

"Then he goes to Michigan or Ohio State. Sure, it's bleak and cold on campus there, too. But the football players may have a tan from a recent week or two in a bowl environment."

Pausing to let that theory sink in, Blackman then continued with added ideas on just why nobody but Woody Hayes or Bo Schembechler could recruit so many blue-chippers in this era: "There is always the assurance of at least one and probably two or three nationally televised games, which include bowl appearances. What do you think this does for a boy? The winter vacation at Los Angeles for the Rose Bowl along with a possible trip to Miami or New Orleans now makes it so much more inviting at Ohio State and Michigan."

Blackman is obviously correct—in part. Ohio State and Michigan seem to perpetuate success with success and bowl games. This became clear as the seventies approached and began slipping by without any team other than Buckeyes or Wolverines finishing on top of the Big Ten football race.

Schembechler came on the scene in 1969 when he moved from head coach at Miami of Ohio to head coach at Ann Arbor. Hayes was well established at Ohio State where the Buckeyes had just beaten out Michigan for the 1968 football title and then gone on to beat Southern California, 27–16, in the January 1, 1969 Rose Bowl. One of the contributing factors that brought Schembechler to Michigan was Ohio State's 50–14 trouncing of Michigan in the regular-season finale that decided the football title. Chalmers (Bump) Elliott was out after ten years as the Wolverines' head football coach, and Schembechler was in.

Don Canham, who had become the director of athletics at Michigan in 1968, was running a multimillion-dollar business at Ann Arbor, and he was going to run it with the best personnel possible and for the advantage of Michigan. Thus he reached down to that well of coaching talent—Miami University of Oxford, Ohio—to bring up Schembechler, who had played under Woody Hayes when Hayes coached the Miami team. Hayes, like Schembechler, had moved ahead to the Ohio State job from Miami in 1951, the year Schembechler was graduated from Miami.

With the arrival of Schembechler things began in earnest between Ohio State and Michigan, or, probably more to the point, between Hayes and Schembechler. Each man, being a tense, hard-working, devoted football coach, drove his team all season but drove particularly hard when the big season final game approached each year. It took its toll on each of these coaches. Both suffered heart attacks but quickly returned to the coaching job during this period of dual dynasty.

The Big Ten was changing through this Hayes-Schembechler era and growing with the times that called for major rules and personnel shifts that had great effect upon all athletics within the league.

Bill Reed, the popular commissioner of the Big Ten, died on May 20, 1971. He had done a valiant job in one of the most trying decades in national college athletic history—the sixties. He was succeeded on August 5, 1971 by Wayne Duke, a former commissioner of the Big Eight Conference and a man who had learned his trade even before that while serving as an assistant to Walter Byers, the executive director of the N.C.A.A.

Less than a year later the Big Ten followed the national guidelines of the N.C.A.A. and permitted freshmen to take part in varsity football and basketball, starting with the fall seasons of 1972. With this allowance came one of the most spectacular young athletes to ever play college football—Archie Griffin. Starting with that freshman season of 1972, this Ohio State tailback ran to a college record for yards gained in a career and became the first man to win the Heisman Trophy twice.

Archie Griffin was a sophomore in 1973 when one of the most controversial Big Ten football games of the seventies was played at Ann Arbor with the two leaders of the league struggling to a 10–10 decision. It wasn't so much a controversy of action on the gridiron as it became a big hassle the very next day when Big Ten athletic directors voted Ohio State into the Rose Bowl. All hell broke loose after the decision that Schembechler said was guided by "petty jealousies."

Both teams finished in a dead heat for the Big Ten championship.

Each finished a season with ten victories, no losses, and that one tie. Only one could go to the Rose Bowl. The previous season Ohio State had gone to the Rose Bowl even though Michigan and Ohio State finished in a tie for the Big Ten title in 1972. But in that 1972 campaign Michigan State had upset Ohio State, 19–12, for the Buckeyes' only regular-season loss, and Ohio State then beat Michigan, 14–11. Since Ohio State won the head-to-head meeting, the Buckeyes got the 1972 nod for the Rose Bowl, January 1, 1973.

But things were different a year later when that 1973 season ended all-even. A previous Big Ten rule had stipulated that if teams were tied at the end of the season, the team that had made the most recent trip to the Rose Bowl would not get the bowl game. Michigan fully expected this to be the guideline for the vote the day after the 10–10 deadlock. But the vote went six to four in favor of Ohio State, with the key vote being Michigan State's decision to send the Buckeyes. Michigan people attributed that to old wounds created over two decades before when the Wolverines tried to keep Michigan State out of the Big Ten.

Schembechler lashed out at the athletic directors and said, "I'm very bitter and resentful."

Commissioner Wayne Duke explained that some athletic directors voted for Ohio State because of an injury to Dennis Franklin, the Wolverines' quarterback. Franklin, who scored the tying touchdown in the fourth quarter when Michigan got its ten points against Ohio State, suffered a knee injury just before the game ended. But Schembechler and Don Canham were not buying that excuse from the Big Ten commissioner.

However, off to the Rose Bowl went the Buckeyes, where they got a big performance from Griffin and a freshman fullback, Pete Johnson, and trounced Southern California, 42–21. But that was the only Rose Bowl victory by a Woody Hayes team in four consecutive appearances that saw the Buckeyes lose at Pasadena in 1973, 1975, and 1976.

Schembechler and Canham may have lost the bid to the Rose Bowl through some politics within the conference, but they created enough of a fuss to have the Rose Bowl selection rules of the Big Ten changed the next year. The Big Ten set up a guide so that if there is a tie for the title, the winner of the game between the two teams tied will go to the Rose Bowl. If these teams play a tie on the field, then the Rose Bowl team will be determined by won-lost percentage of all games played in the season. If there is still a tie, then the most recent team at the Rose Bowl will be eliminated.

Two years before this big tie game and following political mess, Woody Hayes had a big day at Ann Arbor where he created a bizarre situation when Michigan beat Ohio State, 10–7, before 104,016 persons on hand and a television audience of millions, on November 20, 1971.

Neil Amdur of the *New York Times* described it as follows: "In an unusually fiery display of temperament that typified his coaching intensity, the 57-year-old Hayes rushed on the field in the last 90 seconds to protest a Michigan pass interception that thwarted Ohio State's final offensive series at the Wolverine 49-yard line.

"Tom Darden, a Michigan defensive back, had leaned in front of Dick Wakefield, the Ohio State pass receiver, for the crucial interception at the Wolverine 32 with 1:25 left.

"Apparently contending that Darden had interfered with Wakefield, Hayes confronted the referee, Jerry Markbreit, and had to be restrained by assistants and players.

"The Buckeyes were penalized 15 yards for Hayes' misconduct. They lost another 15 yards when Hayes, still shouting at officials on the sidelines, tore up the first-down and sideline markers, to the bewilderment of Lou Lehman, the field judge."

Wayne Duke criticized Hayes for his conduct in that game. It was certainly one of the best-witnessed displays of Hayes' temper, which had become famous because of the Ohio State coach's conduct behind closed doors in the dressing rooms. But here was Woody running rampant over the gridiron at Michigan Stadium with millions watching across the nation in living color.

Woody probably hadn't calmed down by the time, more than a month later, when Stanford edged Michigan by one point—13–12—in the January 1, 1972 Rose Bowl. The Ohio State coach could not get much satisfaction in the Wolverines suffering another of those final defeats of theirs. Because Michigan seemed, in this period, to be unable to win its last game of a total campaign, Woody found no solace. He and his Buckeyes had lost to Michigan by three points way back in November and that was a bitter pill for him to swallow.

The Michigan dilemma about those final games is virtually impossible to explain—unless. . . . Could it be that the powerful Michigan and Ohio State teams of the 1970s were by far the best in the Big Ten but not actually the best in the land, the way Wolverines and Buckeyes sometimes claimed? Maybe the 1976 season pointed out some of this theory by, of course, those persons outside the Big Ten Conference.

The Big Ten finally let down the bars to its runner-up teams in football and basketball in 1975 and permitted strong also-rans to participate in postseason activities. Thus the 1975 Michigan team got to go to the Orange Bowl against Oklahoma, as Ohio State, which beat Schembechler's forces, 21–14, in 1975, went west for the Rose Bowl, January 1, 1976. Both teams were very highly ranked in the nation, and Ohio State was undefeated in the regular campaign while Michigan's only loss was to Ohio State in that finale at Ann Arbor.

Michigan and Ohio State were each whipped in the bowls of January 1, 1976—a shock. Oklahoma had no trouble with the Wolverines and UCLA, which had been trounced by Ohio State in the regular season, turned on Ohio State in Archie Griffin's final game for the Buckeyes and won the Rose Bowl, 23–10.

Then came the 1976 season when Michigan was to be the best in the land because so many of the Orange Bowl players were returning. Despite losing Archie Griffin, Ohio State was going to be strong. No doubt about it. And look at those schedules. The 1976 season was going to be a cakewalk into the bowls for Michigan and Ohio State, with the loser of their annual showdown probably going to the Orange Bowl again.

Michigan, with a backfield the Wolverines felt was one of the best ever assembled, headed into the season behind a brave coach. Schembechler had undergone lifesaving heart surgery the previous spring but was back "in the trenches" when the season began. His only concession was a curtailment of his activities in spring practice and a bit lighter schedule than usual in preseason. But his assistants obviously prepared his team well. The Wolverines broke from the gate ready to comply with predictions. They were ranked No. 1 from the beginning, and kept hold of that spot as the season progressed. Ohio State, unfortunately, was not so impressive as a hot-and-cold Missouri team beat the Buckeyes in the third game and pesky UCLA tied Ohio State the very next week. Both of these shocks to Ohio State's prestige took place at Ohio Stadium.

But those Wolverines. They were tearing everyone apart. That backfield of Rob Lytle, Rick Leach, Harlan Huckleby, Jim Smith, and others had it all. At least they had it all when it came to running with the ball behind a fine offensive line. Leach, the quarterback, seemed to lack a bit in the passing department. But then, with such speed and strength, and Lytle one of the best at tailback following a switch from fullback, Michigan didn't have too much to worry about passing.

Michigan, like Ohio State, had three games outside the Big Ten during the regular campaign. There was nothing for the Wolverines to worry about here since those nonleague opponents in 1976 were Stanford, Navy, and Wake Forest, on three successive weeks. Michigan went through them with ease.

The Navy game, played before another of those 100,000-plus crowds at Michigan Stadium, was a rare contest in a political sense. It matched President Gerald Ford's alma mater, Michigan, against Governor Jimmy Carter's alma mater, the United States Naval Academy, just thirty-eight days before Carter defeated Ford in the presidential election. Only once before in the history of college football that began in 1869 had the alma mater of each of two primary presidential candidates met in an election year prior to the election. That was in 1912 when Theodore Roosevelt's Harvard beat Woodrow Wilson's Princeton. As was the case in 1976, Wilson's alma mater lost but he won the election that was a three-cornered race involving William Howard Taft, the Republican; Wilson, the Democrat; and Roosevelt, the Bull Moose Party candidate. Following the election in the football season of 1912, Roosevelt's alma mater, Harvard, also beat Taft's alma mater, Yale. Roosevelt's Harvard had an undefeated season in that 1912 season.

It all began to look as if history would repeat itself in 1976. A losing presidential candidate could at least see his alma mater go undefeated through the football season during which he lost the big one. But history did not repeat.

It happened on November 6, 1976, at Lafayette, Indiana, that this mighty Michigan team fell—victim of one of the best upset-minded traditions in college football. It was Purdue that did it to Michigan by just two points. Oh, for that good pass that is the big come-from-behind weapon of football. When a steamroller gets into a ditch it may need help getting out. Thus it is with a powerful running team which finds itself behind.

When Michigan fell to the Boilermakers of Coach Alex Agase, Pittsburgh beat Army and jumped from the No. 2 ranking to No. 1, to remain there through the bowl games for the first college national championship in the Northeast since 1959 when Syracuse was champion. Michigan could not regain the heights because Pitt, with Tony Dorsett, the Heisman Trophy winner, remained unbeaten and untied.

And then there was that final loss again for Michigan. The Wolverines were no match for Southern California in the Rose

Bowl, and the once-beaten Trojans took the game at Pasadena, California. Lytle finished his four-year varsity career as a loser in the Rose Bowl. It was a shame for such a fine player and such a fine team as Michigan.

Michigan, of course, had beaten Ohio State in that 1976 regular-season match. It was not too difficult for the Wolverines for a change. So off to Miami went Woody Hayes and his players for a meeting with Colorado in the Orange Bowl. The Big Ten saved some face as Ohio State had few problems beating the Buffaloes in a night game that started just after the Rose Bowl on the West Coast had ended in another Big Ten Rose Bowl setback.

Starting with 1967, when Ohio State beat Michigan, 24–14, in the last game of the regular season, and running through the January 1, 1977 Rose Bowl, Michigan did not win a single last game of a campaign. This eleven-game nonwinning streak in finales included Wolverine defeats in the 1970, 1972, and 1977 Rose Bowl games, and the 1976 Orange Bowl. Michigan lost to Ohio State in the last game of 1967, 1968, 1970, 1972, and 1974. The best Michigan did in these fatal finales was to tie Ohio State in that troublesome 1973 last game, 10–10.

Meanwhile the other members of the Big Ten sort of looked from below as the two behemoths of the league trampled the other eight most of the time, with exceptions such as the Purdue upset of Michigan in 1976. Those teams never seemed to get off the ground in pursuit of Michigan or Ohio State. Coaches came and coaches went. Despite his victory over Michigan in the major upset of the 1976 Big Ten campaign, Agase was ousted at Purdue.

The hopelessness of the battle to catch Ohio State and Michigan in football and Michigan's amazingly successful complete intercollegiate program under Don Canham, the Wolverine athletic director, was pointed up by two major infraction cases in the midseventies. Michigan State and Minnesota ran afoul of the college athletic laws and suffered when caught.

Michigan State's football program was placed on probation by the National Collegiate Athletic Association, and the entire coaching staff changed as a result of this Spartan error. It was embarrassing for the N.C.A.A. itself, as John Fuzak, the Michigan State faculty advisor for athletics, was serving a two-year term as president of the N.C.A.A. (1975 and 1976) when the East Lansing, Michigan, school was caught and punished.

Woody Hayes got into the act again, claiming he was the man

who blew the whistle on Michigan State's recruiting violations. Although Wayne Duke, the Big Ten commissioner, and other officials would not say just who did blow the whistle on the Spartans, it became quite clear that a whole lot of Michigan State's opponents tipped off the cops. As it turned out Woody was just one of many and, as one man close to the case said, "Woody made a call on the thing but he was so far down the list and so late that we had the stuff already well in hand."

Minnesota got into trouble with its basketball program. Again it was a case of bad recruiting, primarily, and a whole bunch of other infractions. The Gophers drew a two-year probation against their basketball team. Then, less than a year later, the N.C.A.A. clamped down on Minnesota again and this time put the entire Minnesota athletic program on probation. This was too much for the Gophers. They felt they had been unjustly treated by the N.C.A.A. and, with some justification, went to court seeking to stay the sentence against their entire intercollegiate setup. The courts gave Minnesota a temporary injunction so that the blanket ban on Minnesota was lifted, leaving the basketball program to finish out its time.

Actually, Minnesota officials felt that the N.C.A.A., while asking for an investigation of three athletes, was not right in saying that those three athletes should be suspended from teams while being investigated. So, while looking into the problems, Minnesota permitted the boys to continue playing on Gopher teams. For this, the N.C.A.A. sat on Minnesota and the university yelled, "Since when is a man not innocent until proved guilty?" The courts agreed to the extent of the temporary injunction and the case went to a higher court.

So it went with those trying to compete with Michigan and Ohio State in the seventies. It was tough!

TEN

The Grand Old Man

While the Big Ten didn't claim to have a monopoly on the great coaches in the early days of college football, the conference did have some of the very best in the business—coaches who were innovative, ingenious in their coaching ways, and disparate in their personalities. The game itself had not yet become sophisticated. It was more a test of strength, endurance, and toughness, and the subtleties which were introduced in the early part of the century were the result of the craftiness and ingenuity of a handful of coaches who rose above the rest.

They were the ones who became the heroes of the day, the ones who turned out championship teams and All-America players, the ones who were most feared by their opponents. Perhaps the most prominent coaches of those early times were a trio who made their marks in the Big Ten—Amos Alonzo Stagg, Fielding Yost, and Bob Zuppke. They were the great innovators, the leaders in a profession which had not yet achieved the prominence it enjoys today.

He was a small giant of a man. And, if that sounds like an unusual description, it is only because the man himself was so unusual in so many ways. Actually, Amos Alonzo Stagg defied mere description. Perhaps the simplest way is merely to call him the greatest college football coach of all time.

That, of course, takes in a lot of time and a lot of coaches—more than a century and men like Yost, Zuppke, Fritz Crisler, Knute Rockne, Bernie Bierman, and Earl Blaik of other days, and Bear Bryant, John McKay, Darrell Royal, Ara Parseghian, Woody Hayes, and Joe Paterno of more recent memory. And there are those who will argue the respective merits of these and other favorites. But no one will deny that Amos Alonzo Stagg had a special place in the world of college football.

Although he stood only five feet seven inches and weighed about 160 pounds, Stagg was an impressive-looking man, whether he was striding the sidelines during a game or making his presence felt at a Big Ten meeting. His shock of white hair served to add to his stately appearance, and everyone who ever was around him, either as a player, official, or even as an opponent, recognized the sense of dignity Stagg brought to the scene.

"Mr. Football," they called him, and with good reason. First, at the University of Chicago for forty-one years until President Robert Maynard Hutchins, who was later to preside over football's demise at the great Midwestern university, thought Stagg was too old and should be retired at seventy. Then for fourteen more years at the College of the Pacific, where he led one of his wartime teams to within a few points of making it into the Rose Bowl and was rewarded by being named "Coach of the Year" at age eighty-one, over Notre Dame's revered Frank Leahy. And then for six more years as an "assistant" to his son, Amos, Jr., at Susquehanna until he finally decided to put away his playbook after the 1953 season. But that adventure into retirement lasted only a few months. Stagg soon turned up as the kicking coach at Stockton Junior College, surely the only ninety-one-year-old kicking coach in the history of football! Seven years later, at ninety-eight, Amos Alonzo Stagg finally called it quits.

Before Stagg hung up his cleats for good, he had amassed a record of 314 victories, more than any other coach in the long history of college football—Glenn (Pop) Warner's 312 wins made him a close second—197 losses and 45 ties in his fifty-seven years as a head coach. It is extremely doubtful if any coach active today will even come close to approaching Stagg's 314 victories.

For the benefit of historians, Amos Alonzo Stagg was born on August 16, 1862 in West Orange, New Jersey, the fifth of eight children of Amos Lindley and Eunice Pierson Stagg. Abe Lincoln was in the White House, the Civil War was raging, Stonewall Jackson was marching on Manassas, and it was seven years before Rutgers and Princeton would play the first college football game.

The elder Stagg supported his large brood by working as a cobbler and general laborer, and the family never had much beyond the bare necessities. Young Lonny, as his parents called him, had to help out by working at a variety of odd jobs and with his father at the cobbler's bench. Most youngsters of that time never progressed beyond grade school, but young Stagg was determined to get an education and, at age eighteen, he announced he wanted to go on to high school. Since West Orange did not have a high school and the nearest one was in the neighboring town of Orange, a tuition fee was involved for nonresidents. However that didn't stop Lonny. He worked to pay the tuition. He also had acquired a deep interest and some skill in throwing a baseball, and played weekends for the town team.

After two years, the ambitious Lonny was persuaded by several of his teachers and his cousin, George Gill, to go to Phillips Exeter Academy in New Hampshire, where he achieved some local fame as a baseball pitcher, and from there he entered Yale, intent on becoming a minister. But fate was to rule otherwise.

The game of football didn't begin with Amos Alonzo Stagg. It just seemed that way since he was involved in it for so long and was responsible for so many of the changes and innovations which took place over a span of more than half a century. The T-formation, unbalanced line, hidden-ball trick, spiral pass, draw play, man-in-motion, criss-cross or reverses, triple passes, ends-back formation, onside kick, fake kick, Statue of Liberty play (Stagg called it the "Whoa-back"), tackling dummy, and the first slip-proof jersey were all credited to Stagg. He also was the first coach to assign numbers to his players, the first to award letters, and the first to take a team cross-country to the Pacific Coast for an intersectional game. There also were many other ingredients that Stagg's genius added to the game.

Although there always has been a controversy over who invented the backfield shift, Knute Rockne, the famed Notre Dame coach, gave Stagg full credit for what became known as the Rockne Notre Dame shift, a slick maneuver that took the backfield out of the T-formation into a box right or left, and disconcerted many an Irish opponent for years. Rockne freely admitted that he got it from Jesse Harper, his coach at Notre Dame, who had been a quarterback under Stagg at Chicago.

"Harper got it from Stagg, who got it from God," said Rockne.

Rockne may not have been too far off at that. Stagg, indeed, did start out in life to be a minister. But after a year as a graduate student at the Yale Divinity School, he began to hear deprecating comments about his ability as a speaker. When he overheard a future Nobel Prize winner say "It's too bad Lonny Stagg can't speak on his feet," Stagg decided it was time to turn his thoughts to another career.

Meanwhile Stagg had become a celebrity as an athlete at Yale. Oddly enough, his number-one sport was baseball and he was good enough at it to pitch Yale to five straight Big Three championships from 1884 through 1889. (Eligibility requirements were much looser in those days.) In 1888 he set a record of twenty strikeouts in one game against Princeton. He later admitted that he might have tried just a little bit harder that day against the Tigers because Mrs. Grover Cleveland, wife of the president of the United States, sat on the Princeton side throughout the entire game. That annoyed the righteous Stagg, who thought she should have displayed less favoritism.

Stagg's pitching prowess—he once struck out the Boston Nationals' Ten Thousand Dollar Kelly, the Babe Ruth of the 1880s, on three pitched balls—attracted several major-league offers, including one in 1888 from the New York Giants, who were willing to pay him the then staggering sum of $4,200 to throw a baseball for them. Lonny, however, turned them down when he learned that there were saloons in major-league baseball parks.

"The whole tone of the game was smelly," Stagg recalled some years later.

It wasn't until 1888, when Stagg began his graduate work at Yale, that he turned his full attention to football. Prior to that, fall baseball practice and an unwillingness to risk an injury to his pitching arm kept the young baseball phenomenon from considering the gridiron as anything other than a part-time outlet for his rather extensive athletic talents. That, and a need to work at a multitude of odd jobs to keep himself going—and, yes, eating—at Yale.

The celebrated Walter Camp, who was to become one of the most notable and influential men in college football, had just been named the Elis' first coach, and he promptly installed Stagg as his right end. Alonzo's teammates on that 1888 team were William Walter (Pudge) Heffelfinger, William H. (Pa) Corbin, and George Woodruff, who became famous Ivy League players in their own right. Woodruff later was one of the game's most astute coaches. With this quartet playing leading roles, Yale swept past thirteen opponents, holding them all scoreless.

Meanwhile, Stagg had begun to take courses preparatory to entering Yale's Divinity School the following year. His instructor for

Biblical Literature was Dr. William Rainey Harper, perhaps the most important man in Stagg's life, although neither was aware of it at the time.

Stagg was in the Divinity School in 1889 and also was back at his end position on the Yale football team. He had learned that football, as it was then being played, was no place for the faint-hearted. Violence was the keynote of the game, particularly when the Big Three—Yale, Harvard, and Princeton—had at each other. Even practice sessions were bloody and bruising, and Stagg, who then weighed a mere 147 pounds, took more than his share of bumps and bruises. So many, in fact, that one day he arrived at practice lugging a huge mattress. It was rolled tightly and held in place by rope.

"I'm tired of being battered about by you guys," announced Stagg. "You can hit this thing from now on."

Thus was born the first tackling dummy, which has since become a fixture on every high school, college, and professional practice field.

Although Yale was to lose to Princeton in 1889, Lonny Stagg was so good at his end position that he was selected by Caspar Whitney for the first All-America team ever picked. That year also marked the end of Stagg's hopes to become a minister. He left Yale to continue his studies at the international YMCA training school at Springfield, Massachusetts, where he was soon doubling as a coach and player on the school's football and baseball teams.

Stagg's teams at the YMCA school didn't exactly set the college football world on fire, but they gave Lonny an opportunity to engage in the innovations and experiments that he had been thinking about during his playing days at Yale. He also became involved with a Springfield classmate, Canadian-born James A. Naismith, who was trying to develop an organized indoor game that could be played by students during the winter. Stagg contributed some ideas from his football experiences, a few other interested folks at Springfield offered their suggestions, and Naismith soon put them all together, along with his own substantial ideas. They nailed up a couple of peach baskets in the Springfield gym and a new sport was born. Naismith called it basketball.

Meanwhile, Stagg's former Biblical Lit instructor at Yale, Dr. Harper, had been named president of a new and still unbuilt college which was to be heavily endowed by multimillionaire John D. Rockefeller and called the University of Chicago. It wasn't long before Stagg heard from Dr. Harper, who told his former student that he wanted him to head up the new university's physical education and intercollegiate athletic programs.

"I'll pay you fifteen hundred dollars a year," said Harper.

Stagg was too stunned to reply and Harper, thinking that he would have to sweeten the pot to get his man, quickly upped the ante. "I'll offer you two thousand and an assistant professorship."

Stagg was speechless. Finally, Dr. Harper said impatiently, "All right, I'll give you twenty-five hundred dollars, an associate professorship, and tenure for life!"

Still overwhelmed by the entire idea, Stagg said he wanted time to think about Dr. Harper's proposal. Soon, after much soul-searching about what he really wanted to do with his life, Alonzo wrote to Harper and agreed to become Chicago's first coach and head of the physical education department. It was a decision that neither Stagg nor the university ever regretted.

When Stagg arrived in Chicago in the fall of 1892 to begin his new job, the sight was hardly encouraging. What was supposed to be the football field was an area littered with cans and broken bottles. The only building near completion was the women's dormitory. When the new coach issued a call for candidates for the football team, a mere thirteen responded. But fortunately, Dr. Harper had the foresight to recruit a strapping young man named Andy Wyant, who had played for Bucknell for four years. Also Stagg himself decided that he would play as well as coach, a fact which hardly caused a stir among Chicago's opponents, since there were no rules prohibiting it. In fact, on at least one occasion he was even asked to officiate when an injury knocked an official out of a game.

"The game was too young and too weak," Alonzo explained, "for such a situation to be thought particularly unusual."

Not only was the game young and weak, it was rough and violent. Newspaper accounts of some of those early games would make even the devotees of today's professional football sit up and take notice. The 1893 game between Chicago and Purdue got so rough and bloody that the district attorney for Tippecanoe County threatened to indict everyone for assault and battery. Wedge, mass, and sheer momentum and strength plays dominated the game, and it was strictly a test of strengths and weaknesses of individuals.

That is, until Amos Alonzo Stagg came along with his startling new innovations and strategy that soon changed the whole face of college football. He introduced finesse into the game and, along with it, trickery. Like handoffs, cross-bucks, reverses, and the hidden-ball play, in which a player would take a handoff while doubled over and then flop to the ground while everyone else on his team continued to run wide to the right or left. Then, when the defenders inevitably took off after the decoys, the man with the ball would suddenly get up and race off in the opposite direction for a huge gain. Stagg called it his "dead man play." Victims sometimes called it cheating.

That first season, 1892, Stagg's sparse squad took on several prep school teams before the coach felt they were ready to engage in intercollegiate competition. The first venture was a scoreless tie with Northwestern, which drew the munificent total of $22.65 at the gate. Then came losses to Michigan State, 18–12, and Purdue, 38–0. The season ended with a doubleheader against Illinois and Chicago split the two games, winning 10–4 and losing 28–12.

Meanwhile, Stagg was attracted to a comely young coed from New York, Stella Robertson, who was a rabid sports enthusiast. They were married in September 1894, just before the start of the football season and, naturally, there was no time for a honeymoon. But Alonzo managed to take care of that little formality in his own way. He arranged for his team to conclude the season by playing three games in California. Not only would it mark the first time that a football team had engaged in an intersectional game, but it also would serve as a honeymoon trip for the Staggs.

Cracked one of Stagg's players, "Gee, the coach must surely love us to take twenty-two guys along on his honeymoon."

Stella Stagg turned out to be one of Coach Stagg's greatest assets. A keen student of football, she charted Chicago's games and even scouted opponents. It became a common sight to see her crashing the Chicago press box so she could get a better view of the game. Long before assistant coaches became fashionable, Stella was Alonzo's unofficial aide in a partnership that lasted seventy years.

From the humble beginnings of that first 1892 season, Amos Alonzo Stagg's coaching genius built Chicago into a football power which was to become nationally famous. He coached his teams to seven conference championships—in 1896, 1899, 1905, 1907, 1908, 1913, and 1924. Four of those teams were undefeated. The stars he produced were legendary—like Clarence Herschberger (Chicago's first All-America in 1898), the great Walter Eckersall, Wally Steffen, Austin (Five Yards) McCarthy, Hugo Bezdek, and Fritz Crisler, just to mention a few.

Of all Stagg's great teams, the one he probably was most proud of was the 1905 club. That was the one that put an end to Michigan's famed point-a-minute, five-year, fifty-six-game unbeaten streak.

For four straight years the free-wheeling Wolverines coached by the feisty Fielding Yost had run over Stagg's Chicago teams by scores of 22–0, 21–0, 28–0,and 22–12. The losses had stuck in Stagg's craw, and his feelings were aggravated in the spring of 1905 when Yost and he had a disagreement at a track meet. Yost testily promised another beating for Chicago the next fall and warned, "We'll give you plenty!"

Just a few minutes before the kickoff, Stagg decided to tell his players about Yost's remark to him the previous spring. The coach's last words to his players were, "Don't let him cram this game down my throat!"

They didn't. In a fierce, bitter struggle, Wally Eckersall, perhaps Stagg's greatest player and then a junior, overshadowed Michigan's great Willie Heston and it was Wally's punt that set up a late safety which gave Chicago a 2–0 victory. The Old Man had been vindicated.

Stagg's relationship with his players was a unique one. Tough, stubborn, and a strict disciplinarian, he had little patience with athletes who did not conform to his rules or were not willing to pay the price for success. Stagg also was a bug on clean living. He never smoked, drank, or swore. However he sometimes was caustic and had ways of showing his dissatisfaction with his players. His favorite, and really only, epithet was to call a player a "jackass." Or, if the offender's violation was flagrant enough, he might be called a "double jackass." It got to be such a distinction that many of Stagg's players during his long tenure at Chicago felt that they were ignored if they didn't make the "Jackass Club," as they referred to it.

Stagg's reputation as a stickler for adhering to the rules was well known and respected. At Stagg's ninety-fourth birthday celebration, UCLA Coach Red Sanders, who had just been caught in a recruiting violation, was heard to mutter sheepishly, "Jesse James will now break bread with a saint."

Despite his total immersion in football, Stagg had other accomplishments. He was also a highly successful baseball and track coach in his early years at Chicago. His baseball teams won five Big Ten championships before he quit in 1909, and his track squads took four titles. He also served on the United States Olympic Committee and coached the middle-distance runners and relay team in the 1924 games in Paris.

After Chicago won the Big Ten championship in 1924, things began to go downhill for the Maroons. Although they sometimes threatened, they never again won a conference football championship. Competition for players got keener and Chicago, one of two private universities in the Big Ten—the other was Northwestern—found it difficult to seduce high school athletes away from state schools.

Then along came Robert Maynard Hutchins in 1929. Although only thirty, he was named president of the university and brought along with him an intensity for Chicago to become a place for the intellectually elite. Football, as far as Hutchins was concerned, was an unnecessary evil and contributed little to the academic excellence of a great university. From the day of Hutchins' arrival, collegiate football at Chicago was doomed.

Hutchins was a young man in a hurry. A graduate of Yale, he had been secretary of the university at twenty-four, a teacher in Yale Law School at twenty-six, dean of the Law School at twenty-eight, and now, two years later, he had been picked to head one of the nation's great universities. Almost immediately, Stagg was perceptive enough to see that college football at Chicago, as he knew, lived, and loved it for so many years, was terminal. In 1930 he advised Fritz Crisler, one of his assistants, to take the head coaching job at Minnesota.

"The game is finished here," the Old Man told Crisler. "This man is going to kill it."

Stagg was right, of course, but before Hutchins completed that task, he got rid of Stagg. Hutchins was merely exercising his right under the university's mandatory retirement law. The school's policy called for mandatory retirement at sixty-five with an extension of five years in "certain cases" where the trustees and the president felt it would be "of benefit to the university." Stagg had been given such an extension in 1927, before Hutchins' arrival at Chicago, but now it was 1932 and he had reached the age of seventy. So Amos Alonzo Stagg, after forty-one years and a record of 129–108–27, was out. Hutchins hired T. Nelson Metcalf of Iowa

ABOVE, LEFT: President James H. Smart of Purdue, generally recognized as the founder, in 1895, of what later became the Big Ten. ABOVE, RIGHT: President J. B. Angell of Michigan spoke out loud and clear in 1905 for reform in college football. RIGHT: Coach Amos Alonzo Stagg of Chicago, the Grand Old Man of college football, played and coached for 72 of his 102 years. He finally hung up his cleats when he was 98! BELOW: Stagg's 1924 Chicago team which won the Big Ten championship.

TOP, LEFT: Major John L. Griffith, the Big Ten's first commissioner in 1922. Among his duties was the job of policing the conference schools. TOP, RIGHT: Commissioner Kenneth L. (Tug) Wilson reigned over the conference from 1945 until his retirement in 1961. It was during Wilson's term that the Big Ten entered into a pact to play in the Rose Bowl. (*Photograph by Shelburne*) BOTTOM, LEFT: William R. Reed, Wilson's successor as Big Ten commissioner. Reed continued Wilson's iron-handed rule until he died in 1971. (*Photograph by Leonard H. Bass*) BOTTOM, RIGHT: Wayne Duke, after a long tenure with the N.C.A.A. and eight years as commissioner of the Big Eight, became the Big Ten's fourth commissioner in 1971. Under Duke's leadership the conference has made changes in philosophy to keep up with the times. (*Photograph by EPS Studios, Inc.*)

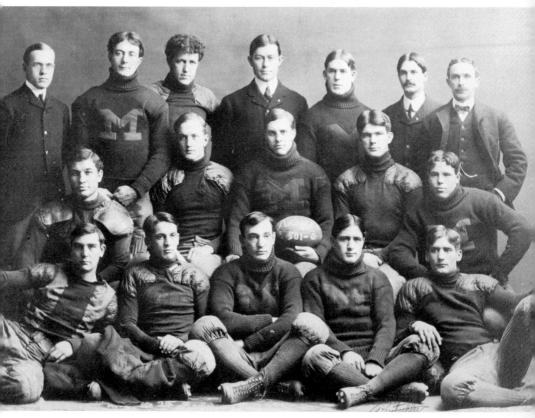

The 1901 Michigan team, the first of the Point-A-Minute machines, which rolled up 501 points to zero for the opposition and played against Stanford in the first Rose Bowl game on January 1, 1902. Star Willie Heston is the first player on the left in the front row.

Coach Fielding H. (Hurry Up) Yost brought football eminence to Michigan in his forty years as coach and athletic director. Yost's "punt, pass, and pray" coaching philosophy produced eight undefeated teams, four national champions, and seven Big Ten titles.

Adolph (Germany) Schultz, Michigan's 240-pound All-America center in 1907, revolutionized football defenses when he decided to move behind the line because "I can see things better back there." Schultz thus became college football's first linebacker.

Willie Heston, the first of Michigan's superstars, ran for more than five miles and scored over 100 touchdowns from 1901 through 1904. Willie was the catalyst of the Point-A-Minute teams.

Although Michigan's 1925 team, starring Quarterback Benny Friedman and End Bennie Oosterbaan, lost one game to Navy, Hurry Up Yost insisted that it was his best team ever.

This grim, determined young man is Jerry Ford, the tenacious center who earned the dubious distinction of being named Most Valuable Player of Michigan's 1–7 team in 1934, went on to greater fame as congressman, vice president, and then president of the United States.

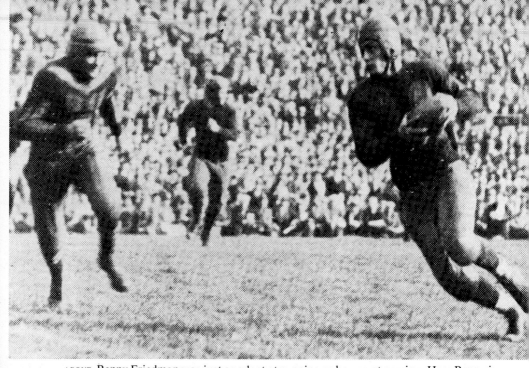

ABOVE: Benny Friedman was just as adept at running as he was at passing. Here Benny is lugging the ball for a big gain against Ohio State in 1926. (*Photograph by Ed Stephan*)
BELOW: Bennie Oosterbaan, Friedman's favorite receiver, latches on to a pass on Navy's 2-yard line despite the clutching hands of a Middie defender. (*Times Wide World*)

Fritz Crisler, Michigan coach from 1938 through 1947 and later athletic director, takes a word of advice from Amos Alonzo Stagg, his coach when he played at Chicago.

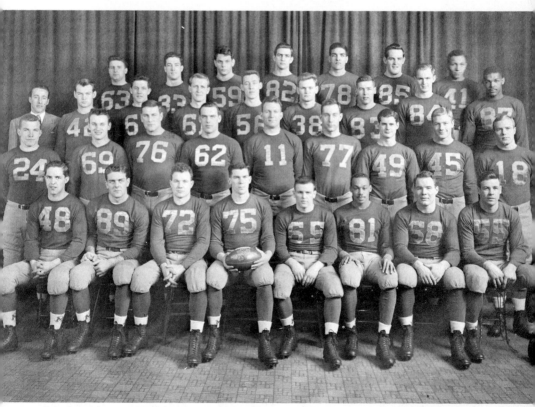

Coach Crisler's best Michigan team was his last in 1947. It was unbeaten and trounced Southern California 49–0 in the Rose Bowl to win the national championship. All-America Halfback Bob Chappuis (third from right, second row) was the star of the high-powered Wolverines.

The Elliott brothers, Bump (left) and Pete, were All-Americas at Michigan in 1947 and 1948, respectively. They also became the only brothers to coach in the Big Ten, Bump at Michigan and Pete at Illinois, where each had Rose Bowl teams.

One of Fritz Crisler's prized mementoes is this inscribed picture of battle-worn All-America Halfback Tom Harmon, "Ole 98," Michigan's legendary football hero. An elusive runner, pinpoint passer, and accurate placekicker, Harmon did it all for the Wolverines in 1938, 1939, and 1940.

Coach Crisler discusses strategy with his great 1938 Michigan backfield, Quarterback Forest Evashevski, Fullback Bob Westfall, and Halfbacks Tom Harmon and Fred Trosko.

On his back, Forest Eva-shevski, acting out his roll as "Harmon's Blocker," watches as Harmon moves around end after Evy cleared the way in big victory over Ohio State in 1939. This photo has become one of college football's most famous action shots. *(Wide World)*

The Wistert brothers, left to right Alvin, Albert, and Francis, were the only three members of the same family ever to win All-America honors at the same school (Michigan) and for the same position (tackle).

LEFT: Ron Kramer, Michigan's two-time All-America end in 1955 and 1956, catches pass against Iowa and falls into the end zone for a touchdown. ABOVE: Michigan Halfback Ron Johnson limps off the field after losing a shoe in the heat of battle. That was about the only thing that ever stopped Ron in 1967 and 1968, when he broke Harmon's career rushing records.

ABOVE, LEFT: Michigan Coach Bo Schembechler conferring with reserve Center Steve Nauta (50) during the January 1, 1977 Rose Bowl game against Southern California. ABOVE, RIGHT: Coach Schembechler and Assistant Coach Chuck Stobart watch the action in the 1977 Rose Bowl game. BELOW: Rob Lytle (41), Michigan's All-America halfback, picks up yardage against USC as Split End Curt Stephenson looks for someone to block in 1977 Rose Bowl. Lytle scored Wolverines' only touchdown in 14–6 defeat.

LEFT: Colorful Francis Schmidt turned Ohio State football into a pyrotechnical display with his free-wheeling offense from 1934 through 1940. (*Courtesy of Kaye Kessler*) ABOVE: A happy Carroll Widdoes, who never wanted to be a head coach (he went back to being an assistant after two years), rejoices with Heisman Trophy winner Les Horvath (22), Jack Dugger (96), and Bill Hackett (rear) after Ohio State beat Michigan 18–14 in 1944 to win Big Ten title and national championship. (*Courtesy of Kaye Kessler*)

ABOVE: One of Ohio State's greatest all-around athletes and football players, Wes Fesler, a three-time All-America, found coaching in Columbus more demanding than playing and resigned in 1950 after only four seasons. (*Courtesy of Kaye Kessler*) LEFT: Halfback Vic Janowicz, who did just about everything for the 1950 Ohio State team, became only the second junior to win the Heisman Trophy.

ABOVE: Young Coach Woody Hayes (far left) and Oldtimer Chic Harley (second from left), the brilliant halfback who made football a national institution at Ohio State in 1916, 1917, and 1919, look on as All-America Halfback Howard (Hopalong) Cassady receives an award in 1955. (*Courtesy of Kaye Kessler*) RIGHT: A sample of the kind of running that earned Hopalong Cassady All-America honors and the Heisman Trophy in 1955. (*Courtesy of Kaye Kessler*)

ABOVE: To pass or not to pass? If that is the question, the answer is probably obvious as Woody Hayes and Quarterback Cornelius Greene talk things over during a timeout in the 1975 Ohio State–Michigan game. (*Courtesy of Kaye Kessler*)

BELOW: Archie Griffin (45), the only two-time Heisman Trophy winner, with a typical move, evades several would-be Penn State tacklers in 1975 game in Columbus. The incredible Archie broke all of Chic Harley's and Hopalong Cassady's records before he finished his career.

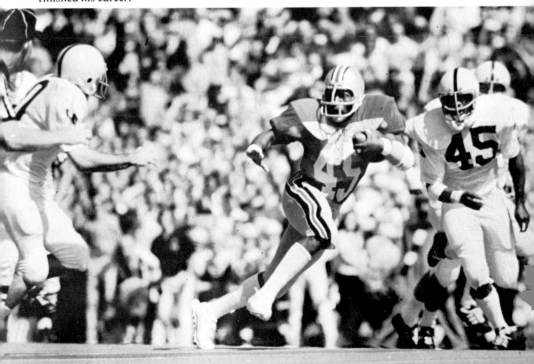

ABOVE: The master strategist and the greatest college runner of them all: Coach Bob Zuppke of Illinois and his star, Red Grange, chat during practice session. BELOW: His sharp eyes covering the field, Red Grange heads for the goal line and one of his five touchdowns in 39–14 victory over Michigan that dedicated Illinois' new Memorial Stadium in October 1924. Red ran for 402 yards that day in one of the most memorable performances of all time.

Alex Agase was an All-America guard wherever he went, in 1942 at Illinois, in 1943 at Purdue, where he turned up in military service, and in 1946 back at Illinois. Agase later coached at Northwestern and Purdue.

Whether he was blocking out opponents as a center on offense or demolishing them as a linebacker on defense, Illinois' Dick Butkus did it with great delight. He was the best lineman in the land in 1963 and 1964.

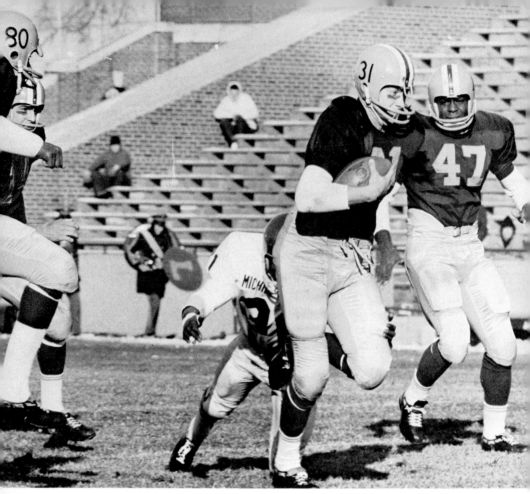

Fullback Jim Grabowski (31) of Illinois off on one of his line-smashing sorties against Michigan. Jim broke all of Red Grange's rushing records before he played his last game in 1966.

Jay Berwanger, the "Man in the Iron Mask," came along at Chicago when the former Big Ten power was on its downhill slide to football oblivion. Nevertheless, Berwanger's running, passing, and kicking skills were so outstanding that he became the first winner of the Heisman Trophy in 1935.

State as his new director of athletics, and Clark Shaughnessy became the new head football coach.

The action roused both Stagg and the populace. Alonzo, still fit and able, wondered out loud why he was being forced to retire. Many of the alumni publicly resented the action on the part of the school, students staged rallies to protest, and even the local newspapers berated Hutchins and his trustees for their decision.

Ralph Cannon wrote in the Chicago *Daily News,* "There are three or four angles of the matter that were a distinct shock to all who are interested in college athletics hereabouts. First, it seemed a little strange that the more or less delicate chore of cutting a man's heart out after all these years of indecision should suddenly have been achieved with the brutal abruptness of a butcher cleaving off another pork chop.

"Second, why was he not retained as director of athletics?

"Third, why was the successor chosen apparently on the theory that the young are always smart while the old are always dumb?

"Fourth . . . William Rainey Harper, father of the University of Chicago, which Stagg more than anyone else had made known to the lay public of America, promised Stagg in writing at the time the retirement clause was adopted, that this would not apply to him and that he could stay there in peace as long as he wished."

The reaction was flattering to Stagg's ego, but it didn't change anything. He was still out as athletic director and football coach. Stagg was offered a couple of jobs by the university, including one with the pompous title of "Chairman of the Committee of Intercollegiate Relations," but Alonzo wasn't having any of that. He saw them as handouts. "I cannot and will not accept a job without work," he said proudly. "I am fit, able, and willing. I refuse to be idle and a nuisance."

There were others, too, who agreed that Amos Alonzo Stagg was "fit, able, and willing" to coach college football, even at the age of seventy. One of these was Dr. Tully C. Knoles, the president of College of the Pacific in Stockton, California, a onetime quarterback at the University of Southern California and a longtime Stagg admirer who confessed that as a youth he had bicycled thirty-eight miles in 1894 to see Chicago play Stanford in Los Angeles.

The two men hit it off and Stagg agreed in the winter of 1933 to come west to coach the Tigers of Pacific. The Old Man soon showed that he had lost none of his coaching genius. Within a few years he had beefed up the Pacific schedule and was playing teams like St. Mary's, UCLA, Southern California, and Stanford. In 1938 Stagg took Pacific "back home" to play Chicago and his Tigers trounced the impotent Maroons. Stagg savored every moment of the one-sided pasting and, according to author Frank Lucia in his excellent book *Mr. Football: Amos Alonzo Stagg,* "He couldn't contain himself on the train, doing an Indian dance and war-whooping up and down the aisles."

Although the impetus was not provided by Pacific's easy victory—Chicago's football fortunes had been going steadily down-hill—a year later President Hutchins dropped a dramatic bomb-shell. The Maroons were giving up intercollegiate football. Stagg's prediction had indeed come true. Seven years later, in 1946, Hutchins made Chicago's athletic demise complete with its resig-nation from the Big Ten. Intercollegiate athletics had become a vic-tim of Hutchins' determination to make Chicago a university for the intellectually elite.

While Chicago was sliding into oblivion, Stagg was turning little Pacific into a team that was feared by its opponents. The Tigers up-set California 6–0 in 1939 and went on to win several Far Western Conference championships.

The 1943 season, however, was one Stagg—and Pacific—never forgot. The Tigers had barely managed to struggle through the 1942 wartime capaign with a combination of naval trainees and 4–Fs, but the next year was something else. Bolstered by a hardy collec-tion of some additional military trainees who were experienced players, little Pacific gained national notoriety by knocking off some of the nation's premier military teams as well as St. Mary's, California, and UCLA. At one point in the season the Tigers even were ranked in the nation's top ten, an exalted position they never hoped to achieve. There was some talk, too, about a trip to the Rose Bowl, but a heartbreaking 6–0 loss to USC—Pacific had two touchdowns called back by the officials—cost the Tigers an invita-tion to Pasadena. Pacific finished the season with a 7–2 record and Stagg, then eighty-one, was voted Man of the Year by the Football Writers Association of America and Coach of the Year by his fel-low coaches. It was still another first in the long life of this remark-able man!

But, like all other good things, Stagg's relationship with Pacific came to an end too. The Tigers' fortunes began to slip after that wonderful 1943 season and so did Stagg's popularity. Soon the alumni, fans, and even some of his players began to grumble. Then came the vocal expressions from his critics. They wanted a younger man to coach the Tigers.

So, after the 1946 season and at eighty-four, Stagg was finished at Pacific. For a second time in his lifetime, he was retired. But not for very long. Almost immediately came the news that Amos Alonzo Stagg had signed a ten-year contract to be an assistant coach under his son, Amos Alonzo, Jr., at little Susquehanna University in Selinsgrove, Pennsylvania. (His younger son, Paul, was the coach at Pacific University in Forest Grove, Oregon.) For the first time the elder Stagg would not be the head coach, but that didn't faze him one bit.

"Of course, I won't have the whole say," Stagg admitted. "Amos, Jr., also will have some ideas. I suppose we'll divide it up by using about three parts of my stuff to one of his."

Whatever the mixture of the ingredients, it worked so well that the two Staggs came up with an unbeaten team in 1951. Finally, in 1953, when he was ninety, Amos, Sr., decided that it was time to quit. His wife, Stella, who had accompanied him East each year for his coaching stint at Susquehanna, and, incidentally, continued to do her scouting and keep her charts, was ailing and unable to make the long trip. So Stagg came back to his Stockton home to live out his years. But the Grand Old Man didn't remain idle for long. For the next seven years, until he was ninety-eight, he coached the kickers at Stockton Junior College.

In August of 1962, when Amos Alonzo Stagg was approaching his 100th birthday, an occasion that was celebrated by 10,000 Americans at extravagant banquets from coast to coast, John Underwood wrote about him in *Sports Illustrated*, "It is not always so grand to be the grand old man. . . . Once he heard the dissonant cry of the football crowd; now it is the muted prattle of old ladies in a rest home in Stockton, California. The jaw that once jutted firm on the sidelines of Chicago Stadium is slack. The blue eyes are clouded by cataracts; the left one droops. His hair is wispy and white as tissue. At 96, he ran laps around the fig trees in his backyard. Now, as if prodded by the uncompromising voice within him that has always demanded Spartan discipline, he insists on frequent walks on the patio of the rest home, out in the sun. But he must be led by the hand . . . he has drawn inward and become occupied with his infirmities. He has become, at last, an old man.

"Typically, Stagg haltingly expressed a wish. 'I would like to be remembered,' he said quietly, 'as an honest man.' "

Less than three years later, on March 17, 1965, just five months short of his 103rd birthday, Amos Alonzo Stagg passed away quietly in Stockton, a victim of the natural infirmities of age. His beloved Stella had preceded him in death eight months earlier at the age of 90.

Amos Alonzo Stagg was many things—player, coach, teacher, innovator, unstinting disciplinarian, humanitarian, father, husband, citizen, Christian, producer of champions, inspirationalist, and, not least of all, a Yale man—but he is remembered above all as "an honest man."

ELEVEN

Yost, Crisler, and on to Bo

What Amos Alonzo Stagg was to Chicago, Fielding Harris Yost was to Michigan. Strangely enough, although these two men spent a quarter of a century together as titans of their profession in the Midwest, their coaching paths crossed only eight times, more than half of them coming in the first years of the century. One reason was Michigan's ten-year defection from the Big Ten, during which time its competition against conference teams was severely restricted. What a pity that Stagg and Yost could not have pitted their skills against each other more often!

If the name Fielding seems to be unusual, consider that his parents' given names were Peremenus and Elzena. And Fielding was called "Hurry Up" by his players because of his impatience to get things done in a hurry. It was common among two generations of Wolverines to hear him shout in practice or during a game, "Ye think we got all day? Hurry up! Hurry up! Let's get on with it. Hurry up!" And thus was born a nickname that was to stick with Yost all his life.

Another thing that stuck with Yost was his West Virginia dialect; you was always "ye," your was "yer," and until his dying day he pronounced Michigan "Meeshegan."

Fielding Yost was a lot of things. Innovative, demanding, unyielding, and wily as a coach; sometimes abrasive and frequently charming in his relations with others, he was an unabashed egotist who enjoyed the limelight and often boasted of his own ability. Yost was not above demeaning an opponent and pointing to his own superior skills. He scorned alcohol and restricted his swearing to an occasional "damn" or "hell." His lone vice was cigars, but he didn't smoke them. He chewed them. Football, except when he

was piling up a modest fortune in various business ventures, dominated his life and more than once he was known to spoil a perfectly
set table in a restaurant by deploying salt and pepper shakers, sil-
verware, dishes, coffeepots, and bread trays to diagram a play.

"Once he even used a full soup plate as a running guard on an
end sweep and washed out the defensive end completely," said
one of his former players.

Yost also was a nonstop talker who rarely ever paused for a deep
breath once he got going on the subject of football, or his other
love, military history.

"Did you ever talk to Hurry Up Yost?" a friend once asked the
late Ring Lardner.

"No," replied Lardner, "my father taught me never to inter-
rupt."

Fielding Yost had his critics and his boosters, but everyone had
to agree that he was one of the great coaches, not only of his time,
but in the history of college football.

Fielding Yost was born in Fairview, a tiny West Virginia hillbilly
town, on April 30, 1871, and he could easily have spent the rest of
his life helping his father run a general store. But Yost went off to
Ohio Normal College for two years and then, when an oil and min-
ing boom hit the West Virginia hills, he took a laborer's job in the
oil fields. Finally, in 1895, at age twenty-four, he decided that he
wanted to be a lawyer and enrolled in West Virginia Law School.
That is where he got his first taste of football as a tackle, and he
liked it. He savored the contact, the hitting and the matching of
strength against an opponent. And Yost had enough muscle packed
on his six-foot, 195-pound body to more than hold his own in the
rough-and-tumble sport.

In 1896 West Virginia's record was a poor 3–7–2 and it played—
and lost—three games in three days to Lafayette, one of the East's
better teams. However, Yost's playing so impressed Parke (Dink)
Davis, the Lafayette coach, that Davis persuaded Fielding to
"transfer" to his school to bolster the Leopards for their big game
with unbeaten University of Pennsylvania. Yost also was supposed
to study engineering at Lafayette.

Penn, with a unique "guards back" formation, had overwhelmed all opposition for three years, racking up thirty-six
straight victories. However, helped by Yost's ferocious play at
tackle, Lafayette upset the favored Quakers. After that there

seems to be a difference of opinion as to what road Yost's educational travelogue took. Some football historians have him getting his law degree from Lafayette, but he chose to give folks the impression that, after a respectable length of time, he transferred back to West Virginia to get his law degree.

However, John Richard Behee, in his fine book *Fielding Yost's Legacy*, uncovered evidence in the form of a letter from one of Yost's former teammates at West Virginia that what really happened was that Yost merely joined Lafayette for the game against Penn and then "returned [to West Virginia] on crutches, head in a bandage. . . ."

It was not uncommon in those days for so-called tramp athletes to switch schools two or three times in a season. That Yost participated in such a subterfuge in his college days becomes significant when it is related to the straightlaced approach that he took to college football many years later.

Anyway, although Yost had his law degree, he became intrigued with the idea of coaching football. In the next four years he coached four championship teams at four different colleges, first at Ohio Wesleyan, where he beat Ohio State and tied Michigan (he even played in the game against the Wolverines) on the way to a 7–1–1 record. The next year he moved to Nebraska and was 7–3, but beat Kansas to win the Missouri Valley championship. In 1899 he went to Kansas and his team was undefeated in ten games, whipping Nebraska and Missouri.

From Nebraska Yost traveled westward to Stanford, where he endeared himself to the alumni by beating California and compiling a 7–2–1 record. Perhaps it was the California climate, but whatever, he managed to keep himself pretty busy out there. He also coached the Stanford freshmen and Lowell High School in San Francisco, and lent a helping hand to San Jose College. All four of his teams won championships in that 1900 season.

Restless by nature, Yost looked for greener pastures to conquer and he heard that Michigan was looking for a coach. After an exchange of correspondence (Yost modestly sent along a ton of scrapbooks and clippings extolling his feats as a player and coach), Yost was summoned to Ann Arbor to start one of the most fantastic coaching regimes in Big Ten history.

When Yost took over at Michigan, he thoughtfully brought along three players. One was Willie Heston, a brilliant running halfback who had played for him at San Jose. Another was Dan McGugin, who later was to become his brother-in-law and the coach at Vanderbilt University. The third was "Dad" Gregory from San Francisco. This trio was to ensure instant success for Yost, who started his new job at the then munificent salary of $2,300 per year, plus living expenses during the season.

Michigan had enjoyed considerable success under Coaches Bill McCauley, Gus Ferbert, and Langdon (Biff) Lea, a Princeton All-America, in the seven years prior to Yost's arrival. In fact, Ferbert's 1898 team was undefeated in ten games. But their records paled by comparison once Fielding Yost took over the coaching reins of the maize and blue. Starting with the 1901 season, the Wolverines trampled almost everyone in sight for the next five years. Their winning scores were astronomical, and they became famous in football lore as the Point-A-Minute teams. Michigan was unbeaten in fifty-five straight games—only a 6–6 tie with Minnesota in 1903 marred the streak—until Amos Alonzo Stagg's Chicago team upset the Wolverines 2–0 in the final game of the 1905 season. Yost's 1901 team also played in what later turned out to be the first Rose Bowl game in Pasadena, stomping all over his former Stanford team, 49–0.

As a coach, Yost was merciless. When the Stanford coach saw that his team was no match for the powerful visitors from the Midwest, he asked that the game be stopped.

"No, sirree," answered Yost happily, "let's get on with it."

However, with about eight minutes left to play, the Stanford captain R. S. Fisher said to the Michigan captain Hugh White, "If you are willing, we are ready to quit." White, it seems, was more of a humanitarian than his coach. He promptly agreed.

Not even Yost's own alma mater escaped. After his 1904 team humiliated West Virginia, 130–0, at Ann Arbor, the *Daily New Dominion* of Morgantown reported in a story headlined "Horrible Nightmare," "Several members of the [West Virginia] team have been interviewed about the affair at Ann Arbor the other day. Some said that there was a team and that several times it stopped long enough for them to distinguish the features of the players. At other times they said they heard a heavy roaring sound as if the air were being split by heavy rushing bodies. . . . At times heavy shocks were experienced and the players were thrown to the ground by the force of the impact and they saw for a moment giant forms which seemed to be clad in football togs. . . . "

Heston, of course, was the mover and shaker of those Point-a-

Minute teams, but the success also reflected Yost's coaching. He was a no-nonsense coach and he worked his players hard. Although he wore starched collars and ties at practice, his style was hardly formal. When a player loafed or didn't seem to be putting out to the best of his ability, Yost got on him as quick as a flash and many a Michigan athlete felt the sting of his caustic tongue.

In his early days, Yost was not above persuading a football player at another school to transfer to Michigan. It also was his determination to increase Michigan's sphere of football influence by playing more teams from other parts of the country, especially the East and South, that led to the school's dispute with and ultimate withdrawal from the Big Ten in 1907, a defection that lasted until 1917. Yet, in later years, as Yost grew into elder statesman status, and particularly after he became athletic director at Michigan in 1921, he became a paragon of virtue and a staunch supporter of amateurism in college football.

Perhaps the most accurate appraisal of what Fielding Yost was and what he became was written by sportswriter Hugh Fullerton after Yost's retirement from coaching. Fullerton wrote, "He had run the gamut of coaching methods from the 'tramp on the injured and hurdle the dead' days to today, when he ranks high as a preacher and practicer of the highest morality in sport. He has developed from a rough fighting coach to an idealist, and is living proof what football can do as a moral force. He is much bigger today than the Yost of 29 years ago. . . ."

Although Yost opposed the introduction of the forward pass, once it came into being he became one of its pioneers and took advantage of it to beef up his attack, which became famous as the "punt, pass, and pray" offense. When things were going well for Yost and Michigan, Wolverine supporters thought it was masterful strategy by the coach. However when Michigan's fortunes faltered, as they did on occasion, Yost's critics were quick to complain about the "dullness" of his style of play. Hurry Up was just as quick to rise to his own defense.

"We play percentage," Yost would say. "We let the other fellow rush the ball and waste his energy in his own territory. Football games aren't won—they're lost. And Meeshegan's record is due to a policy of letting the enemy take the risk of fumbling inside his forty-yard line. Then we cash in on his mistakes. Let 'em holler about a punt, a pass, and a prayer. We generally have the last laugh."

And Fielding Yost and his "Meeshegan" teams generally did. Often enough to give him a record of 164 victories, 29 defeats, and 10 ties, 8 undefeated teams, 4 national champions, 7 Big Ten champions, 21 All-Americas, and a legion of lesser stars in his twenty-five years of active coaching in Ann Arbor. Yost had only one losing season and his overall twenty-nine-year record at five major colleges was a gaudy 196–35–12. Not bad for a coach who relied on "a pass, a punt, and a prayer!"

Yost's game, however, wasn't all just passing, punting, and praying. Classified as a coaching conservative by his colleagues, he frequently came up with the unexpected. One of Hurry Up's most famous plays was something he called "Old 83." Once asked to explain it, he said, "It starts out like a short side sweep, turns into what looks like an end-around play to the long side, and finally winds up with a delayed reverse straight over the spot where the short side defensive end should be, but usually isn't. It's sort of a psychic double-cross."

No wonder Michigan's opponents found it hard to stop. They couldn't even understand it.

Yost's later years as a coach took many twists and turns. He was named athletic director in 1921 and decided to retire as the football coach after an unbeaten 1923 season. George Little, one of Hurry Up's assistants, was named the new head coach for 1924, but Little soon found Yost looking over his shoulder and openly criticizing some of his decisions.

"When we won," said Little, "it was Yost's team. When we lost, it was mine."

Michigan lost only two games in 1924 but Fielding Yost was back as the head coach in 1925. One reason was that he couldn't stay away from coaching. Two others were Benny Friedman, a superb quarterback, and Bennie Oosterbaan, a spectacular end, who promised a glory-filled year for the Wolverines. And no one loved glory more than Fielding Harris Yost.

That 1925 team was worth coming back for. With Friedman and Oosterbaan teaming up as the best pass-catch combination in the country, Michigan lost only to Northwestern, 3–2. Everyone else fell before the rampaging Wolverines, including Red Grange and his Illinois team. Yost had devised some defensive trickery to hold Grange in check, and it worked. Friedman's field goal won for Michigan, 3–0.

Yost coached again in 1926 and turned out another conference

championship team. There was some doubt about who was going
to coach Michigan in 1927. Yost worked with the team and then,
just two weeks before the opening game, he announced that he
would retire again and that Tad Wieman, an assistant, would be the
head coach. Wieman, too, found Yost looking over his shoulder
but he still managed a 6–2 season. Despite this respectable record,
there again was some confusion over who was to coach the team in
1928, Wieman or Yost. It wasn't until the day before the opening
game that Yost announced Wieman would be the coach. The 1928
team had a 3–4–1 record and that was the end of Wieman. Yost,
too, decided that *he* had had enough and Harry Kipke, one of
Michigan's all-time playing greats, who had coached Michigan
State in 1928, was given the job as head coach. This time there was
no doubt, no confusion. Yost made it clear that the job belonged to
Kipke—unless, of course, Hurry Up decided he wanted it again.

Years later, Yost insisted that the 1925 team, even though it had
lost a game, was the best one he ever coached, better even than the
Point-A-Minute clubs of the early 1900s or any of his eight undefeated teams.

"The nineteen-twenty-five team was a hard one to fault," said
Yost. "I don't think the nineteen-oh-one team or any other of my
Meeshegan teams could have beaten them."

Although Yost never returned to coaching, he kept a watchful
eye on the football program until he retired as athletic director in
1941. He died five years later, at seventy-five, of gallstones. Yost,
for all his faults and foibles, was a masterful coach and a truly
great force in the Big Ten. He loved his "Meeshegan," and his
contributions, not only to football, but to the entire physical education and athletic program at Ann Arbor will not be forgotten.

Yost was years ahead of his time in envisioning a huge physical
athletic plant for Michigan, one which would provide facilities for
every student in the university who wanted to participate. When he
first projected his ideas, he was viewed as a dreamer. But the
Fielding H. Yost Field House, now an 8,000-seat hockey rink, and
the many-times-enlarged football stadium, which currently seats
101,701, are a tribute to his foresight and persistence. Now, Don
Canham, the present athletic director, has supervised $10 million
worth of construction of additional facilities and administers an
athletic budget of nearly $5 million a year.

Harry Kipke, meanwhile, after a desultory start in 1929, quickly made his choice by Yost look good. Three of Kipke's next four teams were undefeated and all four of them won or shared Big Ten championships. The 1932 and 1933 clubs also won national championships and Kipke, who had thrilled thousands of Michigan fans with his running and kicking in the early twenties, was being hailed as a miracle man. A major reason, of course, was a succession of All-Americas like quarterback Harry Newman, centers Maynard Morrison and Chuck Bernard, end Ted Petoskey, and tackle Francis Wistert.

But then the honeymoon ended. Kipke and Michigan ran out of superstars and his 1934 team, which featured a center named Gerald R. Ford, won only one game. After four straight losing seasons and some baleful wailing by the usual wolves who turn up when coaches can no longer win, Kipke was fired after the 1937 season. Oddly enough, Kipke was as much a victim of his own success as his failure. Perhaps he had won too much too soon. There also were some other contributing factors. Questions had been raised concerning illegal preseason practice sessions held in Canada, and there were accusations that Michigan football players who also were employed by the Ford Motor Company had been given "working time" to practice football. There were rumors of an alumni "slush fund" to help players. Morale had deteriorated and Harry and his line coach, Franklin Cappon, were at odds, a fact which had been thoroughly aired in the local press. And, finally, Yost had become disenchanted with the coaching of his former pupil.

The timing of Kipke's dismissal was hardly commendable. He was president of the American Football Coaches Association and, ironically, if Harry could have hung on for one more year, he certainly would have regained his "coaching genius." What he left behind on his freshman team were a couple of players named Tommy Harmon and Forest Evashevski and a host of other players who were to become shining stars. Instead, Herbert Orrin (Fritz) Crisler, Kipke's successor, was to reap the rich harvest of Kipke's last planting.

Although Kipke's public comments indicated that his firing came as a "distinct shock," he told a friend, "The more I look at it, the more relieved I feel."

Fritz Crisler, a Westerner born and bred but with a coaching reputation mostly earned in the East, hit Michigan like a breath of fresh air. First, he came without the official sanction of Fielding Yost. Second, he came with a list of demands which were to shake up the entire Michigan athletic structure.

Crisler's football background and coaching credentials were impressive. After playing and coaching under Amos Alonzo Stagg at Chicago, he had coached for two years at Minnesota, where he laid the groundwork for a dynasty that was to be presided over by his successor, Bernie Bierman. Then he had headed east to Princeton where, as the first nonalumnus ever to coach the Tigers, he had lifted them out of their doldrums back to supremacy in Eastern football. In his six years at Princeton he had produced two unbeaten teams and a 35–9–5 record.

When Eastern sportswriters asked Crisler what system he would use at Princeton, he replied tersely, "Blocking and tackling."

Michigan's search for a replacement for Harry Kipke narrowed down to Crisler and Lieutenant Tom Hamilton of Navy. Yost favored Hamilton, but Professor Ralph Aigler, chairman of the Board in Control of Athletics, was taken with the young coach who had brought Princeton back to prominence. There was considerable internal infighting in the Board, but Aigler had the support of President Alexander Ruthven and the job was offered to Crisler.

Before Crisler accepted, however, he laid down several conditions. He asked for the highest salary yet paid to a Midwestern coach; he demanded that the athletic and physical education programs be placed under a single head who would be granted a full professorship and be named head football coach and assistant athletic director and that he (Crisler) would become athletic director when Yost retired; he insisted that there would be no interference from Yost. All of these conditions were met and Crisler took over the job of rebuilding the Wolverines.

Fritz Crisler had come a long way since he "accidentally" became involved with football at the University of Chicago. A skinny six-footer, who weighed a mere 100 pounds, he never even thought about playing high school football at Earlville, Illinois, and later when he transferred to nearby Mendota. He did play some baseball, but most of his time was devoted to accumulating a 93.4 grade average that earned him a full-tuition academic scholarship at Chicago, where he enrolled as a premed student in 1917.

One day that fall, Crisler, decked out in his green freshman cap, stopped by the football field to watch practice. Suddenly the play came toward Crisler and, along with it, Coach Stagg, who nimbly tried to get out of the way. He did, but in the process stumbled over Crisler and they both went down.

"Why haven't you got on a football suit?" growled Stagg as he picked himself up off the ground.

"I'm not big enough," answered the by-now thoroughly frightened Crisler, who then weighed about 150 pounds.

"That's no excuse!" snapped Stagg.

The next day Crisler reported for football practice, was given a uniform, and told to play end. He also was given a good going over by Charlie Higgins, Chicago's 220-pound All-Conference fullback, in a scrimmage. Crisler promptly called it quits and turned in his uniform.

A week later Coach Stagg was pedaling around the campus on his bicycle when he came across his erstwhile freshman candidate, who tried desperately to avoid the coach.

"Weren't you out for football?" asked Stagg.

"Yes."

"What happened?"

"I quit."

"I never thought you'd be a quitter," said Stagg as he rode away.

The next day Crisler was back in uniform and on his way to a football career that was to lead him to the top of the coaching profession. He also was to get tagged by Stagg with a nickname that stuck with him for the rest of his life.

Crisler was no immediate ball of fire as a football player. He played some in 1917, went off to join the army in 1918, and came back to Chicago and the team in 1919. One day, after Crisler had bungled one assignment after another, Stagg stopped practice to make a little speech to him.

"Crisler, there's a celebrated violinist in this country. The name sounds like yours but it is spelled differently—K–r–e–i–s–l–e–r. He's world-renowned because he has certain attributes and knows how to use them. He has genius, brains, skill, coordination. From now on, Crisler, I'm going to call you Fritz, too, just to remind myself that you are absolutely his opposite."

From that time on, although Crisler was to prove many times over that he had "genius, brains, skill, and coordination," both on the athletic field and as a coach, he was known as Fritz. Years later, when the violinist was giving a concert in Ann Arbor, the two Fritzes met and Crisler told him how he got his nickname. Kreisler roared with amusement.

Crisler's football ability improved and by his senior year he was an accomplished end. He also had become an outstanding basketball and baseball player, and won nine letters. As a pitcher he led the Chicago varsity on a tour of Japan in 1920 and was good enough to be offered a tryout with the Chicago White Sox. But when the White Sox hitters began rattling his best pitches off the fences, Fritz decided that his destiny did not lie in the world of professional baseball.

Meanwhile, Crisler was not neglecting the books. He was an honor student and missed making Phi Beta Kappa by a single point. He put in two years at medical school at Chicago but, in 1922, Fritz gave up his aspirations to be a doctor and accepted an offer to join Stagg's coaching staff. Crisler immediately began to absorb as much knowledge as possible from Stagg. In 1924 he was offered the head coaching post at Minnesota but Stagg advised him against it. "Fritz, you're not ready to fly," said the Old Man.

But six years later, in 1930, when Minnesota again came looking for Crisler as a replacement for the resigned Dr. Clarence (Fat) Spears, Stagg recognized that football was on its deathbed at Chicago under the administration of President Hutchins and told Fritz it was time for him to get out. And so was launched a brilliant coaching career.

Crisler was a master organizer and a coaching perfectionist, as his players soon found out. While not an altogether humorless man himself, levity at practice or before a game was not part of his program. He was intolerant when it came to insubordination or if he felt that a player wasn't giving 100 percent. He was aloof with his players and rarely engaged in locker room histrionics, unless it was a carefully plotted ploy to psych his team, or, in some rare instances, to bring them down to earth if he thought they had reached too high a peak. There never was any doubt as to who was the boss. In fact some of his players referred to him as the "Lord." Although seemingly prim and proper in his relations with his players and the public, Fritz was not above letting his hair down with his friends—away from the football field—over a drink or two.

One of his former players, Stu Wilkins, a guard on his 1947 team, said, "Fritz Crisler was not a man with a warm nature. His players never had a brotherly or fatherly affection for him. He remained aloof from the distractions that bothered most of us. Some thought he lacked feeling for us, but I never thought so. He was respected by all . . . he was the most self-possessed man I have ever known."

A confirmed advocate of the single wing, Crisler spent endless hours polishing and perfecting the offense, adding to it whatever he thought would make it more potent. Out of this grew a fairly complex attack that blended power with trickery and included an assortment of spinners, buck laterals, deep sweeps, reverses, multiple-pass plays, and laterals.

When the T-formation became fashionable, Crisler didn't have much faith in it. But he put in a few plays anyway. "We called it the alumni-T," he said, "just to let them know that we were keeping up with the times."

Crisler, for all his urbane manner, was superstitious, almost to a fault. He would wear the same hat, suit, tie, shirt, and shoes to the games when his team was winning, which was most of the time. When Michigan played at home, he and his assistant coaches, Marty Martineau and Biggie Munn, whom he had coached at Minnesota, would always follow the players' bus—and the same route—to the stadium in their own car.

While Crisler inherited some of the greatest talent ever gathered at one school when he arrived in Ann Arbor in 1938, it was raw and had to be developed and molded into his system. The players also had to become used to his personality and coaching ways. Well, none of this took very long. With Tommy Harmon and Paul Kromer, who had been Michigan's running star in 1937, to lead the attack, and Forest Evashevski, who Crisler wisely converted from center to quarterback, and Ralph Heikkinen, a fine guard, to lead the blocking, Crisler's first Wolverine team rode to a 6–1–1 record, losing only to Minnesota, which was to become an annoying habit for Fritz's early teams (the Gophers beat him five straight times), and tying Northwestern.

In the next nine years Fritz Crisler never had a losing season at Michigan, and only twice did any of his teams lose more than two games. Crisler's teams won two Big Ten titles, the first in 1943, two years after he succeeded Yost as athletic director; placed second six times; and the 1947 team, his last and best, went to the Rose Bowl and won the national championship. In ten seasons his record at Michigan was 71–16–3, and eight of his teams finished in the Associated Press's Top Ten. In eighteen years as a head coach Fritz's record was 116–32–9.

One of Crisler's innovations was two-platoon football, but he always insisted that it came about through necessity rather than any ingenuity on his part. His 1945 Michigan team, composed mostly of young players, was getting ready to face powerful Army, with

Glenn Davis and Doc Blanchard, and Crisler was trying to avoid annihilation of his meager troops.

"When the other fellow has a thousand dollars and you have a dime is the time to gamble," said Crisler. "My spindly, rosy-cheeked lads couldn't possibly play that Army team nose-to-nose for sixty minutes, so we had to do something."

The free-substitution rule had been put in in 1941 as a wartime manpower measure, but no one had exploited it quite the way that Fritz Crisler did against Army. What Crisler did was to divide his squad into two units, with the best offensive players on one and the best defensive players on the other. When Army had the ball, Michigan sent in its eight best defensive players. When Michigan took over, they went out to rest and were replaced by eight offensive players. For a while the maneuver worked. Going into the last quarter, Coach Earl (Red) Blaik's heavily favored Army team was locked in a 7–7 tie. Then, the cadets' superior talent exploded for three touchdowns and Army won, 28–7.

"It had worked so well," said Crisler, "that for the rest of the season we platooned complete offensive and defensive teams. By the following year most of the colleges adopted platooning."

Ironically, it was Crisler, as head of the Football Rules Committee, who led the successful fight to kill two-platoon football in 1953. Of course Fritz had retired from coaching by that time and as the athletic director he had a slightly different view of college football.

"Specialization was becoming too pronounced," Crisler explained, "and the all-around skills and objectives were being overlooked."

For a long while Crisler's 1940 team, the one that rollicked its way to a 7–1 season with Harmon, Evashevski, Ed Frutig, and all those other freewheelers, was Crisler's favorite club. That is until the undefeated 1947 team came along to give Fritz some of his greatest coaching moments.

Bob Chappuis and Chalmers (Bump) Elliott were the backfield stars of that team which swept through the Big Ten like a tornado to win the title, then went on to rout Southern California, 49–0, in the Rose Bowl to capture Crisler's only national championship. It was a team of specialists that relied on deception, sleight of hand, the meticulous ball handling which Crisler's single-wing offense demanded, and perfect execution. It was truly Fritz's masterpiece and he was rewarded by being voted Coach of the Year.

It also ended Crisler's coaching career. A few months later, when the Board in Control of Athletics met, Fritz had a surprise ready—his retirement from coaching. He continued as athletic director, however, until he retired from that post in 1968.

Crisler's interest in football didn't end when he stopped coaching. For years he was chairman of the Football Rules Committee and exerted considerable influence in bringing about changes which he believed in, like the abolition of two-platoon football, the optional two-point try after touchdown, and the widening of the goal posts from twenty to twenty-four feet.

As coach and athletic director, Crisler left his considerable mark on Michigan athletics. He continued the building boom started by his predecessor, Fielding Yost. Men's and women's swimming pools and several other facilities were built, and the seating capacity of Michigan Stadium was expanded to 100,001. The "one" seat was for Crisler.

That was Fritz Crisler—a man with class and style.

When Fritz Crisler stepped down as Michigan's football coach in 1947, there was never any doubt as to who his successor would be. It had to be Bennie Oosterbaan, the big, amiable fellow who had spent twenty-four years—more than half his lifetime—at Michigan, first as a three-time All-America end in the twenties and then as a longtime assistant coach under Harry Kipke and Crisler.

Crisler, of course, was a hard act to follow. Fritz's finale—a national championship, Big Ten title, victory in the Rose Bowl, and Coach of the Year—was a show-stopper. Surely no one could top *that!* Well, maybe Bennie Oosterbaan didn't exactly top it, but he equaled it in his very first year as a head coach. Although Bob Chappuis and the entire backfield that had contributed to that super 1947 season was gone, Oosterbaan took what was left, moved Pete Elliott to quarterback, put sophomores Chuck Ortmann and Leo Koceski as the halfbacks, and proceeded to lead them to an unbeaten season. Bennie's first Michigan team did almost everything that Crisler's last one had done. It won the Big Ten crown and the national championship, and Oosterbaan, too, was named Coach of the Year, the first time any college had come up with back-to-back honorees. The only thing Bennie's Wolverines didn't do was win in the Rose Bowl, and that was because they were not permitted to return to Pasadena because of the conference's "no-repeat" rule.

Oosterbaan's troops tied Ohio State for the Big Ten championship in 1949 and won it outright in 1950, but Bennie never had another year quite like that first one. Finally, after a 2–6–1 debacle in 1958, and a respectable 63–33–4 mark for eleven years, Oosterbaan retired and was succeeded by another one-time Michigan All-America, Bump Elliott. Bump's reign as head coach was less distinguished than his playing days, except for two seasons. In 1964 Michigan posted a 9–1 record to take the conference title and went on to wallop Oregon State, 34–7, in the Rose Bowl. Then, in 1968, halfback Ron Johnson led Michigan to an 8–2 record and second place in the Big Ten.

Crisler had retired as athletic director and there had been some talk of Elliott's moving up to the head job. However, while Michigan authorities would never publicly admit it, Bump's chances of succeeding Crisler had suddenly evaporated a year earlier when his brother, Pete, got caught up in the slush-fund scandal which cost him his coaching job at Illinois. Instead, Don Canham, a dynamic promoter who had been the track coach, was named athletic director. One of his first moves was to persuade Elliott to give up his football coaching post in return for being kicked upstairs to associate athletic director. Elliott later went on to become athletic director at Iowa in 1970.

Canham's search for a replacement for Elliott led him almost directly to Miami University in Oxford, Ohio, where a hard-nosed young man named Glenn (Bo) Schembechler had been turning out good football teams in the fast-growing Mid-American Conference for the past six years. Perhaps what turned Canham on was that he saw a lot of Woody Hayes in Schembechler. And why not—Bo had played for Woody at Miami and later was one of his assistant coaches at Ohio State. He also had served apprenticeships at Bowling Green and Northwestern under Ara Parseghian. Although later on Schembechler tried to play down his early associations with Hayes, mostly because the two men *had* to be deadly rivals if they coached at Michigan and Ohio State, there is a great similarity in their coaching styles. Bo, like Woody, is dedicated to a power running game and thinks the pass is a dirty word.

When Canham asked Schembechler if he were interested in the Michigan job, Bo hardly hesitated a second before answering, "Hell, yes."

Elliott had left behind an impressive group of sophomores, among them a pair of offensive linemen, Reggie McKenzie and Paul Seymour, two promising backs, Glenn Doughty and Billy Taylor, and veteran tight end Jim Mandich. Schembechler made the most of this talent. All Bo did that first season was post an 8–2 record and beat Ohio State, 24–12, but he had to settle for a tie with the Buckeyes for the Big Ten title since one of Michigan's two losses had been to Michigan State. The Wolverines also went to the Rose Bowl, where they lost to Southern California, 10–3. However, Schembechler was voted Coach of the Year by the American Football Coaches Association, no mean accomplishment for someone in his first year in the tough Big Ten.

That started an amazing run of victories for Schembechler and Michigan. It also heated up the Michigan–Ohio State rivalry, which the Buckeyes had dominated for so long. With the arrival of Bo the conference championship always seemed to come down to the season's finale between the two old rivals. In the next seven years Schembechler and Michigan won one Big Ten title outright, tied with Ohio State four times, and finished second to the Buckeyes once.

In 1970 Michigan's only defeat came at the hands of Ohio State, 20–7; in 1971 the Wolverines were unbeaten in the regular season but lost to Stanford, 13–12, in the Rose Bowl; in 1972 Michigan was beaten only by Ohio State, 14–11; in 1973 the Wolverines were undefeated, but tied by the Buckeyes, 10–10; in 1974 Ohio State's 12–10 win was the only blemish on Michigan's record. All in all, Schembechler, in his first eight years at Michigan, from 1960 to 1976, had a 76–11–3 record. Not bad for a good old Ohio boy who learned some of his football at Woody Hayes' knee.

Meanwhile, Bo survived a heart attack that hospitalized him on the eve of the January 1, 1972 Rose Bowl game with Stanford, and he underwent coronary-bypass surgery on four occluded arteries leading to the heart in the spring of 1976. Schembechler, however, was back in harness for the 1976 season and going full speed.

"I'm looking forward to coaching this year more than any other season," said Bo. "For the first time in seven years I'm not taking any pills. I'm back to a normal life. I'm not as uptight as I used to be. I know that losing a football game is not the end of the world."

Actually, the 1976 season was more than just a normal one for Schembechler and Michigan. The Wolverines, picked to be No. 1 in some preseason polls, and led by quarterback Ricky Leach, tailback-fullback Rob Lytle, and a halfback with the wonderful name of Harlan Huckleby, rolled over one foe after another until Purdue upset them, 16–14. But they came back from that disappointment to trounce Ohio State, 22–0, in their final game, completing a 10–1 regular season and earning still another tie with the ever-present Buckeyes for the Big Ten championship and a place in the Rose Bowl against Southern California.

Even old rival Woody Hayes praised Schembechler and his team for that accomplishment. "Any team that beats us that badly has got to be Number One," proclaimed Woody. "It is almost unbelievable what Bo has done. It was the most courageous coaching job in football this year."

Although occasionally gruff with the press, sometimes tactless, and frequently short-tempered with his critics, Schembechler is always forthright with his opinions—whether or not they are popular.

"That first year under Bo, everybody wants to go home," said Jim Smith, Michigan's All-America wingback in 1976. "That man will yell at anybody, everybody. But the more you're around Bo, the more sense it all makes. I have grown immensely as both a football player and a human being. Bo has taught us to respect all our teammates . . . Rob Lytle or myself, we're not treated any differently than anyone else."

"Bo is explosive and not very tactful at times," admits his wife, Millie, "but basically he's a very good man. . . . He's very easy to get along with around the house. He can explode, given good reason, but for the most part he's very even-tempered."

Perhaps Bo Schembechler won't win any popularity contests outside his own home, but he wins a lot of football games.

TWELVE

Zuppke of Illinois

The third member of the coaching trilogy which dominated Big Ten football in its early days came along a bit later than Stagg and Yost. Robert Carl Zuppke made his debut at the University of Illinois in 1913 but, unlike his famed rivals, he had never played a minute of varsity football anywhere.

Indeed, there was nothing in Zuppke's early background to indicate that he would become one of the game's foremost coaches. He was born in Berlin, Germany, in 1879 and, when he was two, his parents brought him to the United States, where the family settled in Milwaukee. It wasn't until young Zuppke entered the University of Wisconsin as a philosophy major that he evinced any interest in football. The Badgers didn't have much use for a 140-pound, five-foot seven-inch player, even one as sturdy and determined as Bob Zuppke, a young man who spoke with a German accent. So he spent his entire football career at Wisconsin as a member of the scrubs, taking his lumps in daily scrimmages. But, as it turned out later, it wasn't all in vain.

Zuppke had demonstrated some talent as an artist, and after graduation from Wisconsin he took off for New York City where he got a job in his field. Being a budding artist, however, it wasn't exactly what Zuppke had in mind. He was a sign painter and most of his work was done from a scaffold rather than with an easel. After almost a year of this kind of frustration, Zuppke packed up his palette and took a job teaching history at Hackley Manual Training School in Muskegon, Michigan, where he also was given the assignment of coaching football.

Zuppke quickly demonstrated that he had indeed absorbed considerable knowledge during his days as a scrub at Wisconsin and he was an immediate success as a high school coach. So successful that he soon moved on to Oak Park High School in Chicago and then to Hyde Park High, where he turned out state championship teams while changing the face of interscholastic football with his imaginative and innovative coaching methods.

It wasn't long before Zuppke caught the eye of George Huff, Illinois' athletic director. Illinois had won only one Big Ten championship, in 1910—also its only unbeaten season—in its seventeen years in the conference and Huff was seeking a coach to lead the Illini out of the wilderness. Huff persuaded Zuppke, who had other college offers, to try and in 1913 he was hired for $2,700 a year. That proved to be the best investment ever made by the Illinois athletic department.

Just a year later, in 1914, Zuppke gave the Illini their first outright Big Ten title and the national championship. In 1915 his team shared the crown with Minnesota. During his twenty-nine years as the Illinois coach, Zup had four unbeaten teams, won three national championships, won outright or shared seven Big Ten titles, and had a record of 131–81–13. In his personal rivalries with Stagg and Yost, he held a 13–5–2 edge over the Chicago coach but won only two victories in six games against Yost's Michigan teams. But even when he lost, he always managed to give Yost and his Wolverines a hard time.

Bob Zuppke was perhaps one of the most unlikely looking and sounding coaches in the business. Short and stubby, moon-faced and twinkly-eyed with a hank of hair hanging down over his forehead, he gave the appearance of a quixotic little man. Instead, Zup was philosophical, enterprising, resourceful, persuasive, and could be quite eloquent when he spoke in his German accent. He had a flair for the dramatic and a knack for getting directly to the core of a problem. He also had a wonderful sense of humor, which he exercised on his players and his coaching friends, one of whom was Knute Rockne of Notre Dame. Zup got a big kick out of publicly twitting his good friend about his fame as a football coach. One story Zuppke liked to tell concerned the time he and Rockne were both invited to speak at the same banquet.

"I get off the train," said Zup indignantly in his best German accent. "It's raining. Nobody meets me. My own baggage I haff to carry to the hotel. There is no room reserved for me. I get vun. I go upstairs. I hear a big noise. I look out der vindow. It's a parade. There's a big band, the mayor, the Chamber of Commerce, Rotary Club, Kiwanis—and it's Rockne they bring along. Se ve go to the dinner. Ve speak. Vot do I giff them? Pheelosophy. Vot does

Rockne giff them? High school chokes. Vot do I get? Notting! Vot does Rockne get? Two hundred dollars! Bah!''

Zuppke also took great delight in baiting Michigan's Yost. One memorable occasion in which the Illinois coach indulged in Yost-baiting was the annual convention of the American Football Coaches Association in New York in December 1924. Zup was first vice-president of the AFCA and in the absence of John Heisman, the president, was in the chair when the time came to nominate a candidate for president for 1925.

Yost, who had turned over the coaching reins at Michigan to George Little for the 1924 season, planned to run for the presidency and had prepared a self-nominating speech. When he got up to speak, however, Zuppke refused to give him the floor.

"This organization is for coaches only," said Zup. "Yost is not a coach. He's an athletic director."

Captain John McEwan, the Army coach, then got up to nominate Yost in a flowery speech in which he described his candidate as "a man as tall and as straight and as strong as the timbers which grow in the Northland."

When McEwan finished, Zuppke got up and asked, "Does anyone want to nominate me? Never mind, I'll do it myself."

Then he took off in a wonderfully whimsical speech ending by asking the coaches if they wanted as president a man "as strong as the timbers which grow in the Northland or a little guy like me whom you can push around?"

Zuppke won the election and it was reported that Yost got only a single vote—the one cast by Zup.

They called him, among other things, the "Little Dutchman," the "Dutch Master," and the "Wily Dutchman," appellations which Zuppke never rejected although he was not Dutch, but German. There were even some who suspected that Zuppke's German accent was part of his image.

Zuppke turned out more than his share of outstanding stars during his twenty-nine years at Illinois. His 1914 team, the one he always considered his best, featured George (Potsy) Clark at quarterback, Harold Pogue at halfback, and Ralph (Slooey) Chapman at guard. And there were others through the years, like Perry Graves, Bart Macomber, John Depler, Burt Ingwersen, Charles (Chuck) Carney, Jim McMillen, Bernie Shively, Russ Crane, Robert Reitsch, Butch Nowack, Leroy Wietz, Lou Gordon, and Jim

Reeder, but the greatest of all was Red Grange, who set the college football world on its ear in 1923–24–25.

Grange, or "Grainche," as Zup called him, was Bob Zuppke's masterpiece. Zup had had a couple of bad seasons in 1921 and 1922 and he desperately needed something—or someone—to give the Illini a lift. What he got was one of the game's greatest runners ever. Grange not only supplied the lift in 1923, but gave Illinois its first undefeated season since 1914 and a Big Ten championship.

"I will never have another 'Grainche,'" Zuppke said at the time, "but neither will anyone else. They can argue all they like about the greatest player that ever lived. I'm satisfied I had him when I had 'Grainche.'"

Zuppke was free and easy with his coaching, refusing to stick with a system. He preferred to improvise according to his material and to depend upon his agile mind to dream up new wrinkles with which to torment his opponents. He was the first to introduce the center's short spiral snap, pulling back the guards to protect the passer, and the streamlined, slimmer football to help forward passing.

"I cut the design out of leather in my own workshop," claimed Zup.

Zuppke popularized the huddle and invented the Flea Flicker play, which is still used today. Zuppke's version, which he liked to use from a place-kick formation, was a short pass to the right end, who flicked a lateral to the left half as he went wide around end.

The Illinois coach liked to give exotic names to the plays he conceived. Among them were the Blue Eagle, Corkscrew, Sidewinder, Whirligig, Razzle Dazzle, and the Flying Trapeze. What Zuppke didn't invent, he simply gave a new name.

Zuppke also had a knack for turning an original phrase, many of which have been repeated or claimed by others through the years. The list is endless and these are among the most memorable ones:

Often an All-America is made by a long run, a weak defense, and a poet in the press box.

All quitters are good losers.

If you can't do anything well, try to become an executive.

A coach is always responsible to an irresponsible public.

Plays don't win; it's the men who carry out the plays.

No athletic director holds office longer than two losing football coaches.

When he came to Illinois, Zuppke told folks, "I can win any game you specify, but I can't always win them all."

Well, Bob Zuppke didn't always win them all, but he did manage to win quite a few "specified" games. One of them was a 9–7 upset of Chic Harley's heavily favored Ohio State team in 1919, and another was a 7–0 win over the same Buckeyes in 1921. However, even more notable were Illinois' victories over Minnesota in 1916 and Michigan in 1939.

Prior to the 1916 game, Minnesota was unbeaten in four games and had outscored its opponents by 236 points to 14. The best Illinois had been able to achieve was an even split in its four games and Coach Zuppke's team hardly figured to even ruffle the Golden Gophers' composure. But Zuppke had other ideas about the game.

All week long, Zup scrimmaged his players every day. When they complained, he told them, "We're all supposed to be killed on Saturday, so we might as well have the satisfaction of killing ourselves."

Zuppke's pregame speech was a classic which concluded on a note his players never quite figured out or understood. His closing words were, "I'm Louis the Fourteenth and you are my court. After us—the deluge."

The "deluge" was a 14–9 victory over the shocked Minnesota team, one of the great upsets in Big Ten history.

Even after things began to go downhill for Illinois and Zuppke in the thirties, the wily old man still had an occasional surprise or two up his sleeve for unsuspecting opponents. The 1939 Michigan game was one of those special events.

Michigan had Tom Harmon and Zuppke was particularly annoyed by Coach Fritz Crisler's observation that "Harmon was a better back than Red Grange." So annoyed that he concentrated on only one thing from the beginning of the preseason practice—beating the Wolverines and making Crisler eat his words. To make sure that his team would be familiar with Michigan's favorite plays, Zup put several of them into his own offense. He also junked his defensive huddle for that game and came up with a wide defense, a seven-man line, designed to stop Harmon on sweeps and slants to either side. It left the middle open, but Zuppke was prepared to concede yardage there just so long as Harmon could be reasonably contained.

Meanwhile, Michigan swept to easy victories, including an 85–0 massacre of Chicago, in its first four games. Illinois, on the other hand, had been able to salvage only a scoreless tie with Drake in its four games. The heat had been on Zuppke to quit, and at a pep rally the night before the game he had been heckled by alumni and students who demanded to know, "When are you leaving?"

The next afternoon Zup demonstrated that he wasn't quite ready to leave. Michigan also wasn't ready for his wide defense, which held Harmon to 72 yards rushing, and the Illini upset the Wolverines, 16–7. What made the victory even sweeter was that both Illinois touchdowns were scored on plays taken right out of Hurry Up Yost's book. The first was a "sleeper," with halfback George Rettinger hiding himself along the sideline and then catching a scoring pass from Jimmy Smith. The second touchdown came on Yost's old "talking play." As Illinois lined up on the Michigan 5-yard line, two backs began arguing over the choice of the play which had been called in the huddle. The Michigan defense relaxed, and zap, before the Wolverines knew it, the ball was snapped and Illinois had a touchdown.

After the game, when reporters asked Zuppke about these bits of trickery, he responded with a wide grin, "What was good enough for Yost is good enough for me!"

The tremendous victory in the face of such overwhelming odds even turned some of Zup's fickle hecklers of the night before into admirers. Suddenly, it was "Good Old Zup," the miracle coach, again.

Zuppke's—and Illinois'—good fortunes had begun to turn after the 6–1–1 1929 season. Illinois no longer was automatically getting the blue-chip football players and Zuppke refused to go out and beg high school players to attend his school.

"They tell me that I should go around kissing babies and talking to mothers of poor boys to persuade them to send their sons to Illinois," Zup said. "They say this is one of the duties of a modern coach. I told them that if that was the duty of a modern coach, then I wasn't capable of being a modern coach."

The grumbling about Zuppke started in the early thirties, was interrupted for a while when his 1934 team posted a 7–1 mark, but then reached a crescendo after the 1938 season in which the Illini won only three games. What kicked off the great controversy was a clash between Zuppke and Wendell S. (Weenie) Wilson, who had succeeded the late George Huff as athletic director. Wilson tried to get Zup, then fifty-nine, to resign in exchange for a $6,000 pension. At first Zuppke agreed to the offer which Wilson made on behalf of the athletic board. Then he had a change of heart and subsequently the university's Board of Trustees refused to accept

Zuppke's teams won only four games during the next two years, and in the summer of 1941 Wilson led another attempt to oust the coach. This time a group of Zuppke's former players, led by Red Grange, rallied around their old coach and took their fight to the Board of Trustees. Wilson, meanwhile, charged that Grange had been part of a group which had been trying to get his (Wilson's) job for Potsy Clark. Once again the Board of Trustees refused to fire Zuppke and he was at the helm of the team for the 1941 season. Wilson, however, was replaced as athletic director by Doug Mills, one of Zup's former players.

After a disastrous 1941 season—Illinois won only two games— Bob Zuppke, now sixty-two, finally announced his resignation and retirement from football. *He* had picked the time and the place.

So ended twenty-nine years for Zuppke as the head coach at Illinois. He then turned his full attention to two of his favorite hobbies—farming and painting. Zup raised prize hogs at his farm ten miles east of Champaign, but was more fond of showing off his art. He specialized in landscapes, painting in both pastels and oils, and his works were good enough to hang in respected galleries around the country. His art was frequently referred to as brutal, but Zuppke had a ready answer for that.

"Why shouldn't art be brutal when and if nature is brutal? Why shouldn't I paint the forests as they are? When I go into the forest, the trees scratch and scrape me. Am I expected to come back and paint a lovely scene? Football is brutal, too. But brutes can't play it. The value of all paintings, whether in pigment or in pigskin, lies to some degree in their resemblance to life."

Zuppke was just as positive in his thoughts about football. "There is an awful lot of bunk printed every year about football and it all makes me sick," he once said. "Football is a very complicated game, but it is not the mysterious, romantic, exaggerated game it is cracked up to be. Coaching football is just hard work and patience with a lot of inspiration needed at the big psychological moments. Playing football is just hard work and determination. Guts win more games than unusual ability. If a team can collectively arouse itself and fight like demons it is a football team; if it has a lot of fancy plays and a lot of advertised stars, but it cannot go through real fire without batting an eyelash, it is no good. Guts will always beat individual class."

That, in a nutshell, was Bob Zuppke's coaching philosophy, and he believed in it until he died in 1957 at the age of seventy-eight.

*   *   *

Zuppke's successor in 1942 was Ray Eliot, a balding, affable young man who played guard for the Illini in 1929, 1930, and 1931, and had been line coach under Zup for five years. Eliot had learned his trade well at the feet of the old master, but not even an infusion of fresh blood could cure Illinois, at least not right away.

Actually, Eliot's first season wasn't all that bad. His team won six games and lost four, and one of those wins was a 20–13 shocker over Minnesota, Illinois' first Big Ten victory since 1939. The hero of the game was Alex Agase, the All-America guard who scored two touchdowns on fumble recoveries.

For the next three years, though, things went from bad to worse and the wolves began to howl again. However, Eliot put a halt to that in 1946 when the Illini fought to an 8–2 record, losing only to Indiana and Notre Dame, to win their first Big Ten title in eighteen years and a trip to the Rose Bowl where they trampled UCLA, 45–14.

Eliot put in seventeen years as the Illinois coach and gave the school two more Big Ten championships, one outright in 1951 when only a scoreless tie with Ohio State marred a 9–0–1 season for the Illini, and a tie with Michigan State in 1953. The 1951 team also beat Stanford, 40–7, in the Rose Bowl.

"The nineteen fifty-three team, which had J. C. Caroline as a sophomore halfback, was my favorite," admitted Ray. "We were a small team, but it was a very quick team and a very courageous one. The record [7–1–1] speaks for itself."

The 1953 club was the last of the good ones for Eliot. After that it was all downhill for him and the Illini, and Eliot retired after the 1959 season with an 83–73–11 record.

Pete Elliott, the handsome, blond former Michigan All-America, took over the coaching mantle from Eliot in 1960 and endured three horrible seasons, including a fifteen-game losing streak, before his rebuilding program paid off in 1963. All those freshmen that Pete and his staff had recruited in his first year were now seniors, but they had come off a 2–7 season in 1962 and no one expected that they would be much better. No one, that is, but the Illinois players themselves.

Except for Dick Butkus, an all-purpose center who delighted in hitting people, quarterback Mike Taliaferro, who ran much better than he passed, and Jim Grabowski, a smashing sophomore full-back, the Illini hardly seemed to be the kind of team that would terrify the Big Ten. They played to a 20–20 tie with Ohio State and lost to a mediocre Michigan team, 14–8, but when it came down to the big one with Michigan State, the one which would decide the conference championship and a place in the Rose Bowl, they whipped the Spartans, 13–0. Then, to put the icing on the cake, Illinois beat Washington, 17–7, in Pasadena to complete an 8–1–1 season.

Three years later, before the 1967 season, Pete Elliott was gone, caught up in a slush-fund scandal that cost him his job and, for a while, his career. He was followed by Jim Valek, who bravely took over a sick and dying program. About the only thing notable that happened during Valek's four-year reign was a 17–13 upset of Ohio State in 1967. Also, the university didn't distinguish itself when it decided to fire Valek. School officials announced it during the season. It was tactless timing and drew criticism from all quarters. The athletic board withdrew its announcement but Valek was gone after the 1970 season, succeeded by Bob Blackman, who had been highly successful for sixteen years at Dartmouth.

Blackman, an effervescent man with a positive approach to coaching, had just completed an undefeated 9–0 season at Dartmouth and had won his fourth Ivy League championship. His teams had also tied for the title on three other occasions, and he had produced two other unbeaten teams during his long tenure in the hills of New Hampshire.

Blackman's Dartmouth teams had been noted for the varied and complex offenses and defenses they used and, perhaps, this was responsible for the new coach's bad start in 1971. His team lost its first six games and Illinois officials were wondering what kind of mistake they had made. Then, suddenly, Bob turned it all around, winning his last five games over Purdue, Northwestern, Indiana, Wisconsin, and Iowa to finish in a tie for third place in the conference standings.

There were further signs of improvement in 1974 when Illinois posted a 6–4–1 record, but then disenchantment set in. After the 1976 season, which ended with an emotional 48–6 whipping of Northwestern and a 5–6 overall record, Blackman and his entire staff were fired. He was then replaced by Gary Moeller, who had been an assistant coach at Michigan.

"I don't think I had a fair chance," complained Blackman.

For Illinois the road back to the glory days of Bob Zuppke has been a long and tortuous one, especially in a conference which has been dominated for so long by Ohio State and Michigan.

THIRTEEN

Bernie Bierman,
The Power Master

The myth grew that Bernie Bierman, Minnesota's great coach, would go out into the Minnesota farmlands in the spring looking for big, husky farmhands to recruit for his football team the way Notre Dame and Pittsburgh were supposed to go down into the Pennsylvania coal mines looking for football players. This myth has Bierman going up to any farmhand behind a plow and asking the young husky to point in the direction of the University of Minnesota. If the farmhand pointed with his finger, as most people would, Bierman would get back in his car and drive off. But if the farmhand lifted the plow and pointed in any direction, Bierman grabbed him for his team.

Well, it wasn't exactly that way. But it was power football that Bernard W. Bierman installed at Minnesota. It was to become the famous single-wing behind an unbalanced line that carried Minnesota and Bierman to the greatest string of successes ever enjoyed by a coach and university in the history of football. It all began in 1932 when Bernie Bierman was tabbed as Minnesota's head football coach, after he had served three years establishing Tulane as a national power. Bernie never hesitated in taking the Minnesota job. He was going home—to his native state and to his alma mater.

Bernie Bierman was born March 11, 1894 in Springfield, Minnesota, of German parents. He suffered from a chronic bone defect in his legs but was told to keep active and work at sports to improve the condition. Much like Glenn Cunningham, the great miler who overcame the effects of serious burns to his legs as a child by running, Bierman got active enough to become captain of the 1916 Minnesota football team. After serving in the First World War, Bierman turned to teaching and coaching in high school, and finally got his break as an assistant to Clark Shaughnessy at Tulane. When Shaughnessy left Tulane Bierman stepped in as head coach of the New Orleans university.

Then came the call for home. It was music to Bernie's ears, and the Minnesota fans had a decade of great singing and rejoicing ahead as Bierman compiled a list of victories that topped anything done in football up to that time. Between the time he took over in 1932 and the time he went off to World War II in 1942, Bierman's Minnesota teams had sixty-three victories, twelve losses, and five ties. Strangely enough, four of those ties came in the 1933 season when the Vikings (now called the Gophers) won four games and lost none, but tied four. Bierman had, in that ten-year period, five undefeated teams, seven Big Ten titles, and two victory streaks of twenty-one triumphs in a row.

Bierman's 1934 Minnesota team, undefeated and untied, was considered by many of his contemporaries to be the best team in the history of football. There are still some who believe this Minnesota squad, deep in reserve strength, was the best. It was the best example of Bierman's teachings, with the timing and blocking that he insisted must be done with flawless execution.

But it was later that Bierman's powerful Minnesota teams performed what he is possibly best known for in the way of coaching achievements. For three years in a row—1938, 1939, and 1940—Bierman's Golden Gophers stopped Tom Harmon of Michigan cold. They stopped the mighty Wolverine in his tracks. He never scored a point in three years against Minnesota, and Michigan never beat Minnesota while Harmon was on the team. First Minnesota beat Michigan, 7–6, in 1938 when Harmon was a sophomore. Then the Gophers beat the Wolverines and Harmon, 20–7, in 1939, and finally it was, once again, Minnesota 7, Michigan 6, in 1940. In each of those 7–6 decisions Bierman's Minnesotans came from behind to win after Michigan scored but failed to convert the extra point.

Bruce Smith was the hero of the 1940 victory over Michigan and just one of the many All-America players Bierman coached with the Vikings or Norsemen or Gophers. Whatever the name, it was Mighty Minnesota under Bierman.

Smith, one great runner; Bud Wilkinson, once a guard and then a quarterback for Minnesota; Pug Lund, a halfback; Bill Bevan, a guard; Dick Smith, a tackle—these were among the heroes and All-America players Bierman produced in Minneapolis. These were outstanding athletes, and it was Wilkinson, later the coach at Oklahoma, who became the man to break Bierman's winning streak as a coach.

These athletes were schooled in practice on timing to such a degree that Bierman would inspect their footsteps in the grass to see if they went just where they were expected to run as blockers, tacklers, or runners. And then they got a bit of Bierman's philosophy, whether they knew it or not:

"Only one thing is worse than going into a game convinced you can't win. That's going into a game convinced you can't lose. The best is to feel you can win but will have to put out everything you have to do it."

Bierman was always thinking about new plays to work from that unbalanced line of his. Usually he came up with something such as the reverse that gave Bruce Smith an 80-yard run against Michigan in 1940.

"You cannot design a play that will fool all of the opposition at the same time, or one that will fool them for very long. It is the aim to fool just a few defensive players for a limited time and depend upon our perfect execution to take the split-second advantage of this, which is all we need."

So developed the formula for the best success story in football during the depression years, or during any decade in Big Ten history. Bierman went off to the Marine Corps again in World War II. But when he came back, football had sort of passed him by. He would not convert from his favorite single wing to the T-formation that was then becoming the prime attack. Within a few seasons Bierman ended his football career, retiring from the game after the 1950 season.

A couple of years after Bierman got back to his homeland in Minnesota, Alvin (Bo) McMillin, a colorful Texan who had played and coached his way to fame, became the head coach at Indiana. It was eleven years after McMillin's first season at Indiana in 1934 that the Hoosiers got their first Big Ten championship. McMillin had made it in 1945 with a lot of World War II ex-servicemen and a lot of very young athletes. The Indiana athletic center still has a huge photo of that 1945 undefeated Big Ten championship team plastered over a wall near the football office.

In the picture of that first postwar team of Hoosier football players are Ted Kluszewski, Ben Raimondi, Bob Ravensberg, and others.

In June 1945, McMillin had signed an unprecedented Big Ten college football contract for ten years, calling for a total of $95,000 ($9,500 a year). He produced the big winner in 1945 and two years later stepped down as coach to be full-time athletic director.

This was the man who had quarterbacked the famed Prayin' Colonels from little Centre College in Kentucky that went up to Harvard in 1921 and beat the mighty Crimson, 6–0, to end a twenty-five-game winning streak. McMillin scored the touchdown. Bo McMillin died shortly after quitting the coaching ranks, and Indiana and football lost an exciting and colorful leader.

But Indiana was to get one of the most colorful of all Big Ten coaches in history nearly a quarter-century later when Lee Corso came to Bloomington. He wasn't riding an elephant as he arrived at Indiana. But that wasn't because he had never ridden an elephant. He had done that one day as coach at Louisville where he tried everything to drum up enthusiasm for the football team.

Corso, like McMillin, had been a college quarterback. He had been the quarterback at Florida State under coach Tom Nugent in that coach's rather new I-formation. Corso went on to coach under Nugent at Maryland. Then he moved around until landing the head coaching job at Louisville. He built that little-known football team into a winner as a small halfback, Howard Stevens, did a job setting rushing records that weren't broken until Archie Griffin and Tony Dorsett came on the scene in the seventies.

Success at Louisville earned Corso the Indiana job in 1973, where he joined the ranks of those bucking the big, bad Buckeyes and Wolverines. But Lee Corso was never at a loss for words or inventive ideas. He is the first Big Ten coach to hire a woman as an assistant coach. He made a woman his academic advisor and tutor for the team.

Corso went at everything with spirit. He even attended every banquet offered in his early days at Indiana in hopes of stirring up support and thus some recruits. In his first year at Bloomington, Corso said, "I've attended one hundred fifty banquets this winter and have been served chicken all one hundred fifty times. I don't get a haircut anymore. I get plucked."

Corso sniffed ammonia capsules that he held in one hand while gripping a Saint Christopher medal in the other as he walked the sidelines during games. During one game at Louisville when his team was being trounced and the opposing coach kept his first string in the action, Corso ran out on the field waving a white towel as the signal of surrender.

Corso got to Indiana University during one of those games of musical chairs that afflicts the Big Ten every once in a while. John Pont, the former Yale head coach who had tried for six years at Indiana, left to become head coach at Northwestern as Alex Agase left Northwestern to become head coach at Purdue, replacing Bob DeMoss, who threw in the towel. Pont, a poor automobile driver with a record of accidents that included one on his way to the interview for the Indiana job, drove well as coach in his first season with the Hoosiers. He got them to the Rose Bowl in that 1967 season, was named Coach of the Year, and then could not repeat. He moved on to Northwestern where he also got the athletic director's job, but still was unable to do much against those Buckeyes and Wolverines of the seventies. But he wasn't alone. Agase, who succeeded Ara Parseghian as the Northwestern coach when Ara went to Notre Dame in 1965, was finally finished when Purdue dropped him after the 1977 campaign.

But Northwestern, that private institution that struggles in the conference with nine large state universities, had its heyday amid the climb to great success by Bierman back in the midthirties. The good fortune for the Wildcats came under the direction of Lynn (Pappy) Waldorf, the son of a Methodist bishop. A big, happy man who made friends easily, Waldorf had been a good football player at Syracuse and then a rather successful coach at Kansas State. He took the Northwestern job in 1936 and the Wildcats, expected to do little, were unbeaten in the Big Ten to edge out Ohio State for the league crown. In the course of that season Waldorf's team did so well that he was named Coach of the Year during his first season, the award that is now given by the American Football Coaches Association.

FOURTEEN

Forest Evashevski—
Tough, Controversial,
and a Winner

Forest Evashevski—Wolverine turned Hawkeye. Forest Evashevski—tough guy, controversial coach and athletic director. Forest Evashevski—winner.

The big man burst on the national scene in the role of co-star, the chief blocking back for Tom Harmon, the great Michigan hero of 1938, 1939, and 1940. Evy was supposed to become jealous of all the publicity given to Harmon. But no, Forest Evashevski indicated his forthright temper and fearless approach to touchy subjects. When some of his teammates indicated their displeasure over the celebrity status accorded Harmon, Evy faced up to the problem head-on and succeeded in cooling what could have become an explosive situation.

This was exceptional because Evashevski could have been one of the All-America backs challenging Harmon for prominence if he had played for almost any other team than Michigan. A famous photograph of Harmon sweeping around end against Ohio State in 1939 typifies Evy's contribution to the Wolverines. As "Old 98" makes his turn, there is Evashevski flat on his back with feet raised after another successful block.

Evashevski knew when to be tough. Once in a while he exploded. Once in a while he cooled it. Always he was a man to deal with a sticky problem if one arose.

Possibly the most famous of Evashevski's fight scenes occurred when he never struck a blow or made a block. It occurred when he was Iowa's director of athletics in May 1965. At a Big Ten meeting of football coaches and athletic directors, Woody Hayes, Ohio State's volatile coach, got into a verbal row with Evashevski. The dispute centered around sideline conduct by coaches at the Iowa-Minnesota game in the 1964 season. Hayes was not there and Evy objected to Woody discussing the game when he had not seen it.

Things got hotter and hotter until, apparently, Evashevski questioned the ethics of one Woody Hayes. Hayes bristled, jumped from his seat, and tore off his coat in what was sure to be a physical move on Evy. Evy, who towers above the chubby Ohio State coach, never moved and Hayes suddenly backed off. Word of the incident got out, but none of those present gave the details of just exactly what happened. Finally, David Nelson, Delaware's director of athletics, told the story to these authors. Nelson, who enjoys telling stories of humorous happenings in the world of sports, was a very close friend of Evashevski. Nelson was one of the players on Michigan's team with Harmon and Evashevski.

Nelson obviously got his version of the Hayes-Evashevski confrontation from his long-time friend Evashevski. Maybe it is somewhat prejudiced as a result. Nevertheless, this is the way Nelson told the story:

"When Woody went for Evy, Evy never moved. He just sat back and looked Woody in the eye and said, 'Woody, I'll never bother getting up for a one-punch fight. Now go sit down and shut up.'"

It is known that Woody went back and sat down.

Evashevski went to Iowa amid much fanfare in 1952 as the football coach and turned a mediocre-to-poor team into a champion and took the Hawkeyes to their only two Rose Bowl games as the Big Ten representative. After nine seasons as the Iowa football coach, Evy, who had been made athletic director as well as coach in 1960, stopped coaching to devote full time to being director of athletics at Iowa. Five years later he left Iowa and college athletics in a controversy brought on by his discontent with the way coaches were recruiting athletes.

In his nine years as Iowa's coach Evy's teams won more games—fifty-two—than under any coach in Hawkeye history. Two of these victories were scored in the Rose Bowl. Evashevski's 1956 club beat Oregon, 35–19, while his 1958 team was a 38–12 winner over California. Evy's career was full of turmoil and excitement at Iowa. Wherever Evy went he remained the tough blocker, the man not to waste time clearing the road of hazards or obstacles. He did it in a manner that ruffled many feathers. Maybe he wasn't a diplomat—but Forest Evashevski was all man.

When Evashevski came on the Iowa campus, he shocked many right off the bat but was so refreshing that the majority of Iowa alums and other fans were behind him. Early in his first coaching year at Iowa, 1952, Evy stood before a gathering of alumni and pronounced:

"We will work hard and we will guarantee you interesting football. If that isn't enough, you better get yourself a new football coach."

Then, following a fancy buildup introduction at another alumni banquet, Evashevski got up and said, "Society needs no replacement for the football coach. What it should try to achieve is a system of getting rid of alumni."

When Evy's 1958 team, with Randy Duncan at quarterback, led the nation in offense, the Iowa coach gave credit to his friend and teammate from Michigan, David Nelson. Evy said, "Don't give me any credit. That was Davey Nelson's offense and I'd be guilty of plagiarism if I didn't say so."

Actually it was the fifties version of the wing-T, which Nelson used as head coach at Delaware in those days. Delaware still uses the wing-T to great success. Nelson gives credit for the wing-T to others. But he is the man who has kept the wing-T, which became very popular during the seventies with such teams as Penn State and Notre Dame.

Evashevski created action for Iowa on the field and off the field. As a coach he got as many headlines in the off-season as he got in season. Such was the case when he found himself in the athletic director's chair in the summer of 1960.

For a long time Evy and the Iowa athletic director, Paul Brechler, feuded over many things. Evy finally insisted that the football coach should not be under the control of the athletic director. This was the winningest Iowa football coach talking, and Hawkeye officials were in a predicament. They could not put the football coach on an equal basis with the director of athletics, but they knew that Evy and Brechler could no longer exist at Iowa together.

Finally, support from the faculty members, members of the board of control, fans, and politicos in Iowa swung from Brechler to Evy. Brechler resigned. This made Evashevski the obvious man for the athletic directorship and he was named to that post on June

9, 1960. But since Iowa officials didn't want the athletic director and the football coach to be the same man, Evy had to give up coaching after the 1960 season. Then came his battles with the football coaches at Iowa as he forced out his successor, Jerry Burns, after only one winning season in five years. Evy picked Burns but could not stand a loser.

In came Ray Nagel as head football coach at Iowa and that began a long time of struggle twixt coach and athletic director, despite the fact that Evashevski had been a key man in hiring Nagel. That old Evy bugaboo showed up again. He could not tolerate a loser, and, in five seasons at Iowa, Nagel never had a winning season. Thus, following nine years of unusual success at Iowa under Evashevski, there came ten straight seasons that included only one winning campaign. And Evy let it all go just before the last of those poor years when he resigned amid, as usual, a big stormy situation he helped create in the spring of 1970.

Following accusations back and forth at press conferences, the Nagel-Evashevski battle got very warm when Evy accused Nagel of recruiting violations and Nagel answered back that Evy had approved his moves. So it went until Evashevski stepped down as athletic director, with Nagel to last only one more season. Evashevski, who gave the Hawkeyes a strong football program from 1952 through 1960, left them with nothing but memories.

One of the serious problems toward the end of Evashevski's and Nagel's careers at Iowa was that some of Nagel's players kept saying openly, "What this team needs is a coach like Evashevski." That hurts any coach.

Evashevski was the head football coach at Washington State before he took the job as the head coach at Iowa. Brechler was the athletic director who hired Evy for the Hawkeye job. It wasn't long before Evy got into controversies and, in his second season, he made one of his best-known remarks after the Hawkeyes surprised most people by gaining a 14–14 tie with Notre Dame in the season finale.

"Don't celebrate a tie, celebrate a victory," Evashevski admonished his team and the Iowa fans. "I was there and if ever a team won a game, we did.

"When the one great scorer comes to write against your name, he won't wrote whether we won or lost, but how we got gypped at Notre Dame."

Evy alluded to the method Notre Dame players used in feigning injuries to stop the clock with only seconds remaining in the first and second halves of the game so that the Irish would have time for another play. Notre Dame scored on a play started with only two seconds left in the first half to tie the game at 7–7, and tallied on a pass play with only six seconds remaining in the game to gain a 14–14 tie.

Notre Dame later got into controversies with Syracuse over similar "feigned" injuries in a game won by the Irish on a field goal with seconds to go.

Evashevski went to Iowa just one year after Woody Hayes took over as coach of Ohio State. In Evy's nine years as the Hawkeyes' coach his teams beat Woody Hayes' Ohio State teams four times and lost to them four times. That's not too bad considering that during the seventeen years after Evashevski left coaching Iowa beat Ohio State, coached by Woody Hayes, one time and lost to Hayes' Buckeyes twelve times.

Many persons have said that if Evy hadn't gotten so hot and bothered about his coach–athletic director relationship with Paul Brechler he might have remained the Iowa head football coach for twenty-five or thirty years. Then, once he became the man in the director's office, he had less tolerance for coaches than former athletic directors had for him when he coached.

Certainly, if Evashevski had remained at Iowa as football coach, Woody Hayes might not have dominated the league so long, and Bo Schembechler might not have moved in as the co-force to dominate the Big Ten with Hayes. Evy would not have remained if he began losing. Thus, if he stayed a coach, Iowa would be winning to this day.

Just thirteen years before Evashevski burst upon the Iowa campus to be seen and heard for nearly two decades of controversy, Dr. Eddie Anderson quietly moved into the Iowa head football coaching job to take over the 1939 Hawkeyes after they had suffered three straight losing seasons and generally little football success since Howard Jones' final year as Iowa coach in 1923. Iowa got Dr. Eddie away from Holy Cross where he had been rather successful with the Crusaders, then a strong football power in the East.

Anderson immediately turned the Iowa program around with the help of Nile Kinnick, in his senior season of 1939. That Iowa team of 1939 was known as the "Iron Men," a team that made one of the most amazing reversals of form in Big Ten history. Making an exact 180-degree turnabout, Iowa of 1938 had a 1–6–1 record and in 1939 it had a 6–1–1 record.

This first Anderson team at Iowa earned the Iron Men name because the good doctor got sixty-minute performances out of so many players during the run for the Big Ten title. Kinnick played 402 of a possible 420 minutes in the season.

Anderson, a native of Iowa, had played college football for Notre Dame, where he was one of the many great ones.

Iowa nearly beat out Ohio State for the Big Ten title that first Anderson season in 1939. But a 7–7 tie with Northwestern in the finale prevented the Hawkeyes from gaining the title, as Ohio State, which lost to Michigan the same day, got the top spot. Dr. Anderson remained as Iowa head coach through the 1942 season, left for three years of military service, and returned to coach the Hawkeyes from 1946 through 1949. Never again did his teams threaten to take the Big Ten crown, and Dr. Anderson, always a popular man, returned to Holy Cross where he finished his coaching career with the Crusaders.

Iowa's first taste of football greatness came under Howard Harding Jones, a former Yale end who entered the coaching fraternity at Iowa in 1916. Before he was through as Iowa's coach, after the 1923 season, Jones was to lead the Hawkeyes to their first two undefeated and untied seasons—1921 and 1922. Those were also the Hawkeyes' first Big Ten championships.

That 1921 Howard Jones team was noted for players such as Duke Slater, an All-America tackle. This extremely strong black man never wore a helmet. (it was not mandated by the rules in those days), yet his blocking and tackling were amazing.

That was the senior season for Slater and the likes of Aubrey Devine and Les Balding. But, without them, Jones put together another champion in 1922, and Iowa had its first brush with football greatness in a double serving in those early years of the flapper era.

FIFTEEN

Biggie and Duffy

Dr. John A. Hannah, president of Michigan State College, as it was known then, had a dream in the 1940s. Under his direction, the little land-grant college of 7,000 was growing quickly and he wanted to make it one of the nation's great universities. However, Hannah was having trouble lining up a large and competent enough faculty. Most of the men he wanted had never heard of Michigan State, although it had been in existence since 1855. One way to gain recognition, Hannah reasoned, was to have a good football team.

"If it meant the betterment of Michigan State," Hannah once said, "our football team would play any eleven gorillas from Barnum and Bailey any Saturday."

Also very prominent in Hannah's game plan was a place in the Big Ten, which had been the Big Nine ever since Chicago dropped out in 1936. But that wasn't going to come easy. It was common knowledge that Michigan wanted desperately to keep Michigan State out of the conference. Although Michigan's Fritz Crisler would never admit it, every sportswriter who covered the two schools during Michigan State's bid for the Big Ten was convinced that it was Crisler who tried to keep the then Aggies down on the farm. His reasoning was obvious: both were state schools—Michigan the old, established, and prestigious university, and MSC, the brash newcomer—and competing for funds before the state legislature; another football power in the state might cut into Michigan's athletic income; MSC was a threat to Michigan in recruiting homestate players.

Michigan and Michigan State had been playing each other for years but it was a rare occasion when the Aggies—who were later to become the Spartans—outscored their bigger-time rivals. Nevertheless, the student rivalry has always been keen. Before the Michigan State game, the Michigan campus is usually littered by signs reading, "Cream MOO U," an unkind reference to State's beginnings as an agricultural school. Some years ago, Michigan's humor magazine deftly summarized the students' low opinion of Michigan State by suggesting the following Alma Mater for its rival, to be sung to the tune of "Home on the Range":

> *Oh, give me a school, where the students play pool*
> *Where the cows roam the campus all day;*
> *Where seldom is heard an intelligent word*
> *And the athletes all get high pay.*
> *Chorus:*
> *Moo, moo MSC*
> *Oh, that's the place for me.*
> *Where the chimpanzees can get college degrees*
> *And even a Phi Beta key.*

Despite Michigan's opposition, Michigan State was finally admitted to membership in the Big Ten in May 1949, but it couldn't begin football competition until the 1953 season because of prior schedule commitments by Michigan State and the other teams.

Meanwhile, President Hannah, in line with his drive to make Michigan State a football power, hired Clarence (Biggie) Munn away from Syracuse, where he had been the head coach for only a single year.

Munn's coaching background was impressive. Prior to his year as the head man at Syracuse, Biggie had served four seasons as an assistant under Bernie Bierman at Minnesota, two as the head coach of little Albright College in Pennsylvania, one year as an assistant at Syracuse, and eight as an aide to Crisler at Michigan. He had been associated with winners almost everywhere he coached, and Hannah felt that Munn was the man to bring Michigan State to national prominence.

Not that Munn's immediate predecessors had been failures. Charlie Bachman had coached State for thirteen years, from 1933 through 1946, and retired from East Lansing with a record of 70–34–10 to show for his labors. His 1937 team beat Michigan for the fourth straight time, lost to Manhattan, 3–0, and then went on to win six straight games and a place in the fledgling Orange Bowl, the first postseason bowl game ever for Michigan State. Unhappily

Auburn won that one, 6–0. However, except for a 6–1 season in 1944, State had been through too many mediocre seasons for the image which President Hannah had in mind.

Before Bachman, there was Jim Crowley, one of Notre Dame's famed Four Horsemen, who had four very good years before moving on to Fordham, then a national power. In 1930, Sleepy Jim's second year, his team held Michigan to a scoreless tie, the first time in fifteen years State hadn't lost to their old rivals, and posted a 5–1–2 record. In 1932 Crowley's team lost only one game again—to Michigan—but beat Fordham, and then Jim left to go to the Eastern school, where he developed outstanding teams and produced the "Seven Blocks of Granite," starring the late Vince Lombardi, among others.

However, with all due respect to the success of Bachman and Crowley, Michigan State's schedule was hardly big-time. Oh, the Aggies did play teams like Michigan, Army, Syracuse, Fordham, Kansas, Missouri, Indiana, Purdue, and Penn State, but there were still a lot of Almas, Adrians, Cases, Colgates, Detroits, Grinnells, and Illinois Wesleyans among their victims.

The plan for Michigan State football was for it to be big-time all the way and competitive with Michigan and the other schools in the Big Ten when, and if, it was accepted into the conference. Biggie Munn was just the man for the job.

Munn had been immersed in football, it seemed, almost from the day he was born in Grow, Minnesota, in 1908. He was a fullback at North High School in Minneapolis, had worked his way through Minnesota where he had played guard, tackle, and fullback under Coach Fritz Crisler, and was named All-America as a guard in 1931. Munn was a huge man. Not tall—he was only five feet nine— just plain big. On the field he resembled a bear as he waddled around. He also was an extremely vain man who craved attention and was not at all bashful about his coaching ability. As one of his critics once put it, "Biggie is a man after his own heart."

When Munn arrived from Syracuse he brought along with him as his line coach Hugh Duffy Daugherty, a young man who was to play a prominent role in Michigan State football for the next twenty-six years. Biggie also brought along an intricate multiple offense that featured just about everything in the history of college football—single wing, double wing, wing-T, split-T, straight-T, and even something he called a deep double wing.

Munn's debut as the Michigan State coach in 1947 was hardly a distinguished one. His old boss, Michigan's Crisler, stuck it to his one-time protégé, 55–0, in Ann Arbor, a humiliation Biggie never forgot. To complete the disgrace, as Munn led his broken Aggies off the field after the game, the Michigan band burst forth with a spirited rendition of "Old MacDonald Had a Farm"—an indelicate allusion to the fact that State was widely known in Ann Arbor as "that cow college."

"After that game," recalled Biggie, "we could have had an alumni meeting in a telephone booth."

Despite the opening game tragedy, Munn's club bounced back smartly, losing only once more for a 7–2 season, an event that bordered on a minor miracle, considering the way things had started for Munn and Michigan State. Biggie, however, wasn't quite satisfied. He was determined that never again would Michigan run all over his troops.

Munn began scouring Michigan and the surrounding states for football players and accumulating the sturdy types who would not be at a disadvantage even against Dr. Hannah's "eleven gorillas." Players like Lynn Chandois, Ed Bagdon, Donald Mason, Everett (Sonny) Grandelius, and Dorne Dibble. There were others, too, who were to come later. Along the way the schedule had been beefed up by Athletic Director Ralph Young, and schools like Maryland, Notre Dame, Indiana, Minnesota, Pittsburgh, Ohio State, and Purdue began appearing on Michigan State's schedules.

After two so-so years, 6–2–2 in 1948 and 6–3 in 1948, so-so at least by tough taskmaster Munn's reckoning, Biggie's bold recruiting and hard work began to pay handsome dividends. His 1950 team lost only to Maryland and started a string of four straight victories over hated Michigan. Biggie Munn and Michigan State had arrived in the big-time.

That 1950 season also started a winning streak that established Biggie Munn as one of the game's top coaches. An untiring recruiter, Munn had help from assistant coaches like Daugherty, Forest Evashevski, Red Dawson, Earle Edwards, Steve Sebo, Dan Devine, and Bob Devaney, men who were to go on to become successful head coaches. They all beat the bushes for players and found more than enough skilled ones to run Munn's complicated offense like a well-oiled machine. State swept to two straight 9–0 seasons in 1951 and 1952, and, before the streak ended in 1953, it had won twenty-eight consecutive games. Included were victories over Michigan, Notre Dame, Indiana, Minnesota, Pittsburgh, Ohio State, Penn State, Colorado, Texas A&M, Syracuse, Iowa, and Texas Christian, hardly considered patsies in those days.

The 1951 team, which gave Michigan State its first unbeaten season in thirty-eight years, was quarterbacked by Al Dorow, a superb passer, had runners like Don McAuliffe and Leroy Bolden, outstanding linemen in end Bob Carey, linebacker Dick Tamburo, tackle Don Coleman, and guard Frank Kush, and a premier defensive back in safety Jim Ellis. Along the way they smashed Michigan, 25–0, and Notre Dame, 35–0, but they showed their true worth when they overcame a ten-point Ohio State lead in the last ten minutes to win, 24–20. It was truly a remarkable season and Michigan State was ranked No. 2 behind Tennessee in the AP poll, their highest ranking ever.

It didn't seem possible that Munn, for all his coaching skills, could repeat that job in 1952. He had lost his entire offensive line, a good part of his defense, and his quarterback. But the seemingly inexhaustible supply of talent which continued to find its way to East Lansing managed to fill all the holes more than adequately. Tommy Yewcic, a sub tailback in 1951, was installed at quarterback and he proved to be up to handling Munn's tricky offense. McAuliffe was back to lead the running attack and Biggie found enough rough, tough linemen to support holdovers Kush and Tamburo.

After close victories over Michigan (27–13) and Oregon State (17–14), State hit its stride against Texas A&M. It crushed the poor Aggies, 48–6, prompting Coach Ray George to observe, "It isn't so much what their first and second teams do to you—but the third, fourth, and fifth teams simply murder you!"

Michigan State went on to complete another undefeated season. It won the national championship and Biggie Munn was voted Coach of the Year. That two-year period was a piece of good coaching that has seldom been equaled in college football, largely due to Munn's total dedication to leading Michigan State out of the cow pasture.

Unfortunately, this success was to prove costly to Michigan State. In February 1953, on the eve of State's official participation in Big Ten football, it was placed on probation for one year by Commissioner Tug Wilson. The charge: The Spartan Foundation, an outside organization pledged to help Michigan State athletes, had refused to disclose some details of its collections and disbursements to Commissioner Wilson. Michigan State shaped up quickly, satisfied the commissioner that it was complying with the rules, and the probation was lifted before the year was up.

Even without the probation to worry about, Coach Munn was publicly apprehensive about Michigan State's competing in the Big Ten despite the fact that his substantial troops had indicated for the past three years that they were more than up to the task.

"Honestly," Biggie said, "we can't expect to compete on even terms with Big Ten powers like Michigan, Ohio State, and Illinois, or big independents like Notre Dame. What really worries me is that Frank Leahy or Bennie Oosterbaan might get the erroneous idea that we think we can beat them consistently. If Michigan or Notre Dame ever starts concentrating on us. . . ." The prospect was so terrifying that Biggie couldn't describe it.

So what happened? Well, Biggie Munn's Spartans simply romped to an 8–1 season, a share of the Big Ten title with Illinois, and a trip to the Rose Bowl in their very first year in the conference. The only blemish was Purdue's 6–0 upset in the fifth game, ending State's twenty-eight-game winning streak. Michigan State closed out the season by coming from behind to whip a good UCLA team, 28–20, in Pasadena.

His mission completed, Biggie Munn retired as football coach at the end of the season to succeed Ralph Young in the athletic director's chair. In only seven years Biggie had raised Michigan State from relative obscurity to the status of a national power. His record of 54–9–2 was remarkable, and it is no wonder that, when he was voted into college football's Hall of Fame, he chose to go in as a coach rather than a player.

Munn's record as an athletic director, while not quite as obvious or spectacular, was excellent. Unhappily, Biggie suffered a paralyzing stroke in October 1971. Two months later he resigned as athletic director and was succeeded by Burt Smith. Biggie Munn died in 1975 at the age of sixty-six, secure in the knowledge that he had helped turn Michigan State from a "cow college" into a great university.

When Biggie Munn decided to leave coaching, he handpicked as his successor Hugh Duffy Daugherty, the man who had been his line coach for the previous eight years, one at Syracuse and seven at Michigan State. Things had been so good during those last seven years, there was every reason to believe that the dynasty Munn had begun would continue under the new head coach.

Duffy (the Hugh had been dropped long ago) Daugherty was the direct opposite of his longtime boss. Where Munn took himself seriously and firmly believed that he was the great man of college football, Duffy had neither the portentous air nor commanding presence of the typical big-time football coach. He saw coaching and life in general as a vehicle for happiness. Daugherty was serious about his football but at the same time he found time to joke about it and himself. A rumpled-looking man, cheerfully irreverent and with an Irishman's gregariousness and a leprechaun's sly smile, Duffy's one-liners became legend and interviewers dogged his footsteps, knowing that he was quotable and always willing to talk.

Duffy's appearance and quick wit, however, were deceiving. Although he may have looked—and sometimes acted—like a baggypants burlesque comedian, he was resourceful and resilient, a fighter, tough when he had to be, strong in adversity, and a shrewd football tactician. Daugherty was a demanding taskmaster at practices, but he also wanted his players and himself to get some fun out of football. He showed that he could take defeat, but he despised it. Even when he hurt most, he was gracious.

A native of the coal-mining area of Pennsylvania, Daugherty was born in Emeigh and grew up in Barnesboro, a fact he never has quite lived down or forgotten. In fact, years later, he and his coaching staff at Michigan State used to sing the Barnesboro school song at the slightest provocation, and besides, Duffy insisted upon it. They found its words stimulating. Written by Robert McAnulty and Tom Scollon, it went like this:

> *We're strong for Barnesboro,*
> *B–A–R–N–E–S–B–O–R–O,*
> *Where the girls are the fairest,*
> *The boys are the squarest,*
> *Of any old place that we know.*
> *We're strong for Barnesboro.*
> *Down where the sulphur creeks flow,*
> *We're always together,*
> *In all sorts of weather,*
> *In B–A–R–N–E–S–B–O–R–O.*

Duffy came by his interest in football naturally. His older brothers played the game and his coal-mining father was a dedicated coach-quarterback for the Saint Benedict Athletic Club.

"We used to practice tackling by diving over a coal cart after a rat," Joseph Aloysius Daugherty liked to tell his awed brood. "If we didn't get hold of both hind legs, we weren't any good."

A victim of the depression years, young Duffy had to work while going to high school and then for four years after his graduation to help out at home. In 1936 he entered Syracuse, where the head coach was then Ossie Solem and two of his assistants were Bud Wilkinson and Biggie Munn. Short and slightly round—his teammates called him Stubby—Daugherty was a varsity guard as a sophomore, sat out his junior year with a serious neck injury, and then came back to captain the team in his senior year.

"I was a very, very average player," says Duffy, adding, "I could have been a Rhodes scholar, except for my grades."

After graduation Daugherty enlisted in the army and, in 1942, he met Frances Steccati, an art student, in San Francisco. After a whirlwind courtship, they were married and Duffy spent the next three years in the South Pacific, where he went up the military ladder from private to major and was awarded the Bronze Star.

Daugherty's first taste of coaching came in 1945, after the war, when he got a job at Trinity School in New York City. But the next season he was back at Syracuse as an assistant to Biggie Munn, who had taken over for Solem, and then a year later he and Biggie were at Michigan State.

Duffy Daugherty was a popular choice as Munn's successor, at least until his first season began. When he was Biggie's line coach, his forward walls were known as "Duffy's Toughies," but suddenly a year later folks began calling them much less complimentary names, like "Duffy's Nothings." Daugherty continued to use Munn's multiple offense, adding some refinements of his own. Later in his career, he showed his adaptability by going to other offenses, including the Wishbone.

Duffy's first year as a head coach was a total disaster. Michigan State won only three games while losing six in 1954, and many alumni and fans wondered aloud if the genial Daugherty was up to the job. Biggie Munn's image as a coach also went up about 300 percent. Their wonders ceased, however, in 1955 when Duffy gave them the kind of a team they had become used to—an 8–1 regular season (marred only by a 14–7 loss to Michigan in the second game), a 17–14 victory over UCLA on Dave Kaiser's last-minute field goal in the Rose Bowl, a No. 2 national ranking, and Coach of the Year honors for Daugherty. That was more like it, and *Duffy's* coaching image went up 300 percent. He quickly began to replace Biggie as the hero of East Lansing, all of which was to have its consequences later.

Daugherty had taken the first-year criticism in stride, but he didn't forget it. After the season, while talking to an alumni group, Duffy referred to the 1955 team as "my team." Suddenly he drew back in mock horror.

"I beg your pardon," Duffy said softly. "I forgot. Last year's team was mine. This year's belongs to the alumni."

Two more good years followed and they belonged to Duffy, whose prestige as a coach instead of just a funny man began to grow. His 1956 team was 7–2, while the 1957 club went 8–1. However, for the next seven years, Daugherty and Michigan State were up and down like a yo-yo and so was Duffy's popularity, depending upon his record in any particular season. His 1960, 1961, and 1963 teams lost only three games, but the others either had losing records or barely finished in the black, despite the presence of legitimate All-America stars like Sam Williams, Dean Look, Dave Behrman, George Saimes, and Sherman Lewis.

Meanwhile, the honeymoon between old friends Biggie Munn and Duffy Daugherty had ended. There were signs of a split as early as 1955. The spotlight was on Duffy and he became celebrated as a natural wit. Newspapers and magazines began to write him up. He made the cover of *Time* magazine. Biggie, operating in the anonymity of the athletic director's office, missed the publicity and the back-slapping that went along with his successful days as the head football coach. Not many sportswriters were looking for stories about Michigan State's athletic facilities and programs, which were growing under Munn's skillful guidance. Duffy was the big man and Biggie resented it.

The rift between Biggie and Duffy widened and everybody knew they weren't getting along. Little things became big issues. Duffy would ask for permission to take four assistant coaches on a trip and Biggie would rule only three could go. Incidents multiplied.

Then, in 1958, the feud became public. Michigan State opened with a victory over California, stumbled to a 14–14 tie with Michigan, and beat Pittsburgh. But then a series of injuries wrecked the Spartans and they lost to Purdue, Illinois, Wisconsin, and Indiana.

The next week, Biggie Munn watched in horror as mediocre Minnesota, his alma mater, clobbered MSU, 39–12.

That night Pete Waldmeir of the Detroit *News* and Hal Middlesworth, then of the Detroit *Free Press,* were having dinner in Charlie's Cafe Exceptionale in Minneapolis when Munn walked in with a group of friends. He wore a hurt look as though the trouncing by Minnesota was a personal thing.

Then, as Waldmeir remembers it, "Biggie came over to our table, leaned over between us and said, 'I want to tell you fellows something. What happened out there today was terrible. I've never seen a poorer game. It really hurts to see something you've built, an empire you've made with your own hands, come tumbling down. I clutched and clawed to get to the top. We went into the backwoods to root out players and we got the good ones. It's tough, really tough, to watch things go to pieces like this.''

The implication was quite clear. Munn was being critical of Daugherty and, in effect, charging that Duffy was prodding Michigan State football down the drain. Waldmeir, alert to a story, rushed to a phone and dictated a piece, quoting Biggie, which he thought might run as a sidebar with his story on the game. Instead, the *News* featured it on page one in its Sunday edition and the next day all hell broke loose.

President Hannah summoned both Biggie and Duffy to his office. No one has ever revealed what was said in Hannah's inner sanctum, but it was a fair assumption that he laid down the law to both men and ordered them to cease and desist. Biggie and Duffy emerged from Hannah's office arm-in-arm and the situation was supposedly more or less stabilized. In public, the two men appeared to be the best of friends. But it was more like an armed truce. Biggie didn't go to parties at Duffy's house and Duffy didn't frequent the basement bar in Biggie's new five-bedroom home.

The matter was never really closed. It was common knowledge that Munn had the backing of the "downtown alumni," the guys who put up the money for MSU sports, while Duffy had the players, the press, and the "diploma alumni," those who went to the games, on his side. There were rumors that Daugherty would welcome the opportunity to go to Notre Dame if and when that coaching job became available and that Munn would jump at the chance to succeed Ike Armstrong as the athletic director at Minnesota. Neither happened and the feud never really ended. It simply simmered for the next dozen years.

All the while, Daugherty managed to retain his sense of humor. In 1959, after a 37–8 loss to Iowa, Duffy was asked if the Hawkeyes had come up with anything he wasn't expecting. "Yeah," he said, "thirty-seven points."

Duffy was never at a loss for a quip and some of his best ones came during times of adversity. For example, during one of his bad years, he told the alumni, "The trouble is you get carried away by my enthusiasm."

When Daugherty was questioned about the need factor, he explained, "Our grants-in-aid are based on academic achievement and need. By academic achievement, we mean can the boy read and write. By need—well, we don't take a boy unless we need him."

After 101,000 fans watched one of his teams play Michigan in Ann Arbor, Duffy observed, "That's fantastic. You couldn't get half that many out to see Lady Godiva take her horseback ride. But that's because most people are tired of looking at white horses."

Once, after he spilled a cup of coffee all over his play diagrams during a staff meeting, Daugherty told his coaches, "That's good. We have to learn how to play on a wet field, too."

Duffy even explained why he always looked on the bright side of things. "I've been an optimist since I was a kid," he said. "I can still remember the Christmas morning I ran down to my stocking and found it full of horse manure. I yelled, 'Hey, I got a pony around here somewhere.'"

Daugherty also didn't mind twitting his fellow coaches. One year, during a Big Ten skywriters' spring tour, Ohio State's Woody Hayes ordered the Big Ten commissioner, his assistant, and twenty-four writers off his practice field and kept them waiting outside a locked gate for an hour. Later, Woody explained, "I wanted to give my players hell for their mistakes and I didn't want any outsiders hanging around."

The next day the touring group was in East Lansing and Daugherty threw them out. Ten minutes later, he explained, "I wanted to praise my players for their good work and I didn't want to do it in front of strangers."

But Duffy Daugherty's public life wasn't *all* fun and games. He had his serious side, too. His practices were rough, tough, and hard-hitting, and he demanded perfection from his players. Dave Kaiser, the Rose Bowl hero, once said, "You see a guy and his girl out on a canoe on Red Cedar River and you wonder what you're doing it for. But other times you get out there feeling good and you just want to butt heads for Duffy.''

Daugherty was always refreshingly frank abut recruiting, a subject that causes most big-time coaches to stare blankly at their hands when it comes up. Duffy was a persuasive Pied Piper who ranked with the best in the business.

"There's nothing wrong with recruiting," Duffy said. "It's how you recruit that's important. I think it is a worthwhile thing to help boys through school if you do it the right way, through the proper channels of the school. You want players who can develop a feeling of pride in their team's performance. You want kids who will develop pride in themselves. If you have the right type of boy, he'll win the close ones for you.''

Duffy also did not have any pretensions about his coaching. "We haven't got any secrets. We don't have any magic formula and neither does anyone else in this business. The reason you win is because you've got more good players than the next guy. Most football games aren't won on the field. They are won from December to September when the recruiting is done. Eighty percent of a winning team is material. Ten percent is luck. Our biggest job is getting the boys. The thing we do least at Michigan State is coach.''

Well, however he did it, Duffy Daugherty hit the jackpot big in 1965 and 1966. He got more good players than anyone else—some of the best ever to play for Michigan State—and came up with two of the greatest teams in the school's long football history. Suddenly Duffy was a supercoach again, although he was still coaching the way he did in the poor years. He had an explanation for that, too. "The alumni are always with you, win or tie.''

The 1965 team, which had players like Bubba Smith, George Webster, Bob Apisa, Clint Jones, Ron Goovert, Harold Lucas, Gene Washington, Steve Juday, Jerry West, Jess Phillips, Nick Jordan, Tony Conti, and Dick Kenney, romped past all ten opponents to win the Big Ten championship and the national championship, and Daugherty was named Coach of the Year for the second time. The only blemish on this spectacular season was a 14–12 loss to UCLA in the Rose Bowl, the same team the Spartans had whipped, 13–3, during the regular season.

Duffy and his boys were riding high and they didn't let up in 1966 as they clobbered opponent after opponent to win the Big Ten title again. Michigan State was unbeaten going into the final game of the season with equally undefeated Notre Dame. The only difference was that the Irish were ranked No. 1 and MSU was No. 2 in the polls. The game was a natural. It would decide the national championship and it was variously billed by the media as "The Game of the Year," "The Game of the Decade," and even "The Game of the Century." More than 80,000 people piled into Spartan Stadium for the game, and Fred Stabley, the competent Michigan State sports information director, and Nick Vista, his assistant, somehow managed to fit 745 sportswriters—the most ever to cover a college football game—into their press box.

What happened that afternoon has become a part of history. The two teams battled to a 10–10 tie as the large assemblage of fans watched in astonishment when Coach Ara Parseghian ordered his players to run out the clock and settle for the deadlock in the closing minutes.

"We couldn't believe it," said linebacker George Webster. "We kept watching for the pass in their final series, but all they did was run. We were really stunned. Then it dawned on us. They were playing for the tie."

Parseghian came under fire from all quarters but he staunchly defended his position. "We'd fought hard to come back and tie it up," Ara said sharply. "After all that, I didn't want to risk giving them the game cheap. I wasn't going to do a jackass thing like that."

Regardless of the strong public reaction, Parseghian's strategy paid off. The pollsters decided that the tie preserved Notre Dame's No. 1 ranking and Michigan State finished second. The only consolation for the Spartans came when the National Football Foundation and Hall of Fame voted both teams co-winners of the MacArthur Bowl, emblematic of its version of the national championship.

Duffy Daugherty had his own opinion of how the rankings should have been. "We're Number One and Notre Dame is One–A," he told people.

After those two glory years it was all downhill for Duffy and Michigan State. Somehow the flow of outstanding talent became a trickle and the Spartans went through one mediocre season after another. The "Dump Duffy" cries came alive again, and, along with them, other troubles for the embattled coach.

In 1968 the wave of new militancy among black athletes hit Daugherty and Michigan State football, an unlikely target in view of Duffy's record of recruiting black players. For years the Spartans had recruited more black athletes than any other major school. At one point the majority of MSU's starting twenty-two football players were black and the 1965 national championship team had what it called its soul-brother backfield—three blacks and a Hawaiian.

Nevertheless, during spring practice, LaMarr Thomas, a speedy halfback, led a delegation of fifteen or twenty black players off the practice field and into Athletic Director Biggie Munn's office. They charged, among other things, that blacks were being pressured to take nonacademic snap courses to stay eligible; that the school was not hiring enough black coaches; that the athletic counselor should have a black assistant; that the school did not have a black doctor or trainer for black athletes; that the school discourged blacks from playing baseball; that the school had never had a black cheerleader.

Significantly, none of these charges were leveled directly at Coach Daugherty and the revolt was short-lived. President Hannah, who ironically was also chairman of the United States Civil Rights Commission, got into the situation immediately. He met with Thomas and the matter was settled quickly. However, the entire affair bothered Duffy, whose relations with his players, regardless of their color, had always been good.

Finally, in 1972, after Michigan State had won only two of its first seven games, Daugherty made up his mind that it would be his final year. The Thursday before the Purdue game, Duffy told his players that he would announce his resignation, to take effect at the end of the season, after Saturday's game and swore them to secrecy. But the news leaked out the next day and Daugherty made it official with a public announcement.

"Nobody said much," said All-America defensive back Brad Van Pelt, "but you could see it in the guys' faces. We wanted Duffy to go out a winner."

That Saturday the Spartans upset Purdue, 22–12. During the game, a rickety old plane putt-putted around Spartan Stadium, trailing a sign which read: "We love Duffy and the Spartans!"

Asked if he saw the plane, Duffy replied, "See it? Who do you think chartered it? My mother was flying it and my two brothers were hanging onto the sign."

The next week Michigan State upset previously unbeaten Ohio State, 19–12, on four field goals by Dirk Krijt, a long-haired, skinny, six-foot four transfer student from Bergen, The Netherlands.

While Ohio State's Woody Hayes fumed, Duffy, going out laughing, cracked, "That was my little Dutch treat."

The Spartans split their next two games, losing a rough one to

Minnesota, 14–10, and beating Northwestern, 24–14. Duffy didn't go out a winner, but he didn't go out a loser, either. Michigan State finished the season with a 5–5–1 mark to put Daugherty's nineteen-year record as the Spartan head coach at 109–69–5. He also had given MSU two national championships (Duffy insisted it was two and one-half), two Big Ten titles, and four seconds.

Daugherty retained his title of professor in the Department of Health, Physical Education, and Recreation, and was named a special assistant to Les Scott, Michigan State's vice-president for development. Duffy also had a brief fling as a color commentator on ABC's N.C.A.A. football telecasts.

Dennis Stolz, one of Daugherty's assistants, was named to succeed Daugherty and in 1974 he came up with a 7–3–1 record. A year later Michigan State was put on probation, Stolz lost his job, and in 1976 the Spartans hired Darryl Rogers, who had been the head coach at San Jose State.

Biggie and Duffy—whatever their personal differences, they left their marks on Michigan State football.

SIXTEEN

"Don't Call Me 'Good Ol' Woody'"

There isn't anyone with even a casual interest in college football—and especially those folks in Columbus, Ohio—who doesn't have an opinion of Wayne Woodrow Hayes. They either deplore his autocratic ways or pat him on the back and spoon-feed his ego. They either criticize his style of football or they condone it because it wins games. They either find his outbursts of temper amusing or they become downright blasphemous about him when he unleashes one of his frequent tirades. There is no such thing as being noncommittal about Woody Hayes. You either love him or you hate him, and not necessarily in that order nor with any consistency.

Woody Hayes is a man with a positive talent for controversy. Many of his years in the Big Ten have been stormy ones. He has taken on rival coaches and athletic directors, once even coming to the brink of trading blows with Forest Evashevski when Evy was at Iowa, school officials, Big Ten commissioners, players, football officials, alumni, fans, the press and its component parts like photographers, and anyone else who gets in his way or disagrees with him.

A short, powerful man with silver hair and a barrel chest, Hayes is a familiar sight on the sidelines where he engages in his histrionics in full view of 85,000 or so friendly—or unfriendly—fans every Saturday during the football season. There was a time when he paced the sidelines on the coldest day dressed only in a short-sleeved shirt. With the passing years, Woody has modified that part of his attire. He now wears an Ohio State jacket. But his hands are still balled fists and even when the temperature is in the twenties and thirties perspiration still streams from beneath the black baseball cap with the scarlet O—as in O–H–I–O—that he has worn so long that it seems to be a part of his head. He prowls the sidelines like a bear in a pit, snarling in frustration at his players, his coaches, the officials, and, yes, even at himself. He will yank the cap off his head, slam it to the ground, and stomp on it. He also has been known to do the same with his watch or his glasses in a particularly frenzied time, but somehow he usually manages to miss them with his stomps. He has marched out on the field many times to vent his wrath on an official. Perhaps his finest performance came in 1971 when he demonstrated his feelings about the lack of a pass-interference call during the Michigan game in Ann Arbor by yanking the sideline yard markers out of the hands of the officials, tearing them up, and throwing the remains out on the field.

After that incident, Hayes said, "Those officials up there reminded me of that great poet, Homer."

"You can tell when the old man is building up to an explosion," says one of his players. "When a play goes wrong, he'll whip off his cap with his right hand, push his hair back with his left hand, and put his cap back on. That's an indication trouble is brewing."

Woody Hayes' relations with the press, even his own writers in Columbus, have not always been cordial. He has banned them from his practices, sometimes refuses to talk with them after games, and he almost always keeps them cooling their heels until he is damned well ready to give them a postgame audience. He has been accused of slugging sportswriters and photographers, curiously usually before, during, or after Rose Bowl games in Pasadena.

Back in 1959, after Ohio State lost to UCLA, 17–0, Hayes was less than gentle with one West Coast reporter. "He slugged me," the writer claimed. "I just barely brushed him," said Woody. "Well," said one of the Ohio State assistant coaches, "you might say that Woody showed him to the door."

Just before the kickoff of the 1973 game with Southern California, Art Rogers, a photographer for the *Los Angeles Times*, claimed that Hayes had pushed his camera into his face and yelled, "That ought to take care of you, you son-of-a-bitch."

Rogers filed a complaint with the police, hitting Hayes with a misdemeanor battery charge. Back home in Columbus they were selling scarlet-and-grey bumper stickers which read "Help Woody Hayes—Free the Pasadena One." The charge was later dismissed when Rogers said he had received "an appropriate communication from Woody."

In August 1976, at the annual Big Ten luncheon in Chicago, after Hayes admitted that he had turned in Michigan State for recruiting violations, Woody was approached by Ed Ronders, sports editor of the *State News,* Michigan State's student newspaper, who informed him that he was coming out the following week with a big exposé on Hayes' recruiting practices, including specific instances of where Ohio State was alleged to have paid players.

"Go ahead and print it, but you'd better be ready to prove what you write, and I'll get you now, you son-of-a-bitch!" raged Hayes, heading for Ronders, who headed even more quickly for the exit—and made it.

Ronders printed his exposé but did not name his sources and Hayes, who had cooled down, wisely refused to comment on the accusations.

Subsequently it was revealed that the N.C.A.A. was looking into these and other accusations. But, up until the time this book was completed, no action had been announced.

There have been many other incidents through the years and writers who cover the Big Ten have become inured to Hayes' conduct. It isn't that he dislikes sportswriters, it is just he doesn't care what they think of him. However he once said, "I get along with newspapermen better than I like to admit because it spoils a good myth."

Chuck Heaton of the Cleveland *Plain Dealer* once suggested that much of Hayes' conduct is deliberate and designed to build a legend. "Hayes hasn't mellowed with age," wrote Heaton in 1971, "rather he has become more irascible with success. . . . I've suspected that Woody enjoys the image of the tough football taskmaster who still loves his boys, of a hard-boiled head coach who could be rude to media people and then charm them."

There are some who believe that Woody Hayes is an anachronism. While he has kept up-to-date on everything that is going on among young folks today, he often refers to the past. A voracious reader and student of military history, he will spend hours detailing the activities of famous generals and admirals. Among his favorites are General Patton, Admiral Doenitz, General Rommel, and General von Clausewitz, and he often likens their strategic moves to those used on the football field.

John Hicks, Ohio State's great All-America guard who now plays for the New York Giants, recalls, "Woody once told us, 'You've got to get their respect. I mean, why did Admiral Nelson run into the French fleet and kill himself?' It broke us up and he came over to me and asked what was so funny. I said, 'Well, coach, you said Admiral Nelson killed himself.' So, Woody just turned and walked right onto the practice field, saying, 'All good commanders want to die in the field.' "

A strict disciplinarian, Hayes' practice sessions are often like wars. His players don't dare make the same mistake twice. If they do, the invective comes pouring down on them. Even assistant coaches have been known to cringe once Woody gets going. Some of Hayes' former stars have differing opinions about the coach and his ways.

"You become very wary of Woody at practice," says Doug France, an All-Conference end in 1974. "You left his practices with scars on your helmet. You wanted to get away as far as possible from Woody and football. Really, we hated him. But we didn't let that hatred get in the way of winning football games. What he happens to be is a very successful coach."

Morris Bradshaw, another of Hayes' players, claims, "It's an experience. That's the best way I can describe it. I tend to disagree with the way he handles things, but then when you sit back and look at his record, it speaks for itself."

Randy Gradishar, an All-America linebacker in 1972 and 1973, has a different opinion of Hayes. "A lot of people see him as a very mean old football coach, swearing, kicking, and beating his players," says Randy. "I think that if people got to know him as his players do, if you could sit down and talk with him, you would find out he's a great individual. You would understand that a coach has to holler every once in a while, and maybe swear, in order to get somebody motivated . . . and motivating is what Woody does very well. Woody was a disciplinarian, very strict. When you did something wrong you either got hollered at or kicked in the butt."

Dick Schafrath, a tackle back in the fifties, recalled how Jim Parker, an All-America guard, messed up a blocking assignment in practice three times. "Woody finally belted Parker on top of his helmet," said Schafrath, "but the next day it was all forgotten. That was Hayes, always close to his players. He'd pop off and get mad but wouldn't hold any grudges. Woody was very emotional. His eyes would fill with tears as he talked about Ohio State, mothers, and country. Woody Hayes is about the best thing that ever happened to me outside of my family and my wife and kids."

Parker once paid Hayes the greatest compliment of all. "I sent my brother Al to Ohio State so he could be coached by Woody," said Jim, "and I want my son to learn football from him, too."

There are other former players who have been more vitriolic in their feelings toward the Buckeye coach and some who share the sentiments of Gradishar, Schafrath, and Parker. None of them, however, are neutral.

Woody Hayes' style of football—a crunching ground game with the forward pass considered as only an occasional and unnecessary evil—has been called antediluvian by his critics. Back in 1961, after his Buckeyes ground to a 7–7 tie with Texas Christian, one Texas writer quipped, "We don't know where Hayes went to college, but he must have majored in monotony."

Monotony? Maybe Hayes' football seems to be that to some folks, but his Ohio State rivals don't knock it. They are just weary of having his Buckeyes pound them into submission year after year as they crunch their merry way to one Big Ten championship after another. Woody's system is as uncomplicated as he himself is complex. He just runs his backs up the middle and off tackle more than most other coaches, and he has more ways of doing it than any other coach in the business. And Hayes has done it so consistently by recruiting some of the nation's finest athletes.

Hayes is a charmer when he gets into a young high school athlete's living room. He can be soft-spoken and gracious, and displays a genuine interest in the young man and his family. "I've always regarded recruiting as the first step to coaching," says Woody. "When I tell a youngster something, it better be the same thing I tell him when I'm his coach."

The Ohio State coach also feels very strongly about standards. "At Ohio State, we've had one rule," Woody says. "We give nothing to anybody. The only thing we give them is opportunity. Because anytime you give a man anything he doesn't earn, you cheapen him—you destroy him. And that's what we're never gonna do. And that's why we've had good football teams. Because our kids earn what they get, and they respect what they do and then they respect the man beside them."

One other reason Woody Hayes is so successful is that he is sold on his product—Ohio State and Buckeye football. "Ohio State provides the great athlete more of an opportunity than any other place," he says. "We get more out of a great athlete than anyone else because we set his sights high. A man is always better than he thinks. We prove it.''

Hayes doesn't pay much attention to the material rewards that many big-time coaches seek. Several times he has turned down raises, requesting that the additional money go to his assistant coaches. He does, however, have a TV show, makes a lot of speeches, lectures at clinics, and has written three books. So Hayes does manage to pocket some extra dollars.

"I had a Cadillac offered to me a couple of times," Woody says. "You know how that works. They give you a Cadillac one year and the next year they give you the gas to get out of town."

There have been other ways in which Ohio has demonstrated its feelings for the Buckeye leader. In 1973 Woody Hayes became the only coach in history to be sculpted in butter. He was the focal point of a butter statue, sculpted especially for a display in the dairy building at the Ohio State Fair in Columbus. There was Woody, life-size and complete with baseball cap and silver-rimmed glasses, stomach protruding slightly as he surveyed a buttered cow and her calf. The inscription on the placard inside the huge frozen glass case read, "Woody always looks over the team and goes with a winner." Also prominently displayed was a copy of Hayes' latest book, *You Win With People.*

Although he can be gregarious and personable—and when he is, he likes to remind people, "You must remember that I'm a mean old coach. Don't call me 'good ol' Woody' yet"—basically Woody Hayes is a loner. During the football season, he lives a Spartan-like existence, usually holed up in his tiny, windowless office alongside the practice field, and spends most of his waking hours coaching or thinking football. Hayes does little fraternizing with his colleagues or socializing with anyone. He once said, "When you're winning, you don't need any friends. When you're losing, you don't have any friends anyway."

Despite this preoccupation with football, Hayes is deeply concerned with the changing world and young people. A political conservative and a confirmed supporter of former President Richard M. Nixon, he visited U.S. troops in Vietnam four times. During the campus uprisings in 1970, and particularly after the riots and shootings at Kent State University, Woody tirelessly roamed the Ohio State campus night and day, going into dormitories and even standing on overturned garbage cans to make himself heard, soothing protesting students with the sheer softness, coolness, and eloquence of his logic. He was a calming influence in a situation seething with frustration and turbulence.

It was another side of this volatile, explosive man, one that people rarely get the opportunity to see. His wife, Anne, a gracious, intelligent lady with a wonderful sense of humor, who very often is Woody's buffer and sometimes his alter ego, says, "I tell Woody I have a lot of love to give, but he's never around enough for me to give it. . . . People say there are only two ways to take Woody. You either love him or hate him. Every wife sees her husband that way. Sure, he has his moody times, his eruptions. Really, his emotions run the full cycle. He has a sympathetic side, a compassionate side people rarely see. I admire him for one thing. He's not a phony."

Anne isn't afraid to poke fun at her famous husband, either. She calls herself Woody's "full-time housekeeper and part-time mistress," and once, when asked if she had ever contemplated divorce, Anne answered, "Divorce, no. Murder, yes."

Another time Anne told a gathering, "I've been asked to speak at everything but a Bar Mitzvah. I always say I'm going to talk about sex and marriage, but being a football coach's wife I don't know anything about either."

Asked whether she ever second-guesses Woody, Anne replied, "Sure I do. When I'm sitting in the stands and somebody jumps up alongside me and yells, 'Woody, why in hell are you doing that?' I jump up and yell, 'Yeah, Woody, why in hell are you doing that?' "

Not even Anne Hayes, however, has been able to control Woody's pet hate—the University of Michigan. He rarely ever refers to Michigan by name, preferring to call it "that school up north." One exception was when Gerald R. Ford, that old Michigan center, succeeded the resigned Nixon as president. He told Ford, "I'm going to support you and that's hard for me to say to a man from Michigan." Hayes also had some advice for Ford: "You deserve some blocking when you carry the ball. I just hope you keep it on the ground."

There was never any doubt, though, who was No. 1 in Columbus. In September 1974, when former President Ford came to Columbus to deliver the summer commencement address at Ohio State, Hayes met him at the airport and they had their picture taken together. That evening the Columbus *Dispatch* displayed the pic-

ture on page one with the caption, "Woody Hayes and Friend."
The entire text of Ford's address was printed on an inside page and
headlined, "Friend of Woody Hayes Addresses OSU."

Wes Fesler, one of the best athletes in Ohio State history, had
just completed his fourth season as the head coach at his alma mater in 1950. His 1949 team had compiled a 7–1 record and tied Michigan for the Big Ten championship, and his 1950 club had produced
the Buckeyes' second Heisman Trophy winner—Vic Janowicz.
But the team also had lost three of its nine games, and one of those
losses was to Michigan in what became famous as the Snow Ball.

The fickle Columbus fans were at their headhunting best after
the 1950 campaign and their target was Fesler, whose four years
had produced a 21–13–3 record. That seemed to be respectable
enough, even for OSU, but the big rap against Fesler was that he
had managed only a tie against Michigan in his four years. So the
abuse came tumbling down on his head until Fesler decided that he
had had quite enough and resigned.

Then the politicking and bickering began. There was one strong
faction that wanted Ohio State to rehire Paul Brown, then with the
pro Cleveland Browns, and the group campaigned actively for its
candidate. Other coaches were mentioned and at least eight were
interviewed by a screening committee. The committee recommended to the Ohio State University Athletic Board a man whose
name had not been mentioned at all as a candidate. He was Wayne
Woodrow Hayes, who had been the head coach at Ohio's Miami
University for two years and before that at Denison University for
three seasons. That started a furor among the Brown supporters,
but the Athletic Board submitted the recommendation of the
screening committee to the university's Board of Trustees, who
named Hayes as the new OSU football coach. What the trustees
didn't know then was that they were buying themselves an institution, not just a football coach.

The thirty-eight-year-old Woody Hayes was hardly a household
name in college football ranks. Born in Clifton, Ohio, he went to
high school in Newcomerstown, where his father was superinten-
dent of schools. A big, strong kid, Hayes played tackle on the football team and then went to Denison, where he continued his football career. Woody Hayes may not have been the best tackle in the
state of Ohio, but he was one of the toughest.

Hayes served his coaching apprenticeship as an assistant

at Mingo Junction High School and New Philadelphia, where he succeeded John Brickels, who became one of his closest friends, as the head coach in 1937. Even then, Woody was tough and unrelenting on his players.

Years later Brickels recalled, "Woody was always subject to temperamental outbursts. Maybe it was because he was smart, quick, and a perfectionist. He lacked patience. I tried to tell him that when he corrected a kid he shouldn't make an enemy of the boy, but Woody had a hard time controlling himself and he drove the kids too hard. He'd swear a lot and I told him he was the last guy who should, what with that little lisp of his."

After three seasons as the head coach at New Philadelphia, Hayes entered the navy, married a local girl named Anne Gross, and went to sea where he commanded a patrol chaser and a destroyer escort. By 1946, when he was released, Woody had worked his way up to lieutenant commander.

Hayes then returned to Denison to coach the football team, but his first season was a disaster. While Woody raged, his team lost its first six games before winning the final one. But that was the end of hard times for Denison under Hayes. His next two teams were undefeated and won eighteen straight games, a feat which attracted the notice of Miami of Ohio. There, too, Hayes had to do some rebuilding and he was 5–4 in 1949, his first season. The next year Miami rolled to a 9–1 record, won the Mid-American Conference title, and upset Arizona State, 34–21, in the Salad Bowl.

So then, these were Woody Hayes' coaching credentials when he appeared on the scene in Columbus, where so many coaches before him had seen their spirits and wills shattered because of the vagaries of hypercritical fans. Over the years they would try to do that to Hayes, too, but he was too tough and too cantankerous to pay any attention to them. Besides, early on, Woody made it clear to the alumni and everyone in the athletic hierarchy at Ohio State that he, and he alone, ran the football team. And if they didn't like it, they could lump it!

When Hayes arrived in Columbus, he found as part of the nucleus for his first team a Heisman Trophy winner, Vic Janowicz. But he also brought along a T-formation that just about nullified Janowicz as either an All-America or a Heisman repeater. It also didn't prove to be very successful as the Buckeyes struggled to a 4–3–2 season and the "we told you so" wolves began to howl. It was reported that a member of the Frontliners, which was so influential financially and otherwise in the Ohio State athletic program, was trying to raise $25,000 to buy out Hayes' contract. Crackpots called the Hayes home in the middle of the night to say, "Good-bye, Woody." Hayes, however, simply ignored them and went about the business of coaching the football team his way.

After a pair of 6–3 seasons in 1952 and 1953, Hayes and his ways hit the jackpot in 1954. With Howard (Hopalong) Cassady, who was to become a Heisman Trophy All-America a year later, supplying the offensive impetus, Woody's Buckeyes went all the way to an undefeated season to win the Big Ten title, the national championship, and a trip to the Rose Bowl, where they smashed Southern California, 20–7. All of a sudden Woody Hayes was one hell of a coach and it didn't matter what or how he said or did anything. That was the first of many triumphant seasons for the outspoken, singleminded coach, who defied his detractors and continued to do things his way.

In the next twenty-two seasons, Woody Hayes' Ohio State teams had only two losing years, in 1959 and 1966. The Buckeyes won or shared (all with Michigan—five times since 1969) a total of twelve Big Ten championships, captured two more national titles in 1957 and 1968, had three more unbeaten teams (in 1968, 1970, and 1975) and two unbeaten but tied clubs (in 1961 and 1973). Twice, Woody's colleagues have voted him Coach of the Year. From 1968 through 1976, Hayes' Bucks lost only thirteen games. All-Americas like Cassady, Jim Parker, Aurelio Thomas, Jim Houston, Arnie Chonko, Dwight (Ike) Kelley, Doug Van Horn, Ray Pryor, Dave Foley, Jim Marshall, Bob White, Bob Ferguson, Jim Otis, Rex Kern, Jim Stillwagon, Jack Tatum, John Brockington, Jan White, Mike Sensibaugh, Tom DeLeone, John Hicks, Randy Gradishar, Kurt Schumacher, Steve Meyers, Ted Smith, Tim Fox, Tom Skladany, and the wondrous Archie Griffin came and went.

There have been disappointments, too, like the 1970 team's 27–17 upset by Stanford in the Rose Bowl and the 1975 club's 23–10 defeat by UCLA at Pasadena. Both losses cost Ohio State shots at national championships. There also were many incidents which involved the Buckeyes' feisty coach, some of which have already been recorded here. Perhaps the most prominent of Hayes' faults is his penchant for saying what he thinks. It has been said that Woody passes up more opportunities to keep his mouth shut in one year than most people do in a lifetime.

Few things in life have ever frightened Hayes, but he faced a difficult time on June 6, 1974 when, at age sixty-one, he was carted off to the hospital with a heart attack. It was touch and go for a while and there was some talk that perhaps he would retire. But Woody's indomitable spirit won out and he was back on the field with his team that fall and coached the Buckeyes to a share of the Big Ten title and a spot in the Rose Bowl, where Southern California's late rally nudged OSU aside, 18–17.

"I'm not ready to retire," said Woody. "I had that figured out the morning after my heart attack. I don't know what in the world I would do if I didn't coach. I just want to keep winning. I just love to win."

And Hayes has been winning ever since. His 1975 team swept through eleven games unbeaten and untied before getting upset by UCLA, 23–10, in the Rose Bowl. Woody sulked after that one, refusing to see the press—or anyone else. That, and his unexplained dismissal of tackle Nick Buonamici from the team, incurred the wrath of the *Lantern,* the Ohio State student newspaper, which called for his resignation.

"His fans have made him a God and he has begun to believe it," read the lead editorial. "In spite of the furor it would create among Hayes' loyal fans, the trustees and President [Harold] Enarson should ask for his resignation. Not only would this ease embarrassment for the university and help the players to get a coach who treats them as human beings, but it would help Hayes' legend as well. . . . He would fade away as a martyr before too many more 'incidents' take the polish off his shining armor."

Hayes refused to comment and was back at his same old stand, his usual irascible self, in 1976. Despite the loss of three-time All-America and two-time Heisman Trophy winner Archie Griffin and many of his other All-America stars, Woody's Buckeyes made a first-class run for the championship, losing only to Missouri and Michigan (which was beaten by Purdue) while tying UCLA for an 8–2–1 season. It was good enough to gain a tie with the Wolverines for the Big Ten title and earned Ohio State an invitation to play Colorado in the Orange Bowl. Invigorated by the change of scenery, the Buckeyes broke out of their bowl slump by coming from behind to whip the Big Eight team, 27–10.

Woody Hayes' critics, the same ones who have been complaining about his conservative offense for years, say the game has passed him by, yet he continues to win championships and bowl bids. He is condemned and badmouthed by some players, yet they play their hearts out for him and Ohio State. In thirty-one years of coaching Woody has compiled a record of 221 victories, 65 losses, and 9 ties. In twenty-six seasons at Ohio State his record is 189–54–9 overall, and 139–34–7 in the Big Ten.

Michigan's Bo Schembechler says, "I think he stands tall among coaches to everybody, not just me."

To which Hayes, with tongue in cheek, replies, "That man's a great, great coach and I wouldn't want to argue with him."

For Woody Hayes, the name of the game is winning. "Without winners," he says, "there wouldn't be any civilization."

Woody Hayes hasn't been the only football coach in Ohio State's grand and glorious football history. It just seems that way because he has been the only one to enjoy such a long tenure in Columbus, once known as the graveyard of coaches. Before Woody, the Buckeyes changed coaches almost as often as he wins. Indeed, there were eighteen different coaches in OSU's first sixty years of football, from 1890 to 1950. For a while, they used to meet each other coming and going.

Except for Dr. John Wilce, who officiated over the Ohio State football program for sixteen years, the other Buckeye coaches have had rather limited tours of duty. Wilce's years were particularly distinguished because of the presence of the great Chic Harley, OSU's first true superstar, who raised the Columbus school from obscurity to national prominence. However, Wilce's achievements were not limited only to Harley's time in school. During his term he gave Ohio State three Big Ten championships and had an overall record of 78–33–9.

Wilce may have been the youngest head coach in the history of Big Ten football when he took over in 1913 at the tender age of twenty-five. He had starred in football and track at Wisconsin, had stroked the Badger crew, and was enrolled at Ohio State as a medical student. Young and eager with some new ideas, it took Wilce only a single season to prove that he was a winning coach. His 1913 team was 4–2–1, and after that things got even better. The record was 5–2 in 1914, 5–1–1 in 1915, and then along came Harley and two unbeaten seasons and three Big Ten titles in 1916, 1917, and 1920. The results weren't quite so good after Harley's departure but, meanwhile, Wilce got his medical degree. He finally called it quits after the 1928 season.

Sam Willaman followed for the next five years and, although "Sad Sam," as he was known, had a modicum of success, he failed to do the one thing demanded of every Ohio State coach—beat Michigan every year. It didn't matter that Sam's teams beat the Wolverines twice in his first three years and that his 1935 club lost only one game. That single defeat was by Michigan and so was the 1932 team's only loss. After the 1933 season Willaman was gone, a victim of the Buckeyes' obsession with beating Michigan.

Willaman's successor was Francis A. Schmidt, a former army bayonet instructor who had turned the Southwest Conference upside down with his wild offensive pyrotechnics while coaching at Arkansas and Texas Christian. His seven-year record at Arkansas was 43–19–3 and it was 46–6–5 in five years at TCU. Schmidt's 1929 and 1932 TCU teams were unbeaten, and he had won four SWC titles. So Francis Schmidt wasn't exactly a coaching neophyte.

Colorful in character and language, Schmidt, who had played his college football at Nebraska, introduced the normally staid Big Ten to some of the most exciting offense it had ever seen. For one thing, his offensive formation started out by being unconventional. Schmidt lined up his backs one behind the other—years later it would be called the I-formation—and his team threw the ball often and accurately. Forward passes and laterals filled the air, wide-open offensive sets and tricky reverses were commonplace, and touchdowns came thick and fast. Schmidt also came up with the players to make his system go, backs like Stan Picura, Dick Heekin, Buzz Wetzel, Jack Smith, Tippy Dye, Jumping Joe Williams, and Don Scott, and punishing linemen like Gomer Jones, Regis Monahan, Inwood Smith, Gust Zarnas, Merle Wendt, and Esco Sarkkinen.

Schmidt had earned a reputation in the SWC for being excitable on the sidelines and he never won any awards for tact. He could be crude and profane. Once at a social dinner at the Faculty Club, Francis loudly told a waitress to "take this damned pigeon away and bring me some food."

Big scores never embarrassed Schmidt, unless he happened to be on the short end of one of them. His habit of running up the score on outclassed rivals earned him the nickname of "Close the Gates of Mercy" Schmidt. For example, his first Ohio State team in 1934, a pleasant 7–1 surprise, ran roughshod over little Western Reserve, 76–0.

In 1935 Schmidt had another 7–1 season and tied Minnesota for the Big Ten championship, the first in fifteen years for the Buckeyes. Along the way, Schmidt's juggernaut smashed Drake, 85–0, and Michigan, 38–0. The only loss was to Notre Dame in a game that was to go down in history as one of the great ones of all time. That was the one in which Notre Dame overcame a 13–0 deficit to win, 18–13, in the final seconds. Despite the 7–1 record and the Big Ten title, Schmidt's critics down on High Street, like true Columbus patriots, never quite forgave him for that.

Unhappily for Schmidt and Ohio State, these also were the years when Minnesota football, under Coach Bernie Bierman, was at its very best and consequently the Buckeyes' success dipped accordingly, except for 1939, when OSU's 6–2 mark was good enough to win the Big Ten championship again. But Schmidt's regression in producing top-notch teams didn't stop him from beating up on an inferior rival when he got the chance. New York University got chewed up, 60–0 in 1936, and 32–0 in 1938, while Chicago, then in its death throes, was hammered 44–0, 39–0, 42–7, and 61–0 from 1936 through 1939.

Schmidt's luck finally ran out in 1940. With a bevy of stars returning from the 1939 championship team, the Bucks were picked to rank high in the nation. Instead, they were a disaster. Ohio State was embarrassed by Tom Harmon and Michigan, 40–0, and lost to Cornell of the Ivy League on the way to a 4–4 season. There was dissension between Schmidt and his assistants, and many of the players resented the coach's drill sergeant methods. Even though his seven Ohio State teams had won two Big Ten titles, finished second three times, and he had a very respectable 39–16–1 record, the 1940 season cost the flamboyant Schmidt his job. He went on to coach Idaho for two years and then died.

Meanwhile, Ohio State athletic officials had their eyes on Paul Brown, a young man who was turning out state championship teams at Massillon, Ohio, High School. An intense, well-organized, no-nonsense coach, Brown quickly answered the call when it came, and he turned out to be the opposite of his predecessor in both personality and techniques. Where Schmidt had been dedicated to a wide-open attack, Brown installed his own mixture of single wing, short punt, and the newly fashionable T-formation. A bug on discipline, Brown also ran a much tighter ship. His first OSU team, in 1941, was good enough, posting a 7–1–1 record, but a year later Paul had put it all together and was ready to mount a full-scale challenge for the national championship.

With Les Horvath and Gene Fekete to lead the offense and a trio of linemen—end Bob Shawn, tackle Chuck Cosuri, and guard Lindell Houston—who turned out to be the best in the country at their positions, Brown's 1942 Bucks lost only one game, a 17–7 upset by Wisconsin, and then recovered from that to win the Big Ten crown and the national championship. Brown's college coaching career, however, was short-lived. World War II had turned college football into an unpredictable game for seventeen- and eighteen-year-olds and after a poor 3–6 campaign in 1943, Paul enlisted in the navy and was soon coaching the football team at Great Lakes Naval Station.

With Brown gone, along with a host of players who were in service, Ohio State turned to Carroll Widdoes, Paul's number-one assistant. It appeared to be a thankless job at best, but the soft-spoken, likeable Widdoes built well around Horvath, a halfback who had played for three years and was unexpectedly given a fourth year of eligibility under special wartime regulations; Jack Dugger, a 220-pound end who was deferred from military duty because of bad eyesight; Bill Hackett, a guard who was a veterinary student; Bill Willis, a superb tackle; and a handful of brash seventeen-year-olds, including Ollie Cline, a hard-hitting fullback. Widdoes built so well that his 1944 team was unbeaten in nine games and won the Big Ten title. To top it all off, Horvath won the Heisman Trophy and Widdoes was named Coach of the Year.

Widdoes had another good year in 1945, winning seven and losing two, and then he decided that he had had enough of being a head coach. In an unprecedented action, Carroll asked to return to his post as an assistant coach and recommended that the head job be given to Paul Bixler, one of his aides. Bixler suffered through a 4–3–2 season before leaving to coach at Colgate. His successor was Wes Fesler.

They all had a part in bringing Ohio State to its present position of eminence in the Big Ten and the world of big-time college football, but, love him or hate him, it is Woody Hayes who has been the most dominant—and successful—coach in the conference in the last three decades.

A caption under Woody's picture in the Jai Lai, a Columbus restaurant, says it all: "In the whole world, there's just one."

SEVENTEEN

The Galloping Ghost

There was an aura of excitement in the air in Champaign, Illinois, that Saturday, October 18, 1924. It was Homecoming Day and old Illini by the thousands poured into the college town, mingling with students and townspeople, all in a festive mood. The weather was typical Indian summer, a hot sun pushing the temperature up toward eighty degrees. The occasion was the dedication of the University of Illinois' spanking-new Memorial Stadium on the sprawling campus, and the attraction was Illinois vs. Michigan in an important Big Ten game.

The two schools had tied for the conference championship the year before, but they hadn't played each other. Both Illinois and Michigan had been unbeaten in 1923 and the Wolverines had not lost in twenty-two straight games. Their superb defense had given up only four touchdowns during the streak, a feat unmatched by any other team in the country.

While some 67,000 fans crowded into the new Illinois stadium, Coach Bob Zuppke paced the floor of the Illini locker room. His players fidgeted nervously, waiting for the coach to give them the word to charge out of the locker room and onto the field. Among them was Harold (Red) Grange, a gaunt-looking All-America halfback who had already made his mark as one of the most spectacular and effective runners ever to step on a football field. Suddenly, Zup stopped pacing and turned to his players, who looked up expectantly. They anticipated some final bit of wisdom from the crafty coach, something that would surely help them defeat powerful Michigan.

"Remove your stockings!" barked Zuppke.

The players looked at Zuppke in astonishment. What in the world had gotten into the coach? Had he gone off his rocker? A few of them protested mildly, worrying that their uncovered limbs would suffer bruises and blemishes from contact with the mighty Wolverines. But, at Illinois, Zup's word was law—off came the heavy woolen stockings.

Bereft of their orthodox leg coverings, the Illinois squad rushed onto the field for signal drills, their legs gleaming in the bright sunlight. Moments later, the Michigan squad took the field, ran through a few plays, and then suddenly stopped in wonderment to gaze at their opponents in their bare legs. The people in the stands stood up and Michigan Coach Fielding Yost came over to the Illinois players. He wanted to be sure that a lubricant had not been applied to their legs to make them slippery and harder for his Wolverines to hang onto. Meanwhile, the Michigan players, now more conscious than ever of the heat, began to feel uncomfortable in their heavy woolen stockings. They felt as if their legs were dragging.

That bit of psyching by Coach Zuppke set the stage for one of the most memorable performances by an individual player in the long history of college football.

Michigan's captain, Herb Steger, kicked off, the ball traveling end-over-end in a high arc right into the hands of Red Grange, waiting patiently on the Illinois 5-yard line. Wallie McIllwain and Earl Britton, two of Grange's backfield mates, blocked out the first two Michigan players downfield as Red started upfield and into a horde of Wolverines intent on committing mayhem on No. 77. Somehow Grange burst through the pack, breaking tackles, and suddenly he was in the clear on the Illinois 40-yard line and on the way to a 95-yard touchdown romp.

Minutes later, Illinois had the ball again on its own 33-yard line and once more it was given to Grange. The redhead started around left end, cut back off tackle behind a crushing block by McIllwain, stiffarmed a linebacker, and stormed into the Michigan secondary. There was no stopping the elusive Grange. He simply ran away from all of Michigan's defenders to complete a 67-yard touchdown run. The home crowd went wild, but there was more to come.

After an exchange of punts, the Illini took over on its own 44-yard line. On the second play Grange took a direct snap from center, and whoosh! he was off to the races again. This time Red headed for the right sideline, cut back across the field, and, leaving the Michigan players to grab empty air, raced 56 yards for his third touchdown.

Two minutes later Illinois had the ball on the Michigan 44-yard line after a Wolverine fumble. Everyone in the giant Illinois stadium, including Yost and his Wolverines, knew what to expect, but it hardly mattered. It was Grange again around end, cutting back and outrunning the entire Michigan team for 44 yards and his fourth touchdown. Only twelve minutes of the game had elapsed, but Grange had carried the ball eight times on kickoffs and scrimmage plays and had run 95, 67, 56, and 44 yards for touchdowns. It was incredible, and the fans reacted as if they had just witnessed the Second Coming of Christ.

After scoring his fourth touchdown, a weary Red Grange leaned against one upright of the goalpost, waiting for his teammates and opponents to catch up to him. Indeed, it was practically the only time all that afternoon that the Michigan players ever caught up to Red. Harry (Swede) Hall, the Illinois quarterback, thought it was time that Grange had a rest and several plays later he called for a time-out. When Matt Bullock, the Illinois trainer, came out on the field, he asked Red how he felt.

"I'm all in. Zup better get me out of here," Grange answered.

So Red Grange came out to one of the most tumultuous ovations ever heard in a football stadium. Even the Michigan players had to admire Red's performance, although they probably were relieved to see him join Coach Zuppke on the sidelines.

Zuppke, however, didn't seem to be quite as impressed as either the cheering fans or the Wolverines. When Grange joined him on the sidelines Zup grumbled, "Should've had another touchdown, Red. You didn't cut at the right time on that last play."

Grange didn't reappear until the second half, and then he had slowed down a bit. All he did was gain 85 more yards, including a 13-yard romp for his fifth touchdown, and throw a pass to Marion Leonard for a sixth score. When the busy afternoon ended, Red Grange had played forty-one minutes, carried the ball twenty-one times for 402 yards, completed six passes for 64 more, and the Fighting Illini had vanquished their Michigan rivals, 39–14.

Red Grange, a shy, unassuming young man with a big talent for running away from people while carrying a football under his arm, was the toast of college football, but he wore his fame modestly. While all of Champaign celebrated his spectacular performance and the tremendous victory over hated Michigan, Red and a fraternity brother sneaked out of the tumultuous Zeta Psi house, had a simple meal in an out-of-the-way downtown restaurant, and then went to the movies.

Grange's superb performance that day against Michigan enthralled the entire nation and made headlines from coast to coast. Warren Brown of the Chicago *Herald-Examiner* wrote, "All in all it was a great homecoming for the Illini. They'll have other great ones, to be sure. But the memorial columns of the stadium will be so much dust before they'll ever see another young man run the opposition as dizzy as Red Grange did here today . . ."

Life began for Harold Grange on June 13, 1903 in the small town of Forksville, Pennsylvania, a rustic, isolated whistle-stop which boasted some 200 inhabitants, most of whom worked in the nearby lumber camps. Harold was the third child, but the first boy, born to Sadie and Lyle Grange. However, as it turned out, Forksville had very little claim on Harold Grange. When he was five, his mother died and the family moved to Wheaton, Illinois, where Mr. Grange's four brothers and a sister lived.

Forksville's loss was Wheaton's gain. This bustling Illinois college town was destined to become famous as the home of one of the greatest football players of all time. However, the beginning of Red Grange's football career at Wheaton High School was hardly distinguished.

In the fall of 1918, as a fifteen-year-old, 138-pound freshman, Red played end and recalls, "I was a good tackler, could run and get down fast under kicks and, being tall, I was able to reach up high for passes although, much to my disappointment, no one ever threw any at me during the games."

The next year Grange was switched to halfback and it didn't take long for Wheaton to discover that it had a budding star. Red scored fifteen touchdowns and kicked nine extra points. In his junior year he scored 255 points on thirty-six touchdowns and thirty-nine conversions, and, in one game, Red ran for eight touchdowns and kicked all the extra points!

Young Grange's athletic activities were not confined to football. He also starred on the basketball, baseball, and track teams, and was particularly outstanding in track, where he competed in six events—the 100- and 220-yard dashes, the low and high hurdles, the broad jump and high jump—and often won all of them. He was a center and forward on the basketball team, and, at one time or another, played all positions on the baseball team.

In those days the high school football field was located in an apple orchard a mile and a half from school and it was the job of the freshmen to clear away the stray apples on Saturday mornings before the game. More than once, though, a few apples escaped the freshmen and the players frequently wound up with juice on their faces. There were no seats and the games usually drew a crowd of about 200 folks, who stood around on the sidelines and walked up and down with the plays.

Despite Grange's apparent proclivity for football, his performance really didn't begin to attract attention until his senior year in 1921 when his Wheaton team lost only to Scott High School of Toledo, 39–0. Red was not a factor in that game. He was kicked in the head early in the first quarter and was carried unconscious from the field. However, Red, no longer a puny 138-pounder—he had built up his weight to 170 pounds—came back from that disaster to score six touchdowns against Downers Grove in a 63–14 victory and wound up the season with twenty-three touchdowns and thirty-four conversions for 172 points.

Grange's dad, Lyle, was *the* police force in Wheaton and his salary was barely enough to sustain his family. Red, however, had been supplementing the family income ever since he graduated from grammar school—as an iceman, no less.

It all came about quite accidentally. One day, Luke Thompson, a local ice-truck owner, announced he would offer a one-dollar prize to any boy who could hoist a seventy-five-pound cake of ice on his shoulder. Red, then only fourteen, was the only one to do it and proudly collected his dollar. That little show of strength earned him a summer job working as a helper on the ice truck at $37.50 a week, more money than Red knew existed, and eventually led to a job as wagon boss at $50 per week. It also led to one of the most famous nicknames in college football history. When Grange achieved prominence as an All-America, he was logically called "The Wheaton Iceman" and pictures of Red, wearing a big grin and sporting a cake of ice on his shoulder, appeared in almost every newspaper in the country. The job lasted for eight summers but, in that last summer, in 1926, after Grange completed his first season as a pro football player, his work habits changed slightly. Instead of hitching a ride to work, Red used to pull up in his new $5,500 Lincoln Phaeton.

Red always believed that his summer job lugging ice helped to keep him in condition for the rigorous football seasons ahead, but at one point in his career as an iceman it almost finished his football-playing days.

One July morning in 1919 Red was doing his usual thing, hopping on and off the moving wagon to make his deliveries, when he fell off and rolled under the truck loaded with three tons of ice. One of the back wheels ran over his left leg just above the knee. The leg was crushed so badly that the doctors feared it would be necessary to amputate. A closer examination determined the wheel missed the knee joint by the matter of a scant inch. Although the leg was saved Red was given only a 50–50 chance of complete recovery and it appeared that his football-playing days were over. However, he was back on the gridiron the next fall, as good as ever.

Football recruiting in those days was hardly the major enterprise that it is now. Athletic scholarships were practically unheard of, and college recruiters didn't offer young athletes shiny new cars, under-the-table cash, and fast women as inducements to come to their schools. Instead, the colleges relied upon their alumni to sell prospective athletes on the advantages of their schools.

The first official contact young Grange had from a college came from Carl Johnson, one of Michigan's all-time track stars, who came to Wheaton to try to sell Red on the idea of coming to Ann Arbor. Red, of course, was flattered but he was concerned about how he would manage to pay his way to the out-of-state university.

Meanwhile, Coach Bob Zuppke of Illinois had made a deep impression on Grange in his senior year when the youngster went down to Champaign to compete in the state interscholastic track championships. Zup was warm and friendly and told Red, "If you come down here to school I believe you'll stand a good chance of making our football team."

That may have been one of the understatements of all time. But Grange was impressed by the encouraging words and eventually chose the University of Illinois, mostly because, as a resident of the state, it would be less expensive than Michigan or any other out-of-state college.

So Red Grange wasn't exactly unheralded when he arrived on the Illinois campus in the fall of 1922. But he wasn't sure that he wanted to play football for the Illini. Red felt that his two best sports were basketball and track, and he intended to concentrate on them. But Red's fraternity brothers at Zeta Psi had other ideas.

They knew about his football record at Wheaton High and they ordered him to go out for the freshman team. Red demurred, pointing out that at 170 pounds he was too light for big-time college football. It was all to no avail, however, and Red reported for practice. Once he got a look at the other 150 beefy candidates—including Ralph (Moon) Baker, who later became an All-America after transferring to Northwestern; Frank Wickhorst, a huge tackle who switched to Navy, where he, too, became an All-America; Earl Britton, a six-foot three, 240-pound fullback; and a cadre of high school All-State stars—Red was sure that his first instinct was right and he turned around and went back to his fraternity house. Grange admitted the truth to his frat brothers—that he was scared to death—but he was ordered to return the next day. The alternative was a paddling.

Grange was issued a uniform—it just happened to be No. 77, a number that was to become famous throughout the land—and before the first week was out, Frosh Coach Burt Ingwersen had him in the first-string backfield. In his initial scrimmage against the varsity, Red scored two touchdowns, one when he ran through the entire first team on a 65-yard punt return, while Coach Zuppke licked his chops in anticipation on the sidelines.

Grange's varsity deput as a sophomore in 1923 was even more spectacular. The opponent was Nebraska, a big, tough team from the then Big Seven Conference, and Red startled the unsuspecting Cornhuskers by sprinting away from them on a 35-yard end sweep for one touchdown and then racing through the entire Nebraska team on a 66-yard punt return. For an encore, Grange scored again on a 5-yard run. When it was all over, Red had romped through the Cornhuskers for 208 yards and accounted for all of Illinois' touchdowns in a 24–7 victory.

That was the beginning of a sensational career for the Wheaton redhead, who proceeded to astound every opponent on the Illinois schedule with his tremendous ability as a runner. In seven games that season, Grange scored twelve touchdowns and led the nation in yards gained with 1,260. The Illini were unbeaten, and Walter Camp, then the high priest of All-America selectors, picked Grange on his first team.

From Camp, an Easterner who usually was skeptical of any player who did not do his performing in the Ivy League, came high praise for the Illinois star. Camp wrote, "Red Grange of Illinois is not only a line-smasher of great power, but also a sterling open-field runner and has been the great factor in the offense of Illinois through the midwest conference. He is classed as the most danger-ous man in that section and probably the country over, when all kinds of running must be considered."

Actually, Camp's description of Grange's abilities was under-stated, perhaps because Walter had not seen him in action that sea-son. Red's skills were diverse. He had tremendous speed, and along with it an exquisite sense of timing in changing and control-ling his speed, the power of a slashing fullback, the ability to switch directions in a split second, superb balance and coordina-tion, and amazing footwork that often resulted in opponents' being faked out of their shoes. It was this extraordinary combination of skills and talent that earned him the nickname of "The Galloping Ghost" in his sophomore year. His versatility as a runner was un-matched. He was just as dangerous on defense as on offense. An intent and intelligent defender, Grange more than once picked off enemy passes and returned them for touchdowns or high yardage.

Grantland Rice once described Grange's running ability as fol-lows: "Grange runs as [Paavo] Nurmi runs and Jack Dempsey moves, with almost no effort, as a shadow flits and drifts and darts. There is no gathering of muscle for an extra lunge. There is only the effortless, ghostlike weave and glide upon effortless legs with a body that can detach itself from the hips—with a change of pace that can come to a dead stop and pick up instant speed, so perfect is the coordination of brain and sinew."

Once, when the *Michigan Daily,* deprecating Red's perfor-mance, commented, "All Grange can do is run," Bob Zuppke snorted, "Yeah, and all Galli-Curci can do is sing!"

Zuppke, appreciative of Grange's skills, became almost lyrical whenever he talked about Red in later years. "He was the smooth-est performer who ever carried a pigskin," said Zup. "He ran with rhythm, every movement of his body having meaning and direc-tion. On the gridiron, Red Grange was a football stylist, a sympho-ny of motion. . . . One of Grange's greatest physical assets, be-sides his wonderful pair of legs, was his uncanny peripheral vision, which enabled him to see the sides as well as straight ahead. This made it possible for him to get a panoramic view of the playing field at an instant glance, and probably explains why he had such a great sense of timing and could dodge and twist, both to his left and right, and pick up his interference as effortlessly as he did. . . . He came nearer to being the perfect football player than anyone I have ever known.''

Even as a sophomore Grange wore his fame modestly. He was always quick to credit his teammates for their part in his great success as a college runner. He constantly called attention to the great blocking of Britton and McIllwain, who were responsible for breaking him loose on the patented end sweeps which became his stock in trade. Later, as a senior, when he was shifted to quarterback by Coach Zuppke, he was able to show his appreciation by giving the ball to his teammates when he could very easily have carried it himself and bolstered his scoring and ground-gaining marks. He also paid constant tribute to his linemen, led by tackle Jim McMillen and end Frank Rokusek, whom he credited with opening holes through which he slipped so quickly and adroitly.

Grange also played down his skills. ''The sportswriters wrote I had peripheral vision,'' Red once said. ''I didn't even know what the word meant. I had to look it up. They asked me about my change of pace and I didn't even know that I ran at different speeds. I had a crossover step, but I couldn't spin. Some ball-carriers can spin, but I'd have broken a leg.''

While Red Grange's performance against Michigan in 1924 has to go down in history as the greatest game he ever played, it was hardly the only great one the Illinois star had. Indeed, he was the star of just about every game he played in for the Illini. The only exceptions were when he was suffering from injuries and played only briefly.

After Michigan, even Grange's most rabid rooters wondered what he could do for an encore. Red didn't keep them waiting very long to find out. Two weeks later the Illini went up against one of Coach Amos Alonzo Stagg's better University of Chicago teams, one that featured Austin (Five Yards) McCarthy, so nicknamed because he averaged 5 yards every time he carried the ball.

The game was scheduled for Chicago's Stagg Field and, to help stack the cards against the visiting Illini, it was Homecoming Day for the Maroon. The wily Stagg, fully aware and appreciative of Grange's talented running, figured that his best chance for victory was to keep Illinois—and especially Grange—from getting the ball too often. Stagg's strategy worked early in the game as Chicago got off to a 21–7 lead shortly before the end of the first half. Although the Maroons had done a good job of holding Grange in check, they hadn't managed to stop him completely. Red had sparked Illinois' lone scoring drive, completing three passes for 47 yards, carrying five times for 20 yards, and scoring Illinois' lone touchdown on a 4-yard plunge.

But then, late in the first half, the redhead really got going. He was his usual self, ripping through and racing around the Chicago line, but he added another dimension to his game—pass catching—and soon scored again to bring the halftime score to 21–14.

It seemed that that was the way the game was going to end, with Illinois on the short end of the score, when the two teams played each other to a standstill for a while on the second half. Then, with the ball on the Illinois 20-yard line after a Chicago punt, Red Grange asserted himself again. Taking the ball on a direct snap from center, Red swept left and down the sidelines, cut back to the center of the field, and outran the entire Chicago team for 80 yards and the touchdown that tied the score at 21–21. In the closing minutes Grange ripped off a 51-yard run that ostensibly put Illinois in position to score the winning touchdown. But the run was nullified by a penalty and the game ended in a 21–21 deadlock. All Red Grange had done was gain 300 yards on the ground, complete seven passes for 177 yards, and score all three of Illinois' touchdowns!

"That was the toughest football game I ever played in college," remembers Grange. "Every time I was tackled I was hit hard by two or three men. The entire Illinois team took a terrific beating."

That game took its toll on both Grange and Illinois. In the next game, against Minnesota, Red hurt his shoulder after he had intercepted a pass and the Gophers beat the Illini 20–7 for their only loss of the season. Although that injury kept Grange out of the season's finale with Ohio State, Illinois managed to eke out a 7–0 victory. Despite the unfortunate ending to the season, Grange's year-long statistics read like an All-America's should: 1,164 yards gained, twenty-seven pass completions for 524 yards, and thirteen touchdowns scored. This time it was easy for Walter Camp to pick Red on his All-America team for a second year.

The 1925 season began quite inauspiciously for both Red Grange and his Illinois team. The Illini, weakened terribly by graduation and injuries, was just a hollow shell of the 1924 team that had won all but one of its games. In desperation Coach Zuppke made several position switches which he hoped would bolster his forces. Britton, the hard-hitting fullback and blocker, was shifted to guard, and Grange was moved to quarterback. But nothing helped. Without Britton to clear the way, Grange was shackled by the opposition and Illinois lost three of its first four games.

Meanwhile, back East, where the game had been born fifty-six years earlier, there were still some skeptics who didn't believe that Red Grange was as good as even Walter Camp said he was. The Easterners, however, were destined to find out for themselves. Illinois' fifth game was to be against the University of Pennsylvania in Philadelphia's Franklin Field, on Saturday, October 31. Penn, the cream of the East, was unbeaten in five games and had already beaten mighty Yale and Chicago.

Grange had brooded over his lack of acceptance by the Eastern press and he was determined to give them a show they would remember. But he knew he would have to do it practically by himself because he lacked the superb supporting cast he had had in his sophomore and junior years. To make matters even worse, a hard downpour turned the field into a quagmire of mud. It was hard to envision even Man O'War, another sports hero of the times, being able to trudge through the ooze with any appreciable results.

But Red Grange, his pride stung by the skepticism of Eastern nonbelievers, managed to have one of the greatest days of his spectacular career. Before 65,000 fans, who huddled together in the inclement weather, Red simply destroyed the precocious Easterners. It didn't matter that before very long the No. 77 on his back was completely obliterated by the mud. Everybody knew who Red Grange was. With help from Britton, who by this time was back at fullback, the Galloping Ghost romped merrily among the stunned Penn players for 363 yards and scored three touchdowns on runs of 56, 13, and 20 yards as Illinois unpredictably battered the Ivy Leaguers, 24–2. That made believers out of the skeptics.

Up in the press box, Laurence Stallings, the ex-marine who came out of World War I to write *What Price Glory* and *The Big Parade,* struggled at his typewriter for an hour, got up, read what he had written, tore it up, and threw it away.

"I can't write it," Stallings said. "It's too big."

Grange still had three games left in his college career—two of them against Chicago and Ohio State—but already lucrative offers for his services and name were pouring in. There were inducements for him to lend his name to sporting goods, clothing, soft drinks, cigarettes, and anything under the sun that folks thought they could market. Meanwhile, C. C. (sportswriters later translated those initials into Cash and Carry) Pyle, a local movie theater owner and promoter who had befriended Grange early in the 1925 season, was dreaming up the most lucrative money-making scheme of all. Pyle figured he could market the Illinois star into a multimillion-dollar property. And he did.

Pyle's initial gambit, which he presented to Grange early in the fall of 1925, was a contract to join the professional Chicago Bears of the National Football League immediately after Red's final college game against Ohio State. For playing with the Bears in their final league games and then on a cross-country tour of games against other pro teams, Grange and Pyle were to receive one-half the gate of each contest. That would be split 60–40, with Red getting 60 percent. Red agreed but refused to sign the contract until after his final college game. Despite this, there were persistent rumors that Red had signed even while he was still a college player. There was even some talk by Illinois' opponents that they would question his eligibility. However, no one really did. Coach Zuppke, aware of the rumors, tried to talk his star out of turning pro, but all to no avail.

The day after the Ohio State game, Grange and Pyle met with George Halas and Ed Sternaman, co-owners of the Bears, in Chicago and signed what was the richest pro football contract until the days of the premerger war in the 1960s between the National Football League and the American Football League. It was reported at the time that Grange and Pyle would split $2 million for that deal. Grange later denied that he got all that money, but his take was considerable.

There followed a host of other offers for endorsements which Pyle promptly snapped up for his money machine. Like $12,000 for a sweater; $10,000 for a football doll with red hair (presumably, you wound it up and it scored touchdowns); $5,000 for a soft-drink testimonial. And so it went with Pyle and Grange, turning down very few offers. Also included was a $5,000-per-week contract to make the first of several movies. The money just poured in from all over, and it found receptive hands.

Red Grange had come a long way from his high school days in Wheaton when he lugged ice for pocket money. He was sitting on top of the world. College football had never, and perhaps would never again, see the likes of him as a performer. Thoroughly humble and modest, his marvelous ability as a super-runner had cata-

RED GRANGE'S CAREER, YEAR BY YEAR

Opponent	Touchdowns	Minutes Played	Yards Gained	Passes and Yards
1923 (8–0)				
Nebraska	3	39	208	0
Iowa	1	60	175	0
Butler	2	28	142	0
Northwestern	3	19	251	0
Chicago	1	59	160	0
Wisconsin	1	30	140	0
Ohio State	1	60	184	0
Totals	12	295	*1,260	0
1924 (6–1–1)				
Nebraska	0	60	116	6 for 116
Butler	2	16	104	2 for 30
Michigan	5	41	402	6 for 64
Iowa	2	45	186	3 for 98
Chicago	3	60	300	7 for 177
Minnesota	1	44	56	3 for 39
Totals	13	266	*1,164	27 for 524
1925 (5–3)				
Nebraska	0	51	49	1 for 18
Butler	2	41	185	2 for 22
Iowa	1	60	208	2 for 24
Michigan	0	60	122	0
Pennsylvania	3	57	363	1 for 13
Chicago	0	60	51	0
Ohio State	0	48	235	9 for 42
Totals	6	377	*1,213	15 for 119

*Yards gained includes runs from scrimmage, and return of punts and kickoffs.

RECAPITULATION

Touchdowns scored—31; yards gained—3,637; passes completed—42 for 643 yards.

Grange's single-game records: Most touchdowns—5, against Michigan, 1924; most yards gained—402, against Michigan, 1924; most passes completed—7 for 177 yards, against Chicago, 1924; least yards gained—49, against Nebraska, 1925; longest run—95 yards, with opening kickoff against Michigan, 1924.

HOW RED SCORED

Opponent	Yards	Type of Play
1923		
Nebraska	66	Punt return
Nebraska	5	End run
Nebraska	11	End run
Iowa	3	Line plunge
Butler	22	End run
Butler	7	Line plunge
Northwestern	90	Pass interception
Northwestern	35	Recovered blocked punt
Northwestern	15	End run
Chicago	3	Line plunge
Wisconsin	26	End run
Ohio State	34	Through center
1924		
Butler	13	End run
Butler	48	End run
Michigan	95	Returned opening kickoff
Michigan	67	End run
Michigan	56	End run
Michigan	44	End run
Michigan	15	Line plunge
Iowa	11	Line plunge
Iowa	2	Line plunge
Chicago	4	Line plunge
Chicago	5	Line plunge
Chicago	88	End run
Minnesota	10	End run
1925		
Butler	60	Punt return
Butler	10	End run
Iowa	83	Returned opening kickoff
Pennsylvania	56	Off tackle
Pennsylvania	13	Off tackle
Pennsylvania	20	End run

pulted him into national fame and a household word in a time which was to become known as sports' Golden Era. Red Grange of Illinois had it all—tremendous ability, color, a sense of the dramatic, and a precious knack for rising to the occasion.

Perhaps Paul Sann, in his book *The Lawless Decade,* described best what Red Grange was to the Roaring Twenties: "Red Grange, No. 77, made Jack Dempsey move over. He put college football ahead of boxing as the Golden Age picked up momentum. He also made some of the ball yards obsolete. They couldn't handle the crowds. He made people buy more radios. How could you wait until Sunday morning to find out what deeds Red Grange had performed on Saturday? He was the 'Galloping Ghost' and he made sports historians torture their portables without mercy."

That was Grange of Illinois.

There are a few who will argue that Red Grange was not the greatest player to ever trod the gridiron for Illinois, but the Fighting Illini have had other outstanding stars in their illustrious football history.

Perhaps one of the most notable was Alex Agase, who came to be known as the "wandering guard." A talented lineman who was rarely moved on defense and was a devastating blocker on offense, Alex bounced around like a puppet on a string. During Agase's time in the Big Ten, it was wartime and most players were being shuttled hither and yon by the military.

In 1942 Agase made the All-America team as a sophomore at Illinois after turning in one of the most spectacular performances of all time by a guard against Minnesota. Alex became the only guard in Big Ten history to score two touchdowns in one game. First he stole the ball away from the Gophers' surprised Bill Daley and ran 35 yards for a score. Then, late in the game, he stormed through the Minnesota line to fall on a bad center snap in the end zone for the touchdown that won the game for Illinois, 20–13.

The next season Agase was in the U.S. Marines and he turned up at Purdue for his officers' training. Although Alex was only at Purdue for four months, he played football for the Boilermakers and, naturally, he was named to the All-America team again.

"We thought we were going to get a V–Twelve program at Illinois," Agase recalls, "but we didn't. The programs were at Purdue and Notre Dame. When it came time to assign us, they took the first half of the alphabet and sent us to Purdue. The rest went to Notre Dame.''

One of the teams Agase faced that season at Purdue was Illinois, and Alex's new team was giving it to the Illini pretty good. Purdue was leading in the game by three or four touchdowns and Coach Elmer Burnham took out his starters.

"Coach Burnham told us we were done for the day," remembers Agase, "so those of us who were from Illinois asked if we could go to the other side of the field to visit with our former teammates and coaches. He gave his permission, so we went, trotting around the end zone over to the other side of the field.

"We were sitting over there talking with the Illinois coaches and players and Illinois scored a couple of touchdowns. Burnham was over on the other side waving his arms for us to come back, so away we went again, trotting around the end zone to the Purdue side of the field. He put us back in the game, we took the kickoff and scored, and he took us out again." Purdue won the game, 40–21.

After two years with the marines in the South Pacific, where Agase earned the Bronze Star and Purple Heart in action in Okinawa, the war was over and Alex was back at Illinois in 1946 for his last season of college football. The Illini weren't expected to do much that year but they wound up winning the Big Ten championship and going to the Rose Bowl, where they upset UCLA, 45–14. Alex was a big factor in Illinois' success and, for a third time, was selected for the All-America team to complete one of the most unusual cycles in football annals. Three varsity seasons spread over five years and two schools, and three times picked as an All-America.

That 1946 Illinois team also had three other players who will not soon be forgotten in the Big Ten. Buddy Young, a tiny, fireplug-sized halfback who was as elusive as a firefly, confounded opponents all season long with his darting and dashing through defenses that often came up empty-handed. Buddy, who also was a track star, specialized in breakaway runs. The other halfback, Julie Rykovich, a piledriving line thumper, complemented Young as the other half of the Illinois running attack, while Perry Moss, a smart play-caller who could run *and* pass, ran Coach Ray Elliott's offense with the skill of a magician.

There were other Illinois stars, too, who left their mark on the

Big Ten. Like Dwight (Dyke) Eddleman, an all-everything high school star out of Centralia (Illinois) High School who starred in three sports and accumulated eleven varsity letters. A superb runner, Eddleman's specialty was punting. In 1949 he averaged 43.3 yards on fifty-two kicks. And J. C. Caroline, a long-distance threat whose long runs and hammering plunges set the conference on its ear in 1953 and brought the Illini a tie for the championship with Michigan State. Caroline's stock-in-trade was speed and an alluring flair for the spectacular. He led the conference in rushing with 919 yards (a record) and a 6.9-yard average, and tore off at least one run of 40 yards or more in every game he played.

It was a decade before Illinois returned to the Big Ten wars as a champion under Coach Pete Elliott, who had succeeded Ray Elliot in 1960. The 1963 team wasn't overwhelming but one of its mainstays was Dick Butkus, a fierce center who delighted in demolishing opponents whether he was bowling them over while on offense or smearing them from his linebacking post on defense. Either way, he was the best college lineman in the land in 1963 and 1964. That team also featured Jim Grabowski, a big, hard-hitting fullback who ate up real estate with a vengeance. Before he ended his varsity career in 1966 Jim wiped out all of Red Grange's rushing records and was loudly acclaimed as one of the most productive runners in all of Illinois history.

But there was only one Red Grange.

EIGHTEEN

A Bronko That Was Never Broken

In the fall of 1926, Dr. Clarence Spears, the Minnesota football coach, greeted his squad on the first day of practice with the usual amenities concerning their health, physical condition, and general attitude. Spears' wanderings eventually took him over to where the incoming freshmen were gathered and he amiably greeted each one with a friendly handshake and an introduction, "My name is Spears—what's yours?"

"Mine's Nagurski—Bronko Nagurski," replied a hulking six-foot two, 190-pound youngster, rather hesitantly.

"Bronko, hey? That's a strange name," said Spears.

The big freshman looked Spears right in the eye and blurted out, "Well, Clarence ain't so hot, either!"

It was soon apparent to Coach Spears and his staff that this big, tough young man was a diamond in the rough. And rough was an apt description of the way Bronko played the game. The Gopher varsity found that out the first day it scrimmaged the frosh. Nagurski, playing tackle on defense, fought off the varsity's experienced blockers and slammed down the ball-carrier at the line of scrimmage with a resounding thud. And that was the way it went play after play. Slashing and slamming his way through blockers, Bronko virtually ate up the varsity runners until the first-teamers gladly gave up the ball.

Their ordeal wasn't over, however. When the frosh went on offense, there was that big kid Nagurski at fullback. The varsity went after him with a vengeance, bowling over the green freshmen blockers to get at Bronko. But the young fellow ignored them, booming through the onrushing defenders and shedding tacklers like a man shrugging off mosquitoes. The Minnesota players weren't the only ones impressed. The coaches on the sidelines looked on gleefully, aware that they had a very unusual football player in their midst, but one who might pose problems when he became eligible for the varsity. Like where to play him. But it was a pleasant dilemma and one which Coach Spears found easy to solve—he simply put the Bronk wherever he needed him most.

Before Bronko Nagurski finished his career at Minnesota he was to play end, tackle, and fullback, as well as almost any other position except quarterback, and he was to become one of the greatest players in the history of college football.

Oddly enough Nagurski was never recruited by Minnesota, or for that matter, by any other school. In fact, Bronko hadn't played much high school football because of a combination of peculiar circumstances that cost him his final year of eligibility. And, before that, in his two years of high school ball, he had never played on a team that won a game. It was hardly the kind of a career that would have attracted college recruiters, even in those days.

Nagurski was born of Ukrainian parents in 1908 in Rainy River, Ontario, a short forward pass from the United States border, but when he was three years old his family moved across the Rainy River to nearby International Falls, Minnesota, not exactly one of the best-known communities in the state. It has been said that International Falls' *only* claim to fame is that it is one of the coldest spots in the U.S. "We don't have summer," Bronko once explained, "just a season in the middle of the year when the sledding is poor."

Actually, young Nagurski was christened Bronislau, but his mother had difficulty in communicating in English and, when she entered him in grade school, the teacher didn't understand what she was saying. It sounded like Bronko to the harried teacher and that's the way she wrote it down. So, Bronislau simply disappeared in the confusion and it became Bronko for the record. Somehow, as the years progressed, it seemed to be a more appropriate name for this young man who was to devote so much of his lifetime to imitating a wild horse on the gridiron.

There were only two high schools in the entire Koochiching County and International Falls was not noted for its football teams. The truth is that good old I.F.H.S. had never even scored on the tough teams from the neighboring iron-mining region.

It would be nice to say that Bronko Nagurski turned International Falls into an instant winner when he joined the football squad as a sophomore. Unfortunately it didn't happen. Things improved somewhat, however, because International Falls did manage to score an occasional touchdown as Bronko doubled in brass as a fullback on offense and a tackle on defense. But his team was never able to win a game.

Football wasn't Nagurski's only game in high school. He also was a track man, putting the shot, throwing the discus, high jumping, and running on the relay team, and he played guard and center in basketball. While Bronko wasn't exactly a high school All-America in basketball, it was this sport that cost him his final year of football eligibility. Angered when the high school principal cancelled the team's trip to the district tournament because two other players required disciplining, Nagurski decided to transfer to Bemiji High School for his senior year. International Falls protested that he was not a resident of Bemiji and therefore should not be permitted to play as a transfer student. The state high school athletic commission agreed and Bronko was grounded for football in his senior year.

However, Arnie Oss, a former Minnesota football and basketball star, had met Bronko and was taken with him and his athletic ability. Oss suggested that the University of Minnesota would be a good place for Nagurski to go and he promised to try to get him a job to meet his expenses. So Bronko turned up in Minneapolis, unheralded, unrecruited, and, actually, uninvited, much to the future enjoyment of Coach Spears and the Gophers.

Sans scholarship and with no alumni "angel" to sweeten his pocket, Nagurski had to get a job to help pay his way through school. He managed to get a job with a legal firm in his freshman year, serving papers on litigants. Needless to say, service was almost always accepted. The next year Bronko was a watchman in a lumber yard. "That was pretty good," he recalls. "I got to sleep on a cot in the basement."

Meanwhile, the large Ukrainian with the high-pitched voice was becoming a legendary hero at Minnesota. He eventually grew into a 225-pounder and the toughest Gopher of them all in an era when Big Ten football players were regarded as monsters from another age. His reputation grew and, as it grew, so did Minnesota's string of victories. In Nagurski's three years of varsity football, the Gophers lost only a total of four games, and none of them by more than two points. Despite this magnificent record, however, Minnesota never won a Big Ten title during Bronko's tenure as a player.

Oddly enough, as rough and tough as Nagurski was on the field, off it he was a kind and gentle man. Although he played the game with a fury matched by few other players, he rarely became angered, even when opponents ganged up on him. Coach Spears tried desperately to arouse his amiable giant, but not even his fiercest approaches seemed to work.

There was one game, in Nagurski's sophomore year, when Doc Spears pulled out all the histrionics in the book. The Gophers were trailing Notre Dame 7–0 at halftime in South Bend, Indiana, in a game played in gale-force winds mixed with sleet and rain. Things hadn't been going well at all for Minnesota—a fumble by quarterback Fred Hovde (who later became president of Purdue University) had set up Notre Dame's only touchdown—but then Coach Knute Rockne's Irish hadn't lost a game on its home field in twenty-two years.   .

As Spears sent his Gophers out for the second half, he pulled Nagurski aside, seized him by the jersey with both hands, and shook him.

"Bronk," he shouted, "you should be able to beat that Notre Dame singlehanded. I want you to go out there and tear them apart. You're going out there and kill 'em, kill 'em, kill 'em—aren't you?"

Nagurski looked at the coach, nodded his head gently, and in his squeaky, high-pitched voice, said mildly, "You bet, coach." Then he sauntered out on the field.

As a runner, Nagurski lacked the finesse of a Red Grange, and as a lineman he never bothered with developing the fancy little tricks of the trade that other great linemen of the time employed. He simply used his brute strength and power to overwhelm people. He was about as subtle as a charge of dynamite. When he operated at fullback he simply folded the ball against his belly, lowered his huge shoulders, and charged forward. It wasn't his style to dazzle defenders with his footwork or try to run around them. He just rammed through and over them. When he played in the line all he knew was that, tackling or blocking, the object of the game was to level the man in his path. And he did that with such devastating effectiveness that many an opponent ached and nursed bruises for weeks after contact with the Bronk. It wasn't stylish, but it was certainly extremely effective.

The late Steve Owen, when he coached the New York Giants, once explained that the Giants' defensive strategy against Nagurski was to have the first tackler slow him down, the second one spill him, and the third pin him. "We find we lose fewer fellows that way," explained Steve.

Although Doc Spears knew that in Nagurski he had a superstar who could play almost anywhere, finding a starting spot for Bronko in 1927, his sophomore year, was simplified by the fact that the Gophers already had Herb Joesting, an All-America, at fullback.

Joesting not only was a highly competent fullback, but he was judged to be the best in the country in 1926 and 1927 and was named to the All-America team in both of those years. A compact, rawboned man who weighed in at 190 pounds—they called him the "Owatonna Thunderbolt"—Herb was a hard-hitting line plunger who got most of his yardage inside the tackles. In 1926, his best season, he rushed for 1,011 yards in eight games. Against Wisconsin he rammed through the Badgers for 168 yards, and 114 against Fielding Yost's Michigan Big Ten champions. After that game Yost called Joesting the "greatest fullback I have ever seen." Of course, that was before Yost got a look at Nagurski.

After three years of giving Knute Rockne's Notre Dame teams fits, Joesting so irked the Irish coach that before the 1927 game Rockne offered to buy a suit of clothes for the first Notre Dame player who would throw Joesting for a loss. Rockne never had to pay off on that offer.

In Joesting's three years of varsity football, he totaled 2,018 yards rushing in twenty-three games, averaging 4.53 yards per carry.

Spears decided to play Nagurski at end and that is where the Bronk made his varsity debut against North Dakota State. It would perhaps be an understatement to say that the sophomore's baptismal performance was sensational. Playing both defense and offense, all he did to the poor North Dakotans was mangle their blockers, batter their ball-carriers, and cut down their defenders with crushing blocks as he opened gaping holes for Joesting and the other Minnesota runners. Nagurski, however, didn't stay at end very long. The Gophers already had the two best ends in the league in Bob Tanner and Ken Haycraft. So Spears had to find another spot for the big fellow and Bronko was subsequently moved to tackle for the remainder of the season. He was just as big a hit there as he had been at end, and Minnesota enjoyed an unbeaten season marred only by two ties—with Indiana and Notre Dame.

In 1928 Joesting was gone and it was natural for Spears to move his number-one terrorist to fullback. Bronko had spent most of the summer working in a cement crew in northern Minnesota and he reported for fall practice in excellent condition. He was ready to play anywhere, but obviously was pleased when he learned that he would get a chance to carry the ball. Of course the Minnesota coaches knew that Nagurski also was the best tackle they had and it wasn't unusual for him to slip into the line on defense when the Gophers were threatened.

Fullback Nagurski posed even more of a problem for opposing teams than tackle Nagurski. He shredded enemy lines like a bulldozer ripping up a forest. Bronko frequently gave away the play by looking to the spot where he was going to run. But it didn't matter. His amazing quickness usually got him to the hole before the opposition could adjust its defensive positions. And it always took more than one—usually two or three—tacklers to bring him down. Meanwhile, he would shrug them off blithely.

With Nagurski supplying the power, the Gophers hardly drew a deep breath as they easily ripped through their first three opponents. Then, against a tough Iowa team, the indestructible Bronko Nagurski suffered the only serious injury of his college career. He cracked a transverse vertebra in his back and couldn't bend over to receive the snap from center. So he played tackle for all but about five minutes of the remainder of the game, and, despite his injury, created his usual havoc. However, without Bronko to generate a running attack, Minnesota lost to Iowa, 7–6, one of two games it dropped in 1928.

Nagurski made one concession to his injury. He agreed to wear a corset to protect the cracked vertebra and played only part-time (at tackle) for the next three games against Northwestern, Indiana, and Haskell Indian School.

Wisconsin, Minnesota's traditional rival, was coming up next in the season's final game, and the unbeaten but once-tied Badgers, who had not won a Big Ten championship since 1912, had to beat the Gophers to take the title. With Nagurski still nursing his injury, it seemed unlikely that Minnesota could hold off the high-riding Badgers.

Bronko, however, despite his ailment, was determined to play and he wanted to be at fullback against Wisconsin. He demanded that Coach Spears use him and finally Spears agreed, with the condition that he wear a special brace for his ribs and back to protect his cracked vertebra.

What happened against Wisconsin was that Nagurski put on one of the most courageous performances ever seen on a gridiron. The game turned out to be a bruising battle with neither team able to generate much of an offense in the early going. Nagurski was used mostly as a decoy and blocker for Hovde, the quarterback, and Win Brockmeyer, a speedy 155-pound halfback. Then, early in the second quarter, came the first big break in the game. Wisconsin's Russ Rebholz fumbled and Nagurski—who else?—recovered on the Badgers' 18-yard line.

Quarterback Hovde decided that it was to be now or never for his team and if it was to be now, it would have to be up to Bronko Nagurski, injury or no injury. Bronko understood and he let Hovde know that he was ready for the supreme effort.

Wisconsin also knew that Bronko was coming their way and yet they were helpless. On the first play, Nagurski, head down, legs churning, and his bulging body tensed, blew through the ganged-up Badgers for 9 yards. Then, it was Nagurski again, this time for 2 yards and a first down on the Wisconsin 7-yard line. Two more smashes by Bronko put the ball on the 1-yard line and the embattled Badgers knew that they were going to get the Bronk again on the next play.

Nagurski didn't disappoint his foes. Hovde looked over at the weary Nagurski, who nodded ever so imperceptibly, and the play was set. The ball went to Bronko, who roared through the middle behind center George Gibson and into the end zone for what proved to be the game's only touchdown in a 6–0 victory for Minnesota that ended Wisconsin's championship dreams.

That five-play, 18-yard foray by Nagurski wasn't his only bit of heroics on that November Saturday. On three other occasions during the long, hard-fought afternoon, he saved the day for the Gophers. Once he caught Wisconsin's Bo Cusinier on the 10-yard line from behind to prevent a touchdown. Another time he knocked down a pass on the goal line, and then, on the final play of the game, Nagurski intercepted a Wisconsin pass to shut the door on still another Badger threat. It was an afternoon that old Gophers—and Bronko Nagurski—never forgot!

In 1929 Nagurski posed a difficult problem for All-America selectors. Again he divided his time between fullback and tackle and it was generally agreed that he was the best in the country at either position. Actually, that year he played only 120 minutes at tackle—the equivalent of two full games—and the rest of the time at fullback. Some selectors put him at fullback, others at tackle on their All Americas. The New York *Sun*, however, found a delightful way to settle the dilemma of where to put the Bronk when it picked its All-America team. The *Sun* took the bull—actually, in this case, the Bronk—by the horns and picked only ten men, placing Nagurski at both fullback and tackle! It was a supreme compliment that had never before and has never since been paid to any college football player.

Minnesota lost only to Iowa, 9–7, and Michigan 7–6, in Nagurski's senior year, but it wasn't because anyone succeeded in stopping the incomparable Bronko. For example, against Iowa, he played the first half of the game at fullback, barreling through the entire Hawkeye team for 41 yards and a touchdown. Along the way Bronko met up with Willis Glasgow, Iowa's All-America halfback, and leveled him. A teammate, Duke Johnson, recalled later, "Bronk didn't even try to avoid Glasgow—he just ran right over him and knocked him cold."

Then, when Iowa began to threaten, Nagurski switched to tackle in an effort to contain the rallying Hawkeyes and he did a fearsome job of manhandling their offensive linemen and ball-carriers. But it was all to no avail. Iowa came from behind to nip the Gophers, 9–7.

There were many legendary tales that old Gophers love to spin about the Bronk, some of which have taken on added lore with the passing of time, others factual. Like the time Minnesota had the ball on Northwestern's 12-yard line, fourth down and goal to go, and the great Nagurski smashed everything in his path as he slammed over the goal line, through the end zone, and into a pile of 100-pound bags of cement which were piled up for a construction project. As the tale goes, Bronko even bowled over the bags of cement before he stopped. Or the time when he was playing pro football for the Chicago Bears against the Washington Redskins. In that game Nagurski barreled through center, knocked two linebackers in opposite directions, stomped over a defensive halfback, knocked the safetyman for a loop, then caromed off a goalpost and crashed into a brick wall. A little wobbly from the last shot, Bronko was supposed to have commented, "That last guy hit me awfully hard."

Fact or fancy, one thing is sure—Bronko Nagurski was undoubtedly one of the most versatile and greatest college players of his era.

It was natural that the pros would be vitally interested in acquiring the services of this powerful giant who had such an impressive college career. Several pro teams went after Nagurski, dangling cash offers as an inducement for him to sign. The hottest competitor for his services was George Halas, the owner-coach of the Chicago Bears, who was ready to give Nagurski what he considered to be a small fortune. But, alas, the Bronk was born too soon. He signed with Halas and the Bears for the munificent sum of $5,000, an amount that most present-day pro draft choices use to light their dollar cigars.

"Halas' first offer was thirty-five hundred dollars," remembers Nagurski, "but Dutch Bergman, my backfield coach at Minnesota, told me to ask for sixty-five hundred. So I settled for five thousand, but the next year I got cut. Do you know, it took me seven years to get back up to five thousand dollars."

Nagurski proved to be the biggest bargain that the frugal George Halas ever got. For the next eight seasons he was the scourge of the National Football League. In a time when the emphasis in pro football was on a power game rather than the pass, Nagurski left an indelible mark on the history of the NFL. Playing fullback on offense he piled up 4,031 yards, while destroying almost every defense devised to stop him. And when Bronko wasn't decimating the opposition with his bull-like charges, he was devastating their offenses from a linebacking post on defense.

Meanwhile, Nagurski had become a professional wrestler in the off-season and he was making considerably more money with his grappling efforts than Halas was paying him to play football. Bronko never liked to talk much about his wrestling career, but he became one of the world heavyweight champions in a sport that always had one or more wrestlers carrying that distinction at the same time before he packed in that form of entertainment in 1960 to return to International Falls.

Nagurski retired from pro football after the 1937 season but, in 1943, when the pros were feeling the manpower crunch because of World War II, Halas prevailed upon the Bronk to come back at the age of thirty-five. He agreed, but confined his activity to playing tackle because "I won't need as much speed there." With Bronko back in the fold for that one year, the Bears again won the championship.

In 1958, when he was fifty years old and paunchy, Nagurski returned to Minnesota to play with the alumni against the varsity in the annual spring game. It would be nice to report that, even at fifty, Bronko was still a terror on the gridiron. It wasn't exactly the case, however. He carried the ball three times, gaining 2 yards on one plunge, 4 on another, and was stopped on a two-point try. Not quite the Bronk of old, but still good enough to give him a 3-yard-per-carry average.

The kudos for Bronko Nagurski were endless. Grantland Rice once wrote, "Nagurski may well have been the greatest football player of all time."

Benny Friedman, who played against Nagurski as both a collegian and a pro, said, "He was the greatest fullback I ever played against in college or the pro game. He bucked the line harder than Ernie Nevers. He did everything better. I never saw a greater blocker or a more deadly, brutal tackler."

Now, the Bronk sits in his home in International Falls, Minnesota, "letting my old injuries heal."

While Bronko Nagurski undoubtedly was the greatest of all the Minnesota football heroes, he was by no means the only one who distinguished himself through the years that the Gophers have been cracking heads with rivals in one of the toughest conferences in the country. There was Herb Joesting, of course. Then there was Paul Giel, the handsome halfback who ripped up the Big Ten turf in 1952 and 1953.

Giel (rhymes with eel) had the misfortune to come along just when Minnesota's grid fortunes dipped to one of their lowest levels. Coach Bernie Bierman had just quit after the 1950 season following a distinguished career, and Wes Fesler, the old Ohio State great, took over in 1951—Giel's sophomore and first varsity year. The 1951 team, which won only two games, was so bad that Fesler called it "the world's worst squad."

Despite this, Giel quickly established himself as the golden boy of the Gophers. Although Minnesota was able to win only two of its nine games, Paul, operating at tailback in Fesler's single-wing attack, still managed to break the then-existing Big Ten total offense record with 1,078 yards gained rushing and passing. That, according to Fesler, was one of the miracles of the season, "because the only time we ever got the ball was when we received kickoffs after the other team scored."

Minnesota never did get much better in 1952 and 1953, but Paul Giel stood out like a shining beacon, and, in spite of his team's ineptness, he was twice picked for All-America and became the only halfback ever to win the conference's Most Valuable Player Award two years in a row. And, in 1953, he came within a few votes of beating out Notre Dame's Johnny Lattner for the Heisman Trophy.

Giel's range of talents was extraordinary. He called the plays, passed and caught passes, ran with the ball, and did the kicking. He also blocked and defended with a special kind of ferocity. And, just to add to his wide repertoire of skills, Paul also held the ball for tries for points after touchdowns. He was the complete football player. In fact, in 1952 and 1953, Giel was just about the entire Minnesota team.

One frustrated rival player said of Giel, "It made you sick to your stomach to try to tackle him."

Perhaps Giel's greatest day, however, was against Michigan in 1953. The Gophers hadn't beaten their old rivals from Ann Arbor in ten years, and Michigan was a huge favorite to continue its winning streak over Minnesota. All the Wolverines had to do was stop Paul Giel. And all Paul Giel did that Saturday afternoon was to leave Michigan's players gasping while he put on one of the most spectacular one-man shows ever seen in the Big Ten. Handling the ball on fifty-three of the sixty-three plays Minnesota ran in the game, Giel rushed for 112 yards on thirty-five attempts, completed thirteen of eighteen passes (including his first eleven) for 169 more yards, returned four punts for 49 yards, one kickoff for 24, and intercepted two passes. He scored twice on runs and passed for a third touchdown as the Gophers upset Michigan, 22–0.

Considering the fact that Giel's Minnesota teams won only ten games in his three-year varsity career, his statistics were almost miraculous. Paul totaled 4,094 yards on runs, passes, and kick returns, scored twenty-two touchdowns, and passed for thirteen more.

Football wasn't Giel's only game. He was a superb pitcher on the Minnesota baseball team, good enough to win All-America honors and to attract bonus offers from several major-league teams. There were pro football offers, too, and Giel seriously considered a couple from Winnipeg and Toronto of the Canadian Football League. NFL teams, however, didn't seem to show much interest in Paul, despite his remarkable record as a two-time All-America. Somehow they couldn't get excited over five-foot eleven, 180-pound football players, even one who did so many things so well.

Giel, after much soul-searching, decided to try his hand at base-ball and signed with the New York Giants for a $63,000 bonus, more money than the National League team had ever before shelled out for a college player. For the most part, Giel's major-league career was undistinguished. In the next seven seasons, except for two years when he was in the service, he bounced around from the Giants to Pittsburgh to Minnesota to Kansas City, and finally retired in 1961 after he was bombed for seven hits and six runs in 1⅔ innings while pitching for Kansas City. His major-league won-lost record was an ungaudy 11–9.

After serving stints in the front office of the Minnesota Vikings and as sports director of radio station WCCO in Minneapolis, Giel accepted an offer to return to his alma mater as athletic director in 1971 when the Gophers decided to regroup and reorganize in an effort to improve their lagging football program.

There were many other Minnesota greats, too, among them a pair of halfbacks—George (Sonny) Franck and Bruce Smith—who led the Gophers to Big Ten and national championships in 1940 and 1941. Each had the knack for making the big play, and it took the combined efforts of both of them to extricate Minnesota from what could have become a frustrating season in 1940. Six times the Gophers had to come from behind to achieve victories, and on almost every occasion it was the exciting heroics of Franck or Smith—in some cases, both of them—that pulled Coach Bernie Bierman's team through.

Franck did it in the season's opener against Washington, breaking loose for a 98-yard run and then contributing a game-saving tackle in a 19–14 win; Smith's 42-yard touchdown pass turned the trick against Nebraska; Smith's 134 yards rushing and two touchdowns pulled the Gophers ahead of Ohio State, 13–7, and Franck again saved the day by downing a touchdown-bound Buckeye on the 1-yard line; Franck scored four times in a 34–6 win over Iowa; Smith's 80-yard run contributed to a 7–6 win over Michigan; Smith's touchdown and Franck's 20-yard scoring run with an intercepted pass in the final game of the year against Wisconsin gave the Gophers the Big Ten title and the national championship. And so it went.

In 1941 Franck graduated after winning All-America honors and Smith had the spotlight to himself. Bruce then proceeded to lead the Gophers to their second straight Big Ten title and national championship, and his efforts were rewarded when he, too, was picked for the All-America team and then was voted the Heisman Trophy as America's premier college football player.

For all their individual brilliance, the Joestings, Nagurskis, Giels, Francks, Smiths, and all the other Minnesota superbacks—Pug Lund, Sandy Stephens—who starred for the Gophers couldn't have done nearly as well without the help of superlinemen whose names read like a Who's Who of college football. Players like Biggie Munn, Butch Larson, Bill Bevan, Bud Wilkinson (who went on to coaching fame at Oklahoma), Greg Larson, Ed Widseth, Urban Odson, Tom Brown, Bobby Bell, Carl Eller, Charlie Sanders, Aaron Brown, Bob Stein, the ends, tackles, guards, and centers who provided the offensive blocking and the defensive strength. They didn't capture the headlines, but they were the ones who fought the battles in the trenches. And they were fierce battles indeed when Minnesota's Gophers were more golden than gilded.

NINETEEN

Willie Heston and the Bennies

When the University of Michigan decided to hire Fielding H. (Hurry Up) Yost away from his four coaching jobs in California in 1901, it also acquired one of the biggest bonuses in the annals of college football—a spraddle-legged halfback named Willie Heston.

Somehow, Willie Heston had found his way from his home in Grants Pass, Oregon, to San Jose Normal in California. And, somehow, he found himself being coached by Yost in 1900 when the indefatigable coach spent several weeks with the San Jose team after his Lowell High School and Stanford varsity and freshman teams had completed their seasons. And, somehow, he found himself following Yost to Ann Arbor when the coach decided to accept an offer from Michigan. What followed in the next four years was one of the most incredible careers in college football.

A sturdy 190-pounder, Heston had all the ingredients that go into making a great football player. He ran like a restless wind, he had the kind of speed that made it almost impossible for opposing defenders to catch him once he got into the open, and he had the power to bull his way through even the staunchest defenses. Indeed, he was so fast that he often beat Archie Hahn, Michigan's Olympic sprint champion, in the 40-yard dash. In addition to his physical attributes and talents, Heston also had the earmark of a leader and he was to be the catalyst of one of the most amazing streaks ever chalked up by a college football team.

Yost and Heston arrived at Michigan at a time when the Wolverines weren't exactly the kingpins of the Big Ten. Indeed, Michigan had suffered through so many downright poor and mediocre seasons that almost anything that happened had to be an improvement. What happened was that the combination of Yost and Heston, along with a small band of dedicated and accomplished athletes, picked up the Wolverines and put them right into the athletic history books with four straight unbeaten teams that averaged almost a point a minute while riding roughshod over Big Ten and any other opponents brave enough to face them.

It took only a single game for Willie Heston to establish himself as a superstar. After seeing only limited action in Michigan's opening game 50–0 victory over Albion, the next Saturday he broke away for four touchdowns as the Wolverines crushed Case, 57–0. And that was only the beginning for Willie. Week after week he ran wild, as Michigan piled up yards and points with almost incredible ease.

After ten straight victories, the Wolverines received an invitation to play unbeaten Stanford, the strongest team in the West, in Pasadena, California, on January 1, 1902. The game was to be the major event in the annual Pasadena Rose Festival, a forerunner of what the festival sponsors hoped would become an annual game between the best teams in the East and West. Officially, it had not yet become the Rose Bowl.

Stanford, of course, knew all about Fielding Yost and, naturally, they had heard about Willie Heston, the whiz who used to do his running for nearby San Jose Normal. But none of this helped much. Michigan still walloped the poor Indians, 49–0, as Heston scored once, fullback Neil Snow ran for five touchdowns, and all the Wolverines together gained 1,463 yards.

With Heston supplying the impetus, the Michigan juggernaut continued on its merry way for the next three years—1902, 1903, and 1904. The only blemish on the Wolverine record was a 6–6 tie with Minnesota in 1903. Even after Willie's departure, the streak continued through the 1905 season until Coach Amos Alonzo Stagg's University of Chicago team finally broke it, 2–0, in the final game.

In 1903 Heston became only the third Michigan player ever to be named to the All-America team—Bill Cunningham, a center on the 1898 club, was the first, and Neil Snow, in 1901, was the second—and, going into the 1904 season, Willie had matured into a living legend. That year Heston proved to be the most elusive runner the Big Ten had seen in its short history. He proved to be harder to stop than a runaway locomotive. Among his most notable achievements were runs of 42, 35, 32, and 30 yards in a 48–0 swamping of

Ohio Northern; six touchdowns and more than 400 yards gained in a 95–0 trouncing of Kalamazoo; and three scores against something called the Chicago College of Physicians and Surgeons in a game that lasted only twenty-two and a half minutes because the doctors-to-be cleverly took so many times out that the contest had to be called on account of darkness.

When Heston's playing career finally ended, he had scored more than 100 touchdowns and over 600 points. Heston's exact totals, including his yardage gained in four years, have become hazy with age since no records were kept in those days. It is safe to assume, however, that Willie Heston's yardage figures must have been somewhere in the vicinity of five miles. It makes one wonder what Heston would have commanded as a pro football player in this day and age. However, professional football hadn't yet been invented in 1904 so Heston signed to coach the Drake University team at the munificent salary of $1,200 per year. He later became a judge, as well as one of football's elder statesmen.

Just how great was Willie Heston? Well, Coach Yost said, "Willie never had an equal, not even Jim Thorpe or Eddie Mahan, who was the second and third greatest. He could hit the line as well as any man who ever played and . . . he could do other things equally well. He never let anything slip. He took every chance he could. He was a wonder at maneuvering . . . and he had an uncanny ability to hold his feet."

Grantland Rice, in 1928, more than two decades after Heston played, had even greater praise for Willie. Granny wrote, "Heston was as hard a man to stop as football has ever known. He was off like a flash, starting at top speed and driving through with terrific force. He could break through a line, run an end or hold his own in any broken field. For combined speed and power, Heston has never been surpassed. He was a four-year star and a star in every game he ever played."

There aren't many folks around today who remember Willie Heston, but he left a mark that will never be erased.

One of those players who helped Willie Heston become the scourge of college football in 1904 was Adolph (Germany) Schulz, a huge 240-pound freshman who stretched six feet two inches, and operated at the center position for Michigan. Operate is probably the best way to describe the way Schulz played the game.

In addition to an innate love for combat, Germany had two other things going for him in his jousts with opposing players: he was as strong as a bull and, despite his size, he was as quick as a cat. On offense Schulz went about the job of clearing out defenders like an army tank. He simply blasted people out of his way to make openings for the Michigan backs. On defense he came up with a little trick that caused Coach Yost to shudder the first time he saw it.

Schulz decided that he would be in a better position to size up where the enemy would attack if he moved out of the line. Also, Germany reasoned, he would have a better shot at racking up any ball carrier who dared to challenge the brutish Michigan line. In effect, he turned himself into a linebacker, the first ever in college football.

Yost, as quick as he was to innovate and accept innovations, blanched at this touch of unorthodoxy dreamed up by his big center. He protested at first, but Schulz insisted that his way would work.

"Listen, Yost," he told the coach. "I can see things better back there. If anybody gets by me I'll move back into the line and stay there."

Well, not many folks got by this huge, hard-hitting, and quick man, and Yost finally had to agree that Schulz's way was best. Thus was the linebacker born in college football, and it wasn't too many years before centers on other teams played behind the line on defense.

With this additional fillip added to his repertoire, Germany Schulz became one of the most devastating football linemen of his day. His bone-crushing blocks and shattering tackles earned him All-America ranking in 1907, and eventually Walter Camp called Germany Schulz the greatest center in the history of college football.

One thing Coach Yost prided himself on was his kicking game—in fact, people used to refer to his offense as a "punt, pass, and a prayer"—and in 1922 he came up with one of the premier punters of all time in Harry Kipke, a stocky, thick-legged youngster who could do more things with a football than Houdini could do with a rabbit.

Kipke was a coach's dream. Although an outstanding runner at his halfback position—he was good enough to make All America— Harry's specialty was kicking the football. What Kipke did best with his talented right foot was to kick the ball almost anywhere he wanted it to go, and that was usually out-of-bounds inside an opponent's 10-yard line, a spot that the trade aptly called the "coffin corner" because it invariably put the receiving team in deep trouble. His aim was deadly from any where inside the 50-yard line, giving Michigan's offense an added dimension.

Perhaps Harry Kipke's greatest day came against Ohio State in 1922, when he literally kicked and ran the vaunted Buckeyes into submission. Harry punted eleven times for a 47-yard average that afternoon as Ohio State dedicated its new Ohio Stadium, but, even more important, seven of his kicks bounced out of bounds and the other four simply rolled dead before the OSU safety could pick them up. It was a virtuoso performance that has never been matched, either before or after Kipke.

As if his kicking weren't enough to torment the Buckeyes, Kipke settled Ohio State's doom with two touchdown runs—one for 34 yards from scrimmage, the other for 40 yards with an intercepted pass—and then dropkicked a 24-yard field goal to complete a 19–0 victory for the Wolverines.

Kipke's athletic ability didn't begin and end with football, either. He also starred in basketball and baseball for three years, winning a total of nine letters, and later, in 1929, became the head football coach at his alma mater for nine years.

It was early in the 1924 season and Illinois' Red Grange was having his memorable day against Michigan. The immortal redhead had run wild against the Wolverines and left them for dead on the short end of a 39–14 score, as a crestfallen Coach George Little, who had taken over for Fielding Yost when the old master "retired" after the 1923 season, watched helplessly on the sidelines. With the game hopelessly gone and only two minutes left to play, Little turned suddenly and beckoned to a young player huddled on the bench.

"You," he shouted. "Get in there!"

No one in the stands knew who the lowly substitute was, nor did they care much at the time. Even the fact that he was a quarterback and managed to throw two passes before the game ended didn't impress anyone, except perhaps Benny Friedman, the young sophomore who had finally emerged from obscurity.

During the week after the humbling by Grange and Illinois, Coach Little decided he had to make some drastic moves to get his team back on the right track. One of them was to install Friedman at quarterback for the next game against Wisconsin. It proved to be a fortuitous move. Benny promptly threw a pair of touchdown passes in a 21–0 win over the Badgers, launching Michigan to a four-game winning streak that included victories over Minnesota, Northwestern, and Ohio State. Friedman also launched a personal career that was to bring him fame and glory as one of college football's finest passers and field generals.

Oddly enough, Benny Friedman almost didn't get to play for Michigan at all. In fact, he almost didn't get to play football in high school.

Friedman grew up in Cleveland, the son of orthodox Jewish parents who knew or cared little about football. But Benny, a heady youngster with a deep-rooted urge to excel, decided he wanted to be a football player and the best place to become a good one was East Tech High School, where the highly successful Sam Willaman was the coach. Willaman, however, didn't think much of Friedman's ability and suggested that perhaps it would be best if he went to his neighborhood high school, Glenville, instead.

As it turned out, Willaman, for all his success as a coach, misjudged Benny Friedman. East Tech's loss was Glenville's gain. Friedman developed into a schoolboy whiz as a passer and quarterback, and in 1922 led Glenville to the city championship and a postseason game with Oak Park High School in Chicago for the mythical national scholastic championship. Benny and Glenville won that one, too.

Friedman elected to go to Michigan. "One of its great attractions for me was its tradition," he said years later. "That very first day at practice on Ferry Field was electric. Not only did the turf feel good under my feet but I said to myself, 'This is where Willie Heston played, and Germany Schulz and Harry Kipke!' Just being on the same field where they played did something for me."

Despite the tradition and the good feeling, Friedman was hardly a ball of fire in his freshman year. By this time Benny had grown to five-foot ten and 175 pounds, but he wasn't happy, on the football field or socially. Things didn't improve, either, early in his sophomore year. About the most important assignment Friedman had in the preseason practice was acting as a dummy blocker for Line Coach Tad Weiman's tackles to practice on. Benny learned to block, but that wasn't his goal at Michigan. He wanted to be the varsity quarterback.

After five days of this, Friedman had just about decided to pack his bags and leave for Dartmouth, where some of his Cleveland friends were going to school. He told Weiman he was quitting. "The coach can't see me for dust," complained Benny, "and there is no point in my going on."

Weiman, a gentle and understanding man, had a long talk with the embryo but frustrated quarterback, pointing out that many a Michigan star had suffered similar early problems before making it. "The tradition at Michigan," said Tad, "is that when you're called, you must be prepared."

Well, Friedman decided to stick it out and he was finally called, even though it was born out of desperation by a beleaguered coach who was groping for a way to stimulate his team. What a break it turned out to be for Michigan! All Benny Friedman did was to become the best quarterback in college football and a two-time All-America.

Benny had a knack for throwing the football accurately, and he filled the Big Ten air with his soft, feathery passes that inevitably found their way into the willing arms of Michigan players. He also was a superb field-goal kicker, but perhaps his greatest asset was his intelligence as a play-caller. He knew how to probe enemy defenses until he found a weakness and then he exploited it fully.

Fielding Yost was back at the helm of the Michigan football team in 1925, the same impatient old warhorse who had not been able to abide his brief retirement. He knew all about Benny Friedman, of course, and he knew something about a big, rawboned sophomore kid named Bennie Oosterbaan, who had come to Michigan with quite a reputation as a high school player in Muskegon.

At six-foot two and 198 pounds, Oosterbaan had been just about everything but all-world in four sports at Muskegon, and even in those days, when recruiting was not the way of life in college football that it is today, coaches had an eye out for him. Bennie was an All-State end in football, the star of the basketball team that went to the finals of a national interscholastic tournament in Chicago, a pitcher on the baseball club, and a weightman in track. When he decided to go to Ann Arbor it was big news indeed in Michigan newspapers.

For all his imposing reputation, Oosterbaan also almost never got to play at Michigan. A nagging back injury forced him to pass up freshman basketball and, in the fall of 1925, when he reported for football as a sophomore, he was actually cut from the squad when an assistant coach didn't like the way he lined up for a play.

"You don't even know how to take the position of an end," Bennie was told by the assistant. "Turn in your suit."

However, Oosterbaan's retirement from football didn't last very long. A few days later, Yost asked, "Where's that big Oosterbaan? I need somebody to play end."

The next day Oosterbaan was back in uniform and at the end of the season he was an All-America. And again in 1926 and 1927. He also earned All-America honors in basketball, and won nine letters in the three major sports during his tenure as a Wolverine. Bennie became the second part of one of the most famous pitch-and-catch teams of that era, the Friedman-to-Oosterbaan aerial circus, that Yost unleashed on the Big Ten.

With Friedman passing—and kicking and running—and Oosterbaan catching and playing tough defense—the 1925 Michigan team turned out to be the scourge of the Big Ten. Friedman floated his accurate passes, often on first down, which was almost unheard-of in a time when two runs, then maybe a desperation pass, and a kick was the usual offense, and Oosterbaan made miraculous catches as the Wolverines rolled over Indiana and Wisconsin. Illinois, with Red Grange, was another matter but Michigan managed to hobble the famous redhead and squeaked to a 3–0 victory on a 24-yard field goal by Friedman late in the first half.

Navy was next to fall, 54–0, but then Michigan met its Waterloo against Northwestern at Soldier's Field in Chicago in a game played in the foulest kind of weather imaginable. A driving rainstorm, combined with snow and sleet and a 55-mile-per-hour wind, made running and passing practically impossible for either team and Northwestern edged the frustrated Wolverines 3–2 on a short, wobbly field goal—set up for the Wildcats when Friedman fumbled a punt—and an intentional safety. Needless to say, neither of the Bennies distinguished himself on that miserable day. Perhaps it was only a coincidence, but after that Northwestern didn't appear on Michigan's schedule again until 1932.

Michigan recovered from that mortal blow to beat Ohio State, 10–0, and Minnesota, 35–0, completing a 7–1 season that earned it the Big Ten championship and, in spite of the single loss, national acclaim as the best team in the land. With good reason, too—the Wolverines piled up 227 points and didn't give up a single touchdown. The only points scored against them were from the winning field goal by Northwestern. Years later, Coach Yost called the 1925 team "the best I ever had," and that included those famous Point-A-Minute clubs of Willie Heston's time.

The combination of Friedman and Oosterbaan continued its spectacular shenanigans again in 1926. This time the Wolverines swept past all of their Big Ten opponents, but they had to share the conference title with Northwestern, which also was unbeaten in league play. Michigan's only loss was a 10–0 upset by Navy in Baltimore, even though it was generally agreed that the Middies weren't in the same class with the Big Ten co-champs.

Years later Friedman was still trying to explain the defeat by Navy. "We stopped off in Washington to meet President Coolidge and then we were quartered at the Naval Academy," remembers Benny. "The midshipmen looked at us in awe. 'There's the great Benny Friedman,' they would say. 'There's the great Bennie Oosterbaan.' Everybody got the treatment and we became musclebound from patting ourselves on the back. Swelled heads everywhere. Then the cannon boomed at five A.M. No one slept after that.

"In the game I threw three passes to Oosterbaan. Each should have gone for a touchdown. The total gain was eighteen yards. Those big Navy tackles, Wickhorst and Eddy, were murdering me. This gave me an idea. That big farmer with the hamlike hands, Oosterbaan, could throw a ball the length of the field and I decided to try him. Wickhorst and Eddy smothered him.

"When we pried him loose, Oosterbaan looked at me and said, 'Benny, if it's all the same to you, I'd rather catch passes than throw them.' "

Although he was superb in almost every game in 1926, the most memorable one for Friedman was the comeback 17–16 win over Ohio State. Benny's father was in the stands for that game and he looked in wonderment at the huge crowd packed into the stadium.

"Who gets all this money?" Mr. Friedman asked, and it was explained that the two universities split the gate receipts.

Just about then a couple of Ohio State behemoths broke through, slammed his son Benny to the turf, and sat on him. Time was called, the trainer came in, first aid was administered, and Benny staggered to his feet.

"The players, they get nothing?" Mr. Friedman asked. Not a sou, he was told.

"And for this, my Benny is going to college?" said Benny's dad, with a perplexed look on his face.

The elder Mr. Friedman wasn't the only one in Ohio Stadium who was perplexed that day. The Michigan team was in the same fix but for another reason, when the Buckeyes quickly took a 10–0 lead early in the first half. But then Benny Friedman went to work. First, he threw a beautifully timed 38-yard touchdown pass from a fake placekick formation to Oosterbaan in the corner of the end zone and kicked the extra point. Then Benny demonstrated his intelligence as a play-caller and strategist. Late in the second quarter he turned over the passing to Lou Gilbert and became a receiver. Gilbert promptly passed to Friedman, who lugged the ball to the OSU 35-yard line before he was downed, just about 5 yards in from the sideline.

Only twenty-nine seconds remained on the clock before halftime and Friedman decided to gamble on a field goal in an attempt to tie the score, despite the impossible angle. (In those days, the ball remained where it was downed on the previous play.) With the seconds ticking off, Benny called his players into a huddle, told them what he intended to do, and they headed quickly for the line of scrimmage. All but Bennie Oosterbaan, who stopped and whispered something to Gilbert, kneeling on the 44-yard line to prepare to hold the ball for Friedman's kick.

The Ohio State players, recalling Friedman's earlier touchdown pass to Oosterbaan from a fake placekick formation, reacted predictably. "Fake! Fake!" they yelled. "It's another pass. Watch Oosterbaan."

Instead of rushing the kicker, the Buckeyes fanned out to protect against a pass and Friedman had all the time he needed for the kick. But let Benny tell it himself:

"I knew when my toe touched the ball that I had hit it just right. It rose like a golf ball and kept climbing. It went over the crossbar in dead center to tie the ball game at ten–ten."

Later, the curious asked Oosterbaan what he had whispered to Gilbert. "Oh," laughed Bennie, "I just told him I'd keep my fingers crossed and pray for a strong wind to come along just when you booted the ball."

There was no stopping Michigan—and Friedman—in the second half. Benny threw another touchdown pass to Leo Huffman and kicked the extra point for a 17–10 lead. Ohio State made one last move at the Wolverines, scoring in the fourth quarter, but the extra point try was missed and Michigan came away with a 17–16 victory.

While Oosterbaan made his reputation as a pass receiver and a defender, the play that thrilled him most had nothing to do with either of those specialties. It came in the last game of the 1926 season against Minnesota, a team Michigan had already beaten rather easily, 20–0, once that season. However, because the Gophers had been unable to fill their conference schedule, Coach Yost agreed to play them a second time in Minneapolis, a week after the hard tussle with Ohio State.

Minnesota, surprisingly, was leading the favored Wolverines, 6–0, when a Gopher back fumbled and Oosterbaan, crashing in recklessly from his end position, came up with the loose ball. Once he got over his surprise, Bennie set out resolutely for the goal line 60 yards away with a horde of Gophers in full chase. Oosterbaan went the distance untouched for the tying touchdown and then Friedman kicked the extra point to give Michigan a narrow 7–6 triumph and its second straight Big Ten title.

Oosterbaan, recalling the odd play, called it his biggest thrill in college football. "Every step I took I kept thinking, 'Won't I look like a chump if somebody catches me from behind? Oosterbaan, the All-America end who couldn't beat guys even with a head start!' I guess that made me run faster."

That was Benny Friedman's last game as a Wolverine, but he wasn't finished with football. He went on to an illustrious pro career with the New York Giants and then coached at City College of New York and Brandeis University. Even after his coaching days were over, Friedman kept his hand in the game by running a summer camp for quarterbacks, personally instructing them in the art of passing.

Oosterbaan still had another year to go and was the captain of the 1927 team. However, without Friedman and some of the other great Wolverine players who had been graduated, and without Yost, who had retired again, this time for good, Michigan had only a mediocre season under Tad Weiman, the new head coach. But Oosterbaan was picked as All-America for the third straight year and capped his college athletic career by also winning All-America honors in basketball.

After his graduation, Bennie Oosterbaan never left home. He remained at Michigan as an assistant football coach, became the head basketball coach, then head football coach when Fritz Crisler retired, serving for eleven seasons and producing a national championship team in 1948, and later moved up to assistant athletic director.

Although time, and a constant wave of new heroes, has dimmed the memory of Oosterbaan's accomplishments as a player, there are still a lot of folks around who remember his pass-catching and defensive play with fond memories. Perhaps the best description of Oosterbaan's skill as a pass receiver came from his old pitching mate, Friedman:

"What fluidity of motion he had!" said Benny. "What sneaky and great hands! And we had great confidence in each other. Bennie would tell me exactly where he'd go, and I knew he'd be there, and he knew I would deliver the ball to that point."

That simple statement by Benny Friedman also described his own great talents—the purest passer of his time and a master field general. Together, the two Bennies, Friedman and Oosterbaan, left an indelible mark on Michigan football, one that no other combination has ever been able to match in the Wolverines' long and brilliant gridiron history.

It didn't seem possible that Michigan ever would have another quarterback even to approach Benny Friedman as a passer, but, only four years after Friedman's departure, the Wolverines were singing the praises of Harry Newman, a squat, five-foot eight-inch, 170-pounder who could hit a dime with his pinpoint passes and, in addition, was a superb runner.

Michigan's grid fortunes had begun to flounder under Tad Weiman and Harry Kipke was back in Ann Arbor as the head coach in 1929. Kipke, aware of how important the pass had become in college football, devised a special drill to sharpen his quarterbacks' passing. It consisted of suspending four canvas targets with holes in them in midair in the intramural gym and inviting his passers to throw the ball through the holes. One those who impressed Kipke with his accuracy was Newman, only a freshman at the time. After only a few days, Harry was drilling bull's-eyes with amazing frequency. What Kipke didn't know at the time was that Harry Newman also was a free spirit with the guts of a riverboat gambler.

Kipke, and Michigan's opponents, found out soon enough that Newman was an unorthodox quarterback who delighted in doing the unpredictable. Take the Purdue game in 1930. Harry had spent most of the first half on the bench while the Boilermakers were rolling to a 13–0 lead over Michigan. He was installed at quarterback in the second half with instructions to throw the ball, and one of his early passes went to Bill Hewitt for a touchdown. Harry kicked the extra point and the Wolverines were back in the ball game.

But Newman wasn't finished. Jack Wheeler and Roy Hudson led Michigan down to the Purdue 40-yard line, where the Wolverine attack finally stalled. Two running plays netted only 2 yards and then the precocious sophomore surprised even his own teammates by calling his own number for a run up the middle. He picked up 3 yards—now it was fourth down and five on the Purdue 35-yard line and the situation dictated a punt, or at the very least a long field-goal attempt.

Newman, however, wasn't about to give up a shot at the tying touchdown. He called for a fake punt and promptly threw one of his bull's-eye passes to Norm Daniels, who went in for the score. Then, with the outcome hinging on the extra-point attempt, Harry ignored the advice of his veteran teammates who wanted Stan Hozer, the team's regular PAT kicker, to go for the winning point. Instead, he calmly placekicked the extra point himself and Michigan won the game, 14–13.

That bit of heroics made Harry Newman an instant hero, and he didn't disappoint Michigan fans the rest of the season. The next Saturday he threw two touchdown passes and kicked the extra point in a 13–0 win over Ohio State, then set up a pair of touchdowns with his passes and kicked a field goal to beat Illinois, 15–7, threw for the only score in a 6–3 win over Harvard, and, when a broken right hand kept him from passing, his running led the Wolverines to a 16–0 triumph over Chicago to give his team a tie with Northwestern for the Big Ten championship. It was a spectacular rookie year for the new Michigan star, but there were to be disappointments ahead for young Harry Newman.

The 1931 season began well enough for both Michigan and Newman as the Wolverines swept past Central State Teachers, Michigan State Normal, and Chicago, but then Ohio State unexpectedly whipped the Wolverines, 20–7, and Newman was benched as a starter. After that setback, Michigan regained its winning touch but Newman didn't start another game until the end of one of the strangest seasons ever in the Big Ten.

At the close of the regular schedule, Northwestern was the Big

Ten leader but an unusual set of circumstances gave Michigan a chance for another tie for the title with the Wildcats. The country was in the depths of the depression in 1931 and the Big Ten decided to play five postseason games with the proceeds going to charity, and it was further decreed that the extra games would count in the final standings. In the pairings, Northwestern, unbeaten in the conference, drew Purdue; Ohio State, which had lost once, was matched with Minnesota; and Michigan, also a one-time loser, was scheduled to play Wisconsin. As it turned out, Northwestern and Ohio State both lost, but Michigan defeated Wisconsin, 16–0, to tie the Wildcats for the conference title.

Newman was back as the starting quarterback for Wisconsin, but the game turned out to be a personal disaster for the hero of 1930. Four of his first six passes were intercepted and, just before the end of the first half, Coach Kipke yanked him and Harry trotted off the field with the sound of boos ringing in his ears.

It was a bad time for the erstwhile star, who returned to his room and went into silent retreat. Disconsolate, he debated the possibility of giving up football but was finally persuaded by an older brother that it wasn't the end of the world and that he should concentrate on redeeming himself the following season. Harry finally saw the light and agreed to give it another whirl in 1932. And what a whirl he gave it!

All Harry Newman did in 1932 was to become the nation's most glamorous player. He passed, he ran, and he placekicked with all the great skills he had demonstrated in his rookie year, and the boos he heard in 1931 turned to cheers. With one spectacular performance after another, Harry led Michigan to an unbeaten season, the Big Ten title, and the national championship, and he was everybody's choice for All-America quarterback.

It was just retribution for Harry Newman and a tribute to the tremendous talents he possessed. It would not be fair to say that Benny Friedman had been relegated to the number-two place in Michigan's quarterback history, but Harry Newman belongs somewhere right up with with Benny.

It always has been natural for quarterbacks, halfbacks, and fullbacks to be the headline grabbers. After all, they are the ones who score the points. But even the most gifted passers or ball carriers will readily admit that much of their ability depends upon the guys up front who do the the dirty work of protecting them and thus give them the chance to excel. It was no exception at Michigan, even during the glory years of Heston, Kipke, Friedman, and Newman.

First, of course, there were Germany Schulz and Bennie Oosterbaan, the super end. Then there were the Wistert brothers, a trio who spanned sixteen years at Michigan and each of whom made All-America and contributed some lore of his own to Michigan football. Coincidentally, they were all tackles.

The first was Francis, a big, rawboned fellow they called Whitey, who excelled in 1931, 1932, and 1933. Then there was Albert, who was the star of the 1942 team. His nickname was Ox, in recognition of his strength and stubbornness when he was challenged. And finally, there was Alvin, who won his All-America spurs in 1948 and 1949. They all had one thing in common. They played tackle as if they had invented the position, and they played it with the reckless abandon that is characteristic of All-Americas. They hit with tremendous fury, discouraging opposing ball carriers who dared to run at them; they operated with deadly efficiency as blockers; and they were, first and foremost, team players.

There were others, too, like Jack Blott, the center in 1923, and Chuck Bernard, the pivotman who got the ball to Harry Newman. And Ted Petoskey, a brilliant end in 1931, 1932, and 1933. All three were All-Americas.

Although the 1934 Michigan team had little to boast about in a 1–7 season, it did have one player who impressed both his teammates and his opponents. And, like Blott and Bernard before him, he was a center. He was a fiery, shock-haired young man named Jerry Ford, who defended tenaciously despite the superior opposition he had to face, and was one of the few bright spots on a team going nowhere. Except that he did go somewhere. Despite the Wolverines' inferior record, Ford was named to the All–Big Ten first team, and also was voted Michigan's Most Valuable Player, admittedly a dubious honor considering that the Wolves wound up in last place. After graduation from Michigan he accepted an invitation by Coach Ducky Pond to coach at Yale and he spent six years in New Haven as an assistant while also making his way through Yale Law School. Eventually Jerry Ford went other places. As Gerald R. (for Rudolph) Ford, he became a Republican United States Congressman and minority leader of the House of Representatives, and then was President Richard M. Nixon's choice to succeed Spiro Agnew as vice-president of the United States when that beleaguered Republican resigned his office after pleading no contest to income tax evasion in October 1973.

The late President Lyndon B. Johnson, once asked what he thought of Ford, said, "There's nothing wrong with him except he played football too long—without a helmet."

Ford insisted that the remark never bothered him. To prove it, Jerry showed up at a Washington dinner dressed in formal clothes and carrying his old Michigan helmet under his arm.

As vice-president under Nixon, Jerry Ford showed that he had lost none of the stamina and tenacity he displayed as a football player at Michigan. He proved to be just as adept at blocking for and defending his Watergate-besieged boss as he was back in 1934 at Ann Arbor, even though most Americans thought it was in a much less popular cause.

"As an old center," Ford quipped, "I know what it's like to be number two."

Ten months later, on August 9, 1974, Jerry Ford knew what it was like to be No. 1. When Nixon was forced to resign the presidency—or face almost certain impeachment by Congress—after admitting that he had lied to the American people about his role in the infamous Watergate cover-up, Ford was sworn in as the thirty-eighth president of the United States. He became the leader of a nation that had been torn apart by a political scandal unmatched in the history of America.

Once again Jerry Ford had a chance to be a Most Valuable Player.

However, Ford's tenure as president was to be a short one. He ran for the presidency as the Republican candidate in 1976 but, like his final year of football at Michigan, he was a member of a losing team. Jerry lost to Democrat Jimmy Carter, an ex-navy man, and was benched, becoming a private citizen again on January 20, 1977.

TWENTY

"Old 98"

One day in the fall of 1933, Thomas Dudley Harmon, a callow fourteen-year-old freshman, reported for football practice at Horace Mann High School in Gary, Indiana. Young Harmon was a little late for the opening session that afternoon and he rushed into the locker room, where he was greeted by the equipment manager who brusquely instructed him to "pick a uniform and get out on the field."

Tom quickly spotted a table covered with brand-new jerseys and he grabbed one, pulled it on, and raced onto the field, where Coach Doug Kerr was putting the Horace Mann squad through its paces.

Kerr took one look at the late arrival and screamed, "Hey, scrub, what are you doing with that jersey? Those are for the regulars. Get out of here until you're dressed properly."

That single blast sent Harmon sprinting back into the locker room in search of another jersey. This time, a little wiser, he headed for a pile of old jerseys piled in a corner and deliberately selected the shabbiest one he could find, and the one with the highest number. Now, properly dressed for a lowly substitute, Tom went back on the field and joined the squad gathered around the coach. Pretty soon, the scrubs were lined up against the varsity, ready to undergo the indignities reserved for anonymous freshmen and ragtag nonvarsity players.

However, Tom Harmon's anonymity didn't last very long. The first time the varsity kicked, he gathered in the ball on his own 10-yard line and then, weaving, sidestepping, and running over tacklers, ran 90 yards for a touchdown.

"Hey," yelled an astounded Coach Kerr. "Who is that kid wearing number ninety-eight?"

"That's Tom Harmon," volunteered a student manager.

"Well, tell him he's on the varsity now and to go back in and get a new uniform," said Kerr.

Still remembering, and feeling keenly, the putdown he had suffered only moments before, Tom respectfully declined the invitation. "No thanks," said Tom, "this is my uniform and my number."

And thus was "Old No. 98" born.

Even at that tender age, Tom Harmon's credentials were impressive. He had played on the sixth-grade team at Holy Angels grammar school and in the eighth grade was the player-coach of a club that won all of its ten games, including a victory over the high school freshman team.

"I grew up on the Gary sandlots," says Harmon, "when you played in jeans and sneakers and, if you won, you had to fight your way off the field."

Tom's family background almost assured the fact that he would become a star athlete. His father had been a high school sprinter. Three older brothers had been college stars—Lou in track at Purdue; Harold, who had been a basketball teammate of John Wooden's at Purdue; and Gene, who had captained the basketball team at Tulane. Two uncles, Leo and Doyle, had played football for Wisconsin. Aside from the fact that the Harmon family had an athletic heritage, young Tom was practically weaned on footballs, basketballs, and baseballs. His older brothers saw to that, even putting him through a yelling and hollering drill so he would develop a firm, commanding voice.

"I could have sung bass by the time I was twelve," Harmon observed later.

Well, Tom Harmon never did get to sing bass. He never had time to sing anything. During his years at Horace Mann he developed into one of the most exciting and sought-after athletes of his time. By the time he reached his senior year he was a genuine star who reeled off touchdown runs so effortlessly that college scouts began to bang on his door in increasing numbers.

Harmon didn't confine his athletic efforts to the football field. He won the state high school championships in the 100-yard dash and 220-yard low hurdles, pitched three no-hitters that attracted major-league scouts and an offer from the New York Yankees, and was one of the stars of the basketball team. Tom earned All-State hon-

ors in all four sports and won fourteen letters before he was graduated from Horace Mann.

It was small wonder that colleges all over the country, including
the Ivy League, were hot on Tom Harmon's trail. The offers came
from all over, but Doug Kerr, Tom's coach at Horace Mann, was a
Michigan alumnus and had already planted the Ann Arbor seed in
his brilliant football player. So it was no great surprise when Harmon decided to cast his lot with the Wolverines, leaving behind a
trail of disappointed college recruiters.

Harry Kipke was the coach at Michigan when Harmon showed
up for his freshman year in the fall of 1937, but the former Wolverine star was hanging on the ropes after three disastrous seasons in
which his teams had won only six games. The Michigan athletic
family had become disenchanted and the alumni were braying loud
and clear for Kipke's scalp, and they eventually got it. It was obvious that Harry's days in Ann Arbor were numbered. After a 4–4
season in 1937, while Tom Harmon was playing for the frosh
(which regularly beat the varsity), Kipke was fired and replaced by
Fritz Crisler, a protégé of Amos Alonzo Stagg, who had achieved
notable success as the head coach at Princeton. What a pity Harry
Kipke couldn't have hung around at least one more year to reap the
benefits that were to accrue to Michigan from Tom Harmon!

Crisler walked into a veritable wealth of talent when he arrived
at Michigan. First, there was Harmon. Then there was Forest Evashevski, a husky sophomore from Hamtramck. And Paul Kromer,
a swift halfback who had been just about the entire Wolverine
offense in 1937; Ed Frutig, a sizeable end; and Ralph Heikkinen, a
stalwart guard who had been voted Michigan's Most Valuable
Player in 1937. There were others, too, who were to form the nucleus of Michigan's return to football prominence in 1938.

Crisler also inherited some potential problems, most of them involving the highly publicized Harmon, although he had yet to play
a varsity game. Tom was a cocky young man who recognized his
own talents and wasn't about to let them be hidden—or forgotten.
He was also making a name for himself on campus—they called
him "Terrible Tommy" and "The Hoosier Hammer." A gregarious, lantern-jawed six-footer with a Tarzan physique and a yen for
swing music, he won the University Trophy as the best all-around
athlete in intramural sports. Afraid that he would be considered a
"swelled head," he had a friendly wave or nod for everyone he
met on campus.

Coach Crisler's first crisis came early on, in the winter of Harmon's freshman year, and it put Tom right smack into the middle of the makings of a national scandal. Showing more exuberance than discretion, an assistant coach at Tulane, who had been in the recruiting rat-race for Harmon, sent Tom a telegram suggesting that Harmon was wasting his time and talents at Michigan where there were no athletic scholarships and players had to pay their own way, when he could be playing for Tulane, which in those days was a prestigious Southern football school. To sweeten the suggestion, there also was an offer for a free ride, including tuition, books, room and board, and perhaps a few other goodies.

Harmon was inclined to simply ignore the telegram, but somehow the *Michigan Daily* got its hands on the wire, printed it, and then the pot began to boil. Boil? It began to overflow. Tempers at Ann Arbor flared and the word "piracy" was used to describe Tulane's tactics. And there was Tom Harmon, a mere freshman, the center of a national controversy that promised to blow the lid off college football. Tom may have given the offer a second thought or two, but he reacted publicly with class and style, announcing that he was remaining at Michigan. There were a few red faces in the athletic department at Tulane, naturally, but the whole affair soon blew over.

During spring practice Coach Crisler was faced with the decision of how to fit this hotshot sophomore-to-be, Harmon, into his single-wing backfield. He had Paul Kromer, who had been the tailback the year before—and a darned good one—so Crisler toyed with the idea of using Harmon as a blocking back. But he realized that would be like trying to hide the Hope diamond in a pile of costume jewelry at Woolworth's. Fritz finally decided to keep Kromer at left halfback and put Harmon at right half. That took care of his running game, but the intricate single wing, with its emphasis on timing and execution, required a spinning fullback who would handle the ball on almost every play, either handing off to the halfbacks on reverses or carrying it himself, and, most of all, a quarterback intelligent enough to call the plays, and big and strong enough to provide the super-blocking that would make the whole thing go. So, in a stroke of pure genius, Crisler conceived the idea of converting Evashevski, the big, tough kid from Hamtramck, from a center into a quarterback.

Out of these decisions by Fritz Crisler grew one of the most famous and devastating backfield combinations of all time. With

Evashevski serving as convoy—both on the field and off it—Tom Harmon swept down the glory road to heights hitherto achieved in the Big Ten only by Red Grange. In fact, before Harmon's illustrious career was over at Michigan he was to break several of Grange's conference records, including one "Old 77" cherished dearly—most touchdowns scored in a career.

But Harmon's breakneck dash to daylight was not without its internal problems. It didn't take long for Tom to become a superstar and, naturally, he captured the headlines in the national press. Lines like "Harmon A One-Man Team," "Harmon Greater Than Grange," and "Harmon Wins Again for Michigan," didn't do much to enhance his relations with the rest of the Wolverines who, in their own ways, were making it possible for him to become a superstar.

Harmon, however, was really the innocent victim of circumstances. He knew that his achievements depended upon his teammates and he went out of his way to give the other players credit for the part they played in his touchdown-making. He praised his blockers and pass-catchers, and paid tribute to the defense. But still the resentment was apparent.

Coach Crisler realized he had a problem but it was Evashevski, the strongman on the team and the acknowledged leader, who took direct action to quell what might have been a revolt of disastrous proportions. What Evy did was to try to minimize the situation by treating it with ironical humor. For example, once when the team was dressing for practice and Harmon arrived in the locker room, Evashevski said, "Here comes the team, men. We can practice now!"

Another time, Evy went around the locker room with a stack of dollar bills in his hand, passing them out and saying, "Here it is, men, your chance to join the world's most exclusive organization, the 'I Block For Tom Harmon Club,' and this dollar makes you a bona fide member." The other players went along with the gag, some grabbing the dollar bills and others refusing to "join the club."

Center Bob Ingalls also had a hand in trying to turn Harmon into a mere mortal. In one game Harmon waited impatiently for Ingalls to snap the ball back to him. Instead, Bob suddenly raised up and turned around with a huge grin on his face.

"What's so funny?" asked Harmon.

"I was just thinking," said Ingalls, "how foolish you'd look back there if I never snapped you the ball!"

Despite these obvious putdowns, which Harmon accepted good-naturedly and in the proper spirit, some of the players continued to resent the star treatment, however much it was deserved, that Tom got from sportswriters around the Big Ten and the nation. Yet, it must be pointed out that Harmon himself did nothing to foster this attitude. If anything, he tried very hard to dispel the notion that he and he alone was the Michigan football team. Tom tried to let his teammates know that his skills as a runner would have been diminished without the blocking furnished by Evashevski and the other players. Eventually his colleagues grew to accept the fact that they were playing with a true superstar who had talents that had not been seen in the Big Ten—or anywhere—since the days of Red Grange.

What Tom Harmon had was a combination of skills that were unmatched by anyone of his era. At six-foot one and 195 pounds, he had the strength to run the off-tackle play for first-down yardage, the speed to outrun defenders in the secondary, and the shiftiness and change of pace to sift his way through a broken field. Harmon, legs driving high, his straight arm bowling over tacklers, all coupled with an uncanny knack for shedding opponents, was a sight to behold, as many a Big Ten opponent had ruefully to admit. He had no equal as a runner, but what made him even more dangerous was his ability as a passer. While not quite as great in that department as Benny Friedman or Harry Newman, he could throw with amazing accuracy, and he did it often. And that was not the end of his extraordinary skills. Tom also was an excellent punter and place-kicker, could block efficiently enough when he had to, and was a superb defender.

Harmon fit into Crisler's intricate single wing like the proverbial well-worn glove. An authentic triple-threat, he was the ideal tailback and the player who turned Michigan's pussycats back into Wolverines. During Harmon's three years of varsity play Michigan lost only four games, three of them to Coach Bernie Bierman's Minnesota teams. However, despite Harmon's brilliance and Michigan's superb record, the Wolverines couldn't quite manage a Big Ten championship, a source of frustration to both Tom and his coach, Fritz Crisler. It seemed that every time Michigan was on the verge of winning it all, those pesky Gophers were there to spoil the party.

Tom Harmon didn't exactly burst onto the scene as a superstar in his sophomore year. In fact, he rode the bench during most of the first game against Michigan State, but he got his chance against

Chicago the next Saturday and promptly broke away for a 59-yard touchdown run. After that there was no doubt as to his status as a starter. It was readily apparent that he had all the skills to become a future All-America. One of his passes scored the only Michigan points in a 7–6 loss to Minnesota, his throwing helped throttle Yale, and then he turned in a spectacular performance against Illinois. In that game he sifted through a broken field for 17 yards and a touchdown, and heaved a 40-yard pass to Evashevski for another score in a 14–0 win.

But it was in his junior year that Tom Harmon really came into his own as an All-America. He was switched to tailback, where he really belonged in Crisler's single-wing attack, and he still had the dashing Evashevski to pave the way for him with his crushing blocks. Also, in Bob Westfall, a smallish but sturdy hometown boy from Ann Arbor, Crisler finally had the spinning fullback he needed to make his offense devastating. Westfall, although only a sophomore, became expert at handling the ball and he cracked the line with authority to complement the inside and outside running ability of Harmon and Kromer, now at right half.

With this kind of support in the backfield and a line that delighted in attacking opponents, Harmon quickly made believers out of every opponent he faced. He scored all of Michigan's twenty-seven points against Iowa, including one touchdown on a 90-yard run with an intercepted pass. When the accolades began to pour down on him for that achievement, Tom modestly announced, "Anyone could have done it with that Evashevski and those others in there blocking like that. They don't make them any better than that Evashevski."

Harmon's fame had already begun to spread across the country, but the East got a firsthand dose of his lethal talents when Michigan went up against Yale and Penn. The Elis found him unstoppable. When the long afternoon was over, Harmon had scored three touchdowns, the last on a 57-yard run, kicked three extra points, gained 203 of Michigan's 353 yards, and the Elis had been drubbed, 27–7. Penn was a little more difficult for the marauders from Ann Arbor and it took one of the most fantastic runs of any season by Harmon for the Wolverines to eke out a 19–17 victory. In this one Tom was going head-to-head with Francis X. Reagan, Penn's brilliant runner who had accumulated almost as many headlines in the East as Harmon had in the Midwest.

Harmon scored twice against Penn, but the touchdown that completely enthralled the fans—as well as the embattled Quakers—was a 73-yard run that some folks later referred to as an impossible journey. With the ball on the Michigan 27-yard line, Tom started off tackle and cut to the right sideline, where he was confronted by a trio of Penn tacklers. He ducked and dodged them, and then headed for the opposite side of the field. Again he was hemmed in by Penn defenders, so he simply reversed his field, headed for the right sideline, bowled over still another Quaker, and raced into the end zone to complete what was probably the longest—some people estimated he actually covered 150 yards—73-yard touchdown run ever seen.

"All I know," recalls Harmon, "is that the play started off tackle, the team made two sets of blocks, and I reversed the field three times."

Sounds simple, doesn't it?

The victories over the Ivy Leaguers were tasty morsels for the Wolverines, and especially for Crisler, who made a habit of beating Penn and Yale when he coached at Princeton. They also enhanced Harmon's national reputation, but in between those two games, Michigan suffered a pair of Big Ten defeats that knocked it out of the running for the Big Ten championship. First, Illinois, under the direction of canny Coach Bob Zuppke, upset the Wolves, 16–7, and then Minnesota, with Bruce Smith and George Franck outshining Harmon, bruised them, 20–7.

That brought Michigan down to its annual finale with hated rival Ohio State. The Buckeyes were unbeaten and already had the conference title clinched, but their pride was on the line when they went up against the Wolverines. It looked as if Michigan was going to be easy pickings when Ohio State romped to a 14–0 lead, but then Tom Harmon started to go to work. He scored a touchdown, passed to Evashevski for another, and kicked both extra points to draw the Wolverines into a 14–14 tie. Now it was a new ball game, and Ohio State Coach Francis X. Schmidt began pacing the sidelines nervously. He wondered what Tom Harmon and the wily Coach Crisler would come up with next.

Schmidt didn't have long to wait. With three minutes to go, fourth down, and the ball on the Ohio State 24-yard line, Michigan went into a field-goal formation with Harmon flexing his leg for the placement kick and Fred Trosko getting into position to kneel to hold the ball. Only Trosko didn't put his knee on the ground. As the Buckeye linemen came charging in to try to block the expected field-goal try, Trosko fielded the center snap, straightened up, and took off around right end. Amazingly enough, Harmon was even quicker getting there than Trosko. Tom wiped out a pair of Bucks with a crashing block and Trosko skipped blithely into the end zone for the touchdown that wrecked Ohio State's undefeated season, 21–14.

What Schmidt and Ohio State learned that day, much to their regret, was that Tom Harmon was more than just a great runner and passer. He was a complete football player. Tom's statistics were so impressive—956 yards and fourteen touchdowns rushing, thirty-seven pass completions for 543 yards and six scores, fifteen points after touchdown, and one field goal, and he led the country in scoring with 112 points—that there was no doubt that he was an authentic All-America. Maybe even the best football player in the land!

Harmon's devastating running style even awed his own teammates. In the Northwestern game, one of the Michigan linemen leaned across the scrimmage line and confided to his opponent, "I don't mind telling you, we've just called Harmon's signal over your position. I don't know what you're gonna do, but I'm gonna get the hell out of here!"

If there had ever been any doubt as to Harmon's multiple talents, they were dispelled in the opening game of the 1940 season when he put on one of his greatest exhibitions against the University of California in Berkeley. The fact that that day, September 28, also happened to be Tom's twenty-first birthday made his performance that Saturday even more significant for him.

Harmon began his celebration on the very first play of the game, when he took the opening kickoff and ran it back 94 yards for a touchdown. Before that beautiful afternoon ended, Tom had scored three more times, on a 72-yard punt return, an 86-yard run, and an 8-yard dash, and had thrown a pass to little Dave Nelson for a fifth score as Michigan rolled over the beleaguered Bears, 41–0. It was truly a performance worthy of an All-America.

However, at least one California fan didn't appreciate Harmon's brilliant show. Bud Brennan, a local realtor, decided that his heroes needed some help if they were ever to stop Harmon. So when Tom was pretty-stepping his way through California defenders on his 86-yard run, Brennan leaped out of the stands and onto the field. He made a frantic effort to tackle Harmon on the 3-yard line but Tom nonchalantly sidestepped him and went in for the touchdown.

"It was most embarrassing," Tom said after the game. "Think how I would have felt after slipping past eleven well-conditioned athletes to be downed by a woozy alum."

Oddly enough that little incident grew into a lasting friendship. After the game a sheepish Brennan visited the Michigan dressing room for a more formal introduction to Harmon. For years later, the two unlikely football field protagonists visited with each other whenever their paths crossed in Berkeley and Los Angeles.

The Cal game got Tom off and running to a spectacular last season. He scored all of Michigan's points in a 21–14 win over Michigan State; ran for three touchdowns and passed for a fourth in a 26–0 victory over a good Harvard team which was headed up by Chub Peabody, an All-America guard who was later to become governor of Massachusetts; he ran for one touchdown, passed for a second, and kicked a field goal in a 28–0 trouncing of Illinois; and he scored all of the Wolverines' points in a 14–0 win over Pennsylvania. Harmon had the Wolves rolling and seemingly headed for the Big Ten title and possibly the national championship.

Then came the annual clash with Minnesota and, with it, the usual result, a 7–6 loss for Michigan. Both teams went into the game unbeaten and it developed into a personal duel between Harmon and Minnesota's brilliant Bruce Smith. A muddy field hampered the running activities of both men and Harmon never did get away on one of his by-now patented touchdown dashes. The best Tom could do was a pass to Evashevski for a touchdown and then he missed the extra point. Smith, however, broke loose in the muck for an 80-yard touchdown run and sub halfback Joe Mernik kicked the winning extra point, giving the Gophers both the Big Ten title and the national championship.

It was the only real frustration of Tom Harmon's college football life that he never scored a touchdown against Minnesota and his teams had never been able to beat the Gophers. Years later that loss to Minnesota still nagged at Harmon.

"We had a great team," he insisted. "We thought we were the greatest. Minnesota was a real good club, maybe a great club, too, but on that day no one will ever know. It was the worst slop I've ever seen in my lifetime around football. It poured like maybe they turned Lake Michigan upside down on the stadium.

"We were inside their ten-yard line four or five times. Once there was a six-foot hole from two yards out with two men in front of me. I cut for it and went right on my butt on the four. It was just impossible. Nothing in my life has been more frustrating."

Despite that disappointing loss to Minnesota, there was more than just the usual spotlight on Tom Harmon. He had scored twenty-nine touchdowns in his career and was zeroing in on Red Grange's record of thirty-one with two games left in which to do it.

Perhaps in anticipation, Red Grange was in the stands when Michigan went up against Northwestern in Evanston. Harmon didn't disappoint the old redhead. He scored once to help beat Northwestern, 20–13, and now he had thirty touchdowns.

Fittingly enough, Harmon's last chance was to come against Ohio State, Michigan's oldest and bitterest rival, and on the same Ohio Stadium field where the great Grange had ended his college career fifteen years earlier. With the usual 75,000 Ohio State partisans jammed into the huge stadium, along with a few handfuls of Michigan adherents, it was a perfect setting for what was to happen that Saturday afternoon, despite the rain and a muddy field.

Tom didn't wait very long to provide the first thrill of the day. In the opening quarter, he smashed off tackle from the 8-yard line and plummeted into the OSU end zone to tie Grange's record. Then he threw a touchdown pass to Evashevski and another one to Ed Frutig. The score was mounting, but the fans were still waiting for the big moment.

Suddenly, late in the third quarter, it came. With the ball on the Ohio State 18-yard line after a pass interception, Tom started out wide, cut back over tackle through a gaping hole opened by his efficient crew of blockers, bowled over a linebacker, and outran the secondary on his way to the end zone. A magnificent roar erupted from the large crowd as even the rabid Buckeye rooters voiced their approval. Harmon had his thirty-second touchdown and now Red Grange's old record was only a dim memory.

There was more to come, too. Just to add some icing to the cake, Harmon scored stilll another touchdown late in the fourth quarter, romping over from the 6-yard line after faking a pass to complete a 40–0 trouncing of the hated Buckeyes. That last touchdown also made him the nation's leading scorer, with 117 points, to become the first player to win the scoring title two times.

"I'll never forget the scene after the game," says Tom. "It was like a madhouse. People were stampeding past the guards, climbing

Alvin Nugent (Bo) McMillin coached Indiana to its first Big Ten football championship in 1945.

Possibly the best triple-threat back in Indiana history, Billy Hillenbrand was a 1942 All-America.

LEFT: Known as "Harmon's Blocker" in playing days at Michigan, Forest Evashevski became one of football's most controversial coaches as Iowa mentor, 1952–1960. RIGHT: Evashevski puts his arm around one of Big Ten's best guards in the fifties, Calvin Jones, who was killed some years later in a plane crash.

LEFT: Aubrey Devine, quarterback of Iowa, 1919–1921, played with his brother, Glenn, in Hawkeye backfield during Golden Era of Iowa football. RIGHT: Duke Slater, the rugged tackle on the mighty 1921 Iowa team, played without a helmet.

Nile Kinnick goes in for touchdown against Notre Dame in 1939. Moments later he kicked the extra point in 7–6 Hawkeye triumph over Irish. Kinnick was killed during World War II.

LEFT: Ozzie Simmons of Iowa was first black Big Ten back to become an All-America. RIGHT: Alex Karras, best Iowa tackle since Duke Slater, playing for Hawkeyes in mid fifties.

ABOVE, LEFT: Clarence (Biggie) Munn, head coach and then athletic director at Michigan State, coached the Spartans when they were admitted into Big Ten in 1949. ABOVE: Duffy Daugherty, Michigan State coach, on sidelines during 1966 game against Notre Dame—a battle for No. 1 in nation that ended in a 10–10 tie.

Michigan State's All-America halfback, Sonny Grandelius, who played for Biggie Munn, 1948–1950.

Undefeated and untied national championship 1952 Michigan State team. Spartans, although admitted to Big Ten in 1949, were not permitted to compete for league football title until 1953.

Gene Washington (84), All-America end at Michigan State in 1965 and 1966, making leaping catch—his specialty.

ABOVE, LEFT: Michigan State retired George Webster's number, 90, after his brilliant career as linebacker, 1964–1966. ABOVE, RIGHT: "Kill, Bubba! Kill, Bubba!" was the cry from fans during Bubba Smith's playing days as defensive tackle and end with Spartans, 1964–1966. BELOW: Big Ten and national championship Michigan State team of 1965. Coach Duffy Daugherty is at right end of back row.

LEFT: Dr. Henry L. Williams, first full-time football coach at Minnesota, held the job from 1900 through 1921. RIGHT: Golden Gophers' most famous coach was Bernie Bierman, 1932–1941 and 1945–1950. Minnesota dominated Big Ten in Bierman's first stint.

RIGHT: Bronko Nagurski signed with Chicago Bears after his senior season in 1929. Following his pro career Nagurski returned to his hometown, International Falls, Minnesota, where he ran his own gas station (left).

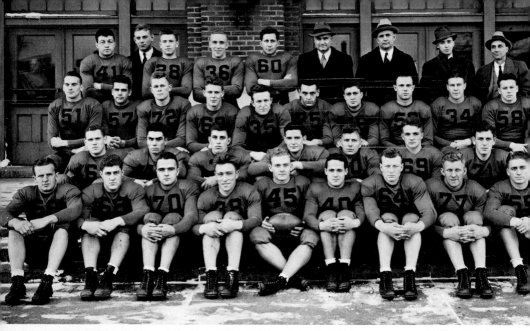

Bernie Bierman's undefeated national championship Minnesota team of 1934. Coach Bierman is fourth from right, back row. Bud Wilkinson is fourth from left, third row.

ABOVE, LEFT: Bud Wilkinson was converted from back to guard by Bernie Bierman at Minnesota and later became one of the most successful coaches in history at Oklahoma. ABOVE, RIGHT: Ed Widseth was just a sophomore tackle on the mighty 1934 Minnesota team that some still consider to be the greatest college team ever assembled. RIGHT: Bruce Smith, Minnesota halfback, won 1941 Heisman Trophy.

Lynn (Pappy) Waldorf began a long and successful career as coach and then athletic director at Northwestern in 1934.

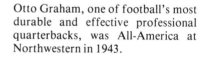

Alex Agase succeeded Ara Parseghian as Northwestern coach in 1965 and then moved to Purdue where things never worked out too well.

Otto Graham, one of football's most durable and effective professional quarterbacks, was All-America at Northwestern in 1943.

Noble Kizer, one of Notre Dame's guards, became Purdue football coach in 1930.

Jack Mollenkopf, Boilermakers' coach, 1956–1969, shown here on way to Rose Bowl after 1967 season. (*Bob Mitchell, St. Joe, Mich.*)

It can't happen now. But Elmer Oliphant played seven varsity seasons of football (1911–1913 at Purdue and 1914–1917 at Army) as a halfback and earned record total of twenty-four letters in seven sports.

Purdue's Ralph Welch, star running back from Texas, earned the nickname "Pest." (*Photograph by J. C. Allen and Son*)

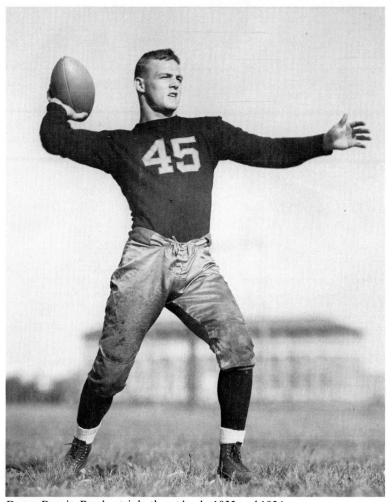

Duane Purvis, Purdue triple-threat back, 1933 and 1934.

RIGHT: Boilermakers' Leroy Keyes was outstanding back and Heisman candidate in sixties.

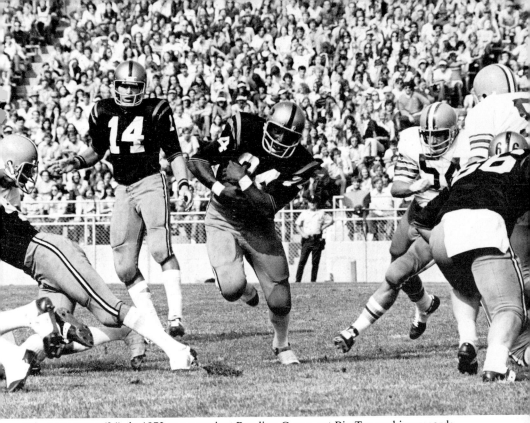

Otis Armstrong (24), in 1972 game against Bowling Green, set Big Ten rushing records for Purdue. (*Photograph by Wayne Doebling*)

Pat O'Dea, an Australian, became famous drop kicker and back for Wisconsin at turn of century. He booted a 60-yard field goal drop kick on the run against Minnesota in 1899.

Wisconsin's Alan (The Horse) Ameche was one of Big Ten's greatest fullbacks. The 1954 Heisman Trophy winner went on to become one of the many heroes of the Baltimore Colts N.F.L. championship teams.

LEFT: Another of Purdue's modern stars who just missed getting Heisman Trophy was Quarterback Bob Griese, who went on to more fame with the championship Miami Dolphins.

Undefeated 1912 Wisconsin team rates as one of the best in college football history. Coach Bill Juneau is first on left in front row.

over the high iron fences leading to the backdoor of the locker room, and even pushing past the cops at the door of the dressing room."

Some members of that crowd trying to get to Tom Harmon were simply fans who wanted his autograph. Others, however, were promoters and fast-buck artists who wanted Tom's name on contracts for testimonials, merchandise, and almost everything under the sun. A fortune was Tom Harmon's for the mere asking, as it had been available to Red Grange years before, but the Michigan star wasn't having any of it. Then came the awards—the Heisman Trophy, Associated Press Athlete of the Year, and numerous others of lesser importance—and a swing on the banquet circuit. There also was an offer to play pro football, a natural outlet for the nation's No. 1 college football player. George Halas of the Chicago Bears, who secured the draft rights to Harmon, dangled a lot of greenbacks before Tom's eyes—but he turned them down.

It was all fitting for a young man who had closed out a brilliant career with such an imposing array of statistics. In twenty-four games, Tom Harmon had carried the ball 398 times for 2,134 yards and 33 touchdowns. He had completed 101 of 233 passes for 1,304 yards and seventeen touchdowns, and had scored a grand total of 237 points on thirty-three touchdowns, 33 extra points, and 2 field goals.

There were many accolades, of course, but one of the most fitting was written by the late H. G. Salsinger, the honored sports editor of the *Detroit News*, who had covered every game in which Tom Harmon played. Salsinger wrote, "Harmon is one of the few who has come up in the last four decades who can truly be called great without abusing a much-abused adjective."

There were many avenues open to Tom Harmon after his graduation from Michigan in 1941, but he had his heart set on a future in radio and television as a sportscaster. However, a lot was to happen to him before he finally got around to his ultimate career. First, Tom went to Hollywood and made a movie called *Harmon of Michigan.*

"It was the biggest bomb I've ever seen," said Harmon. "The only thing honest in it was Bill Henry's introduction and the film clips from our Michigan games."

Tom also played a couple more football games, the East-West Shrine Game in San Francisco and the College All-Star classic in Chicago, before he became sports director of a Detroit radio station. But just as he was beginning to get settled in sportscasting, the rumblings of World War II were becoming more persistent and he enlisted in the Army Air Force as an air cadet barely a month before Pearl Harbor.

The headlines weren't over for Tom Harmon. Less than two years later, in April 1943, came the disturbing news that Lieutenant Tom Harmon, a bomber pilot on submarine patrol over the South American coast, was missing. His plane—appropriately named *Old 98–Little Butch*—had gone down in a rainstorm along with the entire five-man crew.

For a whole week there was no news. Then one day, a gaunt, ghostly figure, covered with cuts, bruises, and sores, stumbled out of the jungle and into an army camp. Harmon, after wandering through the steaming, snake-infested jungle for days, had come across some natives, who obligingly led him to the U.S. base. Tom survived the ordeal in rather good shape, which he attributed to his experiences as a football player. The other crew members were never found.

Tom then switched to flying pursuit planes in North Africa and volunteered to join a group of twenty-five fighter pilots who were being assigned to General Claire Chennault's Flying Tigers in China. He got his share of Zeroes, but on November 30, 1943 came another headline. Tom Harmon was missing in action again. His plane had been shot down by the Japanese in a dogfight over Yangtze in China.

This time it took Harmon thirty-two days to achieve another miracle. Again, he wandered through the jungle before he met up with a band of friendly Chinese guerrilla fighters who smuggled him back to an Allied base.

"I knew the Japanese used chutes for target practice," said Tom, "so I tried to play dead. When I finally hit the ground, there were bullet holes in my parachute."

By the time Harmon was discharged in August 1945, he was a captain and had been awarded the Silver Star and Purple Heart. However, one thing that he treasured almost as much as his awards was a telegram he had received from former teammate Forest Evashevski after he shot down his second Zero.

"Congratulations on your victory, but how did you ever do it without me?" wired his old blocker.

Meanwhile, a year before his discharge, Tom had married Elyse Knox, a beautiful Hollywood star he had been introduced to by actor Alan Mowbray back in 1941 while on a junket to California. Their marriage produced three children, including Thomas Mark, who achieved some football fame of his own as an outstanding Wishbone quarterback at UCLA in the early 1970s.

Pressed for money after his discharge, Harmon had a brief fling at pro football with the Los Angeles Rams, who had traded Dante Magnani and Fred Davis to the Chicago Bears for the draft rights to Tom. He signed for $20,000 a year, big money in those days even for a former All-America halfback. However, he never was quite the runner he had been at Michigan. War injuries had slowed down Tom's once-churning legs and, after two seasons (1946 and 1947), he quit to make his career in radio and television sportscasting. But Harmon's short pro career wasn't a complete bust. He scored nine touchdowns and piled up 547 yards rushing in eighty-one attempts, an average of nearly 7 yards a carry.

Like he did everything else, Tom Harmon worked hard at becoming a good sportscaster and he rose rapidly in his chosen profession to become one of the most respected announcers in the business, covering all of the big events, including college and pro football games and several Olympics.

"Old 98" is still an All-America.

While few players, at Michigan or anywhere else, achieved the fame that Tom Harmon did, the Wolverines have had more than their share of great backfield stars since "Old 98" wreaked his havoc in the late thirties and 1940.

Bob Chappuis, a limber-hipped runner and pinpoint passer, was Michigan's next triple-threat All-America although it took him a little while to get there. Bob's career at Michigan spanned six years, from 1942 through the 1947 season, with time off for military service. Although he was Michigan's bread-and-butter runner and passer in 1942 and then, when he returned from service, again in 1946, Chappuis really didn't hit his peak until the 1947 season. That's when he led what may have been one of Michigan's greatest teams to an unbeaten season and the national championship.

The most talented passer to show up at Michigan since Benny Friedman and Harry Newman, Chappuis had the added advantage of being a superb runner. The opposition never knew whether to expect a run or a pass when Bob got his hands on the ball. What they got in 1947 was a lot of both. Chappuis ran for 1,019 yards and passed for another 665, with thirteen of his tosses going for touchdowns, still a single-season Michigan record. Over three years of varsity competition, the elusive Chappuis piled up 3,458 yards in total offense and threw for twenty-three touchdowns, another Wolverine record that has survived through the years.

Complementing Chappuis and his exceptional talents was one of the greatest brother combinations in Big Ten history—the Elliotts, Chalmers (Bump) and Pete. They had been brought up on a sports diet by their father, Norman, a young doctor who had coached basketball at Northwestern back in 1918, and it was a happy day for Coach Fritz Crisler when the Elliott brothers both decided to attend Michigan.

Bump arrived at Ann Arbor in 1944, Pete a year later, and they left an indelible mark on not only Michigan football but football in the Big Ten. Bump, a brilliant runner and pass-catcher, hit his peak in 1947 as a member of one of the finest backfields ever in the conference, along with Chappuis, quarterback Howard Yerges, the son of an old Ohio State quarterback, and fullback Jack Weisenburger. Bump was the solid man of that crew on both offense and defense. He had a knack for coming up with the big plays. Perhaps his greatest individual effort came against Illinois in 1947. That was the day he returned one of Dyke Eddlemann's booming punts 74 yards for a touchdown and then teamed up with Chappuis on a 52-yard pass play to the Illini 4-yard line that set up the winning touchdown.

While Chappuis captured the headlines for his offensive exploits, Bump earned the plaudits of everyone for his all-around play. Bump scored ten touchdowns and he, not Chappuis, was voted the Big Ten's Most Valuable Player. Also, along with Chappuis, Elliott was named to practically every All-America team.

Brother Pete arrived at Michigan a year after Bump, in 1945, and was immediately eligible for football—and basketball and golf—under wartime regulations then in effect. Like his brother, Pete was a two-way player and he broke into the starting lineup as a freshman. In fact, he led the Wolverines in passing (he threw for three touchdowns in a 27–13 win over Purdue) and total offense that first season. But, for the next two years, his efforts were mostly confined to defense and he became one of the conference's top cornerbacks.

However, when the 1948 season rolled around, Brother Bump, Chappuis, and Weisenburger were gone, and Coach Crisler also had called it a day, moving into the athletic director's chair. Bennie

Oosterbaan became the head coach and one of his first moves was to install Pete at quarterback. Although he ran the Michigan offense with a talented hand—indeed, he led the Wolves to another unbeaten season and the national championship—the versatile Pete still performed double duty as a defensive back and played so well at both positions that he was picked for All-America. It was one of the few times in football history that a pair of brothers were named All-America back-to-back.

By the time Pete finished his athletic career at Ann Arbor, he had become the only twelve-letter man ever at Michigan. No wonder Oosterbaan and his fellow basketball and golf coaches shed a tear or two when he departed!

After their football-playing days at Michigan, the Elliotts went on to become the first set of brothers to coach Big Ten teams, Bump for ten seasons at Michigan before he became athletic director at Iowa, and Pete for seven years at Illinois before he unwittingly got swept up in a recruiting scandal that cost him his job. Both also took teams to the Rose Bowl, where they had played for Michigan in 1947. After several years out of college athletics, Pete became assistant athletic director under Ernie McCoy at the University of Miami in Florida, and, in 1973, the head football coach.

Still boyish-looking despite his years, Pete bubbled over with enthusiasm over being back in coaching. "I love it," he said. "It's like being reborn."

Two years later, Elliott was out of coaching again, but this time to take over as athletic director at Miami.

It took almost two decades for another backfield superstar to come along at Michigan, but it was almost worth waiting for Ron Johnson, later the workhorse halfback star of the New York Giants, to arrive. Johnson, a sturdy, slinky-type runner with graceful moves, was the chief gunner in Coach Bump Elliott's offense in 1967. The Wolverines weren't beating many folks that year, but Johnson was busy piling up 1,005 yards rushing. That, however, proved to be just a whetting of the appetite for what Ron was to accomplish in 1968.

As it turned out, 1968 was to be Coach Elliott's last year at the helm of the Wolverines, and Johnson helped to make Bump's last hurrah a memorable one. Ron smashed through enemy defenses for 1,391 yards, a new single-season record, along the way breaking two of Tom Harmon's Michigan marks—2,440 yards rushing for a career and nineteen touchdowns for a season—as the Wolverines went down to the final game before losing out to Ohio State for the Big Ten title. Johnson also came within a single point of tying Harmon's single-season scoring record of 117 points. In one game, a 34–9 win over Wisconsin, Johnson rushed for an unbelievable 347 yards.

Ron Johnson's bull-lugging record, however, lasted only until Billy Taylor, his successor as the Wolves' running back, came upon the scene. Taylor, a similar type of runner, was made to order for new Coach Glenn (Bo) Schembechler's landlocked offense. Ramming inside and outside the tackles with an occasional foray to the outside, Billy smashed away for 864 yards in 1969, 911 in 1970, and 1,299 in 1971, a total of 3,072 for his three-year career. Gordon Bell and Rob Lytle, a pair of sprightly halfbacks, enlivened things in 1974 and 1975. Bell ran for 1,388 yards and thirteen touchdowns in 1975, while Lytle, a junior then, romped for 1,040 yards.

For Lytle—and his teammates—1976 was an even more exciting year. A compact six-foot one-inch 195-pounder with 9.5 speed for 100 yards, Lytle had power and an assortment of moves to go with his swiftness. He was equally at home at tailback and fullback as he led the Wolverines to one of their finest seasons and a place in the Rose Bowl. Lytle ran for 1,402 yards to bring his career total to 3,250, breaking Taylor's school record. Along the way he also averaged 6.9 yards per carry to surpass a mark held by Tom Harmon for thirty-six years. These efforts earned him a berth on almost every major All-America team.

Lytle wasn't Michigan's only 1976 All-America. Wingback Jim Smith, guard Mark Donahue, and linebacker Calvin O'Neal also achieved that status, while quarterback Ricky Leach and tackle Greg Morton were among others who starred for the Wolverines.

While the passers and the ball carriers basked in the glory, there also was more than enough to go around for a marvelous collection of line stars during the Harmon to Taylor years at Michigan. They were the ones who supplied the juice for the electrifying exploits of the backs—All-America ends like Dick Rifenberger in 1948, Lowell Perry in 1951, Ron Kramer in 1955 and 1956, John Clancy in 1966, and Jim Mandich in 1969. And super-tackles like Alvin Wistert in 1948 and 1949, the last of the All-America brother trio; Allen Wolf in 1949 and 1950; Arthur Walker in 1954; Bill Yearby in 1964 and 1965; Don Dierdorf in 1970; and Paul Seymour in 1972.

There have been others, too—that incomparable trio of guards, Julius Franks in 1942, Henry Hill in 1970, and Reggie McKenzie in 1971 (the same Reggie McKenzie that O. J. Simpson of the Buffalo Bills called "my main man" in the Bills' offensive line that opened up enough gaping holes for the former University of Southern California star to set a new National Football League rushing record in 1973). And linebackers Marty Huff in 1970 and Mike Taylor in 1971; and defensive back Don Dufek in 1975.

All-Americas all, they have helped to make Michigan's football tradition a glorious interlude in the university's long history.

TWENTY-ONE

Ollie, Pest, and Friends

When old Purdue grads gather for Homecoming in West La-
fayette, Indiana, these days, they drop a lot of names—like Alex
Yunevich, Elmer Sleight, Cecil Isbell, Ralph (Pest) Welch, Duane
Purvis, Len Dawson, Bob DeMoss, Leroy Keyes, Bob Griese,
Mike Phipps, Otis Armstrong—but the one the real oldtimers like
to drop most fondly is Elmer Oliphant, a name that has faded with
the passing of time but is still, nevertheless, one of the greatest in
Purdue football history.

Actually, Oliphant is claimed by two schools, and each can claim
him with equal rights. After playing for Purdue for three years, Ollie received an appointment to the United States Military Academy
and put in four more varsity years as the star of the Army team. It
was common practice and perfectly legal in those days, and most
West Point players had seen prior service at another college. Although he was generally recognized as one of the better players in
the country while performing for the Boilermakers, oddly enough
Oliphant did not receive All-America honors until 1916, his third
year at Army. That may sound peculiar, but you must remember
that in the early 1900s the two foremost All-America selectors,
Caspar Whitney and Walter Camp, were based in the East and generally thought that college football began and ended on Eastern
campuses.

A product of the coal mines of southern Indiana, where he had
worked at the tender age of fourteen, Oliphant came to Purdue in
1910 practically unheralded and proceeded to become one of the
finest all-around athletes ever to come out of the Big Ten. While
football was Ollie's forte, it was by no means the only sport in
which he excelled. He starred on the baseball and basketball

teams, and was a world-class sprinter and hurdler in track. At one point in his career at Purdue, Oliphant set a world record for the low hurdles on turf. By the time he was graduated from Purdue, Ollie had accumulated nine letters in four sports.

Oliphant's exploits at Army were even more incredible. In his four years at West Point he earned letters in football, basketball, and baseball, captained a team in each of those sports, also captained the hockey team, won a letter in swimming, broke the school record for the 220-yard hurdles, and captured the Academy's heavyweight boxing championship although he weighed only 178 pounds at the time. All told, he added fifteen more varsity letters to the nine he had won at Purdue.

Hardly more than a stripling—he weighed a mere 145 pounds—when he showed up at Purdue, Oliphant managed to pack 178 pounds onto his stocky five-foot eight body before he finished making history for the Boilermakers, even though he had to work himself to the bone to afford to stay in school. At various times he held down several jobs at once, but he still managed to play a sport in every season. And how he played them!

A superb runner, Oliphant was so tough to bring down that it was a fairly common sight to see him dragging several tacklers for five or ten yards before he was stopped. He also had great speed, the kind that permitted him to outrun folks, sometimes even his own blockers, on sweeps. His stock in trade in an open field was a crackling stiff-arm that brought up short many a would-be tackler. Then there was his kicking—both punting and dropkicking—which won many a game for the Boilermakers.

Oldtimers like to tell about the time that Ollie kicked a field goal against Illinois with a broken ankle, how he scored five touchdowns and booted thirteen out of thirteen extra point attempts for forty-three points in a 91–0 rout of Rose Poly in 1912, or how he ran through four Wisconsin tacklers and then shook off two more on a 32-yard touchdown run that earned Purdue a 7–7 tie with Wisconsin in 1913.

The late Harry Grayson, a sports writer for NEA, was so impressed by Oliphant's performance in that Wisconsin game that he wrote, "Badger rooters used to wake up screaming, nightmared by a herd of pink Oliphants."

A true measure of what Elmer Oliphant meant to Purdue football is the improvement that took place during his three-year varsity tenure. The Boilermakers had been down, having won only a total of seven games in five years, when Elmer appeared on the West Lafayette scene. In 1911, Ollie's first varsity season, the Boilermakers managed a 3–4 record, beating Indiana for their only Big Ten victory. In 1912 Purdue was 4–2–1, beating Northwestern and Indiana, and tying Illinois. Then, in 1913, the record went to 4–1–2, the only loss coming at the hands of Chicago, 6–0, while the Boilermakers beat Wabash, Northwestern, Rose Poly, and Indiana, and played ties with Wisconsin and Illinois. Actually, the 1913 Purdue team was the best to represent the school since 1897. Ollie had turned around the Purdue football program almost singlehanded. How much he meant to the Boilermakers is evident in the fact that only a year after he left they were back in the doldrums.

As great as Oliphant was at Purdue, he was even greater when he played for Army. More mature, and certainly more experienced after three years in the Big Ten, he was so devastating that even his own teammates were happy to stay out of his way when he carried the ball.

"The thing we fear most," said one Army lineman, "is Ollie, with those churning legs of his, running up our backs if we don't charge fast enough."

It was fourteen more years before another superstar appeared at Purdue and then a trio of them came along about the same time— Ralph (Pest) Welch, Elmer Sleight, and Alex Yunevich—and the Boilermakers suddenly began to make the kind of threatening gestures toward the rest of the Big Ten that they hadn't made in years.

Welch, the most spectacular of the threesome and fresh out of Sherman, Texas, a little town due north of Dallas, brought his nickname, Pest, along with him. He explained, "I was always playing with older guys. . . . I was about fourteen at the time and I always wanted to wrestle. The older guys would say, 'You're the darndest pest we've ever seen.' The name stuck ever since."

The Pest burst upon the Purdue scene like a comet in 1927. He did not play in Purdue's opener, a 15–0 win over Depauw, and there was a good reason for it. Coach Jimmy Phelan was saving his sophomore find for Harvard, the next week's opponent and one of the nation's top teams. He hoped to sneak up on the Ivy Leaguers with Welch, and he did.

The Easterners never suspected that Phelan had a secret weapon he would unleash against them. But the Pest was there and he proved to be just what his nickname implied as far as Harvard was concerned. Welch scored on a 3-yard run, passed to Leon Hutton for 40 yards and a touchdown, then ran 13 yards for a third score after Bud Hook blocked a Harvard punt, and Purdue romped off with a 19–0 victory. It was a devastating blow to Harvard's pride and the beginning of a career that was to blossom into one of the brightest in Purdue's long football history.

However, Welch's first year wasn't all peaches and cream. The next week, against Chicago, Ralph fumbled on the second play from scrimmage, on his own 8-yard line. Chicago quickly converted that golden opportunity into a touchdown and Purdue eventually lost to the Maroons, 7–6, for one of its two defeats that year.

For the rest of that year and the next two seasons, 1928 and 1929, Pest Welch proved to be the blood and guts of the Purdue team. A true triple-threat halfback, he ran, he passed, he kicked, he played defense, and he was the rallying point for the entire Boilermaker squad.

Perhaps one of Welch's finest efforts came against Michigan in the second game of the 1929 season, which turned out to be the most successful in Purdue's long football history. Purdue hadn't beaten Michigan since 1892 and the Wolverines were favored to win handily. There didn't seem to be much doubt about the final result when Michigan led, 16–6, at the end of the third quarter. The mighty Wolverines were patting themselves on the back, satisfied that they had the game in the bag. But they failed to reckon with the Pest.

That last quarter was wild and woolly as Welch led a Purdue comeback that produced twenty-four points and a 30–16 victory. The Pest turned on all his brilliance, tearing off runs that Michigan couldn't stop and scoring twice against the helpless Wolves from Ann Arbor. It was a magnificent individual performance, and that game triggered Purdue's first undefeated season since 1892 and the Boilermakers' first Big Ten title.

Although Welch was the ringleader of the Purdue title-bound circus, he also had plenty of offensive help that year from quarterback John White, the field general and prime blocker; Glen Harmeson, who excelled at both running and passing; and Yunevich, a sophomore fullback who loved to pound into the line. Sportswriters of the day, taking their cue from Notre Dame's "Four Horsemen," called them the "Four Riveters." All together, this foursome averaged 4.5 yards per carry as they pounded their Big Ten rivals into submission.

That 1929 team had only one close call as it rolled up 187 points while holding the opposition to 44. Iowa gave the Boilermakers a hard time in the next-to-the-last game on the schedule. Going into the last quarter, the two teams were locked in a scoreless duel until Harmeson's 18-yard touchdown pass to little Bill Woerner broke the deadlock and provided Purdue with a 7–0 victory. Then, in the finale, Indiana fell, 32–0, and the Boilermakers had their undefeated 8–0 season and the Big Ten title.

Naturally the "Four Riveters" didn't do it alone. They had help from the guys up front who opened up the holes for them and held opposing teams to a mere four touchdowns on defense. The star of this group was Elmer (Red) Sleight (pronounced Slate), a six-foot two-and-a-half-inch, 225-pound tackle who specialized in banging heads, something he did so well for three years that he, along with Welch, was named to the All-America team in 1929, the first Purdue lineman ever to achieve that honor.

Although Sleight wasn't big for a tackle by today's standards, he was large enough to raise hell with anyone who got in his way on either offense or defense, and he did so often enough that opposing teams tried to steer clear of him whenever possible.

Sam Voinoff, one of Sleight's teammates, once said, "Red was a leader, but he led by actions rather than words . . . he wasn't a rah-rah guy, but more reserved. He was a real hard-nosed football player who was extremely quick and hard to knock down."

Sleight went on to play a couple of years with the Green Bay Packers and then served as a line coach at Missouri and Lehigh. Welch, of course, followed his old coach, Jimmy Phelan, to the University of Washington as an assistant for twelve years, and then became the head coach for six seasons before he retired from coaching to establish an insurance agency. Yunevich, the precocious sophomore of that 1929 team, starred for Purdue for two more seasons and, from 1939 until he retired at the end of the 1976 season, was the head coach at little Alfred University in New York. His thirty-six-year record was 177–85–12.

Since Pest Welch, Purdue has had a profusion of great running backs who earned All-America honors. First there was Duane Purvis, an imaginative tailback who terrorized Big Ten defenses in 1932, 1933, and 1934 with his brilliant running, passing and pass-catching. Purvis, whose brother Jim had played the same position for Purdue the previous three years, teamed up with Jim Carter to give the Boilermakers a high-powered offense. They also nearly gave Coach Noble Kizer a heart attack in their first season.

Purdue was playing Minnesota and, before the game, Purvis and Carter dreamed up a little play of their own that they would work on the opening kickoff. It went like this: whichever one got the ball would head for the nearest sideline and the other would casually drift to the opposite side of the field. Then, when all those Golden Gophers headed for the ball-carrier, he would simply pass the ball across the field to his teammate, who would surely run for a touchdown. And they would be instant heroes.

"I carried out my part of the bargain," Purvis recalls. "I caught the kickoff and just as I was about to be tackled, I turned to throw a pass to Carter across the field. To my horror, there was a big Gopher right in front of Jim. It was too late to hold back on the pass, so I let it go. By the grace of a kind providence, Carter caught it even though he was downed in his tracks."

"Where the hell did you dig up that one," Kizer demanded when they returned to the bench.

"Why, we saw it work in high school and figured . . ."

"This is not high school, " raged Kizer. "Remember that!"

Purvis remembered alright, but maybe he wondered about a play that Coach Kizer sprang on Chicago that same year. Purdue was leading the Maroons, 30–0, with a minute to play when suddenly Kizer put his varsity back into the game with instructions to pull off "the play." The backfield shifted left, the pass from center went to quarterback Paul Pardonner who handed off to Fred Hecker, coming around from his flanker position. Hecker then lateraled to Purvis, who started dropping back toward his own goal line. Meanwhile, end Paul Moss was streaking downfield. Finally, when Purvis was back to his own 15-yard line, he let fly with a beautiful spiral that Moss pulled in on the Chicago 10-yard line and then carried the ball in for a touchdown. Purvis' pass had traveled 75 yards in the air.

"It was a great play," recalls Purvis, "but the funny thing is that Chicago used the same play against us the next year and scored."

Purvis went on to electrify the Big Ten with his daring running and passing, and became a two-time All-America halfback in 1933 and 1934. Duane was also a javelin thrower on the track team, and won a national championship in the event for Purdue.

Then, in 1935, along came Cecil Isbell, a splendid runner and passer who played for three years with an unusual handicap. In Isbell's very first game against Northwestern he dislocated his left shoulder, and for three seasons Cecil was forced to play with his left arm held by a chain device so it could not be raised above his

shoulder. Despite this, Isbell was one of the top runners and passers in the country. Although he never received All-America recognition, he starred for the Green Bay Packers before coming back to
coach his alma mater in 1944, 1945, and 1946.

Then there was Leroy Keyes, who some folks around West Lafayette think was the greatest Boilermaker of all time. Leroy came
along in 1966 and for three years proceeded to enchant Purdue fans
as well as the rest of the country with both his offensive and defensive pyrotechnics. He was superb at both, and it was a tribute to
his tremendous ability that Coach Jack Mollenkopf, after using Leroy almost exclusively on defense in his sophomore year, switched
him to offense in 1967, but also used him on defense in critical situations. And this was at a time when two-platoon football was the
style. There were very few college football players anywhere who
had the skills to play both offense and defense.

Keyes had the unusual knack of finding holes where
there weren't any and then squiggling through the narrowest opening to burst into the secondary. Leroy also had moves that would
have made a burlesque queen turn green with envy. Once he got
into the open, the opposing secondary was usually at his mercy.
His change of pace, his accelerated bursts of speed, and his power
had defenders lunging and missing. Where he was at his best,
though, was going outside, where he could use his speed to full
advantage.

Purdue's favorite play in those days was a sweep in which the
quarterback pitched back to the halfback. Mollenkopf called the
play "Leroy left and Leroy right," because it usually was Keyes
on the receiving end of the pitch. And how he ran it! Leroy broke
just about every record in the Purdue book in his three years, and
many of them still stand—like the most points in a career (222) and
single season (114), most touchdowns in a career (37) and a season
(19), most career rushing touchdowns (29), average rush for a career (5.97) and a season (6.61), most yards on intercepted passes
returned in a career (166), and the single game mark for yards via
pass-receiving (184, vs. Northwestern). Three of the records he
set—yards rushing in a single game (225), a season (1,003), and a
career (2,090) have since been broken.

It didn't take Purdue fans long to learn that Leroy Keyes was
something special. In only his second varsity game, against Notre
Dame at South Bend, Leroy plucked a fumble by Nick Eddy out of

midair and returned it 95 yards for a touchdown. And remember, he was playing defense then.

In his junior year, Keyes scored four touchdowns against Iowa, two running and two pass-receiving, and then followed that up with three-touchdown performances against Illinois and Minnesota. It also was against Illinois that Leroy pounded the Illini line for 225 yards rushing, and threw a touchdown pass to complete one of the finest afternoons ever enjoyed by a Big Ten back.

Leroy had many great days for the Boilermakers, but most people agree that his best was against Indiana in 1968. The Hoosiers went ahead early but Leroy led a comeback that beat Indiana, 38–35. He scored four touchdowns, three on runs and one on a pass reception, rushed for 140 yards, and caught six passes for another 149 yards. Then there was the afternoon that he scored twice as Purdue upset Notre Dame, 37–22. And the day he rushed for 214 yards against Wake Forest.

There was no doubt anywhere that Leroy Keyes was an authentic All-America and he was a unanimous choice in both 1967 and 1968. He had broken just about every record in the Purdue book, including most of those set by Elmer Oliphant and Pest Welch. Largely through Leroy's efforts, Purdue teams enjoyed three of their best years ever during his tenure, going to the Rose Bowl after the 1966 season and losing only six games in three years.

How did Coach Jack Mollenkopf feel about Leroy and the 1966, 1967, and 1968 teams? "Leroy *was* my team," said Jack.

Like all good things, even some of Leroy Keyes' superlative records came to an end, and it was another Purdue runner who surpassed several of his marks to become the most prolific ground-gainer in Big Ten history until his records, too, fell several years later. Otis Armstrong, a limber-hipped, freewheeling sprinter who combined power with his tremendous speed, came along in 1970 and in the next three years turned the Big Ten into his personal playground.

A product of the Chicago ghetto, Armstrong didn't exactly turn Purdue football around (the Boilermakers were a poor 13–18 during his three-year career), but his individual brilliance undoubtedly kept Coach Bob DeMoss' teams from suffering an even worse fate in their duels with conference opponents. The seventies were not a happy time for Purdue. Coach Jack Mollenkopf had retired after a distinguished career and was succeeded by his longtime assistant, Bob DeMoss, himself one of Purdue's great quarterbacks. With

everyone else in the Big Ten recruiting more intently, the Boilermakers were no longer able to attract the horde of huge, fast high
school stars who used to turn up at Ross-Ade Stadium each fall.
But they did get Otis Armstrong.

In his three varsity years—1970, 1971, and 1972—Otis accomplished what even Duane Purvis, Cecil Isbell, and Leroy Keyes before him were unable to do. Stomping through enemy defenses like
a runaway colt, Otis bolted for 3,515 yards to break the Big Ten career rushing record, even the one that Wisconsin's Alan Ameche
had established in four years. Along the way he set several school
records, for a single game (276 yards), a season (1,361), and the
most attempts (243). It was like Leroy Keyes reincarnated, except
that Otis Armstrong's statistics were even better.

Armstrong already had the conference three-year record in the
bag going into his last game against Indiana, and not even the most
enthusiastic Purdue rooter figured that he would get the 173 yards
he needed to better Ameche's record, which was accomplished in
four years. But Otis did it. He virtually pulverized the Indiana team
with a superb performance that brought Purdue a 42–7 victory. Despite a muddy field, Armstrong pounded the poor Hoosiers for 276
yards on thirty-two carries, sprinting for three touchdowns, including a pair on runs of 71 and 53 yards. It was a fitting farewell performance for this determined young man who managed to pick
himself up by his own bootstraps.

"The odds against my getting anywhere in this world were staggering," observed Armstrong. "There was poverty, unemploy-
ment, dope, and gang wars in my neighborhood, but I managed to
make it out because of football."

How good was Otis Armstrong? Well, after that final game, John
Pont, then the Indiana coach, said plaintively, "We've looked at
him for three years and I can tell you that's enough. He's the greatest, period."

Since then, the pickings have been meager at Purdue. About the
only runner worthy of attention was Scott Dierking, who rushed
for 1,000 yards and scored sixteen touchdowns for the Boilermakers in 1976.

Purdue also has had its share of outstanding quarterbacks over
the years. The first was Bob DeMoss, a tall, skinny kid out of Kentucky who made the varsity as a freshman in 1945 and astounded
even the most rabid Boilermaker fans by leading Purdue to a star-

tling 35–13 upset of Ohio State. In that game DeMoss completed his first six passes, and nine out of eleven in all for 138 yards and two touchdowns. DeMoss made headlines for the next three seasons as one of the premier passers in the Big Ten—192 completions for 2,790 yards and twenty touchdowns—and, after a year of pro football with the old New York Bulldogs, returned to his alma mater as an assistant coach. Bob turned out to be of even greater value to Purdue in his new capacity. He turned out a procession of quarterbacks who proceeded to break all the records he had established from 1945 through 1948.

The first was Dale Samuels, who threw for 3,154 yards and twenty-seven touchdowns in 1950, 1951, and 1952. Then, Len Dawson, who achieved even greater fame later as an All-Pro quarterback with the Kansas City Chiefs, came along in 1954, 1955, and 1956. A slender, quiet, and serious young man who nevertheless possessed unusual leadership qualities, Dawson broke in with a loud bang in his sophomore year. In his very first game, Len threw for four touchdowns as Purdue trounced Missouri, 31–0. Then, just to prove that his debut wasn't a fluke, the next Saturday he passed for four more scores against Notre Dame, and Purdue won, 27–14.

Although Purdue didn't exactly set the world—or even the Big Ten—on fire during Dawson's three-year tenure as the varsity quarterback, Len stood out like a shining light. His passing was just about the Boilermakers' entire offense, and when he had finished his three-year career he had flung the ball 452 times, completing 243 of those passes for a record 3,325 yards and twenty-nine touchdowns. Also, despite Purdue's lowly position in the Big Ten standings—it never finished higher than fourth place—Dawson led the conference all three years in passing and total offense.

It took DeMoss, coaching under Jack Mollenkopf, eight more years to come up with another great quarterback but then, within a six-year span, and back-to-back, he had two—Bob Griese and Mike Phipps, both All-Americas.

Ah, Griese and Phipps, what a pair they were, and they both had the advantage of playing with winning Purdue teams. Griese, who now plies his trade for the Miami Dolphins, was no great shakes as a passer when he came to Purdue as a freshman in 1963. But under the guidance of DeMoss and Mollenkopf he persevered, and, after only a so-so season as a sophomore quarterback in 1964, he became a superb passer as well as a reliable runner—the ideal quarterback for the 1960s, when running quarterbacks were just becoming the new rage. Unlike Len Dawson, Griese had very fine football teams in front of him, including one that was destined to develop into a Rose Bowl winner in 1966.

Perhaps the one game that turned Griese into a college superstar was the clash with No. 1–ranked Notre Dame in 1965. All Bob did that afternoon was complete nineteen of twenty-two passes as he led the Boilermakers to a 25–21 victory in one of the most memorable clashes between these two old state rivals. Then, in 1966, Griese took Purdue to the Rose Bowl, where it upset a favored University of Southern California team, 14–13. Bob's three-year statistics indicated his improvement as his career progressed. In 1964, he completed 76 of 156 passes for 934 yards and five touchdowns; in 1965, it was 142 of 238, for 1,719 yards and eleven scores; in 1966, it was 130 of 215, for 1,749 yards and twelve touchdowns. Overall, he was 348 of 609, for 3,402 yards and twenty-eight touchdowns.

For all these impressive stats, Bob Griese suffered a grievous disappointment in his senior year. Prominently mentioned as an outstanding candidate for the Heisman Trophy, he was asked by the moguls at the Downtown A.C. to stand by the telephone in West Lafayette on the day the votes were counted. But the phone never rang. Instead, it tinkled down in Gainesville, Florida, for Steve Spurrier, the University of Florida quarterback.

As it turned out, however, there was some retribution for the disappointed Bob Griese. He turned out to be a superstar quarterback who led the Miami Dolphins to the Super Bowl championship in 1973. And the last time anyone looked, Steve Spurrier had been traded by the San Francisco 49ers to the new Tampa expansion team in the NFL and then released.

Bob Griese's records as Purdue's greatest passer lasted hardly any time at all. Within three years, Mike Phipps, his successor as the Boilermaker quarterback, had surpassed them all by wide margins. Phipps arrived at Purdue with a greater reputation as a pure passer, and he quickly proved that his rep was genuine. In his three seasons—1967, 1968, and 1969—he threw the football for more than a mile (5,424 yards) and thirty-seven touchdowns, and set single-game records for the most pass attempts (39), most completions (28), most yards gained (429), and most touchdown passes (5). He also set Purdue's all-time total offense mark with 5,883 yards!

Significantly, Phipps' single-game records were established in a game against Stanford's Jim Plunkett, who went on to win the Heisman Trophy. Mike's spectacular performance against the West Coast team in Ross-Ade Stadium in 1969 gave Purdue a 36–35 triumph.

Linemen, those indomitable and frequently anonymous souls who operate in the trenches, rarely receive the publicity that is the natural right of the guys who throw the passes and the runners who sprint through secondaries on their way to touchdowns. But every headliner knows that without them doing the blocking and repulsing the enemy on defense, the stars would be ordinary Joes.

One special breed, the ends, has the opportunity to share the glory with their backfield mates. They catch passes and score touchdowns, giving them one measure of possible immortality. Purdue has had some good ones in this category, like Paul Moss, back in 1931 and 1932; Dave Rankin, an all-purpose end in 1939 and 1940; and Jim Beirne, the split end who was the target of so many of Bob Griese's passes in the middle sixties. They were all outstanding players, but Rankin may have been the best of all the Boilermaker wingmen. A tough, hardnosed player, Rankin did just about everything for Purdue. A superb pass catcher, he was also a fierce defensive player. There was one game, against Michigan State, when Rankin proved just how tough he was. Dave had had his nose broken early in the game but he refused to come out. Instead, the blood streaming out of his injured nose, Rankin kept knocking down Michigan State ball-carriers.

Finally, Mike Layden, the head linesman, whose white official's pants were splattered with Rankin's blood, took matters into his own hands. "Why don't you get the hell out of the game," he yelled at Rankin. "Look at my pants!"

Alex Agase, the traveling guard who played at Purdue in 1943 and earned All-America honors at Illinois both the year before and after, may have been the best of all the Purdue interior linemen, but there are others who deserve to be mentioned in the same breath—like guard Tom Bettis in 1954, Jerry Shay and Karl Singer, the tackles on the 1965 team; Chuck Kyle, an irrepressible middle guard who was an All-America in 1968; and Dave Butz, the big tackle who starred in 1972.

These were men, the kind of men who helped make football a tradition at Purdue.

TWENTY-TWO

Pat O'Dea, Kicker Extraordinary

Patrick John O'Dea—now there is a name that rings bells for old football buffs. It has been three-quarters of a century since Pat O'Dea did such extraordinary things while kicking a football for the University of Wisconsin, yet his name is still in the Big Ten record book for the longest punt and field goal by dropkicking. Those two marks never will be broken.

Pat O'Dea's prowess as a kicker set him aside from all other Big Ten players of his time in an age when college football was still gaining its spurs. O'Dea's towering punts and long field goals brought a new dimension to the game and contributed to some of Wisconsin's most successful seasons. Pat had no equal on the playing field, and he basked in the spotlight for three years from 1897 until 1899.

Like most football stars, Pat O'Dea enjoyed the adulation that came his way. Despite this, however, his post-football life was filled with mystery and intrigue culminating in a strange twist that shook the football world.

One sunny day in the spring of 1896, Andy O'Dea, the University of Wisconsin crew coach, was lounging on the float of the boathouse, contemplating his rowers who were going through their paces. Andy had come to the United States from his native Australia several years earlier, along with Frank (Paddy) Slavin, the Aussie heavyweight champion, who hoped to get a crack at John L. Sullivan, the current world titleholder. Slavin never got his wish, but Andy stayed on in America and eventually wound up at Wisconsin.

Perhaps Andy O'Dea was even thinking about the old days in

Australia while he watched his oarsmen. Suddenly he heard a familiar voice say, "Hello, Andy," and turned to see a tall lanky youth in a blue-flannel lounging suit and tiny cap.

"Hello, Pat," replied Andy matter-of-factly, "when did you get in?" As it turned out, that simple greeting between two brothers who hadn't seen each other in years was one of the best things that ever happened to Wisconsin. The following fall Pat decided to enroll in the university, and thus began one of the most fabulous careers in Big Ten history.

Pat's reputation as a rugby player in Australia had not preceded him to the United States, but folks were going to be learning about it once he began kicking an American football. The Aussie sport was strictly a kicking game, and the only way a team could score was when one of its players booted the ball over the goal. O'Dea had become quite proficient at it in his native country and it didn't take him long to catch on to American football. He just did what he had always done in the Antipodes—kick the hell out of the ball—and his prodigious boots, whether by punting or drop- or placekicking, soon attracted the attention of Phil King, the former Princeton All-America who was coaching the Badgers. Although O'Dea only weighed about 170 pounds, he had the leg power and strength to kick the football farther than anyone King had ever seen before. King also recognized the fact that, with O'Dea's proficiency at kicking long-distance field goals, his team could score almost any time it got within an opponent's 50-yard line.

O'Dea got an opportunity to display his talent in Wisconsin's opening game against Lake Forest in 1896, and he promptly punted the ball 85 yards while both his teammates and opponents looked on in amazement. However, Pat broke his arm in a scrimmage two days later and he didn't get another chance to play until the Badgers, who had won the championship in the Big Ten's first year of competition, played a postseason game with the Carlisle Indians in mid-December in the old Chicago Coliseum.

The dirt floor of the Coliseum had been covered with an additional four or five inches of dirt, but its low ceiling promised to hamper each team's kicking game. It didn't seem to bother O'Dea, however, who got off punts of 50, 45, 55, and 75 yards, the ball tumbling end-over-end in the Australian style rather than the graceful spiral that Americans had become accustomed to. But Carlisle's Bemus Pierce had problems. One of his kicks sailed so high that it stuck in the rafters and, since there wasn't another football available, the game had to be held up for about fifteen minutes until an ambitious official climbed up to retrieve the errant ball.

For the next three years, Pat O'Dea was the greatest kicker in college football. In 1897 he punted the ball 110 yards in a game against Minnesota. In 1898 he dropkicked 65 yards for a field goal against Northwestern. (There is some discrepancy about this mark, though—Big Ten records credit O'Dea with a 65-yard kick but Wisconsin lists the distance at 62 yards.) In 1899 he placekicked 57 yards for a field goal against Illinois. This mark has been broken, but O'Dea's punting and dropkicking records still stand in the Big Ten. Aside from his record-setting efforts, O'Dea consistently punted the ball from 50 to 75 yards, and was deadly on field goal attempts from inside midfield, some of them booted while on the run.

O'Dea's kicking had another feature that no one since has been able to imitate. He could curve a long punted ball right or left, much like a baseball pitcher, and he would signal his ends which direction the kick was going to take. This permitted them to head directly for the spot where the opposing safety man would receive the ball. Who knows what Pat O'Dea would have done if he had been able to kick a spitball!

True, Pat had a longer field to work with than present-day players. In those days the gridiron was 110 yards long. The rules also permitted a field goal attempt on a free kick. All you had to do to get the free kick was to signal for a fair catch on a punt—and Wisconsin usually did if the ball was inside the 50-yard line. Expert kickers like O'Dea had another advantage. Punt receivers who didn't signal for a fair catch, and were lucky enough not to get creamed by opposing ends, were allowed to return the kick with a dropkick attempt for a field goal.

O'Dea took advantage of that quirk in the rules to get off one of his most remarkable kicks against Minnesota in 1899. To fully appreciate it, the stage must be set:

Wisconsin, in the running for the Big Ten title, and Minnesota were locked in a fiercely fought, scoreless tie midway in the second half when the Gophers, backed up deep in their own territory, were forced to punt. Knowlton, the Minnesota kicker, got off a high spiral and there was Pat O'Dea, the Badger safetyman, back on his own 50-yard line (remember, the field was 110 yards long), waiting for the ball. Also, coming fast under a full head of steam were four husky Gophers, led by Gil Dobie, an end who was later to become a great coach at Washington, Navy, and Cornell. To put it mildly, they were bent on mayhem and there didn't seem to be any way that O'Dea could get away from them.

Pat caught the ball, somehow eluded Dobie's diving tackle, and headed for the sidelines on his left, away from the other onrushing Minnesota defenders. The, suddenly, while on the full run, and going away from his target, O'Dea got off a dropkick. While the astonished Minnesota players gaped, the ball sailed across the field and dropped squarely between the goal posts, some 55 yards away, for five points for the Badgers. The accomplishment was all the more miraculous because O'Dea, a rightfooted kicker, was going to his left when he booted the ball!

Dobie said later that O'Dea's tremendous kick was the greatest individual play he had ever seen in football.

O'Dea's career was filled with similar spectacular plays, and Wisconsin fans—and Big Ten opponents—became used to his prodigious kicking feats. There was, of course, Pat's punt against Minnesota in 1897 that traveled the full length of the field—110 yards—a record that will stand for all time. And his 65-yard dropkick against Northwestern in 1898, another mark that will probably never be broken because dropkicking has become a lost art in football. That 65-yarder came under circumstances that were highly unusual, to say the least.

Coming up to the Northwestern game, the final one on Wisconsin's schedule that season, Coach King sensed that his players were overconfident and needed some added incentive. In his pre-game pep talk, King tried to impress his men with the importance of scoring first, and as quickly as possible. Then he came up with the added incentive. He told his players, "You can break training tonight, so if you score in the first two minutes I'll buy you a case of champagne."

When Northwestern won the toss and elected to receive on a muddy field, the Wisconsin players thought they had lost their chance to take advantage of Coach King's offer. Northwestern punched out a first down, but then the Badgers stopped the Wildcats' drive, forcing them to punt, and O'Dea signaled for a fair catch on his own 45-yard line.

Then, with only seconds left before the two-minute deadline set by King, O'Dea called his own signal for a kick. Considering the condition of the field, his teammates thought that Pat was going to punt, but O'Dea had other ideas. When the ball was snapped, he dropkicked it high and true. The ball sailed over the goal posts 65 yards away and didn't stop until it hit the fence another 20 yards away. Pat and his teammates had their bubbly that night, as well as a 47–0 victory over Northwestern.

Pat O'Dea not only had a remarkable ability to kick the ball, he was also one of the smartest and most alert players of his time. In fact, it was his shrewdness and quick thinking that set up his longest field goal by placekick.

On November 11, 1899 Wisconsin was playing Illinois in the old Milwaukee baseball park, and up until game time O'Dea was a doubtful starter. He had suffered a leg injury and hadn't even been in uniform for the twelve days prior to the game. But Pat was a hard man to hold down and he was in the lineup at kickoff time. As usual his long, booming punts kept the Illini pinned down deep in their own territory. One of Pat's kicks had gone into the end zone and, under the rules of the time, Illinois punted out from its own 25-yard line. There was a strong wind sweeping across the field and the Illinois kick was about to go out of bounds on the north sideline when O'Dea shouted to his teammate, Bill Juneau, "Fair catch, Bill, fair catch!" Bill got the message and grabbed the ball just a few feet inside the sidelines and 57 yards from the Illini goal line.

Seconds later, O'Dea made his alertness pay off. He calmly stepped back for a field goal try from placement while even his teammates looked at him in surprise. It seemed there was no way that even Pat O'Dea could kick the ball that far in the face of the wind that was blowing up such a storm. But Pat never gave the stiff breeze a second thought. He simply booted the ball, high and swiftly into the wind, and it never even wavered as it not only crossed the uprights 57 yards away but continued on its merry flight, over the baseball bleachers behind the goal line, over the high fence behind the seats, and into the street outside the ball park. Officially, it was a 57-yard kick, but the ball probably traveled closer to 80 yards before it came to rest. Needless to say, the Badgers won that game easily, 23–0.

Oddly enough, Pat O'Dea didn't consider his football career a completely rewarding one because, while he was the fullback, he was very rarely permitted to carry the ball. Believing that it was more important to keep his valuable kicking property from injury, Coach King used him only infrequently as a ball-carrier. O'Dea didn't take to this strategy very well and often made his views known to the coach. On the few occasions that he was permitted to carry the ball, the opposition recognized that he was pretty good at it. It usually took two or three players to bring him down.

Before Pat O'Dea finished his illustrious football career at Wisconsin, he kicked thirty-two field goals—they were each worth five points in those days—and never had a punt blocked in a game. Unfortunately, punting statistics were not kept in those days so it is impossible to determine what O'Dea's average might have been, but it is reasonably safe to assume that few modern-day punters have ever approached his skill in that department.

After graduation Pat stayed in football for a while, coaching as an assistant at Notre Dame and Missouri, where he taught young kickers his art. Eventually he settled in California, where presumably his fame would live on for years and years.

Then came one of the strangest turn of events in the life of any athlete. For almost two decades, Pat O'Dea dropped out of sight completely, given up for dead, until Bill Leiser, the enterprising sports editor of the *San Francisco Chronicle*, exhumed him and found him very much alive.

O'Dea, who had been practicing law in San Francisco since shortly after his football days at Wisconsin in the late 1890s, simply disappeared from sight around 1917 and not even his brother Andy knew what had become of him. There were rumors, of course, and thirteen years later, in 1930, the *Wisconsin News* reported, "His end was apparently tragic . . . His brother Andy is convinced that Pat joined one of the many Australian troop contingents which went through this country and that he was subsequently killed in action. So Wisconsin's greatest kicker and most colorful football player probably lies beneath an unmarked cross in France or Flanders. May he rest in peace. He was a modest, lovable character, a loyal friend and a super-athlete."

Actually, Pat O'Dea hadn't gone to war. Nor had he really disappeared into thin air. What happened was that O'Dea's law practice had begun to fade, the war had cut off most of his income from business interests in Australia, and he was weary of trying to live up to his fame as a "former" football hero. He didn't like living in what were to him "mere student days of the past." Pat became obsessed with the idea that he was just another big-time football player who had failed in life.

So, O'Dea simply gave up his law practice, packed up and moved to Westwood, a small mountain town in the northeast corner of California, adopted a new identity as Charles J. Mitchell, and went to work for the Red River Lumber Company. As Charles J. Mitchell, he became a highly respected member of the community, secretary-manager of the Westwood Chamber of Commerce and the Westwood Auto Club, a director of the Lassen Volcanic Park Association, and a leader in the fight for new roads. That was his life until a business acquaintance named Walker, who had played football for Minnesota many years before, became intrigued by Mitchell's looks and his apparent knowledge of football although he was always reticent to talk about it. Walker got the truth out of Mitchell and, finally, in 1934, Mitchell agreed to divulge his true identify to Bill Leiser and the resultant story in the *Chronicle* made headlines across the nation.

"Probably I was wrong," O'Dea told Leiser. "Mrs. Mitchell—that is Mrs. O'Dea—always thought I was. But I wanted to get away from what seemed to me to be all in the past. As Pat O'Dea, I seemed very much just an ex-Wisconsin football player. I was very happy as Mitchell for a while. Mitchell was my mother's name and Charley that of a cousin I like. Later, I found it rather unpleasant not to be the man I actually am. So, if you want to write that I'm going to be Pat O'Dea again for the rest of my life, write it.

"Perhaps I should never have been anything else."

Pat O'Dea's return was hailed by the entire football community and especially by his old school, Wisconsin. On November 17, 1934 Pat was guest of honor on Homecoming Day and his presence was saluted by students and alumni alike, most of whom had never seen him play but had been brought up on his legendary feats of thirty-five years earlier. The football team added to the luster of the occasion by beating Illinois, 7–3.

Pat O'Dea was back with the living again.

Since Pat O'Dea, Wisconsin had more than its share of All-America heroes in what the Big Ten refers to as the premodern era—before 1939. Players like Butts Butler in 1912, Tubby Keeler in 1913, Arlie Mucks in 1914, Cub Buck in 1914, Charles Carpenter in 1919, Red Weston and Ralph Scott in 1920, Marty Below in 1923, Milo Lubratovich in 1930—all linemen, by the way—and fullback Howard Weiss in 1938. There have been others, too, in the so-called modern era, but perhaps none as distinguished as a burly freshman fullback who erupted on the Badger scene in 1951 and then proceeded to blast out a four-year career that had people referring to him as another Bronko Nagurski.

Alan Ameche was his name and pounding Big Ten lines was his game. Big, rawboned, and endowed with the strength of a horse, Ameche came along during the Korean War when freshmen were permitted to play varsity football. What a boon that was for the Badgers. Crashing and battering his way through Big Ten lines for 774 yards, the eighteen-year-old Ameche became the first freshman ever to lead the conference in rushing. His biggest day of that season came against Minnesota, when he crunched the Gophers for 200 yards.

Ameche, who was promptly nicknamed "The Horse," wasn't the only offense that Wisconsin had that year. Quarterback Johnny Coatta, who had led the Big Ten in pass completion percentages, was still throwing and still completing the majority of his passes to give the Badgers a varied attack. But it was "The Horse" whom Coatta called upon when the tough yardage was needed.

Ameche led the Big Ten in rushing again in 1952 as a sophomore with 721 yards (he got 964 in all games). From that illustrious beginning Alan went on to carve out 3,212 yards rushing in his four years and also became one of the most feared defensive players in the conference. Forced to go both ways because of the return to one-platoon football, Ameche played linebacker on defense and proved to be just as effective there as he was carrying the ball. He was named to the All-America team in both 1953 and 1954, and then, to the surprise of absolutely no one, was voted the Heisman Trophy after his senior year.

Before Ameche, Wisconsin fielded a pair of irrepressible stars who captured the fancy of Big Ten fans. The 1941 and 1942 teams featured fullback Pat Harder and Dave Schreiner, a two-way end, who helped to make life pleasant for Coach Harry Stuhledreher—the old Notre Dame Four Horseman—who had moved in as head football coach and athletic director in 1934 when an inter-family feud had cost Coach Clarence (Doc) Spears his job.

Harder, a plunging fullback in the Ameche mold, and Schreiner, a superb pass-catcher, blocker, and defensive end, couldn't quite give the Badgers a winner in 1941. They did give Wisconsin a scoring punch but the defense couldn't stop many folks. For example, the 1941 Badgers beat Indiana, 27–25, but lost to Syracuse, 27–20, and Ohio State, 46–34.

But it was quite a different story in 1942 when Harder and Schreiner, with an assist from Elroy (Crazy Legs) Hirsch, who spent one of his wartime seasons with the Badgers, carried Wisconsin to an 8–1–1 season. Despite his team's poor record in 1941, Schreiner had made the All-America team, largely because of his knack for coming through with the big play in the clutch.

In 1942 Schreiner had an even greater year, catching sixteen passes, including the winning ones against Ohio State and Minnesota. Harder devastated Wisconsin's foes with his lunging plunges, while Hirsch's long, limber-legged dashes complemented Harder's inside game. Both Harder and Schreiner made All-America and Hirsch went on to even greater glory at Michigan and with the Los Angeles Rams. Schreiner later lost his life on Okinawa.

There have been other memorable Badgers since then, like Pat Richter, a pass-catching end who rewrote the Wisconsin record books in 1960, 1961, and 1962, and Ron VanderKelen, the passing quarterback who almost did in heavily favored USC in the 1965 Rose Bowl with one of the greatest passing performances ever seen in a college gridiron. Another Badger star was Rufus (Road Runner) Ferguson, a lithe, slippery-hipped runner who combined power with hipper-dipper skittering to break Ameche's one-season rushing record in 1971. The Road Runner piled up 1,222 yards in 1971, added 1,004 more in 1972, and finished a three-year varsity career with 2,814 yards in three years, twenty-six touchdowns rushing (to break Ameche's record by one), and a total of 153 points.

They didn't call him Road Runner for nothing.

The Road Runner, however, was overtaken almost before his records had a chance to get settled in. Billy Marek, who spent his freshman year on the bench watching Ferguson do *his* thing, got his chance at tailback in 1973. Marek, a five-foot eight-inch, 188-pounder, had a knack for ramming through enemy lines, and he did it so well that, by the time he finished the 1975 season, he had made the Badgers forget Rufus Ferguson.

In 1973 Billy carried the ball 241 times for 1,207 yards and fourteen touchdowns to break Ferguson's school record. In 1974 he was even better, battering Minnesota for 304 yards in one game and finishing the season with 1,215 yards and nineteen six-pointers.

Then, Marek topped off his varsity career in style in 1975, rolling up 1,281 yards and scoring thirteen touchdowns to give him career totals of 3,709 yards rushing (he carried once for 6 yards in his freshman year) and forty-six touchdowns.

Unfortunately, Marek played his years in the shadow of Ohio State's Archie Griffin and didn't get his just share of the headlines, but Gus Schrader, sports editor of the Cedar Rapids *Gazette*, recognized Billy's excellence when he wrote, "If there is a back with greater impact, pound for pound, than Billy Marek, well, we'd like to see what he registers on the Richter scale."

Although, lately, Wisconsin has not been one of the Big Ten leaders, the Badgers did come up with a fine quarterback in 1976. Quarterback Mike Carroll did his best to make Wisconsin competitive, completing 132 of 262 passes for 1,627 yards and thirteen touchdowns, and he scored four more rushing. That performance helped the Badgers win five of their eleven games.

TWENTY-THREE

Berwanger and Eckersall

Perhaps he would have been even greater if he had the advantage of performing for better teams than the University of Chicago—then in the embryo stages of a deemphasized program which eventually resulted in the abandonment of football as a varsity sport—was able to field, but John Jacob Berwanger, better known in the trade as Jay, became a legend in his own time.

Six feet tall and 200 pounds, Berwanger was a tough, talented player who did it all for Chicago teams which didn't win very often. Without him it is doubtful whether the once-feared Maroons would ever have won at all. Jay had the power to dent even the toughest Big Ten lines of that era. He had the speed to go outside and an uncanny change of pace that often left would-be tacklers grasping air instead of his flashing legs as he swept past them. While passing was one of Berwanger's lesser talents, he used it as simply another threat to worry the opposition. As a punter he was one of the finest of his time, specializing in kicking the ball out of bounds, thus depriving opponents of the opportunity for runbacks. Berwanger also did the kicking off, and returned punts and kickoffs. In addition, he played defense, and played it superbly as a cornerback. Many a Big Ten carrier and pass-receiver, victims of his bone-shattering tackles, attested to that.

Perhaps the greatest tribute to Jay Berwanger's varied talents, however, was the Heisman Trophy he was voted after the 1935 season, the first time the award named in honor of John Heisman, one-time famed Georgia Tech coach, was given by the Downtown Athletic Club in New York City. That year Chicago had a mediocre season, winning only half of its eight games, and two of those victories came over such Midwestern "powers" as Cornell College of

Iowa and Western State. Yet, despite all this, Berwanger was judged to be the best college football player in the country!

There were few detractors when Jay Berwanger was selected as the winner of the Heisman Trophy. Some people called him the greatest all-around back since Jim Thorpe. That was extravagant praise, indeed, but there was no denying that Berwanger was a superstar. The only speculation was over what he would have done if he had played behind the powerful lines of Minnesota, Michigan, or Ohio State, the Big Ten powers of the middle thirties. Perhaps even Jay himself might have wondered about that a time or two, especially when the porous Chicago front walls he had to make do with left him pretty much on his own. But he never complained, and his performance was all the more remarkable because his heroics were achieved against some of the best Big Ten linemen of all time, men like Bill Bevan, Frank Larson, Bud Wilkinson, and Dick Smith of Minnesota, and Merle Wendt and Gomer Jones of Ohio State.

Berwanger's college football career might have taken a different turn. As an All-State star at Dubuque (Iowa) High School, Jay seriously considered going to Minnesota, Purdue, or Iowa. But he became friendly with Ira Davenport, a former University of Chicago athlete who owned the Dubuque Boat and Boiler Company, where the young Berwanger worked during his high school days. Davenport convinced Jay that Chicago, with its fine academic reputation, was the best place for him to get a good education. Berwanger also was impressed with the fact that Chicago no longer was a big-time football school with all the pressures on winning. He thought football would be more fun and games. So, it was off to the Midway for the young Iowan and, if he ever regretted his decision, it never reached the public ear.

Berwanger holds one other distinction. He was the last University of Chicago All-America. Four years after Berwanger finished his varsity career, following the 1939 season, Chicago finally succumbed to the deemphasis program laid on by President Robert Hutchins and dropped varsity football from its athletic program. It was the end of an era for the university which was once the terror of the Big Ten in the days when the venerable Amos Alonzo Stagg was the coach. Even in 1935, Berwanger's final season, the end was in sight, but that didn't deter the last of the Monsters of the Midway from establishing himself as one of the greats of college football history.

Berwanger's athletic talents were not confined to football. He took a whirl at track during his first two years and, although his best events were the hurdles and broad jump, he demonstrated his versatility by competing in the decathlon at the Kansas Relays, where he finished fourth in his first try at the exhausting event. However he gave up track after two seasons because of the demands on his time. In addition to playing football and hitting the books, he also had to work in his spare time to support himself at the university since there were no such things as athletic scholarships at Chicago in those days.

It didn't take long for Berwanger to break into the starting lineup at Chicago as a sophomore in 1933. Coach Clark Shaughnessy, who later was to become known as the architect of the T-formation, recognized the great talent he had in the youngster from Iowa and soon installed him as the tailback. Although Chicago finished in last place in the Big Ten standings and won only one of its eight games—two ended in ties—Berwanger played sixty minutes in all five of the Maroons' league contests. He carried the ball 184 times, averaging just under 4 yards a shot, scored eight touchdowns, and did all the punting. In one game, against Illinois, Jay was given the ball an incredible thirty-seven times! Despite Chicago's failure to win more than one game—and that against a nonconference opponent—Jay was voted the team's most valuable player, the only sophomore ever to achieve that status.

It was during his sophomore year that Berwanger also became known far and wide as "The Man in the Iron Mask." Jay had broken his nose in his freshman year and it never healed properly. Fearing further injury, the doctors decided that he would not be permitted to play unless his nose was protected. Faceguards, which all players wear today, had not yet been devised, but the innovative Chicago doctors and trainers came up with a device that did the trick for Berwanger. It looked like half a catcher's mask, made of spring steel bars covered by leather. It took a while for Berwanger to adjust to it, but he used the mask in every game he played for three years. Headline writers of the time were quick to dub Jay "The Man in the Iron Mask" and the name stuck with Berwanger throughout his varsity career.

Chicago's grid fortunes picked up in 1934, Berwanger's junior year, largely through the efforts of the classy tailback. While Minnesota and Ohio State were dominating the conference, the Maroons managed an even split in their eight games and climbed out of the Big Ten cellar into seventh place. One game that season, more than any other, epitomized the desire and the drive that Berwanger had to excel, even in the face of adversity.

Chicago was playing Purdue, and late in the game the Maroons were two touchdowns behind the heavily favored Boilermakers. But Berwanger pulled Chicago back into the ball game with his driving thrusts through the line and whirling runs into the Purdue secondary. On Chicago's last touchdown drive, a march of some 85 yards, three times the Maroons found themselves in third down and ten situations. On each occasion, Berwanger tore through the beleaguered Boilermakers for first downs. Chicago lost that one, 26–20, but few folks in the stands will ever forget Jay Berwanger's superb performance that afternoon.

Berwanger's statistics that year were truly amazing. He carried the ball 119 times, averaging 5 yards a carry, completed fourteen passes for 196 yards, and punted seventy-seven times for a 39.3 average, not really an overwhelming statistic except that thirty of his kicks went out of bounds and only five went into the end zone. He also returned eighteen punts for 186 yards, and scored eight touchdowns. Equally important was his work on defense. Against Minnesota he made fourteen tackles in the first half alone, discouraging the Gophers from trying to run his side of the field.

There were many startling individual performances in Jay Berwanger's career at Chicago, but most Big Ten watchers agree that his most spectacular effort came against Ohio State in 1935. The Buckeyes, in a head-to-head battle with Minnesota for the Big Ten championship, had just come off their startling 18–13 upset by Notre Dame in a nonconference game, and they were determined to level Chicago on their way to at least a tie with the then Golden Gophers for the league title.

But there were the proud Buckeyes at halftime, behind 13–0 to lowly Chicago and only because they couldn't stop Jay Berwanger. Jay had scored Chicago's second touchdown on what was perhaps one of the greatest individual efforts ever seen. With the ball on his own 40-yard line, Berwanger slipped off tackle on the soggy field, cut toward the sideline, then back to the middle of the field where he was hemmed in, all the time slithering and sliding on the treacherous turf. For an instant he seemed to be caught, but he back-pedaled a few yards, then made his way between two defenders and headed for the same sideline he had left seconds before. This time he eluded his tormentors and went all the way for the touchdown that gave Chicago a 13–0 lead. Although Berwanger got credit for a 60-yard touchdown run, it was estimated that he ran at least twice that distance before he got to the end zone. It would be nice to record for history that Jay's great run gave Chicago an upset, but it was not to be, at least not on that day. Ohio State came storming back after the intermission to win, 20–13, and the Buckeyes went on to gain a tie with unbeaten Minnesota for the Big Ten crown. But Ohio State knew it had been up against a superstar that afternoon.

When Jay Berwanger's three years of varsity competition ended, he had compiled a set of statistics that convinced the Heisman Trophy voters and All-America selectors that he was indeed the best player in the nation. In his twenty-three varsity games Jay gained 1,839 yards on 439 carries; completed fifty of 146 passes for 920 yards; caught twelve more for 189 yards; intercepted eight for 79 yards, and averaged 37.3 yards on 223 punts, with eighty of them being placed out of bounds. He had averaged 46.3 yards on his kickoffs, and returned fifty-four kickoffs and punts for an average of 31.8 yards per kick. He also scored twenty-two touchdowns and twenty-two points after, for a grand total of 152 points. All that playing for an inferior team that compiled a meager 9–13–2 record in three years!

No less an authority than Red Grange was fulsome in his praise of Jay Berwanger as a runner. Red said that he had "that faraway look," explaining that Berwanger had the unique ability to take in downfield situations while he was cutting, changing speed, and eluding tacklers. "He had a rare gait," said Grange. "He could run hard at full speed and then reach down within his body to get an extra burst of momentum to flash past or between defensive men. Jay also had an uncanny ability to hit a hole that was closing on him. His feet would drum the ground lightly, in momentary hesitation when blockers or tacklers were locked in front of him, then he would be away in a flash when a slit of opening showed."

Coming from the master himself, all of that was quite a compliment. But Clark Shaughnessy, Berwanger's coach, said it all when he observed, "I've never seen a finer football player, and I don't expect to. You can say anything superlative about him you like—and I'll double it."

The Chicago Bears agreed with Shaughnessy. He was their No. 1 draft pick. Berwanger says, "I remember meeting owner George Halas in a hotel lobby. He asked me what I wanted and I said twenty-five thousand dollars for two years and a no-cut contract. We shook hands, said good-bye, and that was it.''

Berwanger, now a successful businessman in Hinsdale, Illinois, didn't really think there was any future in pro football at the time. Some years later, he said, "I was interested in my future because I was there already."

It was twenty-seven years between backfield superstars at the University of Chicago and no doubt you can still get an argument—if there are any Chicago oldtimers around who go back to 1906—on whether Jay Berwanger was better than Walter Eckersall, who was a three-time All-America in 1904, 1905, and 1906. However, it is the kind of an argument that can never be settled one way or the other. Both were stars of great magnitude in their own times, Eckersall in the early days of the game when football was a tough, unruly sport, and Berwanger, when offenses and defenses were much more sophisticated.

There was never any doubt that Walter Eckersall would wind up at Chicago. As early as 1897, Eckersall was lugging a water bucket to Chicago players in their game with the Carlisle Indians. Two years later, this scrawny, little 118-pound youngster was playing end and quarterback for Hyde Park High School in Chicago and doing very well indeed. Hyde Park, bolstered by a collection of older players who found their way into high school to play football, beat everybody in sight and even took on a couple of college teams, beating Chicago and losing to Wisconsin. Eckersall's team also had the distinction of playing the first intersectional high school game in history. Brooklyn Prep came west to meet the Chicagoans in a postseason game, and the result was an utter disaster for the visitors. Hyde Park won 105–0.

Eckersall, although the smallest man on the team even after he bloomed into a 140-pounder, was the heart and guts of both the offense and defense. He ran, he kicked, and he played defense like a 200-pounder, and, despite his lack of size, there were a lot of Big Ten schools that would have liked to get him. But Eckie's choice was Chicago and Coach Amos Alonzo Stagg was happy to see him report for practice on the Midway. Of course Stagg had to wonder whether the little guy would survive against some of the monsters he would have to run against.

Well, Eckersall not only survived but became one of the most feared players in the Big Ten. He was a brilliant quarterback and strategist, a superb runner with 9.8 speed, a skilled field-goal kicker and punter, and a fiery safetyman who saved many a game for the Maroons with his fierce, deadly tackles. Eckersall wreaked his own particular kind of havoc in the Big Ten at a time when Michigan's famed Point-A-Minute teams were the talk of the nation. And all of this from a player who probably wouldn't even get a second look from a coach in this day and age because he was hardly any bigger than the average waterboy. But what he had, in addition to his skills, was a sharp, intelligent mind and a sort of sixth sense that put him a rung or two over the other Big Ten players. That, and the guts of a second-story man.

Eckersall started his varsity career at Chicago as an end and he won All-America honors at that position in 1904, his sophomore year. But for all his talents as a wingman, Coach Stagg soon realized that he would be more valuable to the team playing quarterback and that is where he was stationed when Chicago opened the 1905 season. And what a season that was for Eckersall and the Maroons!

In one game, against Illinois, Eckie kicked five field goals, a feat he was to repeat a year later against Nebraska. In the Purdue game, Eckersall sat on the bench in the first half as the two teams struggled to a scoreless tie at the intermission. He went into action in the second half and, within a ten-minute span, Chicago scored three touchdowns and was well on its way to a victory.

But it was the Michigan game in 1905 that firmly established Eckersall as one of the all-time greats. The Wolverines had been unbeaten in fifty-five straight games, averaging a point a minute against some of the toughest opposition around, and its star runner, Willie Heston, was one of the most heralded backs in the country. Chicago, too, was undefeated coming into the game, which was played on Chicago's old Marshall Field. More than 25,000 fans were on hand for what they hoped would be a titanic struggle between the Big Ten's two powerhouses. Chicago fans, while hardly optimistic about their team's chances against the marauders from Ann Arbor, were nevertheless hopeful.

What transpired that November afternoon in full view of the Chicago partisans was one of the greatest upsets of all time. The Maroons ended Michigan's streak, and even shut out the mighty Wolverines, although the final score was only 2–0. And the hero of the game was none other than Walter Eckersall, the pint-sized human dynamo, who set the stage for the victory with three spectacular plays.

It seemed that Chicago was going to go the way of all Michigan opponents when the Wolverines drove to the Maroons' 2-yard line. But Stagg's determined young men staged a furious goal-line stand and stopped the Michigan drive. What happened next was a play that Chicago fans talked about for years. Back in his end zone to punt, Eckersall noticed that the Michigan ends were playing in tight, hoping to block the kick. So instead of kicking, Eckie simply tucked the ball under his arm and took off around a charging Michigan end in a maneuver that surprised even his own teammates. He was finally nailed by the safety man on the 50-yard line and, suddenly, instead of being in trouble, Chicago was in a position to threaten the shocked Wolverines.

Michigan recovered its poise in time to stop Chicago cold at the fifty, and Eckersall again went back to punt. This time he kicked the ball and got off a tremendous boot that went into the end zone, and Dennis Clark, a substitute Michigan halfback, attempted to run it out. He was hit by Al Badenoch just as he came out of the end zone, and then Mark Catlin applied the finishing touch, booming into Clark and driving him back into the end zone for a safety and two points. Eckersall's daring in running with the ball instead of kicking it and his subsequent 50-yard kick had paid off handsomely.

That, however, wasn't the only bit of heroics that the incomparable Eckie pulled off that afternoon. At one point in the game, Heston, who had been more or less contained by the spunky Chicago defense, broke through the line and seemed to be on the way to a touchdown. The only man in his path was—that's right—that little Eckersall guy. Eckie dove for the speeding Heston's legs but missed and Willie went on his merry way, hell-bent for a score. However, he underestimated Eckersall. After missing Heston, Eckie recovered quickly and took off after his quarry. He overtook Heston on the 20-yard line and brought him down with a lunging tackle to save a certain touchdown, one of the few times in his career that Willie was ever caught from behind.

So, thanks to Walter Eckersall and his individual exploits, Chicago had its 2–0 upset victory and, as an added bonus, the Big Ten championship, its first since 1899.

There was still more to come for Eckersall. In 1906 the forward pass, a newly developed offensive weapon, was made legal and it added still another dimension to Eckersall's already-expansive talents. When considering the possibilities of the pass, Stagg naturally thought first of his quarterback.

"Think you can throw this thing?" Stagg asked.

"Sure," replied Eckie, "just make sure you have someone who can catch it."

The Maroons worked on the pass in practice but it wasn't until the fourth game of the year, against Illinois, that Stagg decided to use the newfangled play. Eckersall's very first forward pass was caught by Wally Steffen, later a coach at Carnegie Tech and a distinguished federal court judge, and the play went for 75 yards and a touchdown. Before the afternoon was over, Eckersall completed every pass he attempted and the demoralized Illini were thoroughly whipped, 63–0.

Walter Eckersall's last game, a 38–5 victory over Nebraska, was duly celebrated by both him and the University of Chicago. Although the Nebraska defenses were stacked to stop his running and passing, Eckie booted five field goals from distances ranging from 18 to 35 yards, from all conceivable angles, to account for twenty points, more than half of the total scored by Chicago.

Menawhile, the university recognized its departing hero in a style usually reserved for men in more distinguished fields than college football. The *Chicago Tribune* chronicled the events of the day as follows:

"Between the halves, Captain Eckersall was the center of all eyes as he was lifted to a bench beside Dr. Goodspeed, the university's registrar, in front of the Maroons' cheering section, and after a special speech bristling with praise by the registrar, was presented with a diamond studded watch, the gift of the students and faculty of the university. . . . When the last whistle blew, the doughty little Maroon hero, whose stature gives no indication of the veritable giant he is, was carried in triumph from the field to the gymnasium by the proud admirers and worshipers who were fortunate enough to reach him first, while thousands fought to get near him, cheering madly all the way."

Eckersall's romance with football didn't really end with that final game. He later became a sportswriter for the *Chicago Tribune* and was roundly acknowledged as the newspaper's leading sports authority. Eckersall also became a football official of note and, in 1923, was involved in one of the most controversial decisions in

Big Ten annals, one that would have had fiery Woody Hayes tearing up more than yard markers if it had happened to one of his teams.

Eckersall was the referee when Michigan played Wisconsin in Madison and the Badgers were on the verge of achieving a 3–0 upset of the powerful Wolverines when they had victory literally snatched away from them in what one local writer called "the biggest robbery ever pulled off in Madison, Wisconsin."

Wisconsin, leading by 3–0 and playing a superb defensive game against heavily favored Michigan, was fighting to preserve its edge. The Badgers punted and Tod Rockwell, Michigan's safety man, ran the ball back about 20 yards before he was nailed by a pair of Wisconsin tacklers at midfield. For all intents and purposes, the play was over. But Rockwell got up, still clinging to the ball, and walked casually away from the mass of players on the ground. Suddenly he took off for the goal line 50 yards away while everyone, including the Wisconsin players, watched in amazement.

Colonel Mumma, the field judge who was on the play, ruled it a touchdown since Eckersall, the referee, had not blown his whistle to signify that the play was over when Rockwell was downed originally. Eckie refused to reverse the decision and then the storm broke. Wisconsin Coach Jack Ryan and his players and more than 20,000 Badger rooters ranted and raved, all to no avail. Eckersall stood firm and Michigan was given the victory, 6–3, which enabled the Wolverines to tie for the Big Ten title. After the game Eckersall had to be escorted off the field by the Wisconsin players to keep the aroused Badger rooters from tearing him apart.

That was Walter Eckersall, indomitable as a player, resolute as an official.

While Berwanger and Eckersall were the most legendary of the University of Chicago's football heroes, they were by no means the only outstanding players who performed for the Maroons, most of them for Amos Alonzo Stagg. The first of Stagg's superstars, oddly enough, was another little guy, Clarence Herschberger, a 158-pound fullback who became the first Chicago player to make All-America when Walter Camp selected him in 1898. Herschberger was a free spirit and, despite his skill as a runner and kicker, often raised Coach Stagg's dander.

Stagg always insisted that one of Herschberger's little peccadillos in 1897 cost Chicago the Big Ten championship. It seems that

Clarence and Walter Kennedy, the captain and quarterback, engaged in an eating marathon on the eve of the Wisconsin game. Kennedy won the gastronomical bout, piling enough goodies into his belly to gain seven and a half pounds, a half-pound more than Herschberger was able to add to his small frame. However, Clarence decided to make up that deficit the next morning and he ate a half-dozen eggs for breakfast. The result was that Herschberger became so ill that he was unable to play against Wisconsin. The Maroons missed Clarence's running and kicking in the game and lost to the Badgers, 23–8, their only loss of the season and just enough to knock them out of the conference title.

Among the other Chicago super-players before Berwanger became the last All-America were Wally Steffen, Paul (Shorty) Des Jardien, Chuck McGuire, Tiny Maxwell, Pat Page, Austin (Five-Yards) McCarthy—and two others, Hugo Bezdek and Fritz Crisler, who later became two of college football's greatest coaches.

What a pity that Chicago's football heritage expired when it did!

TWENTY-FOUR

Kinnick and Devine—Iowa's Best

One night in December 1939 Nile Clarke Kinnick, Jr., a stocky five-foot, nine-inch halfback from the University of Iowa, who had been judged the best college football player in America, stood before a huge throng gathered for dinner in the Downtown Athletic Club in New York City. He had just been presented with the Heisman Trophy, the coveted award for which almost every college player in the land would gladly give his right arm.

Adolf Hitler, the madman of Germany, had already begun his ill-fated campaign to rule the world and Europe was in the early throes of World War II. The combat had not yet touched the United States, but Americans everywhere were apprehensive about the future. However, that evening, at least, those Americans in the Downtown A.C. had put away their worries to pay tribute to this outstanding young athlete from Iowa.

When the applause subsided, Nile Kinnick paid tribute to his coach, Dr. Eddie Anderson, the Iowa assistant coaches, and his teammates. Then he finished his acceptance speech with the following words:

"I thank God that I was born to the gridirons of the Middle West and not to the battlefields of Europe. I can speak confidently and positively that the football players of this country would rather fight for the Heisman Trophy than for the *Croix de Guerre.*"

Two years later Kinnick was in uniform as an ensign in the United States Naval Reserve, destined for duty aboard an aircraft carrier in the Caribbean Sea. On June 2, 1943 Ensign Nile Clarke Kinnick, Jr., was lost at sea when his navy fighter plane crashed in the Gulf of Paria, barely four miles from his aircraft carrier. His fighter plane's engine had failed and he was unable to make it back to his ship.

Nile Kinnick's death touched not only the University of Iowa, where he had distinguished himself as both an athlete and scholar, but created a wave of sorrow across the entire nation. Those who remembered him for his football prowess mourned him as an athlete; those who remembered him as a Phi Beta Kappa mourned him as a scholar; those who remembered him as a budding young attorney mourned him as a man with a tremendous future in his chosen profession.

It was a tragedy that few people have ever forgotten.

Nile Kinnick reached the University of Iowa at a time when the football program was in a turmoil. The Hawkeyes' gridiron fortunes had dipped to an incredible low, and Coach Ossie Solem, under fire from alumni and the administration, resigned to accept the head coaching job at Syracuse University. After weeks of interviewing, Iowa decided on Irl Tubbs, who was then the coach at the University of Miami in Florida. Tubbs had previously coached in Missouri and Wisconsin high schools and put in a nine-year stint at Wisconsin State Teachers College. In his two seasons at Miami, he had compiled an 11–6–2 record.

Tubbs' first two seasons at Iowa were undistinguished. He had Nile Kinnick but, as good as Kinnick was, he wasn't enough to resuscitate the failing gridiron fortunes of the Hawkeyes. In his two seasons, Tubbs' Iowa teams won only two games while losing thirteen and tying one.

Despite this unimposing record, Kinnick shone like a beacon on a lighthouse. He ran, he passed, he kicked, and he defensed so tenaciously, even in a losing cause, that he received mention for All–Big Ten and All-America honors.

Meanwhile, Iowa newspapers were printing things like, "Iowa's football hopes, such as they were, painfully passed away yesterday afternoon, a victim of brutal grid assassins from the East—Colgate's Red Raiders. . . . Interment ceremonies will be held on almost any Iowa City street corner at almost any time you suggest. The sooner the better, however."

One of Iowa's two victories under Tubbs was over the University of Chicago, which was soon to give up football under the prodding of President Robert M. Hutchins. The Chicago *Tribune* noted that accomplishment with the following comment:

"Nearly every Saturday afternoon the gridiron enhanced scholarship and endowed it with new luster at Chicago and Iowa."

It was apparent that Tubbs' days were numbered in Iowa City, and Irl precipitated the decision even before the end of the 1938 season when he informed the Board in Control of Athletics that what Iowa needed to improve its football program was a dormitory for football players and a training table. He was told that Big Ten regulations prohibited both items and, in the words of Walter L. (Stub) Stewart, a member of the Board, "I told him I guessed there wasn't anything for us to do but look for another coach. He agreed."

So the hunt started again, and this time Iowa landed Dr. Eddie Anderson, who had been a star at Notre Dame and was currently the successful coach at Holy Cross in the East. In six previous seasons at the Worcester, Massachusetts, college, Anderson's teams had compiled a 51–7–4 record and were regarded as one of the powers in Eastern football. Getting Anderson was regarded by the Hawkeyes as quite a coup, and they were willing to sign him to a three-year contract at the then-munificent figure of $10,000 per year, a highly respectable figure for a head coach in 1939.

More important, Eddie Anderson inherited a superstar, Nile Kinnick. Between them, they led the Hawkeyes out of the wilderness in one of the greatest turnabouts in a single year ever seen in the Big Ten. Anderson's 1939 team went 6–1–1, finished second to Ohio State in the conference race, and actually had the best overall record of any team in the Midwest. Although Ohio State edged Iowa for the league title, the Buckeyes lost two games, one a nonconference defeat by Cornell.

Anderson had only a handful of players to work with and only a few of them were of the quality that wins football games. The Hawkeyes rarely used more than seventeen men in a game and usually made do with thirteen or fourteen, a feat which earned them the nickname of "Ironmen." But one of them was Nile Kinnick and he led this team to heights never dreamed possible before the season, even by Anderson.

Some football experts, like Bill Osmanski, the Holy Cross All-America fullback and later an All-Pro star with the Chicago Bears, who spent three weeks at Iowa helping out with spring practice, painted a dismal picture of Iowa's prospects for 1939.

When Osmanski returned to Worcester, he said, "Of five thousand male students at the University of Iowa, there are only five real football players."

Osmanski, of course, proved to be a poor prophet. It took only two games for the Big Ten to learn that the Hawkeyes were back and a team to contend with in the race for the championship. Eddie Anderson's coaching had a lot to do with the turnabout, naturally, but the catalyst on the field was Nile Kinnick, the man of varied talents.

Although the opposition was hardly of Big Ten calibre, Kinnick gave folks a preview of things to come in the opening game against South Dakota. He scored three touchdowns and kicked five extra points as the Hawkeyes humbled the modest visitors, 41–0. Perhaps the victory over South Dakota wasn't exactly the most earth-shattering event in Iowa football history, but it was the beginning of what was to be a fantastic season for both the Hawkeyes and Kinnick.

The Indiana game the following week turned out to be a more accurate indication of what to expect from Iowa. The Hoosiers came to town with an outstanding passer in Harold Hursch and a record of not having lost to the Hawkeyes since 1921. Furthermore, Iowa had not won a Big Ten game on its home field since 1933. It appeared that Kinnick and his teammates were overmatched. But the Hoosiers were in for a big surprise.

The game developed into a spectacular offensive show, with Kinnick keeping his team in the game and leading the Hawkeyes back from a ten-point deficit. He threw two touchdown passes and dazzled the Hoosiers with his running. However, with eight minutes remaining in the game, Iowa was behind, 29–26, and it seemed that the Hawkeyes were not going to be able to catch their rivals. Indiana elected not to sit on its slender lead and that bit of strategy led to the Hoosiers' ultimate downfall. Hursch, on target with his passes most of the afternoon, finally threw one too many. It was intercepted by Iowa's Bill Green, who returned the ball to the Indiana 26-yard line.

That was just the break that Kinnick and his opportunistic gang of Hawkeyes needed. Nile broke away for 16 yards, but then the Indiana defenders took charge and threw the Hawkeyes back to the 15-yard line. It was fourth down and Kinnick, an excellent dropkicker, had a choice: to go for the almost certain field goal and a tie or to go for the victory. Nile decided to go for the whole ball of wax, and his decision paid off. He calmly threw to Erwin Prasse for the touchdown—Kinnick's third scoring pass of the game—that gave Iowa a 32–29 victory, and the Big Ten lead.

As it turned out, the enthusiasm in Iowa City was premature.

Michigan, with its wondrous star, Tom Harmon, was next on the schedule and not even Kinnick's heroics, which included a 69-yard scoring pass, could save the Hawkeyes. Harmon had one of his best days, scoring four touchdowns, including one on a 90-yard interception of a Kinnick pass, and all of the Wolverine points in a 27–7 Michigan victory.

Although the loss to Michigan brought Iowa back among the mortals, it actually was only a momentary pause for Kinnick and his astonishing Hawkeyes. Kinnick's three touchdown passes beat Wisconsin, 19–13, two blocked kicks by tackle Mike Enich helped produce a pair of safeties that were enough to defeat Purdue, 4–0, and some late-game heroics by Kinnick produced a 7–6 upset of previously unbeaten Notre Dame.

It appeared that the Iowa bubble was about to burst when Minnesota's mighty Gophers got off to a 9–0 lead in the next game, but Kinnick, with one of his greatest passing exhibitions, brought his team back in the last quarter for a 13–9 victory. He threw 45 yards to Prasse for one touchdown and then heaved a 28-yard pass to Green for the winning score with only a couple of minutes remianing on the clock. It was another superb show by Kinnick.

One Chicago sportswriter, obviously enthralled by Kinnick's performance, wrote, "Nile Kinnick 13, Minnesota 9; tersely that tells the story of the most spectacular football game in modern Big Ten history."

Meanwhile, Kinnick had played nearly every minute of seven straight games, and most of his teammates had played with little or no respite in most games. The wonder of it all was that they were able to stand up to the demanding competition they faced in the Big Ten. Most of their rivals poured in reserves by the hordes in an effort to wear down the undermanned Hawkeyes. But Kinnick and his men hung in there relentlessly, game after game.

Kinnick's string of 402 consecutive minutes of competition was finally snapped in the final game of the season against Northwestern. With the Wildcats leading, 7–0, Kinnick sustained a shoulder separation and was led from the field early in the game. Without their great star, the Hawkeyes battled back to gain a 7–7 tie, a deadlock that cost them the Big Ten championship but gave them a 6–1–1 record for the season.

While Coach Eddie Anderson and every member of that tiny Iowa squad deserved credit for this accomplishment, it was Nile Kinnick who played the biggest role. His personal statistics were simply unbelievable. Of Iowa's nineteen touchdowns scored in 1939, Kinnick passed for 11 of them and scored 5 himself. He also dropkicked 11 points after touchdown to personally account for 107 of Iowa's 130 points scored. He passed for 684 yards (on only thirty-three completions), ran for 374, returned thirty-five punts and kickoffs for 616 yards, and averaged 39 yards on seventy-three punts. And just to add icing to his personal cake, Kinnick also led the nation in kickoff returns with 377 yards, and in interceptions with eight. It was a performance well worthy of recognition and the country's sports aficionados did not stint in paying tribute to the Iowa star.

Kinnick was voted the Heisman Trophy as well as the Maxwell and Walter Camp awards as the nation's outstanding college player. He was named to every major All-America team, and was honored by the Associated Press as Athlete of the Year. Perhaps even more cherished by Kinnick were the awards he won from his own college. In addition to being graduated from the college of commerce as a member of Phi Beta Kappa and of the Order of Artus, honorary commerce organization, Nile won the Iowa Athletic Board Cup for excellence in scholarship and athletics. His coach, Eddie Anderson, also was honored by being selected Coach of the Year.

As a premier football player, Kinnick was fair game for the pros and several teams went after him, dangling lucrative offers as the bait. But Nile spurned them all. This soft-spoken, unassuming young man was determined to become a lawyer and he did not feel that he could divide his efforts.

Unfortunately, Nile Kinnick's early and tragic demise in the wartime service of his country kept him from achieving his ambition and perhaps deprived his countrymen of an outstanding attorney.

Iowa, of course, had its glory years before Nile Kinnick and Hawkeye oldtimers like to recall the exploits of men like Duke Slater, Aubrey Devine, and Gordon Locke, three heroes who starred in the period from 1918 through 1922. They played during a time when college football was less sophisticated than it is now. It was a game that depended less on trickery and more on the durability and strength of its players.

Fred (Duke) Slater was one of those unusual young men who come along about once in a coach's lifetime. The son of a Clinton,

Iowa, minister, Slater was one of the first black men to play in the
Big Ten, and one of the first of his race to achieve All-America recognition. Although not huge by today's standards, Slater was big
for his time. He stood about six-foot two and weighed in at 210
pounds. But, more important, he had the strength and the tena-
ciousness of a tiger, and was the guts of an offensive line that
opened gaping holes for his teammates, Devine and Locke.

Duke wasn't easy to miss on the field. He disdained wearing a
helmet, and he was usually the man who cleaned out defensive
linemen for his runners or smothered opposing ball-carriers. Opponents often put two or three men on him, but Slater merely
shucked them off with his brute strength. Duke also had the kind of
speed that coaches envy. Invariably, he was the first man downfield under kicks, and many a safetyman suffered a moment of an-
guish when he saw this big fellow bearing down on him.

Oddly enough, Duke Slater very nearly didn't make it to Iowa,
or any other college. At fifteen he quit high school to take a job,
and his minister father, perhaps with an ulterior motive in mind,
helped him get a job cutting ice on the Mississippi River for a com-
mercial ice company. Working in subzero weather finally got to
Duke and, just as his dad had hoped, he decided to return to
school. Except for that bit of strategy by the astute Reverend Slater, Iowa and the Big Ten might never have gotten to see one of the
greatest tackles of all time.

Slater made the Iowa varsity as a freshman in 1918, and almost
immediately the Hawkeyes began the winning ways that were
eventually to carry them to the top in the Big Ten. He was joined
by Devine in 1919 and Locke in 1920, and their combined efforts in
1921 earned Iowa its first undefeated and untied season ever.

One of Slater's best games was Iowa's 10–7 upset of Notre
Dame in 1921. It was a game that Coach Howard Jones later called
the "biggest moment of my coaching career." Slater was all over
the field that day, throwing crushing blocks on offense, making
bone-shattering tackles on defense, and harassing Frank Thomas,
the Irish safetyman, on punt returns to help keep Notre Dame at
bay.

"Duke Slater did the work of three men in the line," said Coach
Jones after the game.

In the final estimation of Jones, who before and after coached
other great linemen at Iowa and the University of Southern California, Slater was one of the best he ever had under his wing. "He

almost never made a mistake," said Jones. "He was simply never out of position, never fooled by a fake, never mistaken on where the opposing ball carrier was going, never late on his offensive charge."

Fritz Crisler, who played against Slater while at the University of Chicago, called him "the best tackle I ever played against. I tried to block him throughout my college career but never once did I impede his progress to the ball carrier."

Slater made almost every All-America first team after that 1921 season except Walter Camp's. For some unknown reason, the Eastern sage relegated Duke to his second team, a disappointment which Slater and Iowans were never able to understand.

Despite this slight by Camp, Slater was picked by 600 sportswriters throughout the nation in 1946 as a member of their all-time All-America team, and in 1951 he was voted into the Hall of Fame, the final gridiron accolade for this unusual man, who went on to play pro football with the Chicago Cardinals and then become a distinguished judge of the Superior Court of Cook County, Illinois, until his death in 1966.

While Duke Slater was the big man in the Iowa line, most of the headlines in that superb 1921 season went to Aubrey Devine, the quarterback who was Iowa's first bona fide superstar. In fact, some enthusiasts even went so far as to call the 1921 Hawkeyes "Iowa's Devine Team," and with good reason.

Although hardly a giant in stature—he was only five-foot ten and 175 pounds—Devine was indeed a giant on the playing field. A triple-threat back, he ran, passed, and kicked with élan. He was particularly expert at executing the running pass. Even Coach Jones, who was not the most extravagant man in his praise of his players, admitted that having Aubrey at quarterback was like having a coach on the field.

Devine's rise to stardom was not exactly meteoric. He labored valiantly and with great distinction in the Hawkeye vineyards in 1919 and 1920 when Iowa was building up to its glory year of 1921. He led his team in passing, rushing, and scoring in both of those seasons—as well as the next one—and was recognized as a star of great magnitude as the 1919 and 1920 Hawkeyes lost only four games while winning ten.

But both Devine and Iowa truly came into their own in 1921. The canny Coach Jones came up with an offensive innovation to help diversify his team's attack. He devised a shift in which the ends dropped off into the backfield, and the maneuver paid off handsomely. It was essentially a quarterback-fullback offense with Devine and Gordon Locke doing most of the ball-carrying, while the halfbacks, Glenn Devine, Aubrey's brother, and Craven Shuttleworth, were relegated to the role of blockers. It gave Iowa a devastating attack that confounded opponents and enabled the Hawkeyes to sweep through their schedule for Iowa's first unbeaten and untied season, first Big Ten championship, and first real shot at national honors.

Game after game, it was Devine who supplied the big punch for Iowa. His 38-yard dropkick for a field goal beat Notre Dame, 10–7. His touchdown pass to Les Belding and 33-yard punt return for a score on a field ankle-deep in water after several days of rain accounted for a 13–6 victory over Purdue. Devine's greatest days, however, came in back-to-back games against Minnesota and Indiana.

The Minnesota game in Minneapolis turned out to be a personal showcase for the indomitable Aubrey Devine. All he did that memorable afternoon was account for every single point in a 41–7 triumph. Devine scored four touchdowns himself, passed 43 and 25 yards to Belding for two more scores, and dropkicked five extra points. His personal statistics were overwhelming. He carried thirty-four times for 162 yards, returned seven punts and kickoffs for another 180, and passed for 122, a total of 454 yards for the day. Devine also did all the punting, and twice he quick-kicked over the head of the Gopher safetyman.

After the game, Minnesota Coach Dr. Henry L. Williams shook his head in disbelief at what he had seen. "He is the greatest football player who ever stepped on Northrup Field," said Williams.

A week later Indiana got the Devine treatment from Aubrey. This time he ran for four touchdowns, kicked four extra points, ran for 183 yards, and passed for 102 in the first three quarters before he sat down as Iowa humbled the embattled Hoosiers, 41–0.

Devine finished that season with 895 yards rushing and 1,316 yards in total offense. For his three-year career, he ran for 1,961 yards and had over 3,000 in total offense. Not even Walter Camp could ignore this performance, and Aubrey Devine became the first Iowa player to be named to Camp's All-America first team.

Perhaps the great accolade for Devine came from Howard Jones, who said, "He was the greatest all-around backfield man I have ever coached or seen in the modern game. Others may have been better in individual categories, but I have never known any backfield man whose accomplishments in running, punting, drop-kicking, and forward passing combined equaled those of Aubrey Devine.''

Gordon Locke, who had languished in the background behind Devine, finally came into his own in 1922, his senior year, as Iowa continued to dominate the Big Ten, going through a 7–0 season and winning the conference championship again. The Hawkeyes also ran their winning streak to seventeen straight, and it was to go to twenty before Illinois beat them in the fourth game of the 1923 season.

A durable line-smasher with the power of a tank, Locke became a familiar and dreaded sight for Iowa opponents as, with knees pumping high, his toes barely touching the ground, he pounded enemy lines into submission with his smashing thrusts inside the tackles. Gordon also had remarkable speed, the kind that enabled him to run wide sweeps and outdistance his frustrated pursuers.

In 1922, with Devine gone, it was Locke who carried the Hawkeyes. Twice during the season Gordon scored four touchdowns in a game, against Knox College in the opener and against Northwestern in the final game that clinched the league title. He scored three times in a 28–14 win over Minnesota and both of Iowa's touchdowns in a 12–9 victory over Ohio State.

In his three varsity years, Locke carried the ball 430 times for almost 2,000 yards and lost only 11, scored thirty-two touchdowns and 192 points. His seventy-two points in five games in 1922 set a Big Ten record that survived even the onslaught of the great Red Grange and Tom Harmon. It lasted twenty-one years, until the late Tony Butkovich of Purdue finally surpassed it with seventy-eight in 1943. Needless to say, Locke also achieved All-America recognition.

In between and after the eras of Aubrey Devine, Gordon Locke, and Nile Kinnick, Iowa had other great backs who enthralled Hawkeye fans with their exploits. One of these was Nick Kutsch, a rawboned halfback who was called "Cowboy" because he once had a job prodding cattle down a runway to the slaughterhouse in a packing plant. Kutsch's career at Iowa was short but sweet, and highly productive.

A transfer from little Trinity College in Sioux City in 1925, Kutsch's eligibility at Iowa was limited to two years, 1925 and 1926, but he left quite a mark on Hawkeye football during this brief tenure. So much so that he was one of the few Big Ten players of that time who outshone the great Red Grange in head-to-head combat. If he had done nothing else, the Cowboy would have been remembered for that feat alone.

Kutsch broke into Iowa football with a bang heard around the Big Ten conference. In his first three games in 1925 he scored fifty points, rushed for 427 yards, and averaged 8 yards per carry. But it was the Cowboy's third game against Illinois and Grange that finally established him as a star.

Iowa had won its first two games rather handily, but it wasn't given much of a chance against Illinois. After all, the Illini had Red Grange and who could stop him? And it seemed that Grange was in for one of his typical days when he took the opening kickoff and ran it back 89 yards for a touchdown. However, after that, the game belonged to Cowboy Kutsch. He pounded the surprised Illini line for 144 yards, kicked two 25-yard field goals, and ended his afternoon's work by smashing over for a touchdown in the final minute to give the Hawkeyes a surprising 12–10 victory.

Kutsch was badly injured in the Ohio State game the next week and saw only limited service during the rest of the 1925 season, but he did enough damage to Iowa opponents to lead his team in both rushing and scoring. Back in shape in 1926, the Cowboy continued to ravage the Big Ten. Although Iowa won only three games, Kutsch rushed for 781 yards to bring his two-year average to 6 yards per carry.

It was eight long years before Iowa came up with another super runner, not until Oze Simmons, a lithe, swivel-hipped speedster, arrived in Iowa City in 1934. It wasn't long before everyone knew his name—most people called him Ozzie—and it wasn't long before he reached stardom under the most difficult of conditions. Iowa football had slipped badly under Coach Ossie Solem, and whatever Simmons accomplished in the next three years, he did mostly on his own, except in 1935, when he had the advantage of some hard-nosed blocking by Dick Crayne, who had been the team's leading runner but sacrificed himself—and the headlines—to try to spring Ozzie loose.

Simmons had a style all his own. Possessed of breakaway speed, Ozzie darted through opposing secondaries like a wraith. He would throw a hip at a waiting tackler, shift gears, and then take off in the opposite direction. Sometimes it was a sideways hop; other times it was simply a burst of incredible speed that would leave defenders gaping. He was a marvel to watch.

It took just two games for Ozzie Simmons to impress the fans— and his foes—with his brilliant talents. He virtually singlehandedly wrecked Northwestern, the first Big Ten opponent he faced, with a dazzling performance. That day he ran for 166 yards from scrimmage and picked up 124 more on punt returns as the Hawkeyes leveled the Wildcats, 20–7. That was just the first of many spectacular running days he was to have in 1934, 1935, and 1936, as he piled up more than 1,500 yards rushing and on eight occasions broke away on touchdown runs of 50 yards or more.

Perhaps the best description of Ozzie's running came from Ralph Cannon, who wrote in the Chicago *Daily News* in 1934, "This slithery, rubbery, oozy flyer with his gyrating balance, cool, masterful mental poise, sleek, smooth weaving hips and the most perfect open field pivot probably in the game today, can make his legs talk more languages than even Red Grange's could when he was a sophomore. . . . He is a master, a finished big league runner like Eddie Mahan of Harvard or Eddie Kaw of Cornell, who knows all the tricks of open field progress." And this when Simmons was only a sophomore!

Coach Solem was even more extravagant in his praise of Simmons. Ossie said, "He was one of the two or three greatest backs I've ever coached and the best halfback I've ever seen. He had only one weakness. Sometimes he would think a little faster than his interference and get away from his blockers and get himself in trouble."

It wasn't until twenty years later, when Forest Evashevski was nursing Iowa back to football respectability, that the Hawkeyes again spawned a group of super-backs. There was quarterback Randy Duncan, a pinpoint passer in 1956, 1957, and 1958; Bob Jeter, a fast-stepping halfback in 1957, 1958, and 1959; and Larry Ferguson, the stylish runner who excelled in 1959, 1960, and 1962. In 1958 Duncan gained All-America honors as he led the nation in passing percentage and in yards gained passing, and tied for first in touchdown passes thrown. Randy also was second in total offense and was so highly regarded that he was the runner-up to Pete Dawkins of Army in the voting for the Heisman Trophy. Ferguson, a runner in the mold of Ozzie Simmons, was an All-America in 1960. Then, in the late sixties, there was Ed Podolak, an all-purpose quarterback who went on to star as a running back for the Oakland Raiders of the National Football League.

The Evashevski years also produced a spate of outstanding linemen, the men in the pits who made things easier for the Duncans, Jeters, and Fergusons. The best were Jerry Hilgenberg, an All-America center in 1953, Calvin Jones, Alex Karras, and Curt Merz; but perhaps the greatest of all was Jones, the powerful guard who was a two-time All-America in 1954 and 1955, and called by some the best lineman in Iowa history.

Jones, a ferocious blocker and tackler, almost didn't make it to Iowa City, though. Cal had made plans to go elsewhere, but he decided to visit two of his Steubenville, Ohio, teammates, halfback Eddie Vincent and end Frank Gillian, to see how they were getting along at Iowa. Obviously, Vincent and Gillian, and maybe even Coach Evashevski, did some quick brainwashing because Cal decided to stay, an extremely fortuitous decision for both the Hawkeyes and Jones.

After the 1955 season, during which Jones won the Outland Award as the nation's outstanding interior lineman, Evashevski paid Cal the supreme tribute. He retired his "No. 62" jersey, only the second time in Iowa history that a player had been so honored. Nile Kinnick's "No. 24" had been retired to posterity years earlier.

Less than a year after he was graduated, Calvin Jones met an untimely death, perishing in a tragic plane crash in Canada. It was an odd coincidence that both Jones and Kinnick met an early death in similar circumstances.

Alex Karras, a broad, brawny, and devastating tackle, took over the spotlight in 1956 and 1957, and emerged as the premier lineman in the country. In the spring of 1956 Coach Evashevski had borrowed the wing-T formation from former teammate Dave Nelson, who had developed the offense and had great success with it at little Delaware. The new formation operated from a balanced line and Karras found a comfortable home at a tackle spot, from which he terrorized friend and foe alike. Built like a bull, he was one of the movers and shakers of the 1956 team that went from obscurity to renown as it won the Big Ten title, finished No. 3 in the nation, and went on to beat Oregon State in the Rose Bowl, 35–19.

Karras, later an All-Pro star with the Detroit Lions, was an All-

America in both 1956 and 1957, and was the runner-up to John Crow, the Texas A&M back, for the Heisman Trophy in 1957, the first time a lineman had ever finished that high in the annual balloting. Karras also won the Outland Award, the second time in three years it had gone to an Iowa lineman.

At the same time that Karras was performing his deeds of derring-do for the Hawkeyes, Curt Merz was beginning a career as an Iowa end. A splendid pass receiver and blocker, Merz, too, became an All-America in 1959.

Iowa has had many other fine football players in its illustrious history, but these were the ones who stood head and shoulders above the rest through the good and the bad years.

TWENTY-FIVE

Chic, Hopalong, and Archie

For years, loyal Ohio Staters, and there are no more fierce fans in the entire nation than old Buckeyes, argued the respective merits of two of the brightest backfield stars who ever ruffled the hallowed turf in Columbus—Charles Wesley (Chic) Harley and Howard (Hopalong) Cassady, whose exploits were performed three and one-half decades apart. Who was the greater—Harley, who launched Ohio State on its trip to football fame and fortune back in 1916, 1917, and 1919; or Cassady, the nimble-footed tailback who performed like Nijinski on cleats in 1953, 1954, and 1955? The pros and cons have been discussed in living rooms and bars the length and width of Columbus lo these many years.

Then, in 1972, along came Archie Griffin, a talented young freshman halfback who made even Coach Woody Hayes, an old Cassady worshipper from way back, start singing a different tune. Archie had a little bit of both Harley and Cassady in his style and maybe even a touch more than either in the way of running talent.

To compare the trio is a little like trying to match oranges with apples and pears. Each starred in an era of his own, each had his own little tricks of the trade that made him special, and each played in a game that had changed both in tactics and skills. Harley, Cassady, or Griffin? Take your pick. They were all superstars.

He came out of East High School in Columbus, a quiet, black-haired youngster with high cheekbones who weighed in at a scant 145 pounds and stood barely five-feet seven-inches. Although he looked more like a member of the debating team, Chic Harley was a terror when he was unleashed on a football field. He ran, he passed, he punted, and he dropkicked, and he did them all so well

that Columbus East lost only one game, his last one against Columbus North, in Harley's three years of varsity football. Ohio newspapers acclaimed him as one of the state's greatest schoolboy players of all time.

Needless to say, college recruiters flocked around Chic Harley
like mother hens around a new chick. They clucked with approval
as they tried to induce this young man with many skills to attend
their respective schools. They could have saved their breath. The
only school Chic really wanted to go to was hometown Ohio State,
and that is where he turned up as a freshman in the fall of 1915.

Ohio State had been admitted to the Big Ten in 1912, but, so far,
the Buckeyes had not made much of an impression on conference
football. Local high school games, especially those which featured
young Harley, frequently outdrew the Buckeyes, but things had
begun to look up under Coach John Wilce, who took over the head
coaching post in 1913. Still, Ohio State wasn't exactly feared by its
conference rivals.

Chic Harley turned that all around with astonishing swiftness.
That is, once he won the battle of the books. After spending a year
on the freshman team, bedeviling the varsity in scrimmages with
his running, passing, and kicking, and filling the hearts and minds
of Ohio State followers with illusions of sudden grandeur, Chic almost didn't make it for the 1916 season. He was in trouble aca-
demically and it wasn't until two days before the opening game
against Ohio Wesleyan that his eligibility was approved.

Once free of academic worries, it didn't take long for Harley to
live up to his reputation. Ohio State easily beat Ohio Wesleyan,
12–0, in its first game, and then, with Harley passing and running,
the Buckeyes smashed poor little Oberlin, 128–0. Though both victories were hardly a test for Ohio State, it was apparent that the
Buckeyes for the first time were going to be a team to be reckoned
with in the Big Ten championship race.

The first test came in the conference opener against Illinois in
Champaign. No one ever knew quite what to expect from wily Illini
Coach Bob Zuppke and Wilce was certain that Zup would come up
with something to try to shackle Harley. There *was* something, but
Zuppke really couldn't claim all the credit for it. The something
was rain that turned the Illinois field into a quagmire. Harley and
his teammates were held in check for almost fifty-nine minutes.
Meanwhile Illinois built a 6–0 lead on a pair of field goals by Bart
Macomber.

Harley finally got Ohio State going and, in the final minute, the

Bucks were on the Illinois 12-yard line. Chic went back to pass, found all his receivers covered, and then did the most natural thing. He simply tucked the ball under his arm and headed for the sideline with Illini defenders in hot pursuit. He outran them all and dove into the end zone for the tying touchdown. Now, the outcome of the game depended upon Harley's trusty right leg.

Chic called a time-out and asked for a dry right shoe to replace the mud-caked one he had worn throughout the game. He took his time donning the replacement shoe, carefully tying the laces, then hitched up his pants and calmly dropkicked the ball through the up-rights to give the Bucks a 7–6 victory.

It is fair to say that Chic Harley had a flair for the dramatic. Time and again during his illustrious career he came up with the kind of heroics that snatched victory from defeat for Ohio State. Sometimes with a spectacular touchdown run, other times with a scoring pass or a dropkick. Chic was a daring, imaginative player and perhaps the closest thing to a one-man gang that the Big Ten had seen since the days of Willie Heston of Michigan.

Harley had a style all his own, one that occasionally gave his own teammates some fretful moments and almost always gave the opposition fits. When catching a punt or kickoff, Chic would loaf a little, doing a little dogtrot while viewing his possibilities for a long return. Once he had the field spread and found his opening, he would take off like a rocket, turning on his great speed and utilizing his amazing sense of timing and change of pace to throw tacklers off balance. Despite his slight appearance, Chic also had the power to blast through defenders. Ohio State ran mostly from a deep-punt formation, which gave Harley time to gain momentum before he got to the line of scrimmage. Even with the rounder football in use in those days, Harley was an exceptionally accurate passer. His kicking, too, was faultless, whether he was punting or dropkicking for field goals and points after touchdown. Along with these physical attributes, Chic had an insatiable desire to achieve victory. He was a born winner.

Although he was hardly an unknown in Columbus because of his feats as a schoolboy athlete, Harley became an instant celebrity after his game-winning performance against Illinois. A modest, sincere man, he took his fame gracefully as hero worshippers on and off the campus took him to their hearts.

"He inspired the mother instinct in women," recalls one old Ohio State follower.

Harley didn't wait very long to give a repeat of his sensational performance against Illinois. The very next week Wisconsin was leading the Buckeyes, 7–0, in the third quarter when Chic suddenly began his own fireworks. First he threw a 33-yard pass to his end, Dwight Peabody, to put the ball on the Badger 27-yard line. On the next play he slipped off tackle and slithered and sidestepped his way through the secondary and into the end zone for a score. His dropkick for the extra point tied the score at 7–7. Then, midway through the last period, Harley broke away for an 80-yard touchdown run, breaking tackles like a rodeo bronco and outrunning frustrated defenders. Again he calmly booted the extra point to put Ohio State ahead, 14–7, a kick that eventually was the winning margin in a 14–13 victory.

Harley continued his spectacular playing and Ohio State kept on winning until all the amazing Buckeyes needed was a win over Northwestern to take their first Big Ten championship.

Coach Wilce, Harley, and his teammates knew the Wildcats would not be a cakewalk. Northwestern was also unbeaten, including three conference victories, and had its own superstar in Paddy Driscoll.

The day of the game dawned bitter cold with near-freezing temperatures and lashing winds, but that didn't keep a near-capacity crowd of 11,979 from jamming little Ohio Field when the teams took the field for the kickoff. Since most of them were Buckeye fans, they were in an optimistic and festive mood, their hopes high and their eyes focused on the indomitable Chic Harley and his Northwestern counterpart Paddy Driscoll.

Harley was the first to move into the spotlight, kicking a 34-yard field goal in the opening quarter. Then the defenses took over and neither team was able to move the ball substantially until Northwestern got into the field-goal range early in the fourth quarter. Driscoll promptly booted a 40-yarder to tie the score at 3–3 and, the way things had been going, it seemed fairly possible that the game would end in a deadlock.

However, Chic Harley didn't see it that way. The first time Northwestern punted in the fourth quarter, Chic gathered in the ball on his own 33-yard line, did his inimitable little dogtrot for a few seconds, and then took off for the goal line 67 yards away. Not a single Northwesterner laid hands on him as he went the full route for a touchdown. Moments later the aroused Buckeyes were on the Wildcats' 20-yard line with Harley in the tailback spot and the ends split. It was an obvious pass play and Northwestern's onrushing linemen swallowed the bait. They crashed through to rush Harley, but Chic took off like a shot and almost before the Wildcats knew what had happened he was in the end zone for another touchdown.

Before the game ended Harley set up another score with a long pass to give the happy, undefeated Bucks a 23–3 victory and the conference crown.

There was little doubt about Chic Harley's All-America stature. Walter Eckersall, the old Chicago star, writing in the Chicago *Tribune,* let the Midwestern world know "Chic Harley will be placed on my All-America team. He's one of the greatest players I've ever seen."

Walter Camp agreed with Eckersall and also picked Harley for his All-America team, stating flatly, "He is one of the greatest players the country has ever seen. He is an excellent leader, shifty, fast and one of the best open-field runners in years."

With this first flush of success behind them, Coach Wilce, Harley, and his returning teammates looked forward to the 1917 season with great expectations. But Harley, busy winning letters in basketball, baseball, and track, as well as football, didn't have much time left over for his studies and his eligibility again was in doubt until just before the opener with Case. Eventually Chic managed to get clearance from his profs and he was in uniform for the first game, a 49–0 romp over the Clevelanders. Then Harley scored three touchdowns as the Buckeyes routed Ohio Wesleyan, 53–0.

After these two "breathers," OSU was ready to begin defense of its Big Ten championship against Northwestern. This time it was no contest. While Harley confined his duties mostly to blocking, Gaylord (Pete) Stinchcomb showed *his* talents as a runner, scoring three touchdowns as Northwestern fell, 40–0.

After a 57–0 trouncing of Denison, Ohio State got into the serious part of its Big Ten schedule. Indiana was first and Coach Wilce decided not to start Harley so Chic would have an opportunity to get a good look at his opposition. Scouting of future opponents was not as sophisticated in those days, and game films, an important part of pregame preparation today, were unheard of. However it didn't take Wilce long to realize that he had to get Harley into the fray, and quick. The Buckeyes sputtered like a wet motor and were going nowhere until Chic went into action late in the first quarter. He immediately proceeded to tear up the Hoosiers. Harley ran 40, 8, 11, and 33 yards for touchdowns, and Indiana succumbed rather meekly, 26–3. The next week Chic threw a pair of touchdown passes to Charles (Shifty) Bolen and another to Hap Courtney, kicked a field goal and an extra point, and OSU walked off with a tough 16–3 victory over Wisconsin.

Now only Illinois stood between Ohio State and a second straight Big Ten title and the Illini, still distressed over the previous year's narrow loss to the Buckeyes, were well-prepared for Harley. Canny Bob Zuppke had his defenses stacked to stop Chic's running, and the Illini did a pretty good job of zeroing in on him whenever he got the ball. But Illinois couldn't stop his passing or kicking. He threw 17 yards to Courtney for the game's only touchdown, kicked the extra point, and then booted 14- and 29-yard field goals to give Ohio State a 13–0 win and its second straight conference crown. The triumph also stretched the Bucks' winning streak to seventeen straight games.

Chic Harley, of course, made all the All-America teams—along with Shifty Bolen, the superb end—for the second straight year. There was no doubt about Chic Harley's status as a superstar and Ohio State fans responded predictably. Huge crowds jammed Ohio Field whenever the Bucks played at home. Columbus was beginning to get the fever that would make the Ohio city the self-acknowledged football capital of the United States. And also to make little Ohio Field obsolete for big-time football.

There was to be an interruption, however, in both Chic Harley's career and Ohio State's ascendency to national football supremacy. The United States, by this time, was deeply involved in World War I and after the 1917 season most college athletes began leaving campuses in droves to enlist in the services. Among them were Harley and Stinchcomb, the two shiniest stars in the Ohio State firmament. Because of wartime conditions, the Big Ten approved only a limited schedule for 1918 and some schools around the country even gave up football for the duration.

Without Harley and the other Ohio State regulars who had gone off to war, Ohio State dipped back into mediocrity in 1918, breaking even in a six-game schedule and losing all three of its conference games, to Michigan, Illinois, and Wisconsin.

Happily, World War I ended in November of 1918 and Chic Harley was out of the Army Air Corps and back in school for the 1919 season. Harley quickly showed that his year out of football had not impaired his skills. The first time Chic carried the ball in the opening game against Ohio Wesleyan, he ran 35 yards for a touchdown. Then he scored once, kicked two field goals and three extra points in a 46–0 win over Cincinnati, and ran for three touchdowns as Ohio State rolled over Kentucky, 49–0. It was obvious to all that Chic Harley still had his magic touch.

The stage was now set for the biggest challenge of Chic Harley's meteoric career. Ohio State was going up to Ann Arbor to play Michigan, even then a hated rival and one which the Buckeyes had never beaten. In fifteen games since 1897, the best OSU had been able to get was a pair of ties—a scoreless effort in 1900 and a 3–3 deadlock in 1910. In fact, the Bucks had been able to score only twenty-one points against Michigan in those fifteen games. The Wolverines' dominance over Ohio State had been complete.

Ah, but 1919 was another year. Michigan had never had to face Chic Harley. The two teams had played only once since 1912—in 1918, when Harley was off fighting a war. Buckeye fans sensed that this was going to be *their* year and there were plenty of them among the 27,000 in the stands at old Ferry Field in Ann Arbor that Saturday afternoon in late October. And they weren't disappointed.

Late in the third quarter, with Ohio State holding a slender 7–3 lead and the ball on the Michigan 40-yard line, Harley took charge. With his usual flair for the dramatic, Chic came up with the big play. Tucking the ball under his arm, he started toward right end, cut inside behind a good block, and then proceeded to run through the entire Michigan team for the touchdown that nailed down a 13–3 victory. Although it was not noticeable in the scoring, Harley had quite an afternoon against Michigan. He intercepted four of the Wolves' eighteen passes and averaged 42 yards on eleven punts, one of his kicks flying 60 yards to get the Buckeyes out of trouble. Needless to say the Michigans were impressed, so much so that Coach Fielding Yost, who rarely heaped praise on an opponent, went out of his way to visit the Ohio State locker room to pay his respects to Harley.

The rest of the 1919 season was a series of personal triumphs for Harley—until his final game against Illinois. There was a lot on the line that gray, wet day in late November—a third straight unbeaten season for Harley and a third Big Ten title for him and his Buckeyes. The Illini had lost only one game, a narrow 14–10 decision to Wisconson, and Coach Zuppke, the master strategist, had just about convinced his charges that they could whip the imposing Ohio Staters.

More than 17,000 fans jammed into Ohio Field for Chic Harley's finale. They had no reason to expect anything but another Buckeye victory. And why not? Hadn't they watched the invincible Harley lead his team to nothing but victories in his three varsity years? It would have been nonsense to think anything else. Besides, this was a special game, the last one Chic Harley would play in a Scarlet uniform, and, surely, he would be at his very best.

Even the editors of the Ohio State *Lantern*, the student daily, were aware of the dramatic possibilities of the day and they were prepared to capitalize on them. They planned a special "extra" with coverage of the game which would roll off the presses in time to be rushed to Ohio Field within minutes of the end of the contest for distribution to the fans as they were leaving the old wooden stands. Such was the optimism that prevailed that day in Columbus.

It certainly looked as if the *Lantern* was going to fill its mission in style when the Buckeyes led, 7–6, with only three minutes to go and the ball in their possession. Earlier, Harley's running and passing had carried Ohio State more than half the length of the field to the Illini 2-yard line. From there it was a simple matter for Harley to squirm over for a touchdown and he kicked the extra point. Illinois had come back to score but missed the extra point, and that's the way things stood as the minutes ticked off on the clock.

So secure did Ohio State's position seem that the confident student editor of the *Lantern* gave the word to let the presses roll with the banner headline proclaiming an Ohio State victory and another Big Ten title for the Buckeyes. Celebrating fans would be able to read all about it as they left Ohio Field.

Then came one of the few mistakes Chic Harley ever made on a football field. From deep in his own territory Harley let fly with a pass and it was intercepted by the alert Illini. Coach Zuppke's team mounted one last offensive effort and it took Illinois down to the Ohio 12-yard line. With only eight seconds remaining, the visitors quickly lined up in field-goal formation and Bobby Fletcher's drop-kick floated over the crossbar for the points that gave Illinois a 9–7 victory. Meanwhile, student newsboys were hawking the ill-fated issue of the *Lantern,* whose large and by then ridiculous headlines hailed an Ohio State victory. Thus ended the Chic Harley era at Ohio State.

But what an era it had been! Harley's individual brilliance would never be forgotten. In three years he had scored twenty-three touchdowns, thirty-nine extra points, and ten goals for 201 points, and Ohio State had won twenty-one games, while losing only one and tying one, and captured two Big Ten titles. Chic was a three-time All-America, one of the few ever to be so honored in college football.

More than that, though, the impact Chic Harley had on Ohio State football was rare and almost unbelievable. In three short seasons he had almost singlehandedly lifted the Buckeyes from football mediocrity into a national power, a position it was never to relinquish in the years to come. People in Columbus still claim that football at Ohio State really didn't begin until Chic Harley played his first game for the Bucks. Even years later, when other All-America stars were prancing up and down the field in huge Ohio Stadium—still another result of Harley's imprint on Ohio State football—there were those who insisted that Chic was the greatest football player ever to don a pair of cleats. All of Columbus mourned in April 1974 when Chic Harley, at the age of seventy-eight, died of bronchial pneumonia in the Danville, Illinois, Veteran's Administration Hospital.

If people were still writing epitaphs, perhaps the most fitting one for Charles Wesley (Chic) Harley would have been: "Here lies the man who invented Ohio State football."

Thirty-three years after Chic Harley, in 1952, a slight, redhead-ed, 155-pound youngster sat across the desk from Coach Woody Hayes in his green-walled office in St. John Arena, nervously clasping his fingers together as the Ohio State coach looked him over.

"I weigh only a hundred seventy-five pounds," lied Howard Cassady, "and I don't know whether that's big enough."

"If you're good enough, you're big enough," replied Woody.

That brief exchange was the beginning of a brilliant college career that was to bring Howard Cassady All-America fame and the Heisman Trophy, and Ohio State back-to-back Big Ten championships and a trip to the Rose Bowl. It also was to bring endless arguments among Columbus football partisans on the subject of who was the greater player, Harley or Cassady.

Oddly enough, although Cassady played his high school football in Columbus, he almost never got to Ohio State. Like most youngsters growing up in Columbus, Howard worshipped the Buckeyes. When Ohio State played at home, he would walk from his home on the west side of the city to the huge stadium on the campus and sneak in to watch his heroes perform. His life's ambition was to someday play for OSU.

Cassady got his first taste of competitive football as a 130-pound second-string sophomore fullback at Central High School and, by his senior year, had achieved local and statewide fame as a star runner. It also was a time when Hopalong Cassidy, the famous Hollywood cowboy actor, was prominent in the movies, so it was only natural that young Cassady was dubbed "Hopalong" by a caption writer for the Columbus *Dispatch*.

After Cassady's final high school season, offers from colleges began to pour in. Notre Dame, Wisconsin, and Kentucky, among others, were hot after the Central High star, but Ohio State, where he really wanted to go, was strangely silent. Obviously, the Buck-eyes weren't interested too much in 155-pound halfbacks, even those who ran with a football like Hopalong Cassady. Actually Ohio State should have been interested in almost anyone who could play the game since new Coach Woody Hayes' first season in 1951 had not exactly been a howling success. The Bucks had been able to win only four games while losing three and tying two.

Finally, through the efforts of Lou Berliner, a scholastic sports writer for the Columbus *Dispatch*, Ohio State got around to con-tacting young Cassady. The result was the across-the-desk meeting with Coach Hayes and a subsequent football scholarship for Cas-sady, who entered Ohio State in the spring of 1952 after graduating from high school in December. The fact that Cassady enrolled for the spring quarter turned out to be a lucky break for both him and the Buckeyes. That summer the Big Ten rescinded the Korean War rule that would have allowed freshmen who entered school in the fall to play varsity football. Cassady, however, although a fresh-man, was eligible for the 1952 season because he was already in school.

Almost immediately, Hopalong Cassady established himself as a potential star. In Ohio State's opener against Indiana, Cassady rode the bench until Bobby Watkins, a bull-like runner, injured an ankle. Coach Hayes beckoned to Cassady, the freshman, who pranced onto the field like a young colt and then proceeded to run wild. He scored three touchdowns in the 33–13 trouncing of the Hoosiers, going over from the 4- and 6-yard lines and capping his debut by catching a 27-yard pass from quarterback John Borton for another score.

It was an auspicious beginning for any player, but especially so for a 155-pound halfback who was almost overlooked by Ohio State in the first place.

After that Cassady began to see more action and, although he was unable to duplicate his brilliant opening-game performance, finished the season with six touchdowns and more than 290 yards rushing in sixty-five carries. Ohio State's grid fortunes also improved as the Buckeyes posted a 6–3 record.

Cassady's individual achievements as a runner were particularly notable because, and folks who have become used to Woody Hayes' classic landlocked offense over the years—3 yards and a cloud of dust they call it—may find this hard to believe, Ohio State was a *passing* team in 1952. Indeed, John Borton, the quarterback, set a whole bunch of school passing records which still stand in the books. Borton completed 115 of 196 passes for 1,555 yards and fifteen touchdowns. In one game against Pittsburgh he threw forty-four times and completed twenty-five of his tosses. In another game with Washington State, John passed for 312 yards and five touchdowns!

Ohio State football—Woody Hayes–style—was on the upswing. But Hayes suddenly learned that he was going to have to make some major adjustments in his style for the 1953 season. The N.C.A.A., acting on a recommendation from the Football Rules Committee, abolished two-platoon football and now Hayes had to find players who could play both ways, on offense and defense. He began shifting players around to take advantage of their versatility.

Hopalong Cassady, of course, was firmly entrenched as the starting left halfback—Watkins was switched to right half—and he quickly earned a reputation as one of the most feared runners in the conference. Cassady's extraordinary skills in an open field made him a breakaway threat almost every time he laid hands on the ball. Hoppy averaged 5.9 yards a carry and scored eight touchdowns. He also proved to be adept at playing defense, a new game for him. The Buckeyes duplicated their 1952 record—six wins and three losses—but one of those defeats was a 20–0 shellacking by hated Michigan and the alumni were beginning to become hostile. The heat was on Woody Hayes, but he ignored it. With Cassady still around, Hayes was already looking ahead to 1954.

And what a year 1954 was! With Cassady and Watkins supplying the offensive punch, along with Hubert Bobo, a smashing sophomore fullback, and a beefy line led by end Dean Dugger, who was to gain All-America honors, and Jim Parker, a 248-pound mobile sophomore guard, opening gaping holes on offense and throttling the enemy on defense, Ohio State rolled over its opponents like a huge steamroller. Cassady scored two touchdowns, one on a 68-

yard run after snatching a fumble out of midair, in an opening game 28–0 rout of Indiana, and Hoppy got two more on 26- and 29-yard runs in the next contest as the Bucks outscored California, 21–13. Then Illinois, Iowa, Wisconsin, Northwestern, Pittsburgh, and Purdue fell in quick succession to bring OSU up to the annual finale with Michigan. All the while Cassady and his sidekick, Watkins, had turned the Big Ten into one happy playground.

The unbeaten Buckeyes had to win over twice-beaten (but 5–1 in the Big Ten) Michigan to earn the conference title and a trip to the Rose Bowl. OSU also was playing for the national championship, a pretty bauble which had eluded the Bucks for far too long. They were ranked No. 1 in the Associated Press poll and No. 2 by United Press going into the crucial game.

As the Michigan game approached, Columbus acquired its usual pre-Wolverine tension, except that now it was even more pronounced because of the circumstances surrounding the game. Woody Hayes contributed to it by working his players behind closed doors. Local sportswriters, and even the team doctor, were barred from the practice field. Then, the day of the game, a steady rain poured down on the city, and Hayes, worried about the condition of the field, insisted that the Ohio State and Michigan bands be kept off the turf, both prior to the kickoff and during the halftime. Woody lost that one, but it was the only thing he was to lose that entire afternoon.

Not that Hayes and his Buckeyes had things easy. Michigan stunned OSU with an early touchdown to take a 7–0 lead that lasted until late in the first half. Then Ohio State quarterback Dave Leggett threw a 16-yard touchdown pass to end Fred Kriss, and little Ted Weed, Ohio State's placekicking specialist, sent the teams off at halftime in a 7–7 tie. So far the usually ubiquitous Hopalong Cassady had not been much of a factor in the game.

Indeed, it appeared that Ohio State's dreams of a postseason trip to Pasadena were going down the drain when Michigan pounded to a first down on the OSU 4-yard line at the start of the last quarter. However the tough Buckeye defense, led by big Jim Parker, rose up in all its glory to hold the driving Wolverines, taking away the ball on downs on the half-yard line. And, although few among the crowd of 82,438 in Ohio Stadium realized it at the time, that proved to be the death knell for Michigan's hopes.

Just as he had all season, it was Hopalong Cassady who provided the impetus for an Ohio State comeback that has rarely been duplicated. From the 2-yard line, on second down, the irrepressible Hoppy broke off tackle, snake-hipped his way through a broken field, and wasn't nabbed until he reached the Michigan 37-yard line, 61 yards away from where he started. With the fire appropriately ignited by their star, the Buckeyes didn't stop until Leggett's second touchdown pass of the day, a short 8-yarder to end Dick Brubaker, ended the 99½-yard drive, Weed kicked the extra point for a 14–7 lead, and Michigan's hopes began to ebb.

Minutes later Cassady intercepted a pass by Michigan's Don Cline and returned it 35 yards to the Wolverines' 39-yard line. Then, with forty-four seconds left, Hopalong crashed over from the one, Weed again booted the point after touchdown, and the Buckeyes came off the field with a 21–7 victory.

It mattered very little at the time that Ohio State was only the second team in Big Ten history to go through a seven-game conference schedule unbeaten and the first since Chicago accomplished the feat in 1913. What *did* matter was that Woody Hayes and the Buckeyes had stilled their detractors and Ohio State was on the way to the coveted Rose Bowl to meet the University of Southern California.

After the game, while celebrating Ohio State fans were still snaking around the field and singing, "Oh, We Don't Give a Damn For the Whole State of Michigan, We're from Ohio," Coach Hayes paid tribute to his club, calling it "the greatest team with the finest fighting heart I've ever known."

"Hopalong Cassady is certainly an All-America," declared Woody, "and he deserves the Heisman Trophy award."

Well, Woody's praise for Cassady didn't pay off altogether. Hopalong was picked for practically every All-America team but he didn't get the Heisman Trophy. That went to Wisconsin's Alan Ameche. There was one other frustrating annoyance for Hayes and his team. AP and International News Service both ranked Ohio State No. 1 for the mythical national championship, but the United Press voters, made up of coaches, rated UCLA first with Ohio State second. In those days the final votes were taken after the last day of the regular season instead of after the postseason bowl games.

Unhappily, No. 1 could not be settled on the field because UCLA, although the best team on the West Coast, was not eligible to return to the Rose Bowl under the then-existing rules because the Bruins had played there in the January 1954 game. Ohio State would have to settle its score with USC, the Pacific Coast Conference runner-up, which had finished the season with an 8–3 record.

And settle the score Ohio State did. Although Cassady didn't get a touchdown, he piled up 92 yards in twenty-one carries and saved one USC score by running down speedy Jon Arnett as the superior Buckeyes rolled to a 20–7 triumph.

Still rankled over the snub accorded his team by his fellow coaches, the UP voters, Woody Hayes, with typical candor, hardly endeared himself to West Coast football enthusiasts when he was asked if his team could have beaten UCLA. "I don't know about that," shot back Woody, "but there are five teams in the Big Ten I'd rate ahead of USC. I believe Michigan, Iowa, Wisconsin, Minnesota, and Ohio State are all better than the Trojans."

While everyone got a bit of the credit for Ohio State's fabulous season, it was generally agreed that Hopalong Cassady was mostly responsible for the great success. In his three varsity seasons he had scored 132 points and was only two touchdowns away from breaking Chic Harley's school career record of twenty-three. Cassady still had another year of eligibility remaining—his fourth—so, it was with good reason that the Buckeyes looked forward to another grandiose campaign in 1955.

Although most of the stars of that 1954 team were gone and Coach Hayes was faced with a major rebuilding job, the mere presence of Cassady as an offensive threat and Jim Parker to lead the offensive and defensive lines marked Ohio State as a team to be reckoned with again in the Big Ten race.

Hopalong Cassady didn't disappont his fans. In the very first game of the season Hoppy ran wild against Nebraska to roll up 170 yards on twenty-one carries and scored three touchdowns in a 28–20 victory to break Harley's career record.

Despite temporary lapses against nonconference rivals Stanford and Duke, which resulted in losses, both Cassady and Ohio State proceeded to smash their way through the Big Ten schedule. Hopalong scored twice against Illinois, once against Wisconsin, twice against Northwestern to match Red Grange's career output of thirty-one touchdowns, and twice against Indiana to boost his total touchdowns to eleven for the year and thirty-three for his career. He now had 198 points and was only three shy of Harley's record of 201, with two games still to play.

That next-to-the-last game, against a mediocre Iowa team, was Hopalong Cassady's final one in the monstrous Ohio Stadium, and

82,701 fans turned out to see his farewell home performance. And what a performance it was! Hoppy, rising to the occasion as he had so many times in the past, was simply magnificent. The very first time he carried the ball, he darted off tackle, threw his gyrating hips at a pair of defenders, and ran 45 yards for a touchdown. He scored twice more before that glorious afternoon ended, shattering Harley's scoring record, as Ohio State beat the stubborn Hawkeyes, 20–10, for its twelfth straight Big Ten victory.

For several minutes after the game Ohio State fans and Cassady's teammates engaged in an emotional orgy. The Buckeyes hoisted embarrassed Hopalong to their shoulders and carried him off the field while the fans cheered and applauded. Dr. Howard Bevis, retiring president of the university, was so touched by the occasion that he visited the dressing room to tell Hoppy, "I want to thank you for letting me come in here to say good-bye to you."

Hopalong Cassady—and Ohio State—had accomplished just about everything possible, except one thing. Beating hated Michigan at Ann Arbor. In fact, no Ohio State team had accomplished that feat in eighteen years, since 1937. That is until Hopalong Cassady and his swashbuckling teammates did it to close out that memorable 1955 season. With 97,369 looking on, many of them Ohio State adherents who had made the trip from Columbus, Cassady scored once and the indomitable Buckeyes won, 17–0, in one of the roughest, most violent games in the history of the two old rivals. And Ohio State did it the hard way, smashing out its yardage on the ground against an array of Michigan defenses especially designed to stop the landlocked, nonthrowing Buckeye offense.

When it was all over, Hopalong Cassady had just about every offensive record in the Ohio State book. He had scored 222 points on thirty-seven touchdowns, rushed for 2,466 yards in 435 carries for a 5.7 average, and rolled up 2,530 yards in total offense. He was picked for every All-America team, was voted the Heisman Trophy and the Maxwell Trophy, and was named the Male Athlete of the Year by the Associated Press. Even the pros recognized his expansive talents when the Detroit Lions made him their No. 1 draft choice.

Once again the inevitable comparison between Cassady and Ohio State's first immortal, Chic Harley, aroused passions in Columbus. Actually, there was no fair way to compare the two. While Harley was a runner, passer, and kicker, Cassady was strictly a runner. But what a runner! He had great speed, unusual power for his size, and a tremendous knack for using his skills to their full advantage. Watching Hopalong darting, dodging, and cutting behind his blockers was a joy to see. He was able to quickly size up the entire field of action and plot his course. Once he got up a full head of steam, catching him was like trying to run down a wild mustang.

Woody Hayes' description of Cassady was plain and simple: "Hopalong Cassady is the greatest football player I've ever seen. You can compare him with Red Grange."

Woody Hayes began to change his mind in 1972. That was when the N.C.A.A. voted to make freshmen eligible for varsity football and Archie Griffin, a precocious first-year tailback, came along and almost immediately proceeded to do things with a football that not even those mortals, Harley and Cassady, were able to accomplish in their glory years.

Griffin, a compact, bandy-legged, five-foot-nine-inch 185-pounder with 4.5 speed for 40 yards, incredible power, and all the slithery moves of a snake, broke in with a bang in Ohio State's second game of the 1972 season, a nonconference joust with North Carolina. Archie had played for only a moment or so in the opener against Iowa and didn't get into the North Carolina game until the Tarheels had opened up a 7–0 lead in the first quarter. Then, quite unobtrusively, No. 45 was sent into the lineup at tailback in the Power-I formation that OSU favors these days and all kinds of nice things began to happen to him and the Buckeyes.

On Griffin's first play he went outside for 6 yards. Then inside twice for six each time. When the game was over, Archie had spun off runs of 55, 32, 22, and 20 yards and a lot of assorted dashes of 11, 9, 8, and 6, until he had accumulated 239 yards in all to break the single-game school record of 229 set by Ollie Cline against Pittsburgh way back in 1945. Archie had squirmed through tiny little holes in the line, slid outside and tiptoed down the sidelines, broken tackles and bumped into people from North Carolina and knocked them down, and burst into the secondary and darted this way and that like a hopped-up rabbit. He had scored one touchdown and set up another and a field goal, and Ohio State had a 29–14 win over the shellshocked Tarheels. And the 86,900 fans who filled fifty-year-old Ohio Stadium had a new hero to worship.

It was like a sequence out of an old Jack Oakie football movie. Freshman gets his chance. Freshman makes good. Except that this freshman was so extraordinary. Big in the shoulders, Archie Griffin had demonstrated uncanny instincts, moves, and surprising power. He hit quickly, was shifty enough to juke a defensive back, had a fine change of pace, and could switch his course in a split second. Archie had All-America written all over him, even after a single game. And there were going to be a whole lot more dazzling Saturday afternoons for Archie Griffin.

A quiet youngster with an infectious grin and a strange little shuffle walk that tended to camouflage his running abilities, Archie was a little bewildered by the whole thing. After all, he had been in classes for only three days.

"It's all new," Archie said, "I was lucky. I got in the game when the line was starting to open up holes. I just ran. That's all."

Coach Hayes, too, was somewhat taken aback by his freshman's sensational debut. "I don't know what it is that makes a player that good," said Woody after the game. "He's not big but he has power. He has speed but not great speed. He's just hard to catch. He has a natural knack of knowing what to do, where to run."

For the rest of the 1972 season Archie proved again and again that he knew what to do and where to run. He carried the ball 159 times for 867 yards, including a 30-yard dash that provided the winning points in a 14–11 win over Michigan and gave the Buckeyes the Big Ten championship and what turned out to be a disastrous trip to the Rose Bowl, where USC whomped Griffin and his shocked teammates, 42–17. Archie also added 196 yards on ten kickoff returns and 71 yards on six pass receptions. Yet he scored only three touchdowns, mostly because Woody Hayes' style calls for an offensive switch to what he calls an old-fashioned "high button shoe" or "Robust-T," a tight straight T-formation, when Ohio State gets inside the 20-yard line and that is when the fullbacks carry the ball almost exclusively.

Like Harley and Cassady before him, Archie Griffin was a home-bred from Columbus, where he grew up across town from Ohio Stadium on the east side and was an All-State fullback at Eastmoor High School and captained the football, wrestling, and track teams. He is one of a family of eight children, seven of them boys, three of whom played college football—James at Muskingum, Larry at the University of Louisville, and Daryle at Kent State.

Two younger brothers, Raymond and Duncan, followed Archie to Ohio State. Raymond, a quick, slick runner, was Archie's freshman backup in 1974, but shifted to defense in 1975. Duncan was a freshman linebacker in 1975. The youngest brother, Keith, may turn out to be the best of all the Griffins. In 1974, as a fourteen-year-old tailback at Eastmoor High, he scored 188 points on twenty-one touchdowns, forty-one PATs, and seven field goals. And, with Women's Lib coming to the fore in recent years, don't count out Crystal, their little sister!

So, Archie was hardly an unknown. More than 150 colleges contacted him and, when he narrowed down his choices, Ohio State had to outrecruit Navy and Northwestern to get him to stay at home. It was a happy decision for both Griffin and OSU.

If Griffin's freshman debut was sensational, then his 1973 season was fantastic! Just to prove that he was indeed no mere flash in the pan, Archie ripped through enemy defenses as if he owned them. If possible, he had acquired even more poise and some added skills. Also, since Coach Woody Hayes recognized a good thing when he saw it, Griffin got more opportunities to carry the ball and made the most of them.

Griffin started the season by blasting Minnesota for 129 yards on only fifteen attempts, and that was only the beginning. He ran 68 yards for a touchdown against Texas Christian University, gained 128 yards and scored twice in a win over Washington State, picked up 169 yards in twenty-nine carries against Wisconsin, 130 in twenty-five tries in a romp over Indiana, and ran for two scores in a 60–0 whomping of Northwestern. And so it went, game after game.

Archie's greatest day, however, came against Iowa. The Hawkeyes, having a woeful year, knew they were in over their heads and Coach Frank Lauterbur decided to throw a six-man defensive front, jamming the middle, at the Buckeyes, "so they wouldn't punch us around." So Ohio State simply pitched out to Griffin, who turned the ends with his dazzling speed and ran outside the tackles and anywhere else he could find running room. He found so much of it that he ran the ball for 246 yards to break his own single-game record. Archie scored only once, on an 8-yard dash, but he put the ball in position for fullback Bruce Elia, a converted linebacker filling in for the injured Champ Henson, to plunge over for four touchdowns as hapless Iowa fell, 55–13.

Even Lauterbur appreciated Archie's one-man show. "He's just about the greatest I've ever seen," said Frank.

Griffin wasn't finished, though. The next week Michigan felt the fury of his running as he sprinted and bulled his way through the

Wolverines for 163 yards, setting up the touchdown and the field goal that saved a 10–10 tie before 105,223 hostile but reluctantly appreciative fans in Ann Arbor.

Then came one of the year's biggest surprises. While everyone, including Michigan Coach Bo Schembechler, expected the Wolverines to be picked to represent the Big Ten in the Rose Bowl, conference officials voted that Ohio State would go for a second straight year. Schembechler and Michigan adherents protested the decision vociferously, but all to no avail.

So the University of Southern California got its chance to be victimized by Archie in the Rose Bowl. Despite the defenses that Coach John McKay put together to stop him, Griffin smashed and tiptoed through the shocked Trojans for 149 yards and put the icing on a 42–21 triumph with a 47-yard touchdown burst in the last quarter. This time, 105,267 fans had the opportunity to see Archie run, and even West Coach buffs, who had watched some pretty good backs prance up and down the Rose Bowl turf in years gone by, had to admit they had seen one of the greatest ever.

"You don't stop Archie Griffin," said USC's McKay, "you just sit back and admire him."

When it was all over Griffin had gained 100 yards or more in eleven straight games, something no other Buckeye player had ever done, and rolled up 1,577 yards rushing to break John Brockington's single-season mark of 1,142 by a bunch, as well as smashing the Big Ten record of 1,494 set by Michigan State's Eric Allen in 1971. Archie also ran back seven kickoffs for 221 yards and caught five passes for another 32. And he scored nine touchdowns—seven rushing, one on a punt return, and another on a pass reception. In just two seasons he had rushed for 2,444 yards, a remarkable figure even for Ohio State's cloud-of-dust offense. Griffin, a unanimous All America, also became the first sophomore in half a century to be named the Big Ten's Most Valuable Player.

With two years ahead of him, Griffin was only 98 yards away from Jim Otis' Ohio State career rushing record of 2,542 yards and was within reach of quarterback Rex Kern's total offense mark of 4,158 yards, which was achieved both running and passing, a virtue—perhaps the only one—that Archie's repertoire unfortunately did not include. Griffin was almost a certain bet to break the all-time major college career rushing record of 3,867 yards, set by Oklahoma's Steve Owens in 1969.

Otis' record lasted just about as long as a Michigan drunk in a

Columbus bar. In the very first game of the 1974 season, against Minnesota, Griffin slashed, pounded, and juked his way for 133 yards in twenty-six carries, including a 19-yard touchdown run, as the powerful Ohio State Machine, ranked No. 1 in many of the pre-season polls, smashed the Gophers, 34–19. It was a dazzling performance but one that Buckeye fans had become accustomed to from Archie.

That was the beginning of another superseason for Archie. Playing with what many Big Ten watchers thought was one of Woody Hayes' best teams ever, Griffin treated enemy defenses, almost always rigged to key on him, with disdain. He bruised Oregon State for 134 yards in less than half a game as Ohio State bombed Coach Dee Andros' Beavers, 51–10. And, when Archie went to the bench, Hayes had a surprise for Oregon State—still another Griffin. This one was Raymond, Archie's younger brother, a 175-pound freshman tailback who stung the Beavers for two late touchdowns on runs of 9 and 12 yards.

The Ohio State Machine continued to roll and so did Griffin. He piled up 159 yards and scored twice in a 28–9 win over Southern Methodist University, and then pounded Washington State for 196 yards, all in the first half. It was the fifteenth straight game in which Archie had gained over 100 yards. His *pièce de résistance* in this one was a 75-yard touchdown run that helped bury the home team Cougars, 42–7.

When West Coasters trotted out the kudos for the Ohio State star, Archie reacted with typical modesty. "I don't have it made," he said. "It's more important to win championships."

As the 1974 season progressed it became increasingly obvious that Archie Griffin's sincere modesty was misplaced. He did indeed have it made. While Ohio State piled up victory after victory, Archie also piled up immense yardage totals, even though, most times, he played only part-time. Griffin extended his streak to eighteen games in which he gained over 100 yards or more rushing, breaking the N.C.A.A. record set by Steve Owens of Oklahoma in 1969.

Even Griffin's own offensive linemen, the guys who deserve the credit for making good backs better, had unusual words of praise for their star. "With a back like Archie," said one of them, "you don't need too many blocks. He makes *you* look good."

Wisconsin Coach John Jardine, in a state of shock after his Badgers were manhandled by Griffin and Ohio State, was even more effusive. "Archie Griffin is the best running back I've ever seen," said Jardine. "He's strong, durable, runs tough, and has good speed."

Other opposing coaches tried to describe Griffin's style. Indiana's Lee Corso said, "Archie has unbelievable peripheral vision. I saw him go through a hole in our line that wasn't there."

Washington State Coach Jim Sweeney had still another reason for Griffin's effectiveness. "He has explosive eyes," said Sweeney mysteriously. "In our game, he came running wide toward our bench. Our guys had the angle shut off but then he cut and picked up eighteen yards. Anyway, I got a close look at his eyeballs and they were as big as saucers."

Ray Kennedy wrote in *Sports Illustrated,* "Griffin shimmies along as if there was a wheel or two out of line somewhere. He runs low, pitched forward at a precipitous angle. His shoulders roll one way, his hips another, and all the while his legs keep bowing crazily and to the side while somehow churning forward at the same time. Add to that a center of gravity that is somewhere around his instep and you have a moving target that is like trying to tackle a falling tree in a windstorm."

Perhaps the most simple description, however, came from Archie himself. "I waddle," he said, explaining why his teammates called him "Duckfoot."

There didn't seem to be any team on the horizon that would be able to stop Archie Griffin and what Woody Hayes himself was beginning to call "the best team we've ever had." Then along came Michigan State, on the upgrade again under Coach Dennis Stolz, who had succeeded the resigned Duffy Daugherty. A year later Stolz was out at MSU, the victim of a recruiting scandal. The Spartans couldn't quite hold Griffin in check—he went over 100 yards for the nineteenth straight time—but they did shackle the other Buckeyes often enough to score one of the upsets of the year, 16–13, in a game that ended in controversy.

Michigan State had come back from a 13–3 deficit in the last quarter, scoring on quarterback Charlie Baggett's 44-yard pass to Mike Jones and an electrifying 88-yard run by Levi Jackson with only 3:17 to go to take a 16–13 lead. Then with Griffin and quarterback Cornelius Greene leading the way, Ohio State hacked away at the Michigan State defense until the Bucks reached the Spartans' 1-foot line with only seconds to go. Fullback Champ Henson went diving into the end zone and, while one official ruled it a touchdown, another one was indicating that the game had ended before Henson's desperate plunge. It wasn't until about an hour after the conclusion that Big Ten Commissioner Wayne Duke, following discussions with the officials, ruled that time had expired before the last play and that Michigan State was the winner. A replay of the game film also showed that the Ohio State players were not lined up properly when the ball was snapped. End of argument. The commissioner had the last word and Ohio State's winning streak was just a memory.

The disappointed Buckeyes still had to face undefeated Michigan in the season's finale the next Saturday, and, as usual, the whole season was at stake for both teams. Michigan had its sights set on the national championship, although Oklahoma (on probation and therefore unranked in the United Press International poll in which the coaches vote) and Alabama, both unbeaten, were currently rated ahead of the Wolverines in the Associated Press poll. Also, the winner would almost surely get the Big Ten's nomination to go to the Rose Bowl, the richest postseason plum of them all. For Ohio State it was a chance to retrieve some of its lost prestige and maybe even get another shot at No. 1, depending upon what happened in the bowl games. For Archie Griffin it was a chance to ensure his selection for the Heisman Trophy.

As usual, the game turned out to be a barnburner, the kind Ohio State and Michigan have been involved in so many times before. Griffin went over 100 yards for the twenty-second time, but it was Tom Klaban, an unheralded Czechoslovakian kicker who took kicking lessons from his sister—"she's the only one who understands my soccer style," he explained—who upstaged Archie and booted the Wolverines into submission. A walk-on who didn't even have a partial football scholarship, Klaban kicked four field goals, from 47, 25, 43, and 45 yards, for all the points that Ohio State would score that tense afternoon. It was enough to beat the oppressed Wolverines, 12–10, and force the two old protagonists into a tie for the Big Ten championship.

That started another furor. Michigan supporters, and a few other Big Ten schools, thought that the Wolverines, who had lost only two games in three years—both to OSU—deserved a chance to go to the Rose Bowl despite the narrow loss to Ohio State. However the majority of the conference athletic directors, after a prolonged meeting in Chicago, voted for Ohio State. This time, Schembechler, who had paid for his outspoken and bitter comments the year before when his team was also denied the opportunity to go to Pasadena—Commissioner Wayne Duke had imposed an official two-year silence on Bo's critical public statements—took the disappointing decision calmly, at least outwardly. Michigan fans reacted more strongly, conveniently overlooking the fact that Ohio State had earned its trip to the Rose Bowl by beating the Wolverines in a head-to-head contest for that honor.

Except for that lone loss to Michigan State, the regular season was still another high point in Archie Griffin's meteoric career. Archie had run the ball 1,620 yards, the second-best rushing total in the nation, averaging 6.8 yards per carry and scoring twelve touchdowns. All told, including three pass receptions for 52 yards and 71 yards in kickoff returns, he had accumulated a grand total of 1,743 yards. Along the way Griffin had broken an armful of national, conference, and school records, including his own single-season Big Ten rushing mark and Purdue's Otis Armstrong's career rushing record. In his three varsity seasons Archie had run for 4,064 yards, leaving Chic Harley, Hopalong Cassady, and such other more recent Ohio State rushing stars as Jim Otis and John Brockington, far behind.

Griffin made everybody's All-America team again, and then came the sweetest hour of all. Archie won the Heisman Trophy as the nation's outstanding college football player, overwhelming every other candidate in the field, including USC's Anthony Davis, to become only the fifth junior and the first one since Navy's Roger Staubach in 1963 to finish first in the balloting. He also became Ohio State's third winner and the first since Cassady in 1955.

Griffin accepted the honor with his usual humility. "I always dreamed of winning the Heisman Trophy," he said, "but I never thought I would be good enough."

Small wonder then that Woody Hayes changed his mind about the "best back I've ever seen." Woody said flat out, "Archie is the best back I've ever, ever seen. Hopalong Cassady was a great one, but Griffin is even better. It's not even close."

Griffin's string of 100-yard-plus games finally came to an end in the Rose Bowl where a strong University of Southern California defense "held" him to a mere 75 yards rushing (he picked up 25 more on pass receptions, though) as the Trojans upset Ohio State, 18–17, in a thrilling finish. But Archie, far from being discouraged, was looking ahead to 1975 and his fourth varsity year.

Despite all the personal honors he had already accumulated—

All-America, the Heisman Trophy, and with it recognition as the best college football player in the land—one highly coveted goal had escaped Archie Griffin. He wanted desperately to be a member of a national championship team.

"I'd gladly give it all up for that," said Archie as he and his Ohio State team headed into the 1975 season, Griffin's fourth and last.

The makings for a national championship team were all there. First there was Griffin and the rest of that veteran backfield—quarterback Corny Greene, wingback Brian Baschnagel, and fullback Pete Johnson, bigger and tougher than ever—that had terrorized the Big Ten the year before. Then there was a collection of big, bruising offensive and defensive linemen and the usual horde of quick, tenacious defensive backs. Most of the preseason polls awarded the No. 1 ranking to Oklahoma, but almost everyone had Ohio State in the top five.

The key to the Buckeyes' success, of course, was Archie Griffin. Could he have a fourth straight great year? The answer wasn't long in coming. In Ohio State's opening game, against the Michigan State team which had upset the Bucks a year earlier, Griffin demonstrated that he had lost none of the skills which had made him so special. Indeed, if anything, he had expanded them. All Archie did was run through the bedeviled Spartans for 108 yards as OSU smashed them, 21–0. It was the twenty-third straight regular-season game in which Griffin gained better than 100 yards.

The following Saturday it was Penn State's turn to try to stop Archie. Coach Woody Hayes had a particular interest in throttling the Nittany Lions since he had never beaten them in three earlier tries. In fact, Ohio State had never beaten the Easterners in the four times the two teams played. Woody also knew that Joe Paterno, the nonconformist who coached Penn State, would have a few new tricks up his sleeve, and he worried about what to expect.

What Hayes got was just what he feared—one of his toughest games of the year—as 88,093, the second-largest crowd in Ohio Stadium history, looked on. Leading by only 10–9 early in the fourth quarter, and fearful that Penn State's Chris Bahr, a soccer-style kicker who had already booted three field goals, including a 55-yarder, might kick them into defeat, Ohio State finally got a drive going with the aid of a pass-interference call. Then, just when it appeared that the Bucks would falter, Griffin made the big play to keep the drive alive.

With third down and 11 yards to go at the OSU 32-yard line,

Greene floated a big, fat lob pass that appeared to be going well over Griffin's head. However, Archie made a fantastic diving catch for a 23-yard gain and a first down on the Penn State 45. Then Johnson took over. He carried seven of the next nine times for 39 yards, including the final 11 on a brutal thrust over left tackle that provided Ohio State with its final margin in a tough 17–9 victory.

After that close call, both Archie Griffin and Ohio State ran roughshod over one opponent after another. Archie kept getting his 100 yards plus per game, and the Bucks kept winning. Among the OSU victims was UCLA, which fell, 41–20, as Griffin rolled for 160 yards and caught a couple of passes for 44 more yards. Against Illinois, Archie went over 100 yards, as usual, and became the first college football player to rush for more than 5,000 yards in a career.

Along the way, there were enough fun and games for other Ohio State players. Pete Johnson scored five touchdowns in a 32–7 rout of North Carolina. Against Wisconsin, safety Tim Fox intercepted a Badger pass, ran it back for a touchdown, and then did a forward somersault in midair in the end zone. However, he was accidentally bumped by overenthusiastic linebacker Ken Kuhn and slipped on the wet turf.

"I got tired of people doing all those dances in the end zone after scoring," explained Fox. "I figured this is better than a dance."

Tom Skladany, Ohio State's premier punter, kicked his first field goal ever against Illinois and it was a 59-yarder, the longest placement kick in Big Ten history. (Wisconsin's Pat O'Dea, however, still holds the record for the longest field goal, a 65-yard dropkick.) Skladany, a nephew of old Pittsburgh All-America Joe Skladany, also punted four times for a 56.5-yard average, another conference record, including one kick for 68 yards. Johnson scored twice in the rout of the Illini, giving him twenty-one touchdowns for the season and breaking former teammate Champ Henson's Big Ten mark.

That brought unbeaten and No. 1–ranked Ohio State down to the final game with Michigan. The Wolverines also were undefeated but they had been tied twice in nonconference games, by Stanford and Baylor. Once again the winner would win the Big Ten championship and go to the Rose Bowl. And this time there was a "consolation prize" for the loser, a trip to the Orange Bowl to face No. 2–ranked and once-beaten Oklahoma, the Big Eight champion. Some prize!

For Archie Griffin, his own personal record was on the line. He had now rushed for more than 100 yards in thirty-one consecutive regular-season games and had gained more yards carrying the ball from scrimmage than any other player in the more than 100-year history of college football. He was a sure All-America and was the favorite to win the Heisman Trophy again. Even more important for both Archie and Ohio State, the Buckeyes had to win to retain their No. 1 ranking and a shot at the national championship.

There were 105,543 in Michigan Stadium, the largest crowd ever in Ann Arbor, to watch these two titans have at each other, and they weren't disappointed. Surprisingly, Ohio State's Hayes and Michigan's Schembechler, who allegedly have been known to look with disdain at anyone who has had the effrontery to mention the word "pass' in their presence, both came out throwing—thirty-seven times between them, or about as many passes as one could expect to see in three OSU-Michigan games.

Michigan's defensive strategy was simple: everywhere that Archie Griffin went, a crowd of eager Wolverines were sure to go. For about fifty-three minutes, Michigan's game plan worked like a charm. Griffin hadn't gone anywhere to speak of and the Wolves led, 14–7. Then, suddenly, Ohio State's offense came alive. Greene began hitting with his passes and pretty soon there was Johnson, smashing into the end zone with the tying touchdown. Minutes later, the other Griffin—Raymond—intercepted Michigan quarterback Rick Leach's desperation pass and ran it back 29 yards to the Wolverine three, from which point Johnson pounded away at the weary hometown warriors until he slammed into the end zone again. Klaban's placement kick put Ohio State ahead, 21–14, and another interception by Hopalong Cassady's boy, Craig, an outstanding defensive back for Ohio State, sealed the victory for the Buckeyes, sending them into the Rose Bowl against UCLA.

Along the way, Archie Griffin was held to a mere 46 yards rushing by the swarming Michigan defense, ending his record streak of 100-yard-plus regular-season games at thirty-one, but it was small consolation for the losing Wolverines. Griffin himself wasn't crying about the end of his streak.

"I'd give up all thirty-one of those hundred-yard games for this one," said Archie.

As it turned out, one thing Griffin didn't have to give up was the Heisman Trophy. There were other legitimate candidates, like California's Chuck Muncie, USC's Ricky Bell, Pittsburgh's Tony Dorsett, and Oklahoma's Joe Washington. But Archie's credentials were impressive and difficult for the voters to ignore: he had led Ohio State to an unbeaten season; he was the first college player ever to rush for more than 5,000 yards in a career, totaling 5,176 yards in regular-season games in his four years for an N.C.A.A. record; he had run for 6,003 yards in all categories—rushing, kick returns, and pass-catching—for another mark; and his thirty-one-game streak of 100-yard-plus games was still a third national record.

After making everyone's All-America team for a third straight year, Archie was an overwhelming winner in the balloting for the cherished Heisman Trophy, polling 454 first-place votes to Muncie's 145, to become the first ever to win it twice.

Griffin's unprecedented choice raised the usual questions about the future of the college player selected as the best in the land. Was this five-foot nine (who actually was closer to five-foot seven-and-a-half), 180-pound ball of fire big enough to make it in professional football?

"Well," said Coach Woody Hayes, "maybe he's not as big as they like, but he's as brave as they like."

That question was answered when the National Football League held its delayed draft of 1975 college players. Archie Griffin was the No. 1 draft choice of the Cincinnati Bengals and he proceeded to have a good rookie year.

Predictably, Griffin's national major college career rushing record lasted less than a season. Pittsburgh's Tony Dorsett, an elusive, swift runner with all the moves of a jackrabbit, carried the ball for 1,948 yards (and twenty-two touchdowns) while leading his Panthers to the national championship in 1976. That gave Tony a total of 6,032 yards for his four-year career, surpassing Archie's mark. It also gave Dorsett the Heisman Trophy as Griffin's rightful successor.

Unfortunately, neither Griffin nor Ohio State achieved the goal both wanted so badly—the national championship. UCLA, the same team the Buckeyes had bruised so badly earlier in the 1975 season, found a way to keep Archie from running wild and whipped the Buckeyes, 23–10, in the Rose Bowl at Pasadena. That, coupled with Oklahoma's win over Michigan in the Orange Bowl, gave the Sooners the national title in both the AP and UPI polls.

Meanwhile, surprisingly, Corny Greene, not Archie Griffin—everyone's all-everything—was voted Ohio State's Most Valuable

Player by a single vote at the end of the regular season. "I was really surprised," said Greene. "I was sure it would be Archie."

And who cast the deciding vote for Greene? Just All-America Heisman Trophy winner Archie Griffin, that's who!

"I looked at who we could least afford to lose with an injury," explained Archie. "Somebody could replace me, but we would have had to have a freshman go in for Greene. Corny meant everything to our team."

That was Archie Griffin—superstar, superhero, superguy!

Who was Ohio State's best—Harley, Cassady, or Griffin? On the record, it has to be Archie. And Coach Woody Hayes has the last word on this, too, as he has had on so many other things.

"Archie Griffin is the greatest back I've ever, ever seen or coached," says Woody. "He was a great leader, too. Archie could become the first black president."

Coming from a political conservative like Woody Hayes, that is praise indeed.

TWENTY-SIX

Horvath, Janowicz, and All Those Other Buckeyes

Harley and Cassady, those are the names that Ohio State old-timers like to bandy around as the greatest Buckeye backfield heroes but, in between this illustrious pair, and long before Archie Griffin, at least two others established themselves as bona fide superstars—Les Horvath and Vic Janowicz. Like Harley, they played during difficult wartime years. And, like Cassady, they were All-Americas and Heisman Trophy winners.

Horvath, a slender, unassuming young man who came out of Cleveland's Rhodes High School, played his football under perhaps the most unusual set of circumstances of any other Ohio State player. First, because of wartime regulations, his college career was spread over six years. Secondly, he performed under three different coaches—Francis Schmidt, Paul Brown, and Carroll Widdoes. And, unlike Harley, Cassady, and Griffin, Horvath was *not* an instant star.

After spending the 1939 season on Schmidt's freshman team, Horvath saw only limited varsity duty in 1940 under Schmidt and in 1941 under Schmidt's successor, Paul Brown. It wasn't until the 1942 season, his senior year, that Les became a starter, and even then he was overshadowed by another pair of Ohio State backs, Gene Fekete and Paul Sarringhaus, but he showed enough talent to be regarded as one of the most versatile and valuable members of a team that won both the Big Ten and the national championship. Horvath was the complete player. He could run, pass, catch passes, and block.

Horvath's best game in that 1942 season, which he assumed was to be his last in an Ohio State uniform, came against Michigan. He grabbed a 22-yard pass from Sarringhaus to set up a touchdown, and then passed to Sarringhaus in the end zone for the score. Later, he caught another pass from Sarringhaus for the touchdown that nailed down a 21–7 victory over the Wolverines and clinched the conference title for the Buckeyes.

With his college football career presumably over, Horvath enrolled in dental school at Ohio State in a special army training program and spent 1943 learning how to be a dentist. Meanwhile, after a disastrous 1943 season, Coach Paul Brown left Columbus to accept a commission as a lieutenant junior grade in the navy and was assigned to the Great Lakes Naval Training Center, where he later became the head football coach. Brown was succeeded at Ohio State by Carroll Widdoes, one of his assistant coaches.

With his squad decimated by the draft and enlistments, Widdoes faced a dim future for his maiden season in 1944. That is until the Big Ten adopted a temporary ruling which permitted freshmen to play varsity football and also gave a fourth year of eligibility to any player still working toward a higher degree on campus. Suddenly twenty-three-year-old Les Horvath was available for another year of football and he joined the collection of fuzzy-cheeked seventeen-year-olds that Widdoes had managed to recruit for the 1944 campaign.

Horvath, the only experienced back on the squad, was immediately installed as the quarterback in the T-formation which Coach Widdoes favored. However when the Buckeyes shifted into a single wing, Les was the tailback. His running mates were a trio of freshmen, Bob Brugge, Dick Flannagan, and Ollie Cline. There were enough veterans up front, players like end Jack Dugger, tackle Bill Willis, and guard Bill Hackett, all of whom had been deferred from military service for one reason or another, to brighten Ohio State's hopes for at least a respectable season. What Ohio State fans didn't realize, however, was that Les Horvath would make the difference between a just "respectable" season and a sensational one.

It took a game or two for Horvath to regain his football legs after the year's layoff, and when he did the Buckeyes took off like a comet. With Les running the offensive show from his quarterback and tailback positions, Ohio State rolled over a succession of Big Ten and nonconference opponents to come up to the final game with Michigan unbeaten and untied. Horvath had been devastating all season long, running and passing for touchdowns and pulling Ohio State out of trouble time and again with clutch runs. One of his finest performances came against the powerful Great Lakes Naval Station team coached by Paul Brown. In that one Les broke open a tight game with two touchdowns in the last quarter as the Buckeyes upset their former coach's team, 26–6.

That final game against Michigan, and this time it *was* to be the last time that Les Horvath would wear the Scarlet and Gray, was a personal triumph for the Ohio State backfield star. Twice he brought Ohio State from behind with his slashing runs for touchdowns, the last one giving the Bucks an 18–14 victory, and their first undefeated regular season since 1920, the Big Ten championship, and what everyone in Columbus hoped was a trip to the Rose Bowl in Pasadena to play the University of Southern California. Alas, the last was not to be. The following day, conference faculty representatives met in special session in Chicago to consider a Rose Bowl bid for Ohio State and voted against waiving the league rule against postseason games. The Buckeyes had to be satisfied with a No. 2 ranking in the national polls behind Army's draft-proof veterans.

It would have been nice for Les Horvath to finish his career in the Rose Bowl, but he had achieved enough personally in that final year to put his name up with the all-time Ohio State stars. He had scored twelve touchdowns and rolled up 919 yards rushing, and led the Big Ten in total offense with 953 yards. Les was a unanimous choice on every All-America team and was voted the Heisman Trophy, the first Ohio Starter to receive that honor.

For one season, at least, Les Horvath was the equal of Chic Harley and Hopalong Cassady.

Six years later, in 1950, Ohio State had its second Heisman Trophy winner in Vic Janowicz, a stocky, five-foot nine-inch halfback from Elyria, Ohio, who turned the Big Ten into his personal preserve. A hard, shifty runner with a penchant for getting that extra yard when hemmed in, he was also a superb passer, punter, and placekicker.

Although Janowicz's hometown of Elyria was hardly more than a quick two-hour drive from Columbus, it wasn't that easy to get Vic to Ohio State. His feats for Elyria High School brought recruiters from more than sixty colleges from coast to coast to his doorstep, and they bartered for his services like a pack of fishmongers. Some of the offers went far beyond the legal tenders of room, board, tuition, books, fees, and laundry, and the seventeen-year-old son of Polish immigrants soon found himself bewildered by all the attention being paid to him. There were invitations to visit campuses in practically every state, and even a week in New York City for Vic and his girlfriend (and a chaperone), courtesy of a rich alumnus of one of the schools competing for his services.

"It got to be kind of boring for my mother and father, who didn't speak much English," Vic said. "I remember once hearing my dad mutter that nothing like this ever happened in Poland."

There was more, too, and later Janowicz told *Sport* magazine about some of it in an interview. "They would ask me what my best previous offer had been," said Vic. "I'd explain that I already had the chance to go to this or that place with my tuition, room, board, and books taken care of, plus free laundry service, and free transportation for my family to and from games each weekend. Then I'd tell them about offers of a hundred and fifty dollars or so a month for spending money on top of all that. They didn't seem dismayed. They merely offered to double the spending money.

"My top offer came from a school in the South. . . . At this one place, I was to get the whole works, plus an automobile, plus five thousand dollars they promised to put in the bank for me in my senior year. I'll admit I thought about it for quite a while. It sounded like first prize at bank night."

Janowicz finally narrowed his selection down to a field of four—Michigan, Purdue, Notre Dame, and Ohio State—and that was when the Ohio State Frontliners, a group formed to attract players to Columbus, brought up their big guns. The biggest gun was John Galbreath, a wealthy local realtor, builder, and sportsman, who had made Ohio State athletics his avocation.

Galbreath's pitch to Janowicz was simple and straightforward. He would advance Vic the money to attend Ohio State and provide him with jobs to pay back the loans. Also, he would guarantee Janowicz a job with one of his organizations after his graduation from college, regardless of whether or not he ever played football for OSU. It was an offer that Vic couldn't refuse, so he was on his way to Ohio State.

After a successful 1948 season as a halfback on the freshman team, Janowicz moved up to the varsity in the fall of 1949 but then he learned that Coach Wes Fesler was really not all that enchanted with the budding star from Elyria. Besides, he had his starting offensive backfield set. So Janowicz became the number-two fullback on offense and the starting safety on defense. He was also given the placekicking chores and was the punt and kickoff returner. Then, to make matters worse, Vic suffered a bone separation on his right foot and was sidelined for more than a month. When that injury healed he pulled a leg muscle in practice and was set down again. All in all, it was a discouraging year for him, even though Ohio State won the conference title and a trip to the Rose Bowl, where the Buckeyes beat California, 17–14.

Janowicz finally got his chance in 1950. The Korean War, which President Harry S. Truman insisted on calling a "police action," had cast a pall over the land and the immediate future of college football was uncertain. Nevertheless, Coach Fesler went about building what was to be his last Ohio State team. He started by moving Vic Janowicz to quarterback in his T-formation and single-wing offenses, and surrounded him with a light but fast backfield composed of Dick (Skip) Doyle, Walt Klevay, and Jack Wagner.

Janowicz was an instant success at quarterback. He turned out to be a superpasser as well as a superb runner and kicker, and his multiple talents brought him "star" status in a hurry. Although Ohio State was upset in its opening game by Southern Methodist University, Vic scored once on a 14-yard run and kicked two field goals and three extra points.

That was only the beginning of a meteoric year for the Elyria Flash. The next week, against Pittsburgh, Vic completed all six of his passes for 151 yards and four touchdowns in a 41–7 win over the Panthers. He got off a 90-yard punt against Minnesota and then hit his peak in a 83–21 rout over Iowa. Vic ran 11 yards for one touchdown, returned a punt 61 yards for another, threw four touchdown passes, and kicked ten of eleven points after touchdown to account for forty-six points personally. And all of this in slightly more than half a game!

Week after week Janowicz, who was later moved to left halfback to make room for Tony Curcillo at quarterback, proved to be the catalyst of the Ohio State offense. When he wasn't throwing touchdown passes or running for scores, he was setting the opposition back on its heels with his booming kickoffs and punts and adding points via placement.

Despite Janowicz's personal heroics, Ohio State had lost to Illinois, 14–7, and, like so many times before—and after—the Big Ten championship came down to the final game between the Buckeyes and Michigan. An OSU victory would clinch it; a loss would give the title to either Michigan or Illinois, which had a 4–1 conference record and had to play Northwestern.

The big game figured to draw the usual capacity crowd—82,500 then—to Ohio Stadium despite predictions early in the week for a very cold Saturday afternoon. The weatherman had miscalculated, however, and cold weather wasn't the only thing the fans and the players had to contend with at game time. On Friday it snowed briefly, covering the tarpaulin which had been stretched over the field, and by Saturday morning Columbus was in the throes of a driving snowstorm, the temperature was five degrees above zero, and strong winds lashed the city. There was some talk of postponing the game, but Athletic Director Dick Larkins decreed that the show must go on and so on it went, under the most adverse conditions possible, and with 50,000 brave and hardy souls scattered around the huge stadium. The field was frozen, making running almost impossible; the snow and strong winds ruled out a passing game, and the yard lines on the field were obliterated by the rapidly falling snow.

The game turned out to be one huge nightmare for both Ohio State collectively and Vic Janowicz personally. It developed into a kicking duel between Janowicz and Michigan's Chuck Ortman, who between them punted the ball forty-five times. Unhappily, two of Janowicz's punts were blocked and they cost Ohio State the ballgame.

The Buckeyes were trying desperately to make a 3–0 lead, achieved on Janowicz's 21-yard field goal in the first quarter, stand up when Vic went back to punt. Allen Wahl, a Michigan tackle, broke through the line to block the kick and the ball slithered out of the end zone for an automatic safety to make the score 3–2. Then, with forty-seven seconds to go in the first half, Ohio State found itself backed up deep in its own territory with a third down coming up and 6 yards to go. Michigan wisely called for a time-out to make it harder for the Bucks to run out the clock.

Coach Fesler had to make a decision right then and there: to kick on third down or to try a running play to eat up some of the time remaining. He elected to call for a punt, a decision that was to come back to haunt both him and Janowicz for a long time to come. Vic went back about 7 or 8 yards, less than his usual kicking depth, so he could see the line of scrimmage through the swirling snow. The ball was snapped and with it came a horde of blue-shirted Michigan defenders. One of them blocked the kick and Tony Momsen, a Michigan linebacker, fell on it in the end zone to give the Wolverines a 9–3 lead.

And that was the way the Snow Bowl ended. Just before the final gun, the word came that Northwestern had upset Illinois, 14–7, so the frozen Wolverines limped off the field with the Big Ten title and an unexpected invitation to the Rose Bowl. And they had won it without even making a single first down!

Despite the unhappy ending, Vic Janowicz's statistics for the season—five touchdowns scored, 314 yards rushing, thirty-two pass completions in seventy-seven attempts for 561 yards and twelve touchdowns, three field goals and twenty-six points after touchdown—were so imposing and his year-long performance so scintillating that he made almost every All-American team and won the Heisman Trophy in a runaway vote, one of the few juniors ever to be so honored.

Coach Fesler insisted that Janowicz was the most gifted player he ever saw. "You tell him what you want and he does it," said Fesler. "He had unbelievable football sense."

Ohio State fans had every reason to believe that Vic Janowicz would be an even greater star in 1951, his senior year. But a funny thing happened to Vic on his way to greater fame. First, Fesler, buckling under the pressure of that last game and no longer able to stand the taunts of a segment of the sometimes-fickle Buckeye rooting society, resigned to take a job with the John Galbreath Realty Company in Columbus. He insisted that he was through with big-time college football, but seven weeks later he signed to coach Minnesota. After much jockeying and politicking, Fesler was replaced by Woody Hayes, who had been the head coach at Miami of Ohio.

Meanwhile, Janowicz was having his own problems. An honor student in high school, he found that his sudden fame interfered with his school work. Instead of hitting the books, he was traipsing around the country and basking in the newly acquired limelight. Vic made appearances at banquets, accepted awards, and shook hands with thousands of well-wishers. He also was feeling his oats as the big-time hero. Janowicz and some of his friends got into a publicized fight with some Ohio University students at a local beer tavern. It was reported, too, that Janowicz and his buddies would go into a restaurant, order a meal, and then leave without paying the check. There also was a flap over how much Vic's good Samaritan, John Galbreath, had been doing for him financially.

The result was that Janowicz flunked out of school after the 1950 season. He applied for readmission for the spring quarter and, luckily, was accepted with the provision that he had to raise his grade average to be eligible for football in the fall. Vic buckled down to work and regained his eligibility.

As it turned out, Vic Janowicz's star was doomed to expire anyway. New Coach Woody Hayes brought the T-formation along with him from Miami of Ohio and that was the offense he stuck with all through a mediocre 4–3–2 season. Janowicz was the starting left halfback but he lacked the opportunities to pass and run as much as in the single wing that Fesler had used so much of the time. Vic's field-goal kicking won a couple of games for OSU, but his skills were defeated by the type of offense he had to play and he never reached the same heights he had achieved in 1950.

His coach was the first to acknowledge that Janowicz's opportunities were limited by the T-formation. Hayes said publicly, "I regret more than Vic that he didn't have a great season last fall, but our T-formation was not built to give him that chance."

Even though it was only for one big season, Vic Janowicz had left his mark on Ohio State football.

There were other great Ohio State backfield stars, too. Like halfback Don Scott in 1939, and Bob White, the first in a long line of All-American fullbacks. White played fullback, center, linebacker, and guard in 1957, but had fullback all to himself in 1958 when he set a modern conference record with 178 carries (since broken by several players) to win his All-America spurs. Then there were Tom Matte and Bob Ferguson, who teamed up to make the Buckeye's quarterback-fullback offense such a potent weapon in 1961. Matte was an exceptional option quarterback, who was just as dangerous running the ball as he was passing it. Ferguson, the crunching fullback, was a two-time All-America in 1960 and 1961.

Also, Paul Warfield and Matt Snell, the halfback running stars in 1961, 1962, and 1963. Both made it big in professional football. Warfield, with the Cleveland Browns and the Miami Dolphins as a wide receiver, and Snell as a runner with the New York Jets until he was overtaken by numerous injuries and forced to retire. More recently there was quarterback Rex Kern, an exciting ball handler and passer-runner, and Jim Otis, another one of those hard-hitting fullbacks. Kern set a school career record of 4,158 yards in total offense for his three varsity years (1968–1970) while Otis broke Hopalong Cassady's rushing record with 2,542 yards, but he did it in three years where it took Cassady four years to amass his 2,466 yards. Otis also scored thirty-five touchdowns in 1967, 1968, and 1969.

Another star of that era was halfback John Brockington, later the NFL's 1971 Rookie of the Year with the Green Bay Packers, who ran his way to a couple of school records—1,142 yards rushing in a single season on 261 carries—before he was acclaimed as an All-America in 1970. Then there were Harold (Champ) Henson, who as a sophomore, led the nation in scoring with twenty touchdowns in 1972, and Pete Johnson, a bruising, tanklike line-smasher who was so good that he relegated Champ to the number-two spot in 1974. Pete then broke Henson's touchdown record in 1975, scoring twenty-six for 156 points. He got nineteen more in 1976 to finish his career with an all-time Ohio State record of fifty-two touchdowns and 312 points. Not to mention a group of All-America defensive backs—Arnold Chonko in 1962, 1963, and 1964; Ted Provost in 1967, 1968, and 1969; Mike Sensibaugh, who intercepted twenty-two passes in 1968, 1969, and 1970; Tim Anderson, who starred in 1970; Neal Colzie, a brilliant player in 1973 and 1974; and Tim Fox in 1975. Another potential All-America defensive back is Ray Griffin, Archie's brother.

While he may not be another Archie Griffin, Jeff Logan, his replacement at tailback in 1976, showed signs of stardom. Jeff ran for 1,169 yards and five touchdowns, and was an even greater hit when he was switched to fullback for the Orange Bowl victory over Colorado.

Linemen, usually, are a tough breed of cat, but one of the best ever at Ohio State was a mild-mannered, sensitive young man named Wesley Fesler, an end who was named All-America for three successive years in 1928, 1929, and 1930. You have already read about his sad experience as a coach at Ohio State, but as athletes go he may have been the best all-around one who ever performed for the Buckeyes.

A slim, curly-haired, handsome lad out of Youngstown, Ohio, Fesler spread his talents over three sports and was a star in each. He was an All–Big Ten basketball player for three years, and was a good enough first baseman to attract several major-league offers. In one game, an 11–6 OSU victory over Illinois, Wes drove in all of his team's runs with two grand-slam home runs, another homer, and two doubles. That is hitting in any league!

Although he stood barely six feet and weighed only 180 pounds, Fesler was superb on both offense and defense. He was an excellent pass-receiver and more than once his spectacular catches saved the day for the Buckeyes, who weren't exactly setting the Big Ten on fire in those days. He also did the punting. Defensively, there weren't many opposing runners who dared to try to turn his end. Wes had catlike speed and a brain that was always working on the football field. What's more, he was durable, a sixty-minute player who rarely needed a breather.

"He was the greatest athlete I've ever seen," said Dick Larkins, his old teammate and later on the Ohio State athletic director who hired him as the head coach. "I've never seen a human animal so well coordinated."

While there were many great plays made by Wes Fesler in his three-year career, one that most folks will never forget came in a losing game against Northwestern in 1929. The Wildcats, who already held a 6–0 lead, were driving for another score and had reached the Ohio State 1-yard line with fourth down coming up. The center snap hit Northwestern's Don Calderwood on the chest and bounded into the air. Fesler, who had charged with the snap, grabbed the ball in midair and ran 98 yards for a touchdown almost before the bewildered Wildcats knew what had happened.

In his senior year, 1930, Fesler alternated at end and fullback and proved to be just as efficient at carrying and passing the ball as he was at catching it. He scored on a 3-yard plunge against Indiana, passed for a touchdown in a 27–0 win over Navy, threw for another score against Pittsburgh, and then had his finest day in his final game, a 12–9 victory over Illinois.

Meanwhile, when Fesler wasn't leading the offense from the fullback post, he was plying his trade at end, both on offense and defense.

There was no doubt about Fesler's All-America status at the end of the season. He was picked by almost everyone for the third straight year. Fesler would be followed by other outstanding Ohio State All-America ends—Merle Wendt in 1934 and 1935, Esco Sarkkinen in 1939, Bob Shaw in 1942, Jack Dugger in 1944, Dean Dugger in 1954, Jim Houston in 1958 and 1959, Jan White in 1970, and Bob Brudzinski in 1976—but few approached Wes in all-around ability.

If there had been a Heisman Trophy award in those days, Wes Fesler would have won it hands down.

* * *

Jim Parker came along a quarter of a century after Fesler, in the middle fifties. He was a guard, one of those unsung heroes who do the blocking on offense and the tackling on defense and get their noses rubbed in the dirt instead of the headlines that go to the touchdown-makers. But he wasn't just an ordinary guard. He may have been the best interior lineman ever to play at Ohio State.

There were other Buckeye interior linemen who had achieved All-America status before Parker—center Gomer Jones, who later became the head coach and athletic director at Oklahoma, in 1935; tackle Bill Willis in 1944; and Warren Amling as a guard in 1945 and as a tackle in 1946—and there have been a host of others since, but Jim stood head and shoulders, both physically and figuratively, above the rest.

Parker weighed in at about 240 pounds and was six-foot three when he found his way to Ohio State as a freshman in 1953, and before he finished his varsity career he had gone up to a svelte 255. However, despite his size he had the quickness of a halfback and surprising lateral movement. On offense he got off the ball so fast that he often had a bruising block pinned on his man before the opponent knew what was happening. Jim played linebacker on defense and he was a bone-shattering tackler who rarely let a runner get away once he got his hands on him. Besides all that, he was so grateful to be at Ohio State that he would have blocked or tackled a brick wall if he had been asked to.

Parker had found his way to Ohio State through a circuitous route. Born in Macon, Georgia, one of six children of a poor family, he survived a near-fatal burst appendix and a bout with peritonitis at fifteen, and then, after his junior year, he decided to hitchhike his way north to get a summer job. Parker wound up in Detroit, where he worked for a construction company. At the end of the summer Jim accepted an invitation to live with an aunt in Toledo, Ohio, and finished his senior year at Scott High School. Naturally, young Parker played football and he quickly earned a reputation as a tough, hard-nosed, no-nonsense blocker and tackler. When Ohio State recruiters got a look at Parker's size, they drooled in anticipation of what he could mean to the Buckeyes. And, happily, all they had to do was ask him to go to Ohio State.

"When they talked to me," Jim recalls, "I was willing and ready."

When he broke into the starting Ohio State lineup as a sophomore in 1954, Jim Parker was still willing and ready, as well as very able. For the next three years he was the heart and guts of the Buckeye line, both on offense and defense. Time and again, Jim made the big play, the clutch block, or the vital tackle or fumble recovery. He was picked for the All-America team in 1955 and repeated in 1956, when he also was voted the Outland Trophy as the outstanding interior lineman in the country.

Although Jim Parker had many outstanding afternoons, perhaps the one that people remember best was his performance in that 1954 Michigan game when the Wolverines, locked in a 7–7 tie with Ohio State, marched to a first down on the Buckeye 4-yard line. Four straight times Michigan sent its backs hurtling at Parker's position, hoping the sophomore would make a mistake. But Jim wasn't about to be had by the ill-advised Wolverines. Each time he was the one who repulsed the charge, finally stopping a Michigan back on fourth down on the 6-inch line. Ohio State then marched 99½ yards for the touchdown that sent the Buckeyes on the way to a 21–7 victory. It was a truly magnificent performance by Jim Parker, and the kind he was to give almost every week for the next two years.

Years later, when Parker was inducted into the Pro Football Hall of Fame after a long and distinguished career as a pro lineman, he was still grateful to Coach Woody Hayes and Ohio State for the opportunity to play college football in Columbus.

"Woody was like a father to me," said Jim. "He has always been in my corner." In the years since Jim Parker there were other interior linemen who achieved All-America stature—tackles Jim Marshall in 1958, Jim Davidson in 1964, Doug Van Horn in 1965, Dave Foley and Rufus Mayes in 1968; and middle guard Jim Stillwagon in 1969 and 1970—but it wasn't until the early seventies that any Ohio State player was mentioned in the same breath with the superstar of the middle fifties.

When John Hicks came along in 1970 it was immediately apparent that he was destined for stardom. There was a great similarity between Hicks and Parker. Like Parker, Hicks was an offensive lineman—a tackle—and like Jim, he was six-foot three and weighed about 255 pounds. He had the same catlike quickness, the ability to react in a split second, the same authority when he blocked, and the same desire to be the best. But, unlike Parker, Hicks played only on offense since it was an era of two-platoon football.

Hicks missed the 1971 season because of a knee injury, but in 1972 and 1973 he was the outstanding offensive lineman in the nation and was a unanimous choice for All-America honors. And, like Parker, he was voted the Outland Award after the 1973 campaign.

How did he compare with Parker? Well, in Coach Woody Hayes' opinion, "He is the best lineman I've ever had, and that includes Jim Parker."

Hayes, who had a host of premier linebackers, among them Dwight (Ike) Kelley in 1964 and 1965, and Jack Tatum in 1969 and 1970, had the same words of praise for Randy Gradishar, his All-America linebacker in 1972 and 1973. Gradishar had the ability to smell out plays even before they formed and an uncanny knack of being in the right place at the right time. Then, wham! the ball-carrier would get a message that usually rang his bell.

"The best linebacker I've ever coached," said Woody.

There were many others who have played major roles in Ohio State's football success since the days when Chic Harley elevated the Buckeyes from a cornfield football patsy to a national power, but these were the special ones—the ones who shone brightest of all.

TWENTY-SEVEN

Otto Graham and Other Heroes

To say that the Big Ten, in its long, glorious history, has spawned more great players than any other conference would perhaps be presumptuous and start a legitimate ruckus that would raise howls of protest from coast to coast. However it *is* fair to claim that the Big Ten has had more than its share of super-players over the years. Players who left an indelible mark on college football history even though, in some cases, the teams they played on rarely made a noticeable dent in the rough and ready conference in which they competed.

One such player was Otto Graham, a triple-threat tailback who plied his trade at Northwestern in 1941, 1942, and 1943, and later became one of pro football's greatest quarterbacks. Oddly enough, except for a queer quirk of fate, Otto might never have been an All-America tailback.

Graham came from a musical family. His father had directed the Waukegan (Illinois) High School band for twenty-two years, his mother was a grammar school music teacher, and his older brother, Gene, was an oboe player and soloist with the U. S. Marine Corps Band. Otto played the piano, violin, cornet, and French horn, and was a music major at Northwestern. So it would have been natural to imagine Otto Graham playing one—or maybe even all—of his four instruments in a concert hall somewhere in the country.

The prospect of that happening became even more realistic when Graham suffered a knee injury playing freshman football at Northwestern, requiring surgery. He withdrew from school for the rest of the year and it seemed that his football career was at an end. Because of the injury and subsequent surgery, Otto had just about decided to limit his college athletic career to basketball, a sport in which he excelled while at Waukegan High, with music still his primary interest.

Despite Graham's reluctance to take another shot at football—he feared his operated knee would not stand up under the pressure—some of his friends talked him into reporting for spring practice in 1941, and that was one of the best things that ever happened to Coach Lynn (Pappy) Waldorf and Northwestern, as well as for Otto Graham. The next three years proved to be spectacular ones for the young musician from Waukegan.

Waldorf promptly made Graham the tailback in his single-wing offense, and for the next three years Otto proceeded to give a series of virtuoso performances that dazzled Northwestern fans and frustrated the Wildcats' opponents. He ran like the tailback he was, passed like the T-formation quarterback he was later to become, ran back punts and played defense, and did it all so well that he became a unanimous choice for All-America in 1943, his last season.

More than that, Graham also became one of Northwestern's brightest basketball stars, winning All-America honors, and starred for three seasons in baseball, a sport he never played in high school. Otto was simply a natural athlete who performed with grace and style.

Pappy Waldorf had taken over as the Northwestern coach in 1935, succeeding Dick Hanley, who had given the Wildcats Big Ten championships in 1930 and 1931, but then Northwestern fell on bad times and Hanley became one of the casualties. Pappy coached the Wildcats to a 7–1 record and another conference crown in 1936, his second year (the last time, incidentally, Northwestern won the title), but Waldorf's teams slipped back into mediocrity after that wonderful season. Northwestern, the only private school in the Big Ten, was finding it more difficult to compete with the growing state universities in the recruiting arena and few blue-chip athletes were showing up at the Evanston campus. Ohio State, Minnesota, Michigan, Iowa, and the other conference powers were plucking the high schools clean, leaving the poor Wildcats with the leftovers.

However, when Waldorf got a look at Otto Graham in preseason practice in 1941, he knew that he had an exceptional player. Otto was a superb passer, an even better runner, and an outstanding punter. Pappy meant to make the most of these talents.

"With Otto's sense of timing, his peripheral vision, and his natural gifts of size, strength, and toughness, he was the ideal running-passing threat," said Waldorf.

Graham didn't disappoint his coach, but the rest of the team, unhappily, couldn't match Otto's skills and the 1941 season proved to be another one of those mediocre campaigns. Except, of course, for the excitement generated by Graham and Bill DeCorrevont, the former Chicago high school flash, who was in his final season and led the team in rushing.

Graham broke in with a bang in Northwestern's conference opener with Wisconsin. He scored twice in a 41–14 victory. Otto's finest effort, however, came against Coach Paul Brown's Ohio State team. He threw a pair of touchdown passes that accounted for a 14–7 upset of the Buckeyes, who didn't lose another game that year.

Northwestern finished with a 5–3 record, hardly notable, but two of the losses were by a single point, 8–7, to Minnesota, and 7–6, to Notre Dame, while the other defeat was the one-touchdown decision the Wildcats dropped to Michigan. Graham hadn't actually turned around the Northwestern football program, but without his efforts the season might have been a total disaster.

Not even Otto's immense talents, however, could save Northwestern in 1942. He continued to do his things—running, passing, and kicking—and did them well. Graham completed 89 of 182 passes for 1,227 yards, and was at his best against Michigan, when he was successful on twenty of twenty-nine passes. But a schedule dotted with service teams and the usual tough conference opponents proved to be too much for the otherwise undermanned Wildcats. They won only one game, a 3–0 upset of Texas, and lost nine times. Clearly, there was no joy in Evanston.

In 1943 wartime regulations came to Northwestern's rescue and helped to provide both Otto Graham and the embattled Wildcats with some of their finest hours. Navy and Marine trainees on campus, many of them players who had starred for other schools, including a formidable quartet of former Minnesota players—Herman Frickey, Herb Hein, Larry Halenkamp, and Jerry Carle—joined the Northwestern squad to give Graham the kind of aid he missed in 1942. The net result was that Otto had his best year and Northwestern won six of its eight games to finish second in the Big Ten. Only Michigan, which ironically was led by Bill Daley, another former Minnesota Gopher, was able to beat the Wildcats in the conference.

Graham was simply magnificent all season long. His running, punting, and occasional passing virtually overwhelmed the opposition. Coincidentally, Otto's greatest game was against Wisconsin, the same school which had suffered indignities at the hands of Graham in his first Big Ten game. Running like the All-America he was to become at the conclusion of the season, Otto scored three touchdowns and kicked three extra points in the first twelve minutes of play. He came back later to add a fourth score on a 55-yard punt return and threw a pass to Bob Motl for a fifth as the poor Gophers fell, 41–0.

There was no doubt about Otto Graham's All-America status when the selectors made their picks at the end of the season. For three years he had done just about everything one player could possibly do, and more, considering that he also played on a 1–9 team. Otto completed 157 of 320 passes for 2,181 yards and fifteen touchdowns in an era when the pass was only an occasional weapon, added 823 yards and seventeen touchdowns rushing for a total of 3,004 yards in total offense, scoring 115 points. All in all, he had accounted for almost half of the total points scored by Northwestern in his three seasons.

Big Ten opponents weren't one bit sorry when Graham's college days were over, but Coach Paul Brown, who was busy putting together a team to represent Cleveland in the brand-new professional All-American Conference, recognized a good thing when he saw one. Although Otto had never played a single down as a quarterback in the T-formation, the system then in vogue in pro football, Brown felt that his passing and running skills, along with his intelligence, could easily be adapted to the T and he signed Graham to a contract.

From 1945 to 1955 Otto Graham was pro football's premier quarterback. He led the Browns to four All-American Conference championships and then, when the Cleveland team was absorbed by the National Football League in 1950, Graham helped put the Browns into six straight championship games, winning three of them, before he called it quits as a player at the end of the 1955 season. Otto also was picked for All-Pro honors for ten straight years.

Following his retirement from pro football, Graham entered the coaching ranks, first with the U.S. Coast Guard Academy and then with the Washington Redskins. His career as a pro head coach in Washington was largely undistinguished. Otto was under constant fire by management and the fans before he left the Redskins to be

succeeded by the late Vince Lombardi. Eventually Graham returned to the Coast Guard Academy, where the pressures were
considerably less and winning wasn't necessarily everything.

Perhaps Otto Graham would have been a musical genius if he
had elected to pass up football at Northwestern. Instead, he became a football genius.

"The best quarterback football has ever seen," says Coach Paul
Brown.

For all his magnificence, Otto Graham wasn't Northwestern's
first superstar. Twenty-five years earlier Evanston fans were
cheering a young man named John Leo Driscoll, more popularly
known as Paddy, a triple-threat quarterback who did more things
with a football than Houdini later did with chains. The only thing
that kept him from being the seventh wonder of the college football
world was that Chic Harley played for Ohio State at the same time,
and his exploits—and the more flamboyant success of the Buckeyes—earned greater headlines and conference championships.

Nevertheless, Paddy Driscoll was a genuine star in his own right.
Although he weighed only a scant 145 pounds when he began his
varsity career at Northwestern in 1915, Driscoll astounded everyone with his skill as a runner, kicker, and field general. Paddy was
an exceptionally talented dropkicker and his 30- and 40-yard field
goals soon became a familiar and expected sight around what was
then the Big Nine. (Michigan had dropped out of the conference in
1907 and didn't return until 1917, but Ohio State had joined up in
1912 to make it the Big Nine again.)

When Driscoll came along, Northwestern was the perennial
doormat of the conference. The Purple (they didn't become known
as the Wildcats until 1924, when Wallace Abbey, a sportswriter for
the Chicago *Tribune,* gave them the name after a particularly stirring performance against Chicago) had lost twelve straight games
in the league and their rivals actually looked forward to playing
them, confident that any game with Northwestern could be considered an automatic victory. While the arrival of Paddy Driscoll on
the Northwestern football scene didn't change that situation immediately, there were signs that the Purple might just emerge from
their doldrums. They continued to lose, but they were beginning to
scare people.

Driscoll and Northwestern came into their own in 1916 when
they swept past their first six opponents for the Purple's best start

since 1896. Chicago was the first league foe to feel the newly dis-
covered wrath of the suddenly aroused team from Evanston. The
original Monsters of the Midway, who had not suffered defeat at
the hands of Northwestern since 1901, found Paddy Driscoll simply too much to cope with. Paddy ran for a touchdown and dropkicked a 43-yard field goal, and down went the humiliated Maroons, 10–0.

With Driscoll running, kicking, and directing the offense with the
skill of a battlefield general, Northwestern rolled over Drake, Indiana, Iowa, and Purdue, and came up to the final game with Ohio
State unbeaten and untied. All the Purple Gang had to do was beat
the Buckeyes and they would have their first conference championship. But it was not to be. Chic Harley and the Buckeyes
proved to be too much for even Paddy Driscoll to overcome, and
Northwestern lost, 23–3. It was a disappointing ending but there
was some consolation for the Purple, whose 6–1 record was the
best ever up until then for a Northwestern team, and for Driscoll,
who had demonstrated that he belonged in the same class with Harley, even though he was denied All-America recognition.

Although Northwestern's football history has not always been
so distinguished, Paddy Driscoll and Otto Graham were not the
only authentic stars to come out of Evanston. There were many
others. Like Ralph (Moon) Baker, a big, blond, amiable giant who
had enrolled at Illinois with Red Grange but then decided to transfer to Northwestern. A strong runner and a splendid field-goal
kicker, Baker gave Northwestern's opponents, including Coach
Knute Rockne's famed Notre Dame teams which included the
Four Horsemen—Jim Crowley, Elmer Layden, Don Miller, and
Harry Stuhldreher—fits from 1924 through 1926. Baker also had
the distinction of leading the 1926 team to a share of the Big Ten title, along with Michigan.

Over the years Baker was followed by a succession of superlative runners—Hank Bruder, who might have been the best of all
except for a series of mishaps ranging from a hip injury to smallpox, which earned him the nickname of "Hard Luck Hank," in
1928 and 1929; Lafayette (Reb) Russell in 1930; Pug Rentner in
1931; Don Heap in 1936 and 1937; Bill DeCorrevont in 1939, 1940,
and 1941; Art Murakowski in 1946, 1947, and 1948; Ron Burton,
who holds Northwestern's career scoring record of 130 points, in
1957, 1958, and 1959; Mike Adamle in 1969 and 1970; and defensive
safety Eric Hutchinson in 1971.

Adamle has a special place in the hearts of Northwestern fans. A stubby, five-foot nine-inch fullback who was built like a fireplug and spurted out of the backfield like a firehose, Mike created excitement when he carried the ball. Despite his diminutive stature, Adamle weighed a solid 195 pounds, was broad in the chest and massive in the arms. Outgoing and breezy, he was rarely at a loss for words. For instance, once when he was asked the first time anyone mentioned that he was too small to play football, he answered, "I was in my crib."

Adamle explains, "I have the type of stature that makes a computer regurgitate."

Mike's size never hindered him on the football field. He had a knack for hiding behind blockers and squirting through the barest of openings in the line. Adamle set several school records at Northwestern, including one for 316 yards rushing in a game (against Wisconsin in 1969), 1,255 yards in a single season (1970), and 2,015 in a career. Coach Hank Stram of the Kansas City Chiefs thought enough of Mike to make him his fifth-round draft choice in 1971. Adamle moved from the Chiefs to the New York Jets in 1973, where he gained an instant ally in the then coach, Weeb Ewbank, one of the few men in football that the five-foot nine Mike towered over.

"I don't care if he's three feet tall," said Ewbank, who wasn't much taller himself, "as long as he continues to run to daylight."

Northwestern has also had some exceptional quarterbacks who have made passing history in the Big Ten. First there was Tom Myers, an agile young man who threw the ball more times than anyone else in previous Wildcat history. From 1962 through 1964, playing first under Coach Ara Parseghian and then Coach Alex Agase, Tom heaved 534 passes and completed 281 of them for 3,836 yards and twenty-one touchdowns. Myers' marks, however, lasted only until Maurice Daigneau, a talented flinger with unerring accuracy, came along in 1969. Even as a sophomore, Maurie gave every indication that Myers' records wouldn't last very long. Daigneau completed eighty-five passes for 1,276 yards, and before he was finished in 1971 he had not only surpassed all of Tom's records but added another one, for total offense. In three seasons Diagneau completed 298 of 659 passes for 4,237 yards and twenty-three touchdowns, and posted 3,930 yards in total offense. Some might rightly question the disparity between his passing and total offense yardage, but there were many times when Maurie, lacking the protection to make him inviolable, literally had to run for his life while attempting to throw the ball, a nagging pastime that frequently resulted in his being sacked, and consequently cost him considerable yardage.

The latest in the line of Northwestern's passing quarterbacks was Mitch Anderson, who broke in spectacularly in 1972 as a sophomore. Anderson completed ninety-five passes for 1,333 yards and seven touchdowns, and two of his completions, both to Jim Lash, were the longest in Northwestern history, 94 yards against Michigan State and 81 yards against Indiana. Mitch followed with an even more productive season in 1973. Although he completed four fewer passes (91), twelve of them were for touchdowns, including a record-breaking five against Minnesota. In 1974 Anderson led the conference in passing yardage with 1,098 yards and threw for five touchdowns that gave him twenty-four and broke Daigneau's career record.

Aside from the glamor boys who ran and passed the ball, Northwestern also has produced an impressive list of All-America linemen starting with Tim Lowry, a center who was the first Wildcat to make the honor roll, back in 1925. Among the others who earned their spurs while protecting the backs and defending against some of the most esteemed heroes in college football were tackle Bob Johnson in 1926, guard Henry Anderson in 1929, end Frank Baker and guard Wade (Red) Woodworth in 1930, tackles Dallas Marvil and Jack Riley in 1931, and end Edgar (Eggs) Manske, later a celebrated pro player, in 1933.

More recently there were tackle Bob Voigts in 1938, center John Haman in 1939, tackle Alf Bauman in 1940, end Herb Hein in 1943, end Max Morris in 1945, center Alex Sarkisian in 1948, end Don Stonesifer in 1950, end Joe Collier (who caught eleven touchdown passes before he finished his career in 1952 and shares the school record with Steve Craig, another end of more recent vintage), tackle Andy Cverko in 1958, center Jim Andreotti in 1959, center Larry Onesti in 1961, and guard Jack Cverko in 1962.

You can Purple them all genuine Wildcats.

Indiana, too, while only rarely a power in the conference, has contributed a substantial line of individual stars to Big Ten lore. Two of the best were Corby Davis and Billy Hillenbrand, a pair of backs who helped to give the Hoosiers a reputation of sorts in the middle thirties and early forties.

Davis was one of the finest all-around players ever to represent Indiana. A powerful fullback who blasted through the line like a runaway Mack truck, Corby also had other talents that made him special. He was a superb kicker, blocker, and defensive player, who, unfortunately, played on Hoosier teams that were barely mediocre. Davis, then a sophomore, was just about the only bright spot on the 1935 club that posted a 4–3–1 record, but then he had to sit out the entire 1936 season with a streptococcus infection in his arm.

When Davis returned to action in 1937, the Indiana squad had been decimated by graduation. The year's layoff didn't seem to bother Corby to any great extent. If anything he was even better, good enough to be named the conference's Most Valuable Player, the second year in a row that an Indiana star had won that honor (Vern Huffman was named in 1936), although his team posted only a 5–3 record. One of those five victories, however, was a 10–0 decision over Ohio State which knocked the Buckeyes out of a share of the championship. And it was Davis who was mostly responsible for OSU's only conference loss. Although he didn't score, he pounded away at the Buckeyes to put his team in position for the game-winning points, a 17-yard field goal by George (Sparky) Miller and a 15-yard touchdown pass from Frank Filchock to Frank Petrick.

Four years later, in 1941, Billy Hillenbrand was the leading torchbearer for Indiana. He was even more multitalented than Davis. Billy was a triple-threat halfback who ran, passed, and kicked with exceptional skill. He also played defense and was one of the finest punt returners the Big Ten had ever seen. But, like Davis, he found that his teammates were much less skillful. Except for Lou Saban, who was later to gain fame as a coach in college and professional ranks, and Pete Pihos, a tough, rawboned end, the Hoosiers had little else to offer and, despite the efforts of this trio, they suffered through a 2–6 campaign.

Things were better, however, for both Hillenbrand and Indiana in 1942. Billy proved to be one of the most exciting players around. His slashing inside runs and spectacular punt returns turned the Hoosiers around. They beat Minnesota, 7–0, for the first time on Hillenbrand's touchdown pass to Pihos, and won seven of their ten games for Indiana's best season since 1910.

Hillenbrand was almost everybody's choice for All-America at the end of the season and there are some Hoosiers who still insist that he was the best triple-threat back in Indiana history.

Hillenbrand and Saban were still in school in 1943 but they were enrolled in military training programs and thus ineligible to play. When Coach Alvin (Bo) McMillin greeted his squad of forty-four players for preseason practice, forty-two of them were freshmen! But one of those freshmen was Bob Hoernschmeyer, a fuzzy-cheeked seventeen-year-old who could run and pass. And one of the two returning upperclassmen was Pihos, the fine end.

Although Indiana's fledgling team was barely able to hold its own, Hoernschmeyer proved to be one of the finds of the season. He threw six touchdown passes while completing fourteen of eighteen attempts for 345 yards, and rolled up 458 yards in total offense in a 54–13 rout of Nebraska. In another game his last-minute pass to John McDonnell gave Indiana a 20–14 win over mighty Ohio State. Hunchy's thirteen touchdown passes that season is still the best ever for an Indiana player. He also led both the nation—with 2,669 yards—and the Big Ten—with 873 yards, 596 passing and 277 rushing—in total offense, breaking conference records previously set by Otto Graham and Tom Harmon.

However, Hoernschmeyer didn't stay around Bloomington very long. He committed himself to the U.S. Naval Academy, but was able to remain at Indiana for the 1944 season before entering Navy. That put Coach McMillin in a tough spot, especially since Bob reported for practice later than the rest of the squad. When Hunchy did turn out, McMillin decided to relegate him to the second team. But that bit of strategy didn't last very long.

One day, in a scrimmage, the varsity pushed the scrubs all the way back to their 2-yard line before a fumble gave the seconds the ball. Hoernschmeyer promptly took off around end, dipsy-doodled his way through the entire embarrassed varsity, and ran 98 yards for a touchdown.

Hoernschmeyer trotted back, preening like a peacock, only to hear Coach McMillin say, "Hunchy, you made several mistakes on that run."

"Yes, sir," said Hoernschmeyer meekly. "What were they, sir?"

"Well," said Bo, "when you got around end, you should have straight-armed that halfback instead of rolling your body away from him. And then instead of cutting back, you should have kept running straight ahead. And when you got down near the goal line, you should have cut sharply to fool those fellows chasing you. Understand?''

"Yes, sir,'' agreed Hunchy, "but how was it for distance, coach?''

Hoernschmeyer went on to have another fine year for the Hoosiers. He led the conference in passing and starred as a punt-returner —he returned twenty-eight kicks for 635 yards, still a school record—as he led Indiana to a 7–3 season before he took his exceptional talent to Navy, where he continued his distinguished career.

Despite the presence of all these outstanding individual stars, the one thing that had eluded Bo McMillin and his Hoosiers, as well as every other Indiana team in the past, was a conference championship. Going into the 1945 season it appeared that Indiana would be just another league also-ran again. Hoernschmeyer was now a midshipman, while Pihos, an All-America end in 1943, and Howard Brown, a big, fast guard, were still in service. Ted Kluszewski, who was later to gain renown as a homerun hitter for the Cincinnati Reds, and Bob Ravensberg, a pair of talented ends, were around but it appeared that McMillin would have to be satisfied once again with building character. However, the discovery of some budding young new stars plus a set of unexpected and fortuitous circumstances turned the Hoosiers into an honest-to-goodness title contender.

One bonus was the presence of Ben Raimondi, a pinpoint passer who somehow found his way from Brooklyn, New York, to Bloomington, Indiana. Naturally they called him the Brooklyn Bomber. Another was George Taliaferro, a black freshman halfback who had the moves of a belly dancer and quickly demonstrated that he was going to be a star. In the opening game against Michigan, an opponent Indiana had beaten only three times since 1900, Taliaferro darted and scooted through the Wolverine defenders for big hunks of yardage while Raimondi threw a pair of touchdown passes to Kluszewski and Mel Groomes for a 13–7 victory. It began to look then as if the Hoosiers were going to be better than everyone expected.

Then a funny thing happened to Coach McMillin on his way to the next game with Northwestern. He got a telephone call from Howard Brown, a super-guard, who reported that he was just back from the European war theater, had sixty days of leave, would soon be out of service, and could he please return to Indiana to play football. McMillin could hardly restrain his joy. But there was even more to come. The next day, when Bo went to meet Brown for lunch, there was Pete Pihos, who told McMillin he was on terminal leave and that he, too, wanted to come back, if it was alright with the coach. You can imagine Bo's answer to both of his former stars!

After only a couple of days of practice, both Brown, a superb blocker and defender, and Pihos were ready for Northwestern. But Pihos was no longer an end. McMillin had decided to convert him into a fullback and the move paid off. Pete turned out to be a pile-driving plunger who,. time and again during the season, came up with clutch yardage. He also made a singular contribution in the Northwestern game, scoring on a pass from Raimondi and kicking the extra point to give Indiana a 7–7 tie, the only time that the surprising Hoosiers were not to win in 1945.

With Raimondi throwing passes to big Kluszewski and Ravensberg, a fast, sure-handed receiver, Taliaferro running behind the blocking of Brown, and Pihos making mincemeat of opposing lines, Indiana swept to seven straight victories and came up to the final game with old rival Purdue unbeaten but tied once and with a shot at its first league championship. The Boilermakers could hardly be considered a pushover since they came into the game with a 7–2 record, but there was no stopping the hungry Hoosiers. After a scoreless first half, Pihos plunged for two touchdowns, Raimondi tossed to Kluszewski and Lou Mihajlovich for scores, and Indiana swept to a 26–0 victory to win two big prizes—its first conference title and that coveted relic, the Old Oaken Bucket. Raimondi, Taliaferro, Pihos, Ravensberg, Kluszewski, and Brown—those are names that occupy a special place in Indiana football history.

Although it would be twenty-two years before Indiana would win another league championship, the Hoosiers continued to produce outstanding individual players. There was Gene Gedman, a fine back who piled up 1,562 yards rushing for a school record in 1950, 1951, and 1952. Then there were Earl Faison, a bruising end who was an All-America in 1960; fullback Tom Nowatzke, another one of those crushing line plungers; Marv Woodson, a swift, darting halfback; guard Don Croftcheck; and end Bill Malinchak, who hauled in 115 passes in three seasons. All were premier players in the early to middle sixties.

Indiana's title drought finally ended in 1967 when a rollicking band of young players made their debut under Coach John Pont, who had left Yale to come to Bloomington in 1965. Pont's first two seasons were utter disasters, 2–8 in 1965 and 1–8–1 in 1966, and the Hoosier wolves were beginning to howl ever so slightly. Then, in 1967, came one of the most dramatic turnabouts in Indiana history.

The catalysts for the renaissance were a group of free-wheeling sophomores led by quarterback Harry Gonso, halfback John Isenbarge, and flanker Jade Butcher. This trio, along with veteran tackle Doug Crusan, suddenly became the talk of the conference. They called them the "Katzenjammer Kids."

With Gonso doing the passing, Butcher the catching, and Isenbarger the running, and Crusan, Jim Sniadecki, and Ken Kaczmarek heading up a stubborn defense, this crew of Hoosiers turned the Big Ten upside down. And they did it the hard way, winning seven games by seven points or less, many of them in the final minutes. Their games were no place for a cardiac patient.

Coach Pont suffered, too, mostly because his charges were so unpredictable, but it was a pleasure for John. When Isenbarger, a free spirit if there ever was one, went back to punt, Pont never knew whether he was going to kick or run, as he did on several occasions. Pont rarely got an opportunity to relax on the sidelines, starting with the season's opener against Kentucky and going right down to the final game with Purdue.

The young Hoosiers won that first one, 12–10, and the next seven, too, before Minnesota interrupted the string with a 33–7 trouncing. Undaunted, the Hoosiers hung on for dear life in the finale against Purdue to eke out a 19–14 victory and win their first Big Ten championship since 1945. They also earned Indiana's only trip to the Rose Bowl, where they lost to Southern California's national champions, 14–3.

Gonso, Isenbarger, and Butcher were the heart of the Indiana offense all season long. Gonso was not only an excellent passer, but he could—and did—run the ball with amazing frequency, enough to roll up 1,443 yards in total offense. His favorite receiver, Butcher, a sure-handed flankerback, caught ten touchdown passes. Isenbarger was a versatile runner, a slasher inside, and quick, darting, and elusive on sweeps.

Although Indiana was not to have another year like 1967 before Gonso, Isenbarger, and Butcher finished their careers in 1969, all three set school records that still exist. Gonso completed 250 of 513 passes for 3,376 yards and thirty-two touchdowns, and rolled up 4,448 yards in total offense. Isenbarger rushed for 1,217 yards in

1969 for a one-season mark, and had 2,465 yards in his three years. Butcher scored thirty touchdowns in his three seasons to become Indiana's leading scorer with 180 points, and caught 116 passes for 1,876 yards, to break Bill Malinchak's mark. Jade also caught ten passes against Michigan State in 1969 to tie a school record. Isenbarger and Gary Cassells, the tough-blocking guard, were All-Americas in 1967, while Isenbarger repeated in 1969, along with Butcher.

They were the last of the great ones at Indiana, but there will be others in the future if the present coach, dynamic, outspoken Lee Corso, has his way.

No other college football team, anywhere, had the collection of talent that Coach Duffy Daugherty rounded up at Michigan State in 1965 and 1966. They came from all over the country—from Pennsylvania, Ohio, Texas, South Carolina, North Carolina, and even from Hawaii, a favorite hunting ground for Duffy. He even managed to find a few in the state of Michigan.

The Spartans had had great football teams before under Clarence (Biggie) Munn, who turned over the coaching reins to Daugherty in 1954 to become athletic director. But not even Biggie's super-clubs in the early fifties had as many authentic individual stars as Duffy's bunch in 1965 and 1966.

In 1965 the offense was provided by senior quarterback Steve Juday, a nimble little fellow whose pinpoint passing confounded enemy defenses; halfbacks Clinton Jones and Dwight Lee, both of whom could slash away inside or skirt the ends with equal facility and had the breakaway speed to go all the way; and Bob Apisa, a hard-hitting fullback who reached East Lansing by way of Samoa and Hawaii. Gene Washington, the Big Ten hurdles champion, was the target of most of Juday's passes and he turned out to be the best receiver in Michigan State history. A booming, tough-blocking offensive line, led by tackle Jerry West and center Boris Dimitroff, leveled everyone in sight as they gave Juday the protection he needed and opened gaping holes for the other Spartan backs.

As good as the offense was, the defense was even more forbidding. For openers there were Charles (Bubba) Smith, a six-foot eight-inch, 280-pound giant with a menacing stare who loved to sack quarterbacks, at one end, and Harold Lucas, a 265-pound middle guard who loomed like a brick wall—and was just as hard to dent—when foes tried to run up the gut against Michigan State. Behind them were a group of secondary defenders who were expert at throttling anyone who managed to get through the front line. Linebackers Ron Goovert and Charley (Big Dog) Thornhill didn't miss much that came their way, but the best of all was George Webster, the quick, agile, 218-pound rover back who terrorized enemy ballcarriers with his frequent blitzes and deadly tackling. If anyone did manage to elude this crew of destroyers, they had to deal with cornerback Don Japinga, who roamed the secondary like a lion on the prowl.

Before the season started there was no indication that this Michigan State team would be anything but an also-ran in the conference race. Most of the starters, except for sophomores Apisa and Lee, had played in 1964 when the Spartans muddled to a 4–5 season, prompting some calls for Duffy Daugherty's scalp. The genial coach, however, ignored his detractors and the preseason predictions which tabbed his team for a second-division finish. But Duffy had a gleam in his eye and it turned out to be a prophetic one.

No one paid too much attention as first UCLA fell, 13–3, to the Spartans, and then Penn State, 23–0. But when Michigan State got into the Big Ten schedule, people suddenly began to take notice as the Spartans whipped hated Michigan, 24–7, and Ohio State, 32–7. It wasn't so much the victories that began to impress folks but the way they came about. For example, the rough, tough MSU defense held Michigan to minus 39 yards and Ohio State to minus 22 yards in offense, something which had *never* happened to one of Woody Hayes' teams. Later Notre Dame was limited to minus 12 yards. Bubba Smith, George Webster, Harold Lucas, and their partners were simply devastating as only Purdue gave the Spartans a tussle. MSU had to come back from a 10–0 deficit to win that one, 14–10.

The offense was equally terrorizing. Juday expertly picked apart defenses with his sharp passes, Apisa proved to be a powerhouse fullback, and Jones was a delight to watch as time and again he came up with big runs. And, when all else failed, there was Dick Kenney, the barefoot Hawaiian kicker, to boot a field goal.

Spartan fans took to the team like hungry animals. Duffy Daugherty suddenly became a great coach again, and one of the favorite rallying cries was "Kill, Bubba, Kill" when the huge end took off on one of his many attacks against opposing quarterbacks and ballcarriers. There were some who even thought that Duffy was feeding his defenders raw meat to whet their appetites for headhunting.

When the season was over, Michigan State had swept past all ten of its opponents to win the Big Ten title and the national champion-ship in the United Press International poll. (Alabama, also unbeat-en, was voted No. 1 over the Spartans in the Associated Press poll.) Among other things Michigan State led the nation in defense, holding opponents to an average of 45.6 yards per game, and topped the conference in both offense and defense. Duffy Daugh-erty was named Coach of the Year and accolades poured in from all over for the Spartans, including one from former Oklahoma Coach Bud Wilkinson, who had so many powerhouses himself in Norman in past years.

Bud said flatly, "The Spartans are perhaps the finest team in the history of intercollegiate football."

Jones, Juday, Apisa, Washington, Lucas, Smith, Webster, and Goovert were named to various All-America teams and pro scouts flocked around the Spartans like a horde of vultures, even though they would have to wait another year for most of them. Around ev-eryone, that is, but Juday, the little senior quarterback who had led the offense with his skillful passing and set twelve school records.

Juday, who was named one of the National Football Foundation and Hall of Fame's scholar-athletes, good-naturedly quipped, "I guess I'm the only All-America quarterback in history who wasn't drafted by the pros."

The only sour note was the postseason rematch with UCLA in the Rose Bowl. Perhaps oversatiated with their individual and team accomplishments during the regular season, the Spartans did not play up to their usual standard and were outpointed, 14–12, when Apisa's tries for two-pointers were stopped cold twice by the heady Bruins. But the hay was in the barn before that loss even though the defeat took away some of the luster from the regular season.

There was no doubt in the minds of Big Ten prognosticators as to which team was the one to beat in 1966. Michigan's State's player losses had been negligible. Except for Juday, Goovert, and Japin-ga, the rest of that awesome cast—Jones, Lee, Apisa, West, Wash-ington, Smith, Webster, and Thornhill—were all back. All Duffy Daugherty needed was a quarterback to lead them, and he found one in Jimmy Raye, a little black fellow with a shotgun arm and a talent for scrambling and running with the ball.

If anything, the 1966 team was even more intimidating than its predecessor. The offense was more potent with Raye at quarter-back. His running, added to that of Jones and Apisa, added still another dimension to the attack, while the sight of Bubba Smith, George Webster, and Charley Thornhill sprawled over prostrate ball-carriers was a familiar one as Michigan State bowled over opponent after opponent. Only Ohio State managed to give the powerful Spartans a battle before bowing, 11–8. A 37–19 shellacking of Indiana gave Michigan State its second straight unbeaten conference season and another Big Ten title, and set up a last-game battle with Notre Dame for the national championship.

The Irish, too, were unbeaten and the tussle was variously billed as "The Game of the Year," "The Game of the Decade," or "The Game of the Century," depending upon how much writers let themselves get carried away. Notre Dame had been ranked No. 1 in both the AP and UPI polls, with Michigan State No. 2 for most of the season, and there was no question that the winner would get college football's greatest prize.

What happened in the game is history. The two teams battled to a frenzied 10–10 tie, with Notre Dame electing to run out the clock in the final minutes to save the deadlock and, hopefully, its No. 1 ranking instead of going for a possible victory. Notre Dame Coach Ara Parseghian got a lot of heat from the fans and the press for his obvious conservatism, but it protected the No. 1 ranking for the Irish, although a good many people around the country disputed the polls, including the National Football Foundation and Hall of Fame, which awarded its MacArthur Bowl, symbolic of the national championship, to both Notre Dame and Michigan State as co-champions.

Michigan State, unhappily, was denied another trip to the Rose Bowl because the Big Ten rule then in effect prohibited a team from making two consecutive trips to Pasadena. Instead, Purdue, the conference runner-up which had lost only to the Spartans, represented the Big Ten and did it rather handsomely, squeezing out a 14–13 win over the University of Southern California.

Despite the disappointment of not finishing No. 1 in the polls, individual honors still poured in for the Spartans. Jones, Apisa, Smith, Washington, and Webster all repeated as All-Americas, along with tackle Jerry West, and eleven Michigan State players were named to the All–Big Ten offensive and defensive teams. The six All-Americas were joined by halfback Jess Phillips, tackle Nick Jordan, guard Tony Conti, linebacker Charley Thornhill, and kicker Dick Kenney. Never before had one team so dominated the Big Ten selections.

That was to be Duffy Daugherty's last hurrah, however. Although he produced a batch of individual stars, after that Duffy's teams had trouble winning in the tough Big Ten and the heat from alumni and fans finally forced his retirement from coaching after the 1972 season. But not before he turned out another succession of All-Americas—Allen Brenner, a combination pass-receiver and safety, in 1968; guard Ron Saul in 1969; halfback Eric Allen, safety Brad Van Pelt, and tackle Ron Curl in 1971; and tight end Billy Joe DuPree, guard Joe DeLammiellure, and Van Pelt again in 1972.

Allen and Van Pelt were perhaps the best of the lot. Allen, a little guy who flitted hither and yon through enemy defenses, was promptly and aptly nicknamed "The Flea." Although tiny by big-time college football standards, Eric had tremendous speed, a talent for squeezing through the tiniest of holes, and was at his best once he got into the open. It wasn't unusual for him to leave a trail of bigger, heavier, and frustrated bodies behind him as he skittered and dodged his way through the secondary.

Allen broke in as a sophomore in 1969, and the next season began to show signs of greatness as he punished Michigan State rivals for 811 yards rushing and scored ten touchdowns. Then, in 1971, The Flea really came into his own. Daugherty, like so many other coaches, decided to go to the fashionable Wishbone offense. The triple option was made to order for Allen. It gave him more opportunities to carry the ball and he made the most of it. So much so that he wound up as the number-one single-season rusher in Big Ten history—until Ohio State's Archie Griffin came along.

Allen, with his great quickness, was able to slip off tackle, and his speed on outside plays made him a constant threat to go all the way. He had his biggest day in a 43–10 win over Purdue. Eric ran the ball twenty-nine times for 350 yards, still a Big Ten record for a single game, and scored four times on runs of 24, 59, 30, and 25 yards. The poor Boilermakers never did catch up to him that long afternoon. Iowa and Minnesota also got a few very quick looks at The Flea. He scored three times against the Hawkeyes and four times against the frustrated Gophers. When the season ended, Eric had rushed for 1,494 yards, eclipsing Ron Johnson's single-season Big Ten mark of 1,391, and had scored eighteen touchdowns and 110 points.

Van Pelt was probably one of the best all-around athletes in Michigan State history. Also, he may hve been the biggest defensive back the conference has known. Brad stood six feet five inches, weighed in at 221 pounds, and had the kind of speed that folks didn't expect to go with his size. He towered over most pass-receivers and, when he hit someone, they usually remembered him. Daugherty installed him at safety where he excelled to the degree that he became a two-time All-America. But he could have played anywhere, on defense or offense, and been a star.

Van Pelt also played varsity basketball and baseball, and was such a red-hot prospect as a pitcher that he had to make a choice between pro football and major-league baseball. Brad was drafted by the California Angels after his junior year and turned down a $100,000 bonus. After the 1972 football season he was drafted by the New York Giants and elected to go the pro football route—for a considerably more substantial financial arrangement than he could have gotten from baseball.

Even before the awesome collection of 1965–66 stars, there were other players in Duffy Daugherty's regime who left their cleat marks on Michigan State football. The 1955 team, which ranked second to Oklahoma nationally, produced four All-Americas—quarterback Earl Morrall, who went on to achieve stardom in pro football; fullback Jerry Planutis; tackle Norm Masters; and center Buck Nystrom. Although Morrall was best known as a passer, both in college and with the pros, he also excelled as a punter at Michigan State. He still holds school records for the longest punt—71 yards—and the best season average—42.9 yards per kick. And just to demonstrate his versatility, Earl is also in the record book for the longest return of a fumble, 90 yards, for a touchdown against Purdue.

There were others, too. Fullback Walt Kowalczyk and center Dan Currie were All-Americas in 1957, and they were followed by end Sam Williams in 1958, quarterback Dean Look in 1959, guard Dave Behrman in 1961, fullback George Saimes and guard Ed Budde (later a longtime All-Pro in the National Football League) in 1962, and fullback Earl Lattimer and halfback Sherman Lewis in 1963.

Just a few words about Sherm Lewis. He was another one of those little scatbacks that Michigan State seemed to specialize in attracting to East Lansing. An exciting runner and talented pass-catcher, Lewis specialized in making the big play. In 1963 Sherm tore off an 87-yard touchdown run against Northwestern and another for 85 yards against Notre Dame. He also was on the receiving end of the two longest pass plays in the MSU record book, both from quarterback Steve Juday. One was an 88-yarder against the University of Southern California and the other went for 87 yards against Wisconsin.

While Michigan State did not get into the Big Ten until 1953, the "farm boys," as their bitter rivals from Michigan liked to call them, were playing football, rather haphazardly to be sure, as far back as 1884 and the game became a recognized sport in 1896. Then known as Michigan Agricultural College, the Aggies pursued the sport diligently, if not well, until 1903 when they made their first breakthrough and began a series of successful seasons that endured for a dozen years. However it wasn't until 1915 that the Aggies came up with their first All-America player—Neno (Jerry) DaPrato, a hustling halfback who led the entire nation in scoring with 188 points in just six games.

By 1926 Michigan Agricultural College became Michigan State and the Aggies became the Spartans, but they had to wait until the thirties to come up with a couple more All-Americas—Sid Wagner and Johnny Pingel. Wagner, a slashing, no-nonsense guard of rather modest physical proportions who blocked and defended with unexcelled zeal, was the star of the 1935 teams. Pingel, a triple-threat halfback who did everything but sell tickets and peanuts, led the 1937 Michigan State to the Orange Bowl, where it lost to Auburn, 6–0, but Johnny had to wait until 1938 to get his justified All-America ranking.

Perhaps the greatest overall era for Michigan State football came with the arrival of Biggie Munn as the head coach in 1947. The Spartans, striving desperately to achieve major college football respectability and hoping just as desperately to be accepted into what had become the Big Nine with the resignation of Chicago in 1936, suddenly began to make their presence felt in big-time circles and with it came a procession of individual stars who began to show up on All-America teams with pleasing frequency.

There was quarterback Gene Glick, whose passing was phenomenal for an era when college football teams just didn't throw the football with reckless abandon. From 1946 through 1949 Glick threw eighteen touchdown passes, eleven of them in the 1948 season. He was surpassed only by Al Dorow, who passed for nineteen scores in 1949, 1950, and 1951, and was named All-America for his quarterbacking. Tom Yewic, who took over when Dorow graduated, proved to be a fitting successor, passing for eighteen touchdowns in his three varsity seasons. Perhaps the best of the most recent Spartan quarterbacks were Charlie Baggett, who ran and passed for 1,713 yards to pace the 1974 team to a 7–3–1 record, and Ed Smith, who completed 132 passes for 1,749 yards and thirteen touchdowns to lead the Big Ten in 1976.

Then there were the runners. Lynn Chandnois, a marvelous half-back from 1946 through 1949, may have been the best of all time at Michigan State. A stylish, all-purpose runner, Lynn set five school records and four of them have withstood the assault of time and fu-ture stars. His thirty-one touchdowns and 186 career points were new high marks for Spartan football, and his 90-yard touchdown run against Arizona State in 1949 is still the longest in MSU histo-ry. Chandnois also rushed for 2,093 yards in his career, a record that lasted twenty-two years until Eric Allen broke it in 1971. Lynn was just as valuable as a defensive player, intercepting twenty passes in his four years. There was no doubt about his selection as an All-America in 1949, even in a year that produced stars like Doak Walker of Southern Methodist University, Emil Sitko of Notre Dame, Charlie Justice of North Carolina, Eddie Price of Tu-lane, McClendon Thomas and Darrell Royal of Oklahoma (yes, the same Darrell Royal who, after twenty years, retired in 1976 as the head coach at the University of Texas), and George Sella of Princeton.

When Chandnois left, Michigan State had a more than adequate replacement in Everett (Sonny) Grandelius, a stocky fellow who hammered his way to All-America honors in 1950. Sonny could hit hard and was an artful dodger once he got into the secondary. He did it for 1,068 yards in 1950 to become the most productive one-season performer the Spartans had ever seen—again, until Allen surpassed him. Grandelius, too, found himself in elite company in the All-America ranks. Some of his colleagues were Dick Kazmai-er of Princeton, Vic Janowicz of Ohio State, and Kyle Rote of Southern Methodist.

The succession of super-runners followed with halfbacks Don McAuliffe and Leroy Bolden winning All-America honors in 1952 and 1953. McAuliffe also was awarded the Walter Camp Trophy as Back of the Year.

There was no scarcity of outstanding linemen, either, during those good times. In 1949 Don Mason and Ed Bagdon were the best pair of guards in the country, providing the blocking for Chandnois and Grandelius. Indeed, Bagdon was so good that he was voted the Outland Trophy as the nation's best interior lineman. Dorne Dib-ble, a two-way end, was an All-America in 1950, while Bob Carey, another wingman, was picked in 1951, along with tackle Don Coleman, one of the all-time great Spartan heroes, whose No. 78 jersey was retired when he concluded his career at Michigan State.

The 1952 team produced two All-America linemen, center-linebacker Dick Tamburo, a bruising blocker and tackler, and guard Frank Kush, a tough little 180-pound guy who took on all comers regardless of their size. Kush went on to become one of college football's winningest—and toughest—coaches at Arizona State. In 1953 Don Dohoney, who had been shifted from offense to defense, was picked as one of the country's best ends.

Perhaps the best measuring stick for determining the greatest of all the Spartans was a poll conducted in 1970, on the occasion of the Big Ten's seventy-fifth anniversary observance, by ballots which appeared in the 1969 Homecoming Game program, the *Michigan State Alumni Magazine*, and the *Michigan State News*. Alumni, students, and fans voted George Webster the All-Time Greatest Player, Gene Washington the best end, Don Coleman the best interior lineman, and Earl Morrall the greatest back.

The All-Time Michigan State team had Washington and Smith at the ends; Coleman, Currie, Masters, Behrman, and Budde as the linemen; and Morrall, Jones, Webster, and Chandnois in the backfield.

The voting also broke down the All-Time team into offensive and defensive units. The offensive team listed Washington and Carey at the ends; Coleman, Masters, West, Budde, and Behrman as the linemen; and Morrall, Jones, Pingel, and Grandelius in the backfield. The best of all the defenders were Williams and Smith, ends; Bagdon, Jerry Rush of the 1964 team, and Lucas, the linemen; Curry and Kush, linebackers; and Webster, Chandnois, Saimes, and Herb Adderley, who became one of pro football's most celebrated defensive backs with the world championship Green Bay Packers, in the backfield.

Then, just so the Old-Timers would not be slighted, a pre-1940 all-time team also was picked. It had Ed Klewick (1934) and Blake Miller (1915) at the ends; Wagner, Hugh Blacklock (1916), Frank Butler (1934), Gideon Smith (1915), and Lyle Rockenbach (1939) as linemen; and Pingel, Bob Monnett (1932), George (Carp) Julian (1914), and DaPrato in the backfield.

There were others, too, who just missed All-America ranking but, nevertheless, made major contributions to Michigan State's football lore. But these were the very best, Spartans all—except for those who starred as Aggies.

TWENTY-EIGHT

Big Ten Football Will Live On

Starting with 1964, Big Ten football teams were losing more games than they were winning against opponents from outside the league. Despite those previously mentioned big upsets at the hands of surprise teams in nonconference games, the league, as a whole, had only two losing campaigns in nonleague play from 1939 through 1963. Then there were ten such losing campaigns in a row. Why?

Two basic factors seemed to have caused the decline in Big Ten strength against the outside world—the short-lived need-factor scholarship period in the late fifties and the end of red-shirting in the sixties, when players were required to complete their eligibility in four academic years. At least coaches and athletic directors blamed these rules for much of the decline. Rarely did they mention that other teams might just have gotten better coaches and better players.

The Big Ten teams obviously recruit their talent from many of the same high schools that Big Eight institutions look to for players. At least the two leagues recruit in the same areas. The Big Eight is composed of Nebraska, Iowa State, Oklahoma, Oklahoma State, Kansas, Kansas State, Missouri, and Colorado. These fellows are in the same general middle section of the nation. And, like the Big Ten, the Big Eight will go after anyone worthwhile in the whole center of the nation, and anywhere else they can find big, fast, strong players.

When the Big Ten had the need factor and athletes had to pay some of their own way through college, the Big Ten may have lost athletes to the Big Eight where the full athletic scholarship was in use. Also, when the Big Ten stopped red-shirting (the practice of having a boy sit out a season to get older and better, and thus spend five years in college), the Big Eight kept right on red-shirting. The full scholarship and the red-shirting gave the Big Eight teams an attractive edge over the Big Ten teams. There were also numbers limits on scholarships at times in the Big Ten that were lower than the Big Eight limit, although this numbers game is generally accepted as false. Outstanding football teams such as Penn State recruited far less than the Big Eight or Big Ten teams did during this "decline" of the Big Ten teams.

Actually, the future may be that legislation through the N.C.A.A. will resolve some of these differences. The Big Ten, to its credit, has attempted to continue faculty control over athletics even if, in some cases, in name only. It is hard, for instance, to control an athletic director who makes a going thing of a $4-million annual program that shows a profit.

The N.C.A.A. may someday arrive at rules that put a blanket over all of these big powers in college athletics whether the faculty or someone else runs the intercollegiate athletic show. An example is the strong possibility of a national need-factor scholarship. In the midseventies this idea gained support as a money-saving device throughout the N.C.A.A. It would put the Big Ten, the Big Eight, and the Pacific Eight on an equal scholarship basis.

Also, the N.C.A.A. has established limits on the number of scholarships a college may give out for football, basketball, soccer, track and field, etc. This has been counter to conference action of the past years that resulted in some colleges' stockpiling athletes who would never be used, just to keep them away from the other colleges or conferences.

It may come to a time when the N.C.A.A. will even prohibit red-shirting, that is, insist that an athlete's eligibility run out in four years.

Certainly the day is coming when there will be something resembling a super-conference of the major football powers in the nation. There is so much difference between the Ohio State, Nebraska, Notre Dame, Southern California, and Alabama teams, and the Williams, Amherst, Columbia, and Wichita State teams, that the big fellows will draw ever closer in order to be the big moneymakers and the big TV attractions. Once the large group of major powers resembles a super-conference it will have rules for those schools which will put everyone on an equal basis. It was the difference between what the Big Ten faculty reps insisted upon and what the other conferences permitted that led to the losing record in the sixties by Big Ten teams against nonconference foes. That would be leveled off and maybe eliminated in a super-conference future.

Although Duffy Daugherty said he did not want to be forced to cheat again by putting the need factor back in, the need factor may one day—despite major opposition now—return as a national scholarship plan. Then there may be no cheating. Most Big Ten coaches will say that Daugherty spoke of a problem that was forced upon coaches in order for them to be able to attract boys away from the Big Eight and other conferences where a full scholarship was always given out to the athlete. It is what led to the Indiana University scandal. If everyone has to do the same thing, then maybe no one will cheat. But then, again, maybe there will always be cheating coaches who just want the edge on winning a game.

But the Big Ten will live on. In its conception this conference was the first to formalize athletic and academic togetherness on more than just a single-campus plan. The Big Ten drew together athletic and academic worlds within the concept of a group of colleges and universities in a formal, organized system of working rules. When the Big Ten went into the twentieth century, other leagues were still working as loose, informal groups. The Ivy League, for instance, remained informal and with little true direction until the fifties. Even now, the Ivies are hardly as well organized in league form as the Big Ten.

For better or worse, many of the concepts of the Big Ten have served as the groundwork for N.C.A.A. legislation. It is not difficult to imagine the N.C.A.A. getting stronger and stronger in years to come in its control over the truly large football powers of intercollegiate athletics. The N.C.A.A. may lose a bit of its strength over the smaller schools in football and other sports since these schools believe at times the N.C.A.A. does them no benefit. But if a grouping of the major powers is to exist, it must exist under guides that serve for one and all, and not under rules that let one conference outrecruit and outplay another to a point of impossible imbalance. Certainly the Big Ten will again be a useful text for those making rules for such a super-conference if it comes into being.

The major football powers have been threatening to move in that direction, but even they do not have a clear idea of what they want to be or how they want to achieve exclusivity. The rumblings are there, however, and only time will determine the ultimate future of big-time major college football.

But, one way or another, the Big Ten will live on!

Index